Gerard Manley Hopkins and the Language of Mystery

Gerard Manley Hopkins

and the Language of Mystery

Virginia Ridley Ellis

University of Missouri Press

Columbia and London

Library of Congress Cataloging-in-Publication Data

Ellis, Virginia Ridley, 1934–
  Gerard Manley Hopkins and the language of mystery / Virginia
Ridley Ellis.
    p. cm.
  Includes bibliographical references and index.
  ISBN 0-8262-0769-3
  1. Hopkins, Gerard Manley, 1844–1889—Criticism and
interpretation.   I. Title.
PR4803.H44Z625 1991
821'.8—dc20   90-22095
                                                                  CIP

Designer: Liz Fett
Typesetter: Graphic Sciences Corporation
Printer: Thomson-Shore, Inc.
Binder: Thomson-Shore, Inc.
Typeface: Garth Graphic

In memory of Katharine Scott Ridley
for the legacy of her "towery city"

and of

Ben L. Reid, for light through
many dark passages

Contents

Abbreviations

FL   *Further Letters of Gerard Manley Hopkins*. Edited by Claude Colleer Abbott. 2d ed. London, 1956.

JP   *The Journals and Papers of Gerard Manley Hopkins*. Edited by Humphry House and Graham Storey. London, 1959.

LB   *The Letters of Gerard Manley Hopkins to Robert Bridges*. Edited by Claude Colleer Abbott. 2d ed. London, 1955.

LD   *The Correspondence of Gerard Manley Hopkins and Richard Watson Dixon*. Edited by Claude Colleer Abbott. 2d ed. London, 1955.

MS   Manuscripts A, B, D, DN, H, and others: see Appendix A.

P   *The Poems of Gerard Manley Hopkins*. Edited by W. H. Gardner and N. H. MacKenzie. 4th ed. London, 1967.

PB   *Poems of Gerard Manley Hopkins*. Edited by Robert Bridges. London, 1918.

SD   *The Sermons and Devotional Writings of Gerard Manley Hopkins*. Edited by Christopher Devlin, S.J. London, 1959.

Preface

A READER OF CRITICAL commentaries may often be dazzled by their intricate and brilliant answers but left wondering what the questions were, or even whether the questions were worth asking in the first place. In the case of this study, the questions are quite simple, though I hope worth asking still: what are the sources of the special power of Hopkins' poetry? what special resources of eye and ear, mind and feeling, do these works require of us, and reward? what sort of approach, what manner of reading, what kind of knowledge is useful not merely to the specialist, but to any reader who responds in some way to this extraordinary voice and wants to hear and understand it more deeply?

My attempted answers to these basic questions are likewise basic, radical only in the sense that I have tried to return to the roots of the poetry's thought, language, vision, impact. The focus on Hopkins' particular concept of "mystery" offers some challenge to the various critical arguments that his deepest need, and deepest loss, was certitude, theological or linguistic or both, and the approach involves more use of the manuscript revisions than appears in most commentaries, but this study makes no high claim to a wholly new unraveling of Hopkins' "realty." Nor does it centrally engage in the many theoretical conflicts among contemporary schools of criticism. Though my governing questions make some declaration of allegiances and some civil argument unavoidable, I have relegated theoretical debate mainly to this preface and to notes and throughout have tried to bear in mind Dr. Johnson's Olympian irony on these matters: "It is not easy to discover from what cause the acrimony of a scholiast can naturally proceed. . . . The various readings of copies, and different interpretations of a passage, seem to be questions that might exercise the wit, without engaging the passions."[1]

1. "Preface to Shakespeare," in *Johnson on Shakespeare*, ed. Arthur Sherbo (New Haven and London: Yale University Press, 1968), 7:102.

This commentary therefore aims less at critical militancy or ingenuity, more at a combination of detail and synthesis, attempting an
exploration of the major poetry in the context of Hopkins' thought
and time. It issues from the belief most critics entertain, I suppose,
overtly or implicitly, that not everything has been seen and said on the
subject, or not in this way, and embodies the hope that something
here may add to any reader's appreciation of this poet and these
poems. Above all, it tries to reflect both Hopkins' own "passion for
explanation" and his belief that clear formulation may intensify, not
diminish, our sense of what finally remain great mysteries.

Three assumptions should be acknowledged from the start,
two of them more or less technical, the third critical. This study assumes, first, that the reader has near at hand, or in the mind, the
poems themselves, and preferably access to the prose also; the
mode of discussion will usually expect a mutually self-correcting
exchange of mind and eye between critical remarks and the actual
texts. Second, in attempting to address two somewhat different au-
diences, I must hope to assume tolerance from both: asking the
specialist to bear with some recapitulation of what is well known to
scholars in the field; asking the nonspecialist to pursue (or ignore)
the notes indicating central factual and critical sources and to show
forbearance toward the "much-debated" or "notoriously obscure"
sort of phraseology into which I sometimes fall.

Finally, my central critical assumption is that anyone who pre-
sumes to write about works of literature, instead of writing them,
owes first allegiance to that literature, which to me involves primarily an attempt to understand, by all available means, its content, context, ways and workings, and, so far as is possible, its
designed intent. Evaluation, critical theory, personal delight, and
other wider critical or individual positions may follow upon, or be
an inevitable part of, such an approach, but the task of understanding comes first: the attempt to earn for criticism the right to make
Ruskin's most basic but most essential claim for the artist, "Vidi."

Though some contemporary critics regard as passé the notion
that interpretation is a critic's main function, arguing that this area
of the field has been worked out, as it were, and that autonymous
new worlds await the venturesome,[2] I do not take so lofty a view of

2. The archetypal, in every sense, argument against the centrality of interpretation appears in Northrop Frye's *Anatomy of Criticism* (Princeton: Princeton University Press, 1957). For one of the best and fullest recent arguments, see Jonathan
D. Culler, *The Pursuit of Signs: Semiotics, Literature, Deconstruction*, 3–17 and
passim.

the powers of criticism at the present time. With some notable exceptions, such as Coleridge, the critic and the processes of criticism seem to me not usually interesting enough to be their own subject, or object, at least not to many readers beyond academe. I therefore continue to share what used to be J. Hillis Miller's Arnoldian position, and to an extent still is: "I still believe that the aim of criticism is to get inside the works criticized and to convey as intimate a sense as possible of what goes on there."[3]

"What goes on there," however, and especially what one means by "there," are often debatable and ambiguous issues, requiring early clarification of some further aspects of procedure and related assumptions. Having used the phrase *designed intent*, a red flag in some critical arenas, I acknowledge first my assumption that such a thing exists in good writers, and that evidence for its existence may be found and must be explored. My comments on the relationship between the poems and their manuscript variants are therefore especially marked by something close to that cardinal sin in New (now old) Criticism, the "intentional fallacy": the notion that the poet's intended meaning and motives can be discovered or approached, and that these constitute the one legitimate standard and main critical test of a poem.[4]

No one will sensibly deny to poetry, and to Hopkins' poetry in particular, the possibility of richnesses and excellences beyond provably "meant" meaning. Since Hopkins was so persistently and earnestly precise, however, sometimes pedantically and fussily precise, about his own precisions, a critic of his poems is, in my view, particularly challenged to seek these out first, whatever further dimensions the poems may and do have for individual readers. What the seabird's great wuthering of wings embodies in "Henry Purcell," and what Hopkins wrote of that sonnet's meaning, applies to all his poetry, and may serve as a critical guide to it: a fine act, or piece of music, or poem, may very well reveal more than was consciously intended, is certainly more than limited self-expression—in Hopkins' crisper words, "My sonnet means 'Purcell's music is none of your d_____d subjective rot' (so to speak)" (*LB* 84)—but it cannot mean less or wholly other than what is consciously intended. If it "means motion" but shows more, both that "meaning" and that "more" need attention.

3. Revised preface (1975) to *The Disappearance of God: Five Nineteenth-Century Writers*, viii.

4. For the germinal definition and argument, see W. K. Wimsatt, *The Verbal Icon: Studies in the Meaning of Poetry* (Lexington: University of Kentucky Press, 1954).

I shall therefore at times be testing the extent to which the "intentional fallacy" is indeed fallacious and the extent to which it is legitimate. In opposition to one direction in contemporary criticism, I shall also usually assume that absence of evidence cannot be presumed to constitute evidence, whether of a consciously secret or unconsciously suppressed subtext. Without wholly rejecting the enticements of speculation, my readings will reflect a belief that it is possible to read, or at least try to read first, what a poet wrote rather than what he did not write, or what my personal experience, expectations, critical leanings, may make him seem to write as I read in changing stages of my life. I especially retain a rather straightforward, if currently unfashionable, attitude toward Hopkins: what an intensely intelligent, intensely self-critical poet says in and of his work, and what his whole life bears testimony to, I accept as the primary evidence for, and business of, his critics. Recognizing all the pitfalls inherent in the attempt, one can still try "to see the object as in itself it really is."

This seemingly clear-cut aim has generated so much critical discussion, often such critical contempt, in recent times, that I must pause on one assumption inherent in it, and in this study of Hopkins. Fraught though it is with difficulties about the meaning of "really," Arnold's phrase clearly and crisply assumes what seems to me essential: that "the object" a critic can most validly and usefully examine is the artifact, the made thing, not the maker's psyche, nor the making mind of the reader, nor even the conjunction of the two. Though I shall often draw upon what is known of Hopkins' thought and intentions, and shall often attempt, through use of the manuscripts, speculation on what he was after in the poems, and why, and with what aim and effect, recognition of the object as constant, and of the maker as ultimately irrecoverable, seems to me crucial, especially to any critic who is not a poet. The necessity of focus upon the artifact rather than upon the autobiography of the artist will be particularly important to my treatment of the "terrible sonnets" (Chapter 9). While also particularly problematical in a chapter on such private and unfinished poems, the governing assumption will continue to be that the sonnets are made things, the record of a poet's mind at work on the actual psyche's experience, not uncontrolled confessions or *cris du coeur*.

In sum, I take Hopkins to have been what he knew and thought he was, a complex and often deeply troubled human being, but a deeply committed priest and Christian poet, for whom faith was life, and art the voice and instrument of faith. While the instrument was important to him, obsessively so at times, my readings do not accept the view that poetic language and linguistic processes displaced God as his central subject, and they will consciously neither construct nor deconstruct, though they will often attempt a reconstruction of the processes and stages of creation. Though perhaps all criticism risks being in the end like Lucifer's song, "a sounding of [its] own trumpet and a hymn in [its] own praise" (November 1881, *SD* 200-201), the readings that follow aim at a degree of critical chameleonism and try to remember that "a critic is one of those candles by which we behold the sun."[5]

Because many previous scholars and critics have made sillion shine in this field, no attempt is made here to comment on every poem Hopkins wrote, not even on every finished poem; in order to look closely at the workings of poetic wholes, I have made some selections among, not within, the poems. Mature works passed over briefly or wholly omitted fall into one of three categories: those that seem relatively slight and unsuccessful, or at least relatively uninteresting in method ("Penmaen Pool," "In the Valley of the Elwy," "At the Wedding March," "Brothers, "Inversnaid," "The Soldier," for example); those that are either so relatively accessible or so well discussed by other critics that only brief comment, if any, seems needed ("Pied Beauty," "The Sea and the Skylark," "Binsey Poplars," "Duns Scotus's Oxford," "To R. B."); and finally, those in which specifically doctrinal concepts are the clear and obvious center ("The Silver Jubilee," "The Blessed Virgin compared to the Air we Breathe," "The May Magnificat," "The Loss of the *Eurydice*," among others). The decision to omit the poems in this third category, the last of which is one of Hopkins' most polished finished works, was based both on the premise behind this study, that Hopkins' religion affected his poetry in ways deeper and more complicated than that of supplying obvious Catholic content, and on my sense that these are on the whole minor achievements. Hopkins himself seems to have suspected that his specifically devotional Catholic poems were not his best—"it is too true that the highest subjects are not those on which it is easy to reach one's highest," he wrote of "The Blessed Virgin compared to the Air we Breathe" (May 11, 1883, *LB* 179)—and especially feared that the artistic attempt to "make capital" of the highest might well approach sacrilege (February 15, 1879, *LB* 66). While the poet was

5. Richard Le Gallienne, "Some First and Second Principles of Criticism," *Retrospective Reviews: A Literary Log*, 1:xv.

always the priest, the great poems in my view are those in which he was not merely the didactic priest, and it is mainly on those poems that I shall be concentrating.

Acknowledgments

MY MANY DEBTS of gratitude go back to the late Walter E. Houghton, in whose class at Wellesley I first encountered "The Windhover," and discovered that teaching and scholarship could be both rigorous and joyful; to Howard Nemerov, formerly of Brandeis University and director of my initial study of Hopkins, for being not only "a good writer on paper" but a lasting inspiration; to Norman H. MacKenzie for generously sharing the manuscripts when I was a wholly unknown upstart to him; to the late Father Basil Fitzgibbon, former librarian at Campion Hall, Oxford; to Patricia Stubbs Bielec, with whom I first worked closely on the dark sonnets in directing her undergraduate honors paper "Cliffs of Fall," which was and remains an influence on my ideas; to my sister, Alison Evans Garfield, for proofreading and for being there; to my mother, Katharine Ridley, who "watched the door," and opened many.

I am grateful to the Oxford University Press and the Society of Jesus for permission to quote from the Hopkins material, both published and in manuscript; the Bodleian Library, Oxford, for manuscript photocopies reproduced here; Dr. Judith Priestman, Department of Western Manuscripts at the Bodleian; the Faculty Grants Committee of Mount Holyoke College for financial assistance at various stages; Yvonne Nicholson, for editorial intelligence as well as expert and long-suffering preparation of the typescript; and to Beverly Jarrett, Director and Editor-in-Chief, and Jane Lago, Managing Editor, of the University of Missouri Press.

With special gratitude I thank two arch-especial colleagues. First, Ben L. Reid, mentor, exemplar, goad, friend of many years, without whose constant encouragement, refusal to tolerate my diffidence and laziness, and practical initiative this book would not exist. Second, my husband, James Ellis, keen critic, ruthless editor, eagle-eyed proofreader, shoulder-companion, whose selfless help on both substance and mechanics was indispensable, and who has shown in the midst of great trial "patience, hard thing."

Finally, it seems right to end these remarks with a word of thanks to my students over the years. Their responses to Hopkins have sustained, challenged, and renewed my own, especially because they usually began by knowing nothing of Scotus or "priest-poet conflicts" or paeonic feet, but knew and felt a poem when they saw it. It is especially for and to such readers that this commentary hopes to speak.

Obscurity I do and will try to avoid so far as is consistent with excellences higher than clearness at a first reading.

—To Bridges, May 30, 1878

We should explain things, plainly state them, clear them up, explain them; explanation—except personal—is always pure good;
without explanation people go on misunderstanding; being once
explained they thenceforward understand things; therefore always
explain: but I have the passion for explanation and you have not.

—To Bridges, May 25, 1888

I

Background and Theory

1

Introduction

Our generation already is overpast,
And thy lov'd legacy, Gerard, hath lain
Coy in my home . . . .
Go forth: amidst our chaffinch flock display
Thy plumage of far wonder and heavenward flight!
　　　　—Robert Bridges, Dedicatory Sonnet, *Poems*, 1918

WHEN BRIDGES GAVE the whole of the long-kept "lov'd legacy" to its new inheritors in a new generation, he rightly judged that he was loosing upon the world poems that would seem lovelier perhaps, but also more dangerous to standards of intelligibility and decorum, than current chaffinch taste could easily admire or tolerate. His severe critical preface in the first edition is therefore a preemptive tour de force in taking wind from the sails of yet severer critics, and it was in the dedicatory poem that he summarized his imaginative response to the poems as poetry. His attempt may perhaps evoke a slight uneasiness in us—a sense of something strained, and something lost—but the metaphors do loyally try to capture more than the oddities of Hopkins' merely outward plumage. It was upon those oddities, however, that critical attention was first fixed. Whether in wonder, or in baffled fascination, or in condemnation, or in a combination of these responses,[1] the initial reaction was

　　1. "You fight your way through the verses yet they draw you on," wrote the reviewer for *TLS* in a representative reaction, which deplored an "effect almost of idiocy, of speech without sense and prolonged merely by echoes" but also found "authentic fragments that we trust even when they bewilder us" ("Gerard Hopkins," January 9, 1919, 19). For full citation of contemporary responses, see W. H. Gardner, *Gerard Manley Hopkins (1844–1889): A Study of Poetic Idiosyncrasy in Relation to Poetic Tradition*, 1:212–24; Todd K. Bender, *Gerard Manley Hopkins: The Classical Background and Critical Reception of His Work*, 5–10; *Gerard Manley Hopkins: The Critical Heritage*, ed. Gerald Roberts, 77–139.

3

mainly to technique, to poetic outscape, as it were, a reaction that set the course and focus of the first decades of Hopkins' influence and of Hopkins criticism.

Yet more damning, however, were some early responses of readers who did try to look beneath manner and moonmarks for passion and vision and content, but found only a plentiful deal of technique. Exemplifying this contemporary response, the reviewer for the *Oxford Magazine*, writing more in sorrow than in anger, it would seem, lamented the absence of "some more direct vision and more complete expression than it was given to Gerard Hopkins to attain."[2] Two decades later, this century's greatest poet expressed the same view far more devastatingly, and may here speak authoritatively for the many contemporary and subsequent detractors of Hopkins as an empty practitioner of art for art's sake. "I read Gerard Hopkins with great difficulty," wrote Yeats in 1936. "I cannot keep my attention fixed for more than a few minutes; I suspect a bias born when I began to think." The reformed Aesthete goes on to say, perhaps with a convert's extreme severity: "He is typical of his generation where most opposed to mine. His meaning is like some faint sound that strains the ear, comes out of words, passes to and fro between them, goes back into words, his manner a last development of poetic diction. My generation began that search for hard positive subject-matter, still a predominant purpose." This comment on the seeming absence of content and tough intellect is coupled with a cut not only at the technique of the poet but also at the temperament, perhaps even the masculinity, of the man, in the remark on sprung rhythm: "this stoppage and sudden onrush of syllables were to him a necessary expression of his slight constant excitement."[3]

Nevertheless, in spite of such heavy arms ranged against them, the poems have of course survived not only critical blame, and searching analysis, but also critical praise. As has often been remarked, Hopkins was his own prophet in the long run, though without much honor even from Bridges at the time, when he wrote, "If you do not like it it is because there is something you have not seen and I see. That at least is my mind, and if the whole world agreed to condemn it or see nothing in it I should only tell

2. *Oxford Magazine* 37 (May 23, 1919): 311.
3. Introduction to *The Oxford Book of Modern Verse, 1892–1935*, chosen by W. B. Yeats, xxxix, xl.

them to take a generation and come to me again" (April 1, 1885, *LB* 214).

Though the "it" in question here was a musical work, the remark clearly applies also to the poetry's fate and present standing, as successive generations have come to it with new eyes. But it is especially that phrase "something you have not seen and I see" that is quietly potent and important here, for it is what and how he "saw," not merely the flash of technical novelties, that seems to speak increasingly to readers now (and I suspect spoke also to ordinary readers then). Certainly more than ingenious stylistic mannerism is necessary to account for what is probably a commonly experienced but still surprising fact, as teachers of Hopkins can especially testify: he continues to waken in new readers a sense of extraordinary discovery, not simply of clever technique or "slight excitement," but of passion, and living reverence, and a quality of vision intensely conveyed. Even in our climate of poetic experimentation, density, difficulty, Hopkins' poems retain their utterly distinctive "taste"—"more distinctive than the taste of ale or alum, more distinctive than the smell of walnutleaf or camphor" (*SD* 123)—their explosive pressure, and their power, even at their most perverse, to fan fresh our wits with wonder. This is poetry that still compels us to say, as Hopkins said of any individual's selfhood, "Nothing else in nature comes near this unspeakable stress of pitch, distinctiveness, and selving" (*SD* 123).

Yet distinctiveness alone is not what Hopkins himself most valued in art, nor an absolute touchstone of poetic excellence in general, nor, I think, what commands the passionate attention, even passionate devotion, of new and unbiased readers. It may be what touches them first, and to readers of a classical persuasion may seem suspect and merely emotional in impact; it is certainly obvious that Hopkins' style is marked less by what he called "*candorem*, chasteness" than by "brilliancy, starriness, quain, margaretting" (*JP* 290), sometimes by what he termed mere "idiom" rather than inscape.[4] I must admit myself to a somewhat guilty admiration for some of the poems, of the sort Hopkins described in writing of his own liking for some oddities in Dixon's poems—admiration, "but with a vicious taste, as for Stilton or high game" (October 3, 1881, *LD* 68). Nevertheless, what makes the poems not only strange and

---

4. "I have no other word yet for that which takes the eye or mind . . . which not being beauty nor true inscape yet gives interest and makes ugliness even better than meaninglessness" (*JP* 195).

beautiful—"beautiful to individuation" (*LB* 210)—but also a genuine source of wonderment to new readers, is more than distinctive "selving," more than masterful and daring technique, more than powerful feeling, and more even than the intensity and intelligence of priestly faith. Or perhaps one should say not "more than" but "deeper than" these, and with that the circle returns to "I see," and to the purpose and focus of this study.

The basic subject here is simply, and complicatedly, Hopkins' way of seeing: the presence, nature, and consistency of his "direct vision," which I shall argue was also a vision of indirection, and the translation of that vision into his "authentic cadence" as a poet.[5] In 1886, writing to Canon Dixon a spirited defence of the Immortality Ode, Hopkins placed Wordsworth with a few other strange and great geniuses who have "*seen something*," with the result that "human nature in these men saw something, got a shock; . . . is in a tremble ever since" (October 23, 1886, *LD* 147–48). If Hopkins' own poetry continues to have something of this electrical effect, to be more potent than critical language can easily account for, and to evoke a response to more than linguistic oddity, it is because of the special nature of what he himself had "seen," which Bridges, and the Oxford reviewer, and Yeats, and most other early critics did not see. He wrote as he did, and not merely what he did, because of what and how he saw, and because this vision so completely informs and governs every aspect of his thought and method.

I am referring here not merely, or mainly, to the doctrinal elements of his Catholic and specifically Jesuit faith, ably and thoroughly discussed by other critics,[6] but to his concept and vision of "mystery," a large and somewhat elusive term, but a crucially suggestive one. The concept is related of course, organically related, to his faith, but subsumes his specifically Ignatian and Scotist beliefs, and I believe that it pervasively affected both his aesthetic, critical, and philosophical theories and the content, structure, and language of his poems.

My concern, therefore, is both with Hopkins' way of seeing

5. "Let me be to Thee as the circling bird" (*P* 19). Except where quotations and their metrical notations are from the original manuscripts, all references to Hopkins' poems will be to the Gardner-MacKenzie edition, indicated by poem number, not page. Line numbers are cited only for a few of the longer poems.

6. See especially Christopher Devlin's many fine studies, including the introductions and notes to *SD*; David A. Downes, *Gerard Manley Hopkins: A Study of His Ignatian Spirit*; Alfred Thomas, S.J., *Hopkins the Jesuit: The Years of Training*; John Pick, *Gerard Manley Hopkins: Priest and Poet*.

and with a way of seeing what he created: the two concerns are in fact one, since the poems are, and compel the reader to take part in, an act of seeing in a special way, an act of insight. They consistently demand of us what he believed God expected of him and of all human beings: an attempt to read rightly and to "utter outright" the mysterious and manifold eloquence of the world as it is "news of God" (August 7, 1882, *SD* 129); to penetrate its density of structure and metaphor and seeming paradox; to understand its often complex but precise syntax; to tolerate, and rejoice in, its multiplicity and complexity, but not vagueness, of meaning; to recognize that the literal is always metaphorical, and that the metaphorical in turn embodies a higher literal truth; and to do all this without violating either the essential reality or the essential mystery of creation and Creator. They are poems that, at their best, can at least partially transform the world for us, whether we are believers or nonbelievers, as Christian faith wholly transformed it for Hopkins: "Suppose God shewed us in a vision the whole world inclosed first in a drop of water, allowing everything to be seen in its native colours; then the same in a drop of Christ's blood, by which everything whatever was turned scarlet, keeping nevertheless mounted in the scarlet its own colour too" (1882, *SD* 194).

Hopkins here exactly describes the nature and effect of his own religious vision, a vision of life, both outer and inner, given not only intensity, but coherence, beauty, being itself, by Christ's sacrificial act. And that splendidly bizarre heraldic phrase, "mounted in the scarlet," suggests with equal accuracy something of how our world appears in the world of his poems: minutely observed, true to its own colors indeed, but with the flat colors of common reality intensified, heightened, vibrant with new energy, vividly sharp but never static, redeemed from mere actuality by the mysterious presence in them of Hopkins' mysteriously ungraspable but revealed God.

I shall be attempting to explore some of the ways in which Hopkins' work, in method as well as content, in prose as well as poetry, is permeated by this vision. Although, like Bridges, one tends instinctively to think of Hopkins in images of height and flight and the flash of strangely wondrous plumage, there was also in his art, as in his life, the stiller "deep down" vision, the steadiness of a faith fed by deep sources. "Religion, you know, enters very deep," Hopkins wrote to Baillie in 1880 (*FL* 245), and it may be that exploration of his concept of mystery can offer one way of reading the poems, of entering into them, that brings us close to those deep sources. His unmistakable "authentic cadence" is the voice of that vision, the voice of his spiritual "eye-witness" to the realities and mysteries of the world and of God, a vision which, like Ruskin's, begins in exactitude, begins with "Vidi,"[7] but reaches toward "the treasure never eyesight got" (P 28.26), the God beyond all seeing and all saying and all grasp. Like Saint Winefred's Well, which so impressed and moved him, the body of Hopkins' poetry is "the sensible thing . . . uttering the spiritual reason of its being . . . and the spring in place leading back the thoughts by its spring in time to its spring in eternity: even now the stress and buoyancy and abundance of the water is before my eyes" (October 8, 1874, JP 261).

---

7. "Nothing must come between Nature and the artist's sight, nothing . . . . between the universe, and the witness which art bears to its visible nature. The whole value of that witness depends on its being *eye*-witness. . . . All its victory depends on the veracity of the one preceding word, 'Vidi.'" John Ruskin, *The Stones of Venice* in *The Works of John Ruskin*, 11:49.

2

Mysterious Certainty

Let me be to Thee as the circling bird,
Or bat with tender and air-crisping wings
That shapes in half-light his departing rings,
From both of whom a changeless note is heard.
I have found my music in a common word,
Trying each pleasurable throat that sings
And every praisèd sequence of sweet strings,
And know infallibly which I preferred.
The authentic cadence was discovered late
Which ends those only strains that I approve,
And other science all gone out of date
And minor sweetness scarce made mention of:
I have found the dominant of my range and state—
Love, O my God, to call Thee Love and Love.
                    —October 1865 (19)

BECAUSE BOTH CIRCULARITY and mystery govern this study's organization as well as its content, a glance at some common aspects of the early poems, and a close look at the keynote sonnet quoted above, may serve as a somewhat oblique but concrete means of entry into major and continuing aspects of Hopkins' thought and method.

With two exceptions ("Elected Silence" and "Saint Dorothy," probably the second version), Hopkins wrote of the early poems, both finished and fragmentary, "I disavow those things" (September 30, 1884, *LB* 198). They nevertheless do show the embryonic beginnings of his thought and style, while also, in what they lack, dramatically suggesting the radical effect his full Catholic vision of a world "mounted in the scarlet" would have upon his mature poetry. The stylistic difference between the early and the later poems is the result not merely of growth in years and skill, but of a passage

9

of the spirit through crisis and revelation, "from the grace to the grace."

In content, however, the early poems not only cumulatively reflect the continuing though groping search for God but also specifically dramatize two aspects of that search that will remain central in later poems: the attempt to reconcile intense sensuous response to natural beauty with a need for the divine principle of order that creates and justifies beauty, and the attempt to balance acknowledgment of a "shrouded" God with the hope and thirst for total sight: "Some day to gaze on thee face to face in light" (168).

"I have been writing numbers of descriptions of sunrises, sunsets, sunlight in the trees, flowers, windy skies etc. etc." Hopkins wrote airily to E. H. Coleridge in 1862 (*FL* 13), but even the earliest of these sensuous, descriptive, and usually derivative poems at least hint at the attempt to reach through nature to God, and the later undergraduate poems make that attempt explicit. "Nondum" (23), for example, written in 1866, laments, "We see the glories of the earth / But not the hand that wrought them all," and concludes with the somewhat melancholy, and very Tennysonian, prayer that God's hand may reach down through dark vacancy to touch his own: "And lead me child-like by the hand / If still in darkness not in fear." But the grim resignation to present darkness and blindness in this poem, the forlorn acceptance of the "not yet" of the title, is countered in many of the early poems by a hunger to see now, a longing implicit, and often explicit, in what Hopkins himself identified to E. H. Coleridge, and what Miller was the first to emphasize in criticism: the surprisingly consistent imagery of the sun and of the various yearning watchers or seekers of the sun.[1]

Admittedly, some of the poems in which this motif appears are not only imitative but explicitly imitations ("Il Mystico," among others), so that it may be suspect to look to them for firm biographical evidence. I am not sure, for example, that the lushly Keatsian schoolboy poem, "A Vision of the Mermaids" (2), as yet identifies the sun as "a symbol for the divine center, that absent God whose unattainability darkens Hopkins' early poetry,"[2] but it does anticipate later uses of this image and also expresses what will remain

1. *Disappearance of God*, 275–76.
2. Ibid., 275. For an alternative and subtle reading of some of the preconversion poems, see Howard W. Fulweiler, *Letters from the Darkling Plain: Language and the Grounds of Knowledge in the Poetry of Arnold and Hopkins*, 95–103. See also Norman H. MacKenzie's splendid facsimile edition of *The Early Poetic Manuscripts and Note-Books of Gerard Manley Hopkins*.

deeply characteristic: a strange longing and a strange pain in the presence of mystery. In "Il Mystico" (77) of 1862, which actually owes almost nothing of its imagery to its model, "Il Penseroso," he longs to see "the mystery of those Things / Shewn to Ezekiel's open'd sight" (ll. 47–48), longs specifically to be a lark who attains the sun-heights, "And when the silent height were won, / And all in lone air stood the sun, / To sing scarce heard" (ll. 75–77), or again, longs to gaze upward until he penetrates the meaning of the rainbow, a rainbow seen, perhaps significantly, both as "a sevenfold-*single* gem" and as "Ending in sweet *uncertainty*" (ll. 116, 121, italics mine). In "Winter with the Gulf Stream" of 1863 (3), he again gazes at the sunset, whose "waxen colours weep and run" (l. 29) until they vanish into darkness; in "I am like a slip of comet" of 1864 (103), there is a momentary coincidence of the sun and the comet-poet, who "sucks the light as full as Gideon's fleece" (l. 11), but soon must fall away, and away, "into the cavernous dark" (l. 16); the Alchemist in "The Alchemist in the City" of 1865 (15), hungering for the "One spot" of the sun on the horizon (l. 32), yearns to "pierce the yellow waxen light / With free long looking, ere I die" (ll. 43–44); the more somber, slightly later poem "My prayers must meet a brazen heaven" (18) and the very Herbertian and more hopeful "The Half-way House" (20) respectively rebel against the apparently sunless indifference of heaven and try to draw down into the present darkness of earth the now-named sun of God: "To see Thee I must see Thee, to love, love; / I must o'ertake Thee at once and under heaven / If I shall overtake Thee at last above" (ll. 14–16).

If such recurrent imagery does validly show something of the consciousness that wrought it, if it reflects the persistent attempt to find in sunlight Son-light, a second, and counter, point also needs to be made about it. "To see Thee I must see Thee," the hope and possibility of direct sight, is not the burden of the imagery in most of these poems. All but one of them are sunset, if not actually twilight or night, pieces: the sun is sinking, or misted, or blurred by rain or cloud, or somehow melting into invisibility or "uncertainty," even when the poem is not centrally or at all a poem of frustrated vision or outright despair. Latent in such imagery therefore may be more than the obvious point of human blindness and divine elusiveness. The imagery may reflect already Hopkins' sense of the nature of religious vision, which can neither be, nor be expressed in terms of, clear daylight sight.

This point becomes explicit in "The Habit of Perfection" (22)

of 1866 (which Hopkins referred to as "Elected Silence" and
would not "disavow"), in its distinction between the physical and
the "uncreated light" that he seeks in physical "double dark" (ll.
9–10); it was explicit also in the earlier "Il Mystico," which may
not owe wholly to Milton its prayer that revelation come in pre-
dawn darkness, because paradoxically then, and not in sunlight,
"most thinly lies / The veil that covers mysteries" (ll. 35–36). It is
dramatized, and nearly explicit, in the one early poem to be discussed here in detail, "Let me be to Thee as the circling bird" (19),
a sonnet that is a poem both of twilight and of dawning.

Though the sonnet laments the "lateness" of his discovered
dedication, with characteristically extreme remorse for past fail-
ings, Hopkins was only twenty at the time of writing it in October
1865; it would be almost a year before his formal conversion to Catholicism, and three years before he entered the Jesuit order. Yet
among all the early poems, this one seems to me most useful for
full discussion, because it is openly lyric and personal, and because
it is pivotal, looking both before and after in concept and method.
It is not only a clear announcement of the increasingly urgent and
total dedication to God that was to lead to his two crucial religious
decisions, but in aspects of language and method it also hints at the
ways of sensing, feeling, speaking, and especially of seeing and not
seeing, that will be characteristic of his mature vision and mature
"authentic cadence" as a poet.

Most obviously characteristic is of course the opening image of
the circling bird, and the entire overt statement that emerges from
it. Affirmation of God as love and as eternal center, emphasis in
statement and image on the homing instinct of the heart in flight,
the imperious need not only to "be" true to that central God but to
express him, "to *call* Thee Love and Love" (italics mine)—to
"utter Thee outright" in *The Deutschland*'s later phrase—these
dominate in various ways and keys all Hopkins' later works, whatever complexities and desolate fears enter to baffle the certainty
and deepen the ground-melody of faith. Even when the name
changes, when "Love and Love" has become "thou terrible," the
basic and ultimate impulse of the poems is to "say yes" to the God
of lightning as to the God of love; they are always perceived as essentially one and, even when darkly "away," are felt to be, as here,
"my God."

Somewhat more specifically, this sonnet, like some of the early
poetry and much of the prose, expresses a double will and need: the
need to retain a "me" while replacing the self as center with God as

center; the need to turn to the single and changeless One, rejecting the "minor sweetness" of intellectual knowledge, poetic achievement, and all the pleasing variety of this world—all the false gold from which the Alchemist had also turned to the horizon's "One spot" of true light. The sonnet announces that the decisive choice has been made on both counts and, at least in statement, is therefore a culmination of a process, and a turning point.

The earliest writings embody not only a young Ruskinian's meticulously detailed and delighted response to the world's variety but also a young Romantic's tendency (or perhaps simply any young person's tendency) to view the self as the center of that variety: "me" still precedes "Thee" quite boisterously in such lines as "The earth and heaven, so little known, / Are measured outwards from my breast. / I am the midst of every zone / And justify the East and West" (130), or again, though here a fictional character speaks, "And I must have the centre in my heart / To spread the compass on the all-starr'd sky" (102, 3.7–8).[3] Yet even some of the early poems, as seen, and especially the early diaries, reflect a longing for an objective source of unity, focus, law, governing and ordering the world's variety.

The entire search for what he would soon call "inscape" was essentially a search for law, and the word is constantly repeated in the early journals: "I have now found the law of the oak leaves" (July 19, 1866); "Those tretted mossy clouds have their law more in helices, wave-tongues, than in anything else" (July 2, 1866); and so forth. The search is always for what he sees and emphasizes in the budded lime tree, "the *form* speaking" (April 6, 1868)[4]—a phrase that may help explain why the later terms *instress* and *inscape*, when used as verbs, often seem to overlap, sometimes to be interchangeable, in Hopkins' thinking.

Even seemingly casual remarks reflect uneasiness, regret, when some unifying source of meaning and focus is lacking: "May 6. . . . boated with H. Dugmore to Godstow, but the warm greyness of the day, the river, the spring green, and the cuckoo wanted a canon by which to harmonise and round them in—e. g. one of feeling"

3. See Miller's discussion of the influence of Pater's subjective impressionism, *Disappearance of God*, 274, and Alan Heuser, *The Shaping Vision of Gerard Manley Hopkins*, 14–17, on Hopkins' training of the senses with the perceiving self as center.

4. *JP* 146, 142, 163. See also Norman H. MacKenzie, *Hopkins*, 6–7, on Hopkins' probable debt to Ruskin's consistent use of the word *law* to explain the "ideal form" of a species.

(1866, *JP* 135). And on trees in new leaf he comments: "beautiful, but distraction and the want of the canon only makes these graceful shapes in the keen unseasonable evening air to 'carve out' one's thought with painful definiteness" (1866, *JP* 136).

There seems to be some swift and perhaps multiple punning in the first entry, but whether taken in its musical or in its other more legalistic senses, this "canon" appears still to be thought of as a unifying force that must exist in and emanate from the perceiving, and in this case feeling, self; this will change, in part, as God replaces self as center, and as Hopkins discovers a body of laws external to the self. But the dissatisfaction with individual beauties, however beautiful, whose separate lines of melody remain unbound into a whole and recurrent song, will remain constant. So also will the sense of "painful definiteness" of the second entry, a major point to be returned to later.

The search for a center that, however mysterious, was absolutely certain, and for the informing law underlying complexity, was finally resolved, of course, in total commitment to God: the opening line of *The Wreck of the Deutschland* will make dramatically clear that the "me," though still potent, bows to, and follows, the mastering "Thou." This was a commitment that seemed at first to require an austere and total rejection of all other beauties. "The Habit of Perfection" explicitly rejects the sensuousness on which its language lovingly dwells. In "Let me be to Thee" sensuousness has been almost entirely eliminated: the vocabulary insists far more abstractly on the "changeless," the "infallible," the "dominant," the "only"; already "*Ipse*, the only one" demands and receives a dedication so absolute that "each" and "every" and "all" other beauties and knowledge are swept aside as insignificant. And the journal shows that Hopkins tried to practice for a time what the poems austerely preach: "On this day by God's grace I resolved to give up all beauty until I had His leave for it" (November 6, 1865, *JP* 71).

Leave for it was found when Hopkins arrived at the sacramental view of the world that made variety coherent and beauty legitimate. Having found the center and informing law in God, he was to find in Ignatius, and later in Duns Scotus—who was indeed for Hopkins "a mercy from God"[5]—further "laws" to justify his own

5. From the entry on his first discovery of Scotus, when he was "flush with a new stroke of enthusiasm. It may come to nothing or it may be a mercy from God. But just then when I took in any inscape of the sky or sea I thought of Scotus" (August 1872, *JP* 221).

instinctive response to the world's loveliness. Its various pied beauties, however "minor" their sweetness, need no longer be rejected
or suspect, since they speak of and point to a creator "past change"
and beyond variousness.

His speculative thought was then also freed to develop what
the "circling bird" of the sonnet partly implies, an attempt to reconcile God, self, and world in a rather complex system of overlapping circles and radiations from various centers, ultimately
envisioning a system of concentric circles. God is always the center
of the world, sending forth his own all-informing radiations, dis-
playing himself in his all-inclusive "outsetting," but the human self
also "will consist of a centre *and* a surrounding area or circumference, of a point of reference *and* a belonging field," and the object-
world will be partly one with that center, and partly external to it:
"If the centre of reference spoken of has concentric circles round it,
one of these, the inmost say, is its own, is óf it, the rest are tó it
only" (August 1880, *SD* 127). This attempt to reconcile subjective
self and objective world will be pursued further in the context of
the period (Chapter 3); here it suffices to say that the sonnet's initial and central image dramatizes, though in simple form, the habitual and increasingly complex tendency of Hopkins' mind to
think in terms of various concentric circles.[6]

That Hopkins found in God a fixed and constant center did
not mean, however, that he found that center itself clearly visible,
or comprehensible, or apprehensible, and I now return to what
seems to me the really crucial image of the early sonnet, the somewhat odd and startling image of the bat. That it immediately replaces the initial generalized "bird" as the more adequate and the
only sensuously developed image reveals, of course, Hopkins' keen
attention to the specific, even in a poem filled with important generalizations. It probably reveals also his awareness of the beauty in
oddity, and perhaps even some consciousness of his own already
somewhat strange "music" and eccentric wings. Certainly in context it vividly conveys his awareness that he himself is still unable to
see, or hope to see, God clearly.

Beyond this, however, I think it may be viewed as a suggestive
emblem of what I am calling Hopkins' vision and method of mys-

6. See James Finn Cotter's discussion of this tendency in relation to Hopkins'
studies of Parmenides and other pre-Christian thinkers and myths (*Inscape: The
Christology and Poetry of Gerard Manley Hopkins*, 16–17), particularly the intriguing statement, "One of his Jesuit superiors many years later was to observe that
Hopkins's own mind moved 'in concentric circles'" (17).

tery, a vision and method in which certainty and uncertainty combine to be and to express faith. What the bat suggests here is something that remains consistent, I believe: his sense that it may always be in dim half-light that human beings circle the certain but mysterious center, shaping their course, the patterns of their lives and belief, not by clear "sight"—whether intellectual or mystical—but by a finely tuned sensing of that center's charge of stress, a devotion to it, and a homing response to it.

I am suggesting, in short, an alternative, or at least a qualification, to some major critical arguments that Hopkins' driving search was for certitude, for mystical union with God, or at least for full understanding and expression of his mysteries. In its most simplistic form, this argument appeared in Elsie Elizabeth Phare's early (1933) comments that the "side" of Hopkins that was the intellectual Catholic thinker lived in the "tidy, cut-and-dried mental world of the Jesuit," and that "the world as viewed in the light of Catholic dogma is a riddle solved." It takes a more persuasive form in such statements as Robert Boyle's that "union with the Word is the central desire and concern of Hopkins' life, the motive force behind his being a Jesuit and his being a poet," and especially in James Finn Cotter's entire, and impressive, argument that Hopkins not only searched for gnosis, but actually "discovered the arcane key that unlocked his universe." It is also the basis of Miller's analysis of Hopkins' linguistic theory and practice, which intricately argues that "the whole structure of his thought and textual practice—theological, conceptual, or representational—is put in question by the fact that there is no master word, no word for the Word, only endless permutations of language."[7]

It is certainly unquestionable that Hopkins needed, and created, certainty in the form of "laws" of various kinds. Nor do I question the intensity and persistence of his longing for spiritual enlightenment, even spiritual union with God. And no one will deny that he strained language to its limits in the poetic attempt to express the inexpressible. I am simply suggesting that balancing that longing and attempt there was from the beginning a not necessarily despairing sense—in fact an intellectually sensible and spiritually humble sense—of the impossibility of full consummation in this life. "Asking for perfect understanding" according to Ignatian

7. Phare, *The Poetry of Gerard Manley Hopkins: A Survey and Commentary*, 10; Boyle, *Metaphor in Hopkins*, 70; Cotter, *Inscape*, 296; Miller, *The Linguistic Moment: From Wordsworth to Stevens*, 263.

instruction, "desiring to know more of the Eternal Word incarnate, in order to serve and to follow Him more,"[8] seems to me always to have involved for Hopkins emphasis on the asking, not the
finding, on the service, not the expectation of total knowledge.
The certain existence of God did not carry with it a guarantee that
he was susceptible to full comprehension, even in moments of
near-mystical or otherwise ecstatic insight, or to adequate expression in logical, priestly, or even poetic language. It is my sense, in
short, that Hopkins not only knew that "Gnosis ends in mystery,"
as Cotter allows,[9] but knew that it so began as well. Against the
critical emphasis on absolute certainty, and therefore against those
arguments that trace his conflicts as priest and poet to the impossibility of total union with God, spiritual or linguistic, I would set
Hopkins' own concept of "incomprehensible certainty," of certitude that remains mystery, and accepts mystery.

A general concept of mystery probably informs the thought of
any religious believer to some extent; a Catholic, and a Jesuit in
particular, will also specifically understand the word in its technical application to the episodes in Christ's life, presented in the
form of points for meditation in a major section of the *Spiritual
Exercises* ("The Mysteries of the Life of Christ Our Lord").[10] An
equally specific influence may also have been Cardinal Newman's
logically argued concept of "mental certitude" in religious matters,
resulting from "accumulated" or "converging" probabilities that
may ultimately lead "to a certitude which rises higher than the logical force of our conclusions."[11] But in Hopkins, while training,
logic, influence were certainly important, what converged was not
only an intellect in need of certitude, but a temperament and way
of seeing instinctively sympathetic to what is not wholly or easily
clear and graspable.

Even before fully formulating his concept of religious mystery
he seems to have had a natural, perhaps partly aesthetic and

8. Saint Ignatius of Loyola, *The Spiritual Exercises*, translated by Elder Mullan,
S.J., 124, 67–68.

9. *Inscape*, 262.

10. A sense of the word that Hopkins specifically includes and explains in the
letter to Bridges on Catholic mystery (*LB* 188).

11. *Apologia Pro Vita Sua: Being a History of His Religious Opinions*, 31, 180–
81. That Hopkins does not adopt Newman's careful distinction between "certitude," a habit of mind, and "certainty," a quality of propositions (31), may reflect
his own faith's absolute fusion of the two, or may simply result from his attempt to
make a complex concept clear to Bridges, a not wholly receptive correspondent on
such matters.

Ruskinian,[12] perhaps even partly physical, affinity for the visually mysterious, a dislike or at least a distrust of the visually clear. I have quoted one comment expressing his almost physical aversion to the "painful definiteness" of a landscape's effects. Scattered through the early journals are similar comments: "The straight quains and planing of the Alps were only too clear," for example, and "But too bright" (*JP* 171, 181), and of course in both journals and poems he remains fascinated with what is "pied," not primary, in color and nature. These are secular hints and reflections of what the bat flying in half-light implies more spiritually: a rejection of the blank, bright, too-distinct, too-garish colors of flat reality, untransmuted by an informing vision that could give them both greater distinctness and the complex vibration of mystery.

His particular concept of Catholic mystery, which is what I take to be crucial not only to the thought of the priest but also to the method of the poet, is clearly set forth in his "remarks" on the subject to Bridges in 1883, from which I must quote at some length.

> But by the way you say something I want to remark on: "Even such a doctrine as the Incarnation may be believed by people like yourself", as a mystery, till it is formulated, but as soon as it is it seems dragged down to the world of pros and cons, and *"as its mystery goes*, so does its hold on their minds". Italics the present writer's. You do not mean by mystery what a Catholic does. You mean an interesting uncertainty: the uncertainty ceasing interest ceases also. This happens in some things; to you in religion. But a Catholic by mystery means an incomprehensible certainty: without certainty, without formulation there is no interest (of course a doctrine is valuable for other things than its interest, its interestingness, but I am speaking now of that); the clearer the formulation the greater the interest. At bottom the source of interest is the same in both cases, in your mind and in ours; it is the unknown, the reserve of truth beyond what the mind reaches and still feels to be behind. But the interest a Catholic feels is, if I may say so, of a far finer kind than yours.

12. See Alison G. Sulloway's illuminating and detailed discussion of Ruskin's influence in *Gerard Manley Hopkins and the Victorian Temper*, 64–114. Especially pertinent to Hopkins' developing aesthetic, and in part religious, ideas about mystery is one of Ruskin's emphatic summaries of his consistent argument: "EXCELLENCE OF THE HIGHEST KIND, WITHOUT OBSCURITY CANNOT EXIST" (*Modern Painters*, quoted by Sulloway, 100).

The letter then proceeds to drive the point home through a carefully lucid comparison in secular terms of the lay and the Catholic "interest":

> Yours turns out to be a curiosity only: curiosity satisfied, the trick found out (to be a little profane), the answer heard, it vanishes at once. But you know there are some solutions to, say, chess problems so beautifully ingenious, some resolutions of suspensions so lovely in music that even the feeling of interest is keenest when they are known and over, and for some time survives the discovery. How must it then be when the very answer is the most tantalising statement of the problem and the truth you are to rest in the most pointed putting of the difficulty!

Finally, Hopkins goes on to speak specifically of the two central religious mysteries, in one of the rare moments in the whole of the correspondence in which he does so. Of the doctrine of the Trinity he argues that if it could be explained logically, "by grammar and by tropes," it would cease to be "the true mystery, the incomprehensible one," but that, as it is, the doctrine provides for Catholics both certainty and vital tension: "their knowledge leaves their minds swinging; poised, but on the quiver." And lastly, "So too of the Incarnation," the utterly crucial belief to Hopkins, so much so that he can dare to say that it is "a mystery less incomprehensible, it is true," than the Trinity, but one which again, to a Catholic, is both absolute fact and absolutely incomprehensible: "birth and death are not mysteries, nor is it any great mystery that a just man should be crucified, but that God should fascinates—with the interest of awe, of pity, of shame, of every harrowing feeling." This section of the letter then abruptly ends with a statement one can only regretfully disagree with: "But I have said enough" (October 24, 1883, *LB* 186–88).

It is my belief that Hopkins' poetic method, like every other aspect of his life and thought, is intimately related to, even dictated by, this concept of God, and all his mysteries, as "incomprehensible certainty," requiring and receptive to formulation—and "the clearer the formulation the greater the interest"—but always requiring also that human beings acknowledge their sense of the ultimate mystery, of "the unknown, the reserve of truth beyond what the mind reaches and still feels to be behind."

No introductory summary can do justice to the details of Hopkins' poetic style, but in central qualities it reflects exactly the ideas of the letter. It is a method that both clarifies and obscures its subject, characterized on the one hand by concreteness, distinctness, precision, vividness of language, sharpness of form, and on the other by complexity, density, multiplicity of meaning, even obscurity of meaning. Whether deliberately, half-deliberately, or simply instinctively and inevitably, given the poet-priest's vision of the world, it is a sacramental method, a visible sign of the invisible God, in all its aspects working to incarnate the great mystery in words that give it intensely precise "formulation," but a formulation that in the successful poems never gives us the sense of "the trick found out," never fails to make us feel that "the truth you are to rest in [is] the most pointed putting of the difficulty."

In method as well as content, the Real Presence is thus celebrated as real.[13] Divinity in Hopkins' poems informs what represents it, never wholly or neatly contained by its "symbols" of language, rhythm, form, movement, music, but so permeating them that it is felt to be both tangibly immanent and ungraspably transcendent. As a result, the effect of this poetry at its best is "to leave our minds swinging; poised, but on the quiver." I would therefore suggest that what Miller has come to see as tragic—"the tragic limitation of poetic language lies in the fact that the Word itself cannot be said"[14]—Hopkins accepted as essential mystery: a God who could be wholly grasped would not be God; a God who could be wholly named would not generate nor be worthy of either faith or poetry.

To draw toward an end of this beginning, I must circle back one final time to the early sonnet for some brief comment on three aspects of its method. These are elements that presage in a muted way what will be typical in Hopkins' later poems, all of them revealing, in still fairly straightforward ways to be sure, a working toward complex unity, a "formulation" that is clear, but not static. The first of these elements is paronomasia, or serious punning, through which multiple meanings of words—which he will later call "moments" of words—are fused into newly compounded complex meaning. The second is the fusion of multiple times and time schemes into one time, and the third is the handling of the sonnet structure so that it exactly dramatizes statement, creating both a progression and a circling.

The grave wit of this poem may be too carefully contrived and

13. On this doctrine, see letter to E. H. Coleridge, June 1, 1864, *FL* 17; Miller's profoundly suggestive summary of its centrality to Hopkins' basic view of being and general view of language in *Disappearance of God*, 311–15; Jeffrey B. Loomis, *Dayspring in Darkness: Sacrament in Hopkins*.

14. *Linguistic Moment*, 260.

cerebral, yet there is a quiet elegance to its ingenuity of conceit, and especially of wordplay: the musical puns on "minor," "dominant," "cadence," "range," and possibly "strains," are perhaps self-evident, but even here there is a somewhat complex vibration of "moments": "range" would seem to emphasize the paradox of the space and freedom discovered in limitation, in the circle's pattern; "state" not only carries its normal meaning, but acknowledges fealty to a higher royalty than himself; above all, "cadence" anticipates something of the complexity of the later Hopkins. Combining the dominant musical meaning (conclusion of a musical movement or phrase) with the secondary linguistic one (concluding rhythmic unit of a rhetorical period), it fuses in one word the two sorts of music a poet creates. Through its root meaning of "falling," combined with the initial imagery of flight, it may possibly also suggest the paradox that will be central to "The Windhover" and other later poems, because central to Christian belief, that of a falling that is also a rising, an ending that is also a beginning. Even in this relatively restrained and conventional sonnet, in short, Hopkins is experimenting with what his great Protestant predecessors, Milton, Herbert, and Donne, had long since known and used, and which Hopkins will carry to its furthest extreme: the possibilities, even the necessity, of the serious pun in the service and expression of faith.[15]

Second, while this sonnet's handling of time is by no means as intricate as that of later poems, it already shows a characteristic manipulation of tenses, and especially of present participles. The verbs not only range very freely in time but also consistently work to make the past and present, if not quite one, at least on a continuum: "And know infallibly which I preferred" (possibly, one admits, merely the result of the rhyme scheme's demands), and "is heard." More importantly, they make the present and the future one; the present participles of the octave and the infinitive of the final line create a present and ongoing action that neither begins nor ends, a "cadence" that is not merely an ending, but a "changeless note," now and always.

Finally, the handling of the structure is allied with this effect, and with the full meaning of "authentic cadence" in ecclesiastical

---

15. More than Donne or even Herbert, Milton was a major influence on Hopkins, explicitly on the theory and practice of counterpointed and sprung rhythms (April 3, 1877, *LB* 37–38; October 5, 1878, *LD* 13–14, 15), but I suspect also on the manipulation of multiple meanings of words and multiple times (both well illustrated in the opening lines of *Paradise Lost*).

music, "The Perfect Cadence, or Full Close." Within the traditional Petrarchan structure, the sonnet's movement compels the reader as well as the poet to discover "late" the full meaning; building toward the climactic final cadence, "Love and Love," it ends the sonnet with what is simultaneously a new discovery and a perfect closing of the poem's circle, a turning back to "Thee."

The sonnet is about arrival, discovery, and a turning home, while being at the same time about leave-taking: something of the sadness of parting is to be heard in it, I think. Although those "departing rings" in their context do not cancel the emphasis on the "changeless" commitment, since only the air-drawn shapes of action are ephemeral and vanishing—not the center, nor the singer, nor the song—the line does convey, to my ear at least, a strange loneliness, close to sadness. It may be that the phrase and image carry something of Hopkins' awareness that departings in a different sense were imminent, that coming home to the true center must and would demand a departure from former ones, that the "authentic cadence" was indeed an ending, a "close" as well as a new and true beginning.

Nevertheless, the emphasis is of course on the quiet joy of discovery, and while this careful and deliberate sonnet lacks the exclamatory vibrancy of some later poems of affirmation, certainly lacks the most un-"common" words and rhythms of his later music, it is typical at least of the heart and focus of his thought. It is also typical of many of the later poems in final tone, because of the quietude and firmness of its ending; here as later, discovery, revelation, may require no exclamation, merely commitment. Above all, it is typical of his thought, and in part of his method, in its use of twilight, and a creature of twilight, to express his discovery of final and ultimate vision. Night will later hold both vivid beauties and spiritual terrors for Hopkins, and bright dawns and bright harvest skies will bring him exuberant news of God, but the poise of spiritual twilight, what he will later call "not-to-call-night" (137), the condition of both seeing and nonseeing, knowing and not knowing, was I believe the inner climate in which and from which he shaped his life and poetry.

The "One spot," then, the one center, was not a neat solution to the riddle of the world, but a majestically revealing and still inscrutable new riddle, an "incomprehensible certainty," and I take it to be this special form of religious conviction that informs all aspects of Hopkins' critical and poetic method. Because it did so, because his "brilliancy, starriness, quain, margaretting," had their origin deep in religious conviction, his best poems manage to reconcile what he once presented to Dixon as irreconcilable for a Jesuit: "show and brilliancy do not suit us ... we cultivate the commonplace outwardly and wish the beauty of the king's daughter the soul to be from within" (December 1, 1881, *LD* 96). In the poems, the beauty of the king's daughter is indeed from within, but finds an equal beauty in the uncommonplace words that express it, words that are, in Longinus's phrase, "the light of thought," the light, in this case, of a vision of mystery.

3

"Things Real"
Vision and Revision

> The intelligible forms of ancient poets,
> The fair humanities of old religion,
> ....
> They live no longer in the faith of reason!
> But still the heart doth need a language, still
> Doth the old instinct bring back the old names.
> —Coleridge, *The Piccolomini* (Schiller), 2.4.123–31

THOUGH WRITING SPECIFICALLY of the new value of old mythology, Coleridge here summarizes the larger search, and some of the central losses, not only literary, of the nineteenth century. This chapter turns to Hopkins' relation to four aspects of his period's "overthought," his own term in a different context (*FL* 252).

Some of Hopkins' early critical defenders praised him at the expense of his century, as though he stood alone for intellect and discipline in a time of flabby-minded music-makers and dreamers of dreams,[1] but to elevate him by debasing his context misrepresents both his own achievement and the great achievements of his age. Since his originality did not spring full-fledged from the brainthroe of some sportive and "modern" end-of-century zeitgeist, identification of some fundamental concerns that he shared with his predecessors and contemporaries brings his sometimes radical divergences into sharper focus. Recognition also of the fact that he was writing when for some of the major endeavors and ideals of the century "The times are nightfall, look, their light grows less; / The

---

1. F. R. Leavis, *New Bearings in English Poetry: A Study of the Contemporary Situation*, 10, 193; Gardner, *Hopkins*, 1:193; William Empson, *Seven Types of Ambiguity*, 22, 27.

times are winter, watch, a world undone" (150), makes the more remarkable that life with which he newly charged some aspects of a great but darkening world.

Though we may agree with Hopkins that "Romantic is a bad word"—and one that he himself applied only to Keats, Hunt, Hood, and Scott (*LD* 98)—it is now the best available to describe the dominant intellectual, literary, and spiritual movement of the century as a whole, as well as Hopkins' particular relation to it. While in literal time he of course belongs to the Victorians, the Romantics of the second and third generation, and while persuasive arguments have been made for his essentially Victorian temperament and intellectual position,[2] in my view it is in the line and spirit of the firstborn, the great early Romantics, that Hopkins stands.

The Romantic movement, impulse, way of seeing—all words are "bad" words for it—had sprung from the urgently felt need not to escape reality, but to rediscover and re-create a cosmos out of the chaos "reality" had become. This was the search that caused so many major writers of the century to look for new access to new sources of vision, coherence, permanence—and specifically to look to the self as a first and possibly representative reality, and to the imagination as the possibly redemptive faculty within the self. It is also the search that generated the basic attempt of Transcendental philosophy in its various forms: opposing the dead hand of Lockean and post-Lockean empiricism, this was the attempt to posit a theory of objective reality, even divine Reality, that would yet leave room for the creative action of the human mind.

Intense consciousness of individuality and complexity, therefore, "pied beauty" at best, chaos and confusion at worst, combined with the longing for a key to complexity, led to the central aspiration of the Romantic mind, the desire to be, like Wordsworth's skylark, "true to the kindred points of Heaven and Home." The belief that these were, or should be, kindred points, together with the acute awareness, felt by all Byronic heroes and most Romantic writers, of the intolerable difference, produced the century's persistent aspiration: the attempt to reconcile this

2. See especially Sulloway, *Victorian Temper*, and Wendell Stacy Johnson, *Gerard Manley Hopkins: The Poet as Victorian*. For discussion of the specific influences of Wordsworth, Keats, Shelley, the Pre-Raphaelites, and Tennyson, see Gardner, *Hopkins*, 2:34–40, and the excellent concise summary of these and other influences in Norman H. MacKenzie's indispensable *A Reader's Guide to Gerard Manley Hopkins*, 210–20.

world's complexities, inner and outer, with some ideal source of coherence above the temporal world, yet somehow, somewhere, intersecting with the temporal to give it meaning.[3]

While these broad generalizations validly apply to the over-movement of the century as a whole, by Hopkins' time the terms in which the search was conceived had undergone several, sometimes radical changes. Some of the potential sources of spiritual reality still available to the Romantics seemed, and were, denied to the mid-Victorians. Pre-Darwinian and Darwinian nature was no longer spiritual nurse or guide or guardian or minister of beauty, though it was perhaps still a minister of fear. Beauty could no longer—with an easy conscience—be called Truth: the Palace of Art, even though Tennyson could not bring himself to tear its towers down, could be seen as a stagnant and sinfully selfish pleasure-dome, not as Kubla Khan's visionary ordering of, and amid, dark realities. The dialogue of the mind with itself, and even the reaching of the self toward something other, larger, higher, than self, came to seem in some cases sterile, suspect, guilt-laden. The pied possibilities of a richly varied world could be merely Arnold's chaotic and paralyzing "multitudinousness." Dream vision might reveal not only deep insights and high grandeur through magic casements or Moneta's veil, but also the insubstantiality of idle singers and their dream ideals, or Childe Roland's landscape of reality as nightmare. Even the past, whether of mythology or of childhood, could reveal not only heroic archetypes and saving origins but also the modern tragedy of an Empedocles, the adulteration of Camelot, the corruption and death of innocence in all the satanic mills of England's mines and city ghettos. Above all, the problems of this world, urgently demanding responsible social action, not self-expression, nor even inspired vision, however high-magical or heart-deep, exerted a sobering and, as it were, lowering pressure on mid-Victorian aspiration; the roads from Xanadu were many and various, but on the whole led downward from the palace to the valley. Nevertheless, until the Aesthetic movement severed art from life, and tried to make art itself the one eternity, the attempt to achieve moments, at least, of intersection between mortal and immortal worlds continued, although it increasingly took the form either of a liberal and undogmatic Christianity (Tennyson, Ruskin,

3. For the best full discussion of this whole point, see David Perkins, *The Quest for Permanence: The Symbolism of Wordsworth, Shelley, and Keats*, to which my allusive summary is indebted.

the Brownings, Carlyle, Dickens) or of the elevation to godhead of something other than the "old name" of God: Culture, and eventually poetry (Arnold); human morality and decency (Eliot); humanity itself (Swinburne); art itself (Aestheticism).

Hopkins was an early Romantic by instinct, a Victorian by birth, a Catholic priest by choice. He shared with his Romantic predecessors their intense attempt to penetrate and order reality in new ways, while also being conscious of its mystery. He obviously shared their search for the ideal penetrating this world but above it. He shared their passionate response to the variety and richness of the temporal world, the streaks in the tulip, "all things counter, original, spare, strange." He shared their attempt to make the special self a starting point for the discovery of much more than self, their almost obsessively acute awareness of mutability and pain, and, with the one major exception of reliance on mythology and dream-vision,[4] most central aspects of their poetic procedure.

Obviously, however, his answers to shared questions, his sensibility, thought, and poetry, were governed by his commitment to an "old religion" that was not an unformulated faith, or hopeful trust, or wistful reminiscence. For him, the "old instinct" brought back the oldest of names to resolve the tensions of the world's dichotomies and fragmentations, to make Beauty one with Truth again. The ideal, for him, while transcendentally and massively mysterious, was nevertheless intensely present, eloquently "worded" by heaven and earth. Though the "terrible sonnets" reflect a special crisis of loss, and though throughout his mature life he wrote out of the difficult certainty of paradox,[5] not the comfort of vagueness, neither as man nor as poet was he characteristically in the condition of other poet-pilgrims of his time. His road was not unclear, though it was difficult; his divinity was not unclear, though it was ungraspable; he was not groping blindly toward what might be behind the veil or at the height of the great world's altar stairs, but never quite sure what was there, if it was there. "Swinging" and "on the quiver" his mind was, but with the complex clarity of a faith that gave it "poise."

More specifically, the precise formulation given that faith by

4. Among the mature poems, none employs dream-vision, only "Andromeda" has a mythological subject, and only *St. Winefred's Well* turns to the historical past, perhaps because his own central "myth" was both a timeless and present reality.

5. That Hopkins would not have considered either his faith or his poems "paradoxical" in any merely literary or rhetorical sense is discussed in the context of *The Wreck of the Deutschland*, Chapter 5.

Ignatian thought helped clarify for him, and to an extent resolve, two related issues that haunted the age: the relation between humanity and nature, and the relation between mind and world. Ignatian teaching allowed him, first, a view of nature unblurred by pantheistic confusions. He did not need to find in stones the sermons he had already hidden there, as Wilde cattily but perceptively remarked of Wordsworth's practice; he did not share the dilemma of those Transcendental thinkers, both English and American, who sought to find, or put, some sort of God in nature, but "who, if they got Him in, could not get Him above it,"[6] in David Downes's concise summary.

Hopkins understood quite clearly that the created world "is word, expression, news of God" (SD 129), a visible sign of its invisible creator, and therefore to be studied, rejoiced in, loved, but never to be identified with the creator, nor to be loved or worshiped in his place. Accepting as fundamental the Ignatian First Principle that "Man was created to praise, reverence, and serve God Our Lord, and by so doing to save his soul," he also understood Ignatius to allow that a proper response to nature, "a proper use of creatures," is one of the means, and not a hindrance, to this end: "And the other things on the face of the earth were created for man's sake and to help him in the carrying out of the end for which he was created" (SD 122).[7] He could therefore delight in the natural world without confusion or guilt, and without endowing it with moral or redemptive powers. Windhovers, kingfishers, dappled skies, stooks in harvest, stars and bluebells and ashtrees, could point beyond themselves to the God who made them, but they could not, for Hopkins, knowingly serve, prove, or wholly embody God: "'The heavens declare the glory of God.' They glorify God, *but they do not know it*. The birds sing to him, the thunder speaks of his terror, the lion is like his strength, the sea is like his greatness, the honey like his sweetness; they are something like him . . . they give him glory, but they do not know they do, they do not know him, they never can . . . . But man can know God, *can mean to give him glory*. This then was why he was made, to give God glory and to mean to give it" (SD 239).

Second, Hopkins' faith governed his response to that larger dilemma, probably the dominant philosophical dilemma in

6. *Ignatian Spirit*, 76–77.
7. For an argument that Hopkins' understanding of this "First Principle and Foundation" and his entire sacramental view of the world are actually at odds with the central emphasis of Ignatius, see Fulweiler, *Letters*, 137–40.

nineteenth-century overthought, of the relation between the mind and the external world. For the poets, the new emphasis in philosophy and science on the problems of perception, on the perceiving mind's part in making the world it perceives, took the form of attention to the imaginative faculty specifically, as Coleridge brilliantly exemplifies.[8] But this emphasis was combined with that other persistent need for an objective reality external to mind, which the imagination might recognize (or "seize" on, in Keats's phrase) as well as create. Romantic theory therefore emphasized, and Hopkins inherited and developed, a concept of the creative reciprocity between creating mind and the existent world: a relationship in which our consciousness is "creator and receiver both,"[9] recognizing an external world called into being by Coleridge's Ancient of Days "at the first creative fiat," but also newly creating it by the constant, and godlike, act of individual perception.[10]

This concept no longer dominated, if it even survived, by the end of the century, but Hopkins' concepts of the imagination in general, and of "inscape" and "instress" in particular, make him something of a throwback to the attitudes of his Romantic forbears. Since there is no need here to retrace the ground broadly surveyed above, and explored in detail by Harold Bloom, Bell Gale Chevigny, and others,[11] my comments here will merely focus briefly on two successors of Wordsworth and Coleridge, two known and major influences on Hopkins, Keats and Ruskin.

Keats's "speculations," unsystematic though they are, "straining at particles of light in the midst of a great darkness,"[12] often prove more swiftly illuminating on some of the dark matters in question than more formal Romantic theories, and it was the

8. M. H. Abrams' *The Mirror and the Lamp: Romantic Theory and the Critical Tradition* remains a definitive study of this fundamental aspect of Romantic thought. Also see Fulweiler, *Letters*, 11–23, for a concise summary of the post-Lockean revolution in theories of reality and language and of its bearing on this issue of the relation between mind and world.

9. William Wordsworth, *The Prelude*, ed. Ernest de Selincourt, rev. Helen Darbishire, 2.258.

10. Samuel Taylor Coleridge, *Biographia Literaria*, ed. J. Shawcross, 1:59, 202.

11. Bloom, *The Visionary Company: A Reading of English Romantic Poetry*, 120–91. Chevigny's "Instress and Devotion in the Poetry of Gerard Manley Hopkins" includes a particularly helpful summary of the parallels between Coleridge's two forms of imagination and Hopkins' two kinds of instress (143–45).

12. Keats, to George and Georgiana Keats, March 19, 1819, in *The Letters of John Keats*, ed. Hyder Edward Rollins, 2:80.

promise of Keats's critical thought, more than the poetry, that Hopkins explicitly admired.[13] "The Imagination may be compared to Adam's dream—he awoke and found it truth," Keats had written in a famous early letter, and he had tentatively explored in the same letter the workings of a mind and power that can both "seize" and create from realities here the Reality—"the Prototype"—hereafter.[14] It is this power's power that later letters and poems explore, following it both into the "dark passages" of pain and heartbreak and toward the possibility that it reveals "on earth" all we need to know. It is this power that Ruskin then systematically developed, far more elaborately than Keats or even Coleridge, and with an explicitly Christian emphasis. For Ruskin, not only was the imagination the power that penetrates reality and finds Truth—"a piercing, pholas-like mind's tongue, that works and tastes into the very rock heart"[15]—but intense study of reality was justified by his belief that all things of beauty in the phenomenal world bespeak a personal and governing Divine Presence behind and within them.

Hopkins is clearly at one with these, and earlier, Romantic thinkers in his concept of the imagination's possible doubleness ("either energetic or receptive"),[16] and in his view of it not as a fiction-making faculty, but as one means of penetrating inmost reality. Indeed, the *Spiritual Exercises* support and command this latter view: "The imagination is employed to realise truth, not error, but under its own imagery" (*SD* 179, translating the Ignatian Latin). But also, one must add, obviously under a different aegis from that of most Romantics, and with different premises and ends. Hopkins is filled with "loathing and horror" at the thought "of man setting up the work of his own hands, of that hand within the mind the imagination, for God Almighty who made heaven

13. See especially "He was, in my opinion, made to be a thinker, a critic, as much as a singer or artist of words" (to Coventry Patmore, May 6, 1888, *FL* 386–87).

14. To Benjamin Bailey, November 17, 1817, in *Letters of Keats*, ed. Rollins, 1:185.

15. "Of the Imaginative Faculty," *Modern Painters*, in *Works*, 4:251. Also related to Hopkins' procedures in both journals and poems are such characteristic statements as, "The imagination sees the heart and inner nature, and makes them felt, but is often obscure, mysterious, and interrupted, in its giving of outer detail" (*Modern Painters*, in *Works*, 4:253).

16. To Baillie, September 10, 1864, *FL* 216. The phrase in context specifically describes "inspiration," the highest source of the highest poetry, but I think he is making no real distinction between the two terms in this early letter.

and earth" (October 23, 1886, *LD* 146). He is making more than a nod to the ancestry of the Muses, or to Wordsworth, in subordinating imagination as he does within the larger faculty of memory;[17] above all, the truth aimed at in Ignatian meditation is not vivid realization of human possibilities or sufferings, but an intense and humble recognition of God's.

More specifically, Hopkins' concepts of "inscape," *haecceitas*, and "instress" show likeness, perhaps debt, to Romantic theories, though again with Ignatian, and particularly Scotist, differences. Hopkins' search in all areas of being for "inscape" exactly parallels the Romantic attempt to "draw a kind of quintessence from things,"[18] the attempt, as Robert Langbaum puts it, "to open a channel from the individual to its archetype by eluding the rational category of the type."[19] But for Hopkins, it was the Scotist formulation of this concept, or Scotist confirmation of Ruskin's ideas, that was crucial.

Since Duns Scotus, unlike Aquinas, allowed *haecceitas* (special individuality, "this-ness," what makes any thing or person an intensely special self) to be part of the individual's ideal form, and a pointer toward the divine creator, the pied beauties that Hopkins instinctively loved were sanctioned as more than isolated or isolating or secular oddities; for him as for Keats, "the Prototype must be hereafter," but what is special here bespeaks that high ideal. For him also, as for Keats, though perhaps coincidentally, and with the usual difference in emphasis, great truths do not depend on literal present existence: of Beauty's reality and meaning Keats had written, "What the imagination seizes as Beauty must be truth— whether it existed before or not";[20] of *haecceitas*, Scotist thought held that "a *haecceitas* is a reality whether it exists or not . . . because it is a distinct intention in God's will" (*SD* 303*n.186.2*). In both cases, what is apprehensible in and by the mortal particular bespeaks immortal reality. In Graham Storey's helpful summary of Scotus, the point is "that the mind could come to know the universal (the *summum* of all medieval philosophy) through apprehend-

17. Influenced by Scotus, Hopkins defines imagination as that form of "memory" that is directed toward the future or the unknown and goes on to say that memory "on the strain . . . gives rise to *reverence*" and to "the sense of the *presence* of God" (*SD* 174).

18. Coleridge, *Biographia Literaria*, ed. J. Shawcross, 2:13.

19. *The Poetry of Experience: The Dramatic Monologue in Modern Literary Tradition*, 66.

20. November 17, 1817, in *Letters of Keats*, ed. Rollins, 1:185.

ing an individual object's 'this-ness' (*haecceitas*), and that such apprehensions ultimately reveal God."[21]

Whether or not *haecceitas* and inscape should be equated is a matter of some debate. Devlin crisply and brusquely rejected the identification early on (*SD* 293n.146.5); Miller has pursued the point more recently, arguing that "inscape" for Hopkins was not individual specialness, but the opposite—what a number of individuals have in common.[22] In my view, however, the exact equation or nonequation of the terms seems less important than Hopkins' basic concept of the relation of special self to larger universals. That he did not himself see inconsistency between "own, abrupt self" and the universal seems clear in the headnote to "Henry Purcell" (45): "he has . . . uttered in notes the very make and species of man as created both in him and in all men generally." As I understand it, this is a Scotist formulation of the central Romantic assumption that the special particular, deeply understood and fully revealed, may speak for and of the many; like the "I" of *The Prelude*, and of so many other nineteenth-century works in prose and poetry, the intense singular is both singular and representative. It is what Ruskin very precisely called the "specific" ideal, "not the individual, but the specific."[23]

Similarly, one aspect of Hopkins' concept of "instress," its verbal use and meaning, is closely allied to that central Romantic concept of energetic reciprocity between mind and world, though again with a crucial distinction. And again, both kinship and difference show a close parallel to Keats. Musing on the sources of reality of "Things real—things semireal—and no things," Keats speculated that while there are things so "real" that they require no action of the mind upon them, the insistently great and unquestionable facts of the world ("Sun Moon & Stars and passages of Shakespeare"), and "no things," wholly dependent for their value "on the ardour of the pursuer," there is also the crucial second category: "Things semireal such as Love, the Clouds etc. which require

21. *Gerard Manley Hopkins*, 11.
22. *Disappearance of God*, 282–83, 293. The weight of the evidence seems to me to support the near identity of the terms to Hopkins, but Miller's argument may well identify some slippery logic in his thinking, and even in Scotus.
23. "The true ideal of landscape is precisely the same as that of the human form; it is the expression of the specific—not the individual, but the specific—characters of every object, in their perfection. There is an ideal form of every herb, flower, and tree; it is that form to which every individual of the species has a tendency to arrive" ("Preface to the Second Edition," *Modern Painters*, in *Works*, 3:27).

a greeting of the Spirit to make them wholly exist."[24] Not only is the whole Romantic concept of the mind's creative action on the world summarized in that one swift phrase, "a greeting of the Spirit," but, specifically, Keats's distinctions may have found a receptive listener in Hopkins: to Keats's somewhat whimsical list of "things real," Hopkins simply and seriously added "God."

Whether or not there was any direct Keatsian influence on this particular point, instressing did involve for Hopkins mutual, reciprocal energies in object and beholder, a "greeting" and correspondence between the receptive consciousness and what it sees, an act of bringing fully into being what the senses have perceived and pointed toward. It is an act of spiritual interpretation beyond sense perception, as was the similar functioning of the imaginative eye and spirit for the Romantics. And for Hopkins as for them, when instress given off by any object is answered by the beholder's power to instress—"which two when they once meet" (38)—the flash of revelation comes, but without that response, never.

The crucial distinction involved here, however, is that for Hopkins the power of any created thing to give off instress and to instress derives specifically and absolutely from an original and divine source, God's stress of energy, which charges the world with life, sustains it, keeps inscapes tautly at tension, prevents disintegration of being. Instress is thus both the life-giving energy in any object, derived from God, and the energy given off by that object, news of its selfhood and of its maker, when it is perfectly fulfilling its God-given function. It is the outgoing energy of inscape, "the *form* speaking."

From this central belief much follows, both in theory and in practice, that distinguishes Hopkins from even his closest kindred among the early Romantics. "What you look hard at seems to look hard at you" (March 1871, *JP* 204): this is Hopkins' way of phrasing the persistent Romantic concept of reciprocal energies, "Of action from without and from within."[25] But Hopkins does not end his statement where I have ended the quotation, and the additional phrase is crucial: "What you look hard at seems to look hard at you, hence the true and the false instress of nature."[26] "False instress" I

24. To Bailey, March 13, 1818, in *Letters of Keats*, ed. Rollins, 1:242–43.
25. Wordsworth, *The Prelude*, ed. Selincourt and Darbishire, 13.376.
26. For an opposing reading of this statement see Chevigny, "Instress and Devotion," 143. For further discussion of the complications of inscape, instress, and *haecceitas*, see especially W. A. M. Peters, S.J., *Gerard Manley Hopkins: A Critical Essay towards the Understanding of His Poetry*, 1–28, and Devlin, *SD* 283–84, 293,

take to be what is "imposed outwards from the mind as for instance by melancholy or strong feeling" (September 14, 1871, *JP* 215), a falseness Ruskin had labeled "pathetic fallacy" and that Keats had intuitively rejected in part in his acknowledgment of "Things real," but one that most Romantics accept. These relatively early statements by Hopkins already point toward the strenuous intellectual determination of his mature thinking to preserve the objective reality of the God-created world, its integrity apart from mind. While he consistently believed that for full revelation the viewer must bring his powers of instress to bear, he believed also that even if the human mind did not answer to the world or to God, God is still there, the world is still there, the freshness is still "deep down things," the bright wings sustain; these are "Things real" in the most absolute sense. Only temporarily and to the subjective eye, governed by subjective mood, does the world sometimes seem to fall apart and inscape to fail;[27] if inscaping did mean to him "hitting the mark," as Cotter persuasively argues,[28] only briefly and to the darkened vision is individual failure to do so allowed to seem equivalent to *hamartia* and its resultant tragic and cosmic destruction.

In short, not the human mind in general, nor the imagination in particular, nor the imagination's creations, could be for Hopkins, as for some of his predecessors and contemporaries, the creative divinity to replace a lost God. While recognizing the potency of mind—recognizing it most desolately in "that night, that year" of 1885—he characteristically insists on the objective reality of God-created things, and of their Creator, center and encloser of all the world's concentric circles: "The universal mind is outside of my inmost self and not within it" (*SD* 126).[29]

This respect for the realities outside mind, combined with his interest in the mind itself, produced in Hopkins' best poems a third characteristic, a particular kind of Romantic subjectivity, which as-

---

303, 338. For further discussion of Ruskin's influence, and for illuminating readings of major poems according to Ruskinian principles, see Sulloway, *Victorian Temper*, 105–14.

27. See especially two comments that will have special bearing on "Spelt from Sibyl's Leaves": "being unwell I was quite downcast: nature in all her parcels and faculties gaped and fell apart, *fatiscebat*" (August 16, 1873, *JP* 236), and "It is not that inscape does not govern the behaviour of things in slack and decay as one can see . . . even in a skeleton but that horror prepossesses the mind" (June 19, 1871, *JP* 211).

28. Cotter, *Inscape*, 18–21.

29. The full context of this statement should be consulted, *SD* 122–29.

pires to and achieves a new objectivity. Though again the "terrible sonnets" are a special case, most of Hopkins' poems reflect an attitude that is at once inward and outward directed, both private and dramatic, self-assertive and self-denying. Individuality and the special taste and expression of self obviously mattered to him, but he did not equate inscape, *haecceitas*, or any of his other terms for particular selfhood with mere ego, or even with subjectivity. No more than Purcell's music is Hopkins' own verse "d____d subjective rot" (*LB* 84), but like Keats, he tends to achieve objectivity in the way Langbaum has explored in detail in *The Poetry of Experience*: not by standing far back from his subject, but by so penetrating it that the personal self is annihilated by entering and becoming other selves. He could not therefore have agreed with Arnold's sad summary of the Romantic method: "such a price / The Gods exact for song: / To become what we sing";[30] for Hopkins, as for Keats, and for any dramatic poet, the "price" was also the achievement.

Again, however, Hopkins' kinship with a major Romantic tendency resulted from more than artistic or temperamental inclinations, and from more than a good Victorian sense of altruism or philosophical respect for "disinterestedness." It was dictated and channeled in special ways by the doctrinal demand of self-sacrifice and the doctrinal hope of self-discovery in Christ. Because in Hopkins' thought "Christ plays in ten thousand places" (57), because he informs and is all true selves, all true acts, "to become what we sing" is in a special way to come close to being one with him without losing individual identity. Because any being, especially any human being, that "Selves—goes itself" (57) is glorifying not its own ego but the divine origin of its function and selfhood, it approaches oneness with that origin; self-assertion and self-annihilation become curiously synonymous.

Fourth and finally, while Hopkins' poems are haunted from first to last by a painfully acute and characteristically Romantic awareness of the mutability of beauty, happiness, and above all innocence in its fullest sense, Romantic sensibility speaks in them with a Catholic difference. An undated but almost certainly early poem, "Spring and Death" (4), a derivative but charming small allegory, ends with a poignant couplet whose thought sounds again and again through later poems: "It seem'd so hard and dismal

30. "The Strayed Reveller," lines 232–34. In connection with Hopkins' dramatic method, see the discussion of its "miming" elements in Geoffrey H. Hartman's "Introduction: Poetry and Justification," in *Hopkins: A Collection of Critical Essays*, 1–14.

thing, / Death, to mark them in the Spring." It is of flowers marked in their prime that these lines speak; later, only a few poems will lament transience in the natural world. Nature will almost always be viewed as not only beautiful in all its seasons but also invincibly eternal in its cycle of death to rebirth, and the flowers marked in spring will be the Margarets and Bugler Boys and Felix Randals of the world, all who are or may be doomed to loss of "innocent mind and Mayday" (33), all who are spiritually threatened by the "dark tramplers, tyrant years" (157), all who have been marked in the world's spring by Adam's fall.

That all mortal things end Hopkins knew as well and mourned as elegiacally as his fellow poets in a century peculiarly characterized by great voices of loss and ending, but that knowledge was both intensified and resolved for him by his Christian faith: by his belief both in the Fall, an irrevocable end at time's beginning, and in the new spiritual beginnings without end offered daily and hourly to each person's choice, making possible the ultimate hope that "mortal trash" may become the bright permanence of "immortal diamond" (72). In his mature poems, therefore, sorrow's source is no longer the dying flowers or falling leaves of this cosmic Goldengrove, nor even the physical death of beauty and of human beings that these deaths symbolize for so many of his contemporary poets, nor is it the bittersweet philosophical knowledge of Yeats's "Man is in love, and loves what vanishes." Hopkins' sorrow springs from the acute fear that man may indeed choose to love what vanishes instead of the saving God "past change," that the "hell-rook ranks" (48) of the world may therefore corrupt and conquer him in life, and that, dying unsaved, he may be their victim hereafter. It takes a vision that assumes so terrible a permanence as hell, so splendid a permanence as heaven, to make of the age-old but peculiarly Romantic problem of mutability a matter of more than philosophical and poetic sorrow, of more than philosophical and poetic acceptance, to make it a matter of moral terror and of spiritual hope, and it is with such a vision that Hopkins, unlike most of his major contemporaries, did view it.

The century's persistent dilemmas and dualities were not irrelevant or forgotten in Hopkins' Catholic vision and poetry but found in them new resolutions, and a new voice. And if one sees with Hopkins' eyes for a moment, it may seem particularly satisfying and appropriate that it should have been when the Romantic movement had all but spent its force, when the times were growing nightfall for any convinced faith of any kind, that Hopkins' belief in the oldest of "old names" for "Things real" gave Romanticism a new and vital poetic form, so new as to seem "modern" to our century, and answered in a new-old way the heart's old need for a language.

4

"The Synthesis of the Succession"
Cadence and Its Theory

IT WAS THE young Hopkins' opinion that "the most inveterate fault of critics is the tendency to cramp and hedge in by rules the free movements of genius" (September 6, 1863, *FL* 204), yet as man, priest, and poet he was himself intensely in need of "rules," doctrine, authority, and as critic, extremely prolific in formulating poetic laws and principles. "Where there is much freedom of motion the laws which limit it should be strict" he wrote to Patmore in relation to sprung rhythm (*FL* 335), a comment that also reflects his larger critical and religious views. This chapter examines a few of his own "strict laws" in order to explore some of the ways in which the priest's vision underlies the critic's language and the poet's practice.

This discussion is necessarily speculative, since the critical remarks are almost invariably couched in secular terms, and Hopkins rarely theorized about specifically religious poetry. Possibly it would have seemed semi-sacrilegious to him to lay down rules about a style adequate to "word" God, or at least futile, given the religious views of his major correspondent. Possibly also his basic subject and vision were so central that they did not require constant laboring; in a rather painful letter to Bridges, replying to what he took as a charge—or perhaps hope—that he was not himself in earnest with his religion, he puts the point plainly: "However a man who is deeply in earnest is not very eager to assert his earnestness, as they say when a man is really certain he no longer disputes but is indifferent. And that is all I say now, that to think a man in my position is not in earnest is unreasonable and is to make difficulties" (November 26, 1882, *LB* 163).

Above all, he may simply have been reflecting in his theoretical

38

and critical writings the distinctions that were always crucial to him even from undergraduate days. "The Origin of Our Moral Ideas," probably written for Walter Pater in 1865, distinguishes clearly between the aims of art and the aims of morality, and concludes with a point central to Hopkins' mature thought and poetic practice: "In art we strive to realise not only unity, permanence of law, likeness, but also, with it, difference, variety, contrast: it is rhyme we like, not echo, and not unison but harmony. But in morality the highest consistency is the highest excellence" (*JP* 83). This clear and early recognition of the distinction between the two realms is not sufficiently weighted, in my view, by those critical theories that see in Hopkins' later linguistic experiments a reflection of theological confusion, frustration, even despair, a view most fully developed in Miller's argument that linguistic and artistic multiplicity necessarily undermined, at least challenged, a theological belief in unity.[1] The available and recurrent evidence seems to me to suggest that on this one point, at least, Hopkins remained perfectly clear in his own mind: art is art, God is God; multiplicity is mortal, unity is divine; language is human, Logos is God.

From these fundamental distinctions much follows, in theory and in practice. Letter after letter emphasizes not only the dangers of fame to him, the priest, and his perfectly practical as well as moralistic sense that "I cannot in conscience spend time on poetry" (February 15, 1879, *LB* 66), but also a further, and double, point. Noble as art is, or should be, important as its fame and permanence should be to true artists, nevertheless "art and its fame do not really matter, spiritually they are nothing, virtue is the only good; but it is only by bringing in the infinite that to a just judgment they can be made to look infinitesimal or small or less than vastly great" (October 13, 1886, *LB* 231).

The generous, though perhaps slightly condescending, duality of this comment is not a sign of intolerable conflict in him, I think, but a clear-eyed reflection of his considered values and choices. Bridges, Dixon, and Patmore, Hopkins apparently felt, could and should value their art and do what good they might through it, but for himself the infinite was always there, setting the higher goal, lowering the claims of art by widening perspective. For him, "the only just judge, the only just literary critic, is Christ" (June 13, 1878, *LD* 8), and he did not discuss with any other critic the extent

1. *Linguistic Moment*, 242–66.

to which his own poetic theory reflects his habitual practice of "bringing in the infinite."

Since to many early readers, as seen, he appeared not to bring in the infinite or anything else in the way of content, the first question tackled here is the issue of "meaning": the degree to which Hopkins' own theories advocate or deny its importance to poetry, the degree to which they justify or refute those critics who treat him as an advocate and practitioner of art for art's sake, poetry for sound's sake, and hence as a poetic champion of beauty only, divorced from "morality." In a passage tirelessly quoted by these critics, Hopkins does parenthetically state, "Poetry is in fact speech only employed to carry the inscape of speech for the inscape's sake—and therefore the inscape must be dwelt on." What immediately precedes this parenthesis, however, makes clear that he is not denying the importance of meaning altogether, but simply exploring what is special to poetry's way of "meaning": "Poetry is speech framed for contemplation of the mind by way of hearing or speech framed to be heard for its own sake and interest even over and above its interest of meaning. Some matter and meaning is essential to it but only as an element necessary to support and employ the shape which is contemplated for its own sake" ("Poetry and Verse," *JP* 289).[2] He then proceeds to a rather opaque distinction between poetry and verse, but clearly emphasizes the necessity of both meaning and artistry: verse is "speech wholly or partially repeating some kind of figure which is over and above meaning, at least the grammatical, historical, and logical meaning"; "But is all verse poetry? . . . it [verse] might be composed without meaning (as nonsense verse and choruses—'Hey nonny nonny' or 'Wille wau wau wau' etc) and then *alone* it would not be poetry but might be part of a poem. But if it has a meaning and is meant to be heard for its own sake it will be poetry."

Taken as a whole, this passage seems to me an almost irreproachable statement about the nature of poetry, at least lyric poetry. Like numerous critics before him, including Aristotle, Hopkins is simply maintaining that the distinctive value and impact of poetry do not derive from paraphrasable content alone, but from its ways of conveying content, its interest "even over and

2. That I and other critics make such heavy weather of what were probably early lecture notes (1873–1874) will earn Hopkins the sympathy of any teacher. For more on the central theory, see Humphry House, "Introduction," *JP* xxvi–xxvii, and Donald McChesney's concise and perceptive "The Meaning of 'Inscape,'" 55–57.

above its interest of meaning." Its immediate end is what Words-worth and Coleridge had risked calling "pleasure" not "truth," but this is by no means a suggestion that it is or should be wholly de-void of "truth."

Pattern, sound, technique, virtuosity of execution were cer-tainly important to Hopkins, in theory as in practice. His unwill-ingness to slight their value in any work of art is reflected, for example, in his reply to Bridges' dismissal of technique in painting: "'The first touch of decadence destroys all merit whatever': this is a hard saying. What, all technical merit—as chiaroscuro, anatomical knowledge, expression, feeling, colouring, drama? It is plainly not true. . . . Go to" (February 23, 1889, *LB* 300).[3] But neither accu-racy of observation and representation nor a design only of the sur-face constituted "inscape" for Hopkins. Since inscape meant for him the essence of any thing or experience made visible, apprehen-sible, articulate (and since perhaps "its own *sake*" already carries its later, similarly expressive, meaning),[4] the inscape of which he speaks in defining poetry could not have been for him merely a weaving of pleasing sounds and repeated "figures." That "shape which is contemplated for its own sake" would necessarily be the translation of inscaped sight, encounter, thought, feeling, into the new, heightened, but still accurate inscape of the work of art. The statement that "design, pattern or what I am in the habit of calling 'inscape' is what I above all aim at in poetry" (February 15, 1879, *LB* 66) seems therefore not at all irreconcilable with a concern for "truth" in its deepest sense.

Whether or not my interpretation of these early notes is valid,[5] it is plain fact that Hopkins elsewhere stressed constantly the im-

3. See also his comments admiring English poetry for its "insight and inspira-tion" but lamenting its weakness in "rhetoric," in execution, control of structure, control of language (August 7, 1886, *LD* 141).

4. Suggested by Michael Sprinker, *"A Counterpoint of Dissonance": The Aes-thetics and Poetry of Gerard Manley Hopkins*, 69. The idiosyncratic meaning was fully developed some years after the quoted lecture notes (stanza 22 of *The Deutschland*, 1875), and not explained to Bridges until four years later still (May 26, 1879, *LB* 83), but the combined meaning of inward specialness and outward speaking might have been germinating in his mind much earlier.

5. It is certainly open to challenge. Miller, for example, derives from these notes only one of the three poetic theories he finds in Hopkins' writings, that of the poet who is simply "a skilled craftsman" (*Disappearance of God*, 284). The argu-ment that Hopkins tried to reconcile incompatible theories of poetry, but ulti-mately failed, is still more strenuously pursued in *Linguistic Moment*, 249–50, 262–66.

portance of thought, of high seriousness, to poetry. "But words only are only words" he comments on Swinburne's *Locrine* (July 29, 1888, *LD* 157), and he sees in Swinburne's poetry in general "a perpetual functioning of genius without truth, feeling, or any adequate matter to be at function on" (April 29, 1889, *LB* 304). Of Dixon's *Mano* he says "it either has not or else I have hitherto missed finding a leading thought to thread the beauties on" (October 24, 1883, *LB* 189), and he objects to Richard Crawley's *Venus and Psyche* on the grounds that "it is not serious; the scenes are scarcely realised; the story treated as a theme for trying style on" (June 1, 1886, *LB* 225). At least in Hopkins' theory, therefore, the first essential for the poet, and the poem, was not technique but substance, thoughtful engagement with a subject, for whose absence no amount of technical skill could compensate. In a thoroughly "Victorian" and Arnoldian statement he summarizes this point: "This leads me to say that a kind of touchstone of the highest or most living art is seriousness; not gravity but the being in earnest with your subject—reality" (*LB* 225).

That Hopkins was deeply "in earnest" with his reality, and that his language expresses it, may now seem so obvious that it is easy to sneer at those critics—and their names are legion, and often distinguished—who found his muse unconverted, his thought thin or absent, his ultimate achievements—or failures depending on the point of view—merely technical.[6] Yet unless one condescendingly assumes that they were one and all less sensitive and less intelligent than modern critics, there must be reasons for their reaction worth speculating on.

One such reason is suggested in a comment by F. R. Leavis, an early and consistent defender of Hopkins. One of the few critics in the first four decades of Hopkins criticism to recognize in the poems "a vitality of thought, a vigour of the thinking intelligence," he also defended them as poetry as follows: "His use of words is not a matter of *saying* things with them; he is preoccupied with what

6. "Hopkins' muse, I believe, never underwent conversion," James Reeves, "Introduction," *Selected Poems of Gerard Manley Hopkins*, xvi. A roll call of other such critics includes, in addition to Yeats: J. Middleton Murry, *Aspects of Literature*, 58; T. S. Eliot, *After Strange Gods: A Primer of Modern Heresy*, 51–52; Harold Whitehall, "Sprung Rhythm," 52, 54; Austin Warren, "Instress of Inscape," 88; Yvor Winters, in whose side Hopkins seems to have been a painful but inoperable barb, "The Poetry of Gerard Manley Hopkins, II," 79–80; Geoffrey H. Hartman, *The Unmediated Vision: An Interpretation of Wordsworth, Hopkins, Rilke, and Valéry*, 171–73, 156; and even Boyle, *Metaphor*, xviii.

seems to him the poetic use of them, and that is a matter of making them do and be."[7] This is wholly in accord with Hopkins' own early statements on poetry, but it is perhaps exactly because he was so successful in making words "do and be" that it was, perhaps still is, possible to overlook the fact that he also has something profoundly serious to "say": something not reducible to "message" or abstractable from the work, but organic, duplicating and dramatizing a whole way of seeing and being as well as thinking. And it may be because his religious beliefs and ideas are so fused with style in the best poems, exert so constant and alchemical a pressure on it, seem so like "the air we breathe" (60) when we enter the world of any poem, that it has been possible for readers and critics to suppose that ideas are not there at all; the very omnipresence of Hopkins' complex religious thought can sometimes make it invisible.

The difficulty one encounters, therefore, or should encounter, in attempting to isolate "meaning" in any of the best poems is an indication of Hopkins' success in meeting his own demand that thought and feeling must wholly "flush and fuse the language" (May 26, *LB* 82), rather than evidence that either is thin or absent. This peculiarly intimate welding of meaning and language, the inseparable locking of idea into image and music, of course offers enormous and frustrating difficulties to the dissecting critic, but the critic's defeat is simply the poet's victory.

Beyond the issue of "meaning," four other topics central to Hopkins' critical theory are also, though less obviously, related to his religious vision: obscurity and clarity; intensity and emphasis; "current language heightened"; and variety and order.

Hopkins' critical remarks on obscurity in poetry are themselves somewhat obscure and seemingly contradictory, but they make sense when related not merely to technical considerations but to his guiding concept of "incomprehensible certainty." "The obscurity is a great fault: from remarkably clear speaking he [Dixon] will lapse into gibberish" (*LB* 74) is a remark typical of Hopkins' frequent and stringent attacks on lack of clarity in the works of his three poet-friends. But when it comes to his own poetry, an apparently quite different point is stated and reiterated. In the most often quoted of such comments, he wrote to Bridges of *The Wreck of the Deutschland*: "Granted that it needs study and is obscure, for indeed I was not over-desirous that the meaning of all should be

7. "Metaphysical Isolation," 121, 125.

quite clear, at least unmistakeable, you might . . . have nevertheless read it so that lines and stanzas should be left in the memory and superficial impressions deepened, and have liked some without exhausting all" (May 13, 1878, *LB* 50). A similar statement on "The Loss of the *Eurydice*" is both crisper and more general: "Obscurity I do and will try to avoid so far as is consistent with excellences higher than clearness at a first reading," a statement followed by the tantalizing promise, "This question of obscurity we will some time speak of but not now" (May 30, 1878, *LB* 54).

Many critics have related Hopkins' advocacy of "excellences higher than clearness at a first reading" to merely, or mainly, artistic considerations, to the intellectual and dramatic effects of difficulty on the reader's mental muscles. In his influential article of 1926, I. A. Richards condemned contemporary verse for its blandness, its lack of "resistance," but praised Hopkins' poetry for having sufficient friction so that "the effort, the heightened attention, may brace the reader."[8] In 1930 Charles Williams expressed a similar admiration for Hopkins' obscurity, and for similar reasons; well before later critics made the same point, he argued that the devices obscuring meaning are valuable because they "suspend our attention from any rest until the whole thing, whatever it may be, is said."[9] And this approach to the intent and effect of Hopkins' obscurity is in part justified by his own comment, which clearly favors the second alternative he suggests: "One of two kinds of clearness one shd. have—either the meaning to be felt without effort as fast as one reads or else, if dark at first reading, when once made out *to explode*" (October 8, 1879, *LB* 90).

Yet important as intellectual tautness and dramatic impact were to Hopkins, neither, I think, was the basic philosophical source of his respect for obscurity. A rare example of critical comment that approaches direct statement on his own particular subject and style offers some support for this view:

> Epic and drama and ballad and many, most, things should be at once intelligible; but everything need not and cannot be. Plainly if it is possible to express a sub[t]le and recondite thought on a subtle and recondite subject in a subtle and recondite way and with great felicity and perfection, in the end, something must be sacrificed, with so trying a task, in the process, and this may be the being at once, nay perhaps even the being without explanation at all, intelligible. (November 6, 1887, *LB* 265–66)

8. "Gerard Hopkins," 195.
9. "Introduction," *Poems of Gerard Manley Hopkins*, 2d ed., xii.

Even this prose passage reflects in its tangled and difficult syntax Hopkins' habitual stylistic response to "subtle and recondite thought," and I would suggest again that the major subject of his poetry, the most recondite "thought" of all, dictated a poetic method that could acknowledge God's mystery, revealing but not claiming to resolve, leaving the reader with the residual sense of seeing much "without exhausting all." While there is a persuasive, more pragmatic, less nebulous explanation of his specific comment on *The Wreck of the Deutschland*, first offered by Elisabeth W. Schneider, and subsequently accepted by later critics,[10] I am not convinced that doctrinal nervousness can fully account for his general statements on the limitations of clarity. The deeper, more central source of his belief in "excellences higher than clearness" would seem to me the deep and central recognition that his subject was not susceptible to "unmistakeable" clarification, that mere clarity could only insult and shrink it.

Related to his respect for mystery, and hence for stylistic complexity as well as precision, are some of Hopkins' specific theories of diction and of the nature of language in general. While acknowledging the too-specific, too-limiting tendency inherent in the English language itself—"This seems in English a point craved for and insisted on, that words shall be single and specific marks for things, whether self-significant or not" (December 1, 1882, *LB* 165)—he also postulates a theory of the "moments" of words, and of whole works of art, which reconciles richness and multiplicity of suggestion and meaning with precision of meaning and wholeness of impact.

This early but germinal theory, from an undergraduate essay of 1868, is based on an initial general assumption that is in itself relevant to Hopkins' later poetic practice: "All words mean either things or relations of things: you may also say then substances or attributes or again wholes or parts. E. g. *man* and *quarter*" (February 9, 1868, *JP* 125). This somewhat opaque distinction seems clear on one point: it is not simply a grammatical distinction—as between nouns and prepositions, "fire" and "toward"—but one

10. Schneider proposes that Hopkins was announcing an actual miracle in the appearance of Christ to the nun (stanza 28) and hesitated to make so bold a theological assertion too bluntly and clearly (*The Dragon in the Gate: Studies in the Poetry of G. M. Hopkins*, 30–31). Also Paul L. Mariani, *A Commentary on the Complete Poems of Gerard Manley Hopkins*, 67; John Robinson, *In Extremity: A Study of Gerard Manley Hopkins*, 116–17; and somewhat indirectly, Sprinker, "*Counterpoint*," 115–16.

based on the relative fullness, substance, and density of the ideas conveyed in individual words. This general assumption will be specifically dramatized in the poems, where individual words are constantly used to function as wholes, not parts, and where words that "mean things" are especially central: nouns, obviously, and verbs (acts that are things), but also and above all forms that combine grammatical functions to form new, larger, and usually active and tangible wholes ("the hurl and gliding"; "the achieve of"; "O unteachably after evil"; "my comfortless," and so on).

The essay then goes on (*JP* 125) to present the three "moments" or "terms" of a word that means a thing: "prepossession," "definition," and "application." The "passion or prepossession or enthusiasm" belonging to a word allows the most individual freedom of association, while typically seeming to have some roots in a more objective origin: it is everything a word originally meant and still may mean and convey emotionally, in itself or to an individual. Though not viewed as constant, either historically or individually—though "not always or in everyone" will the word carry the same prepossession—this "moment" comes the closest of the three to being the word's "form," analogous to "soul," its living, almost spiritual, power and specialness. Devlin's useful suggestion that this aspect of words is "some remnant of the original power that first matched them with reality" may further explain Hopkins' use of the term *form* for this moment, and has a bearing on his later poetic practice.[11]

"Definition," seemingly the most straightforward of the terms, proves actually to be the most complex, because in itself multiple, but appears first and basically to be the word as almost pure denotation, almost an abstraction uncluttered and unenriched by associations or extensions, something cerebrally grasped, equivalent to the most limited "meaning." It is distinguished both from "prepossession," which is "not a word but something connotatively meant by it," and from the third moment, "application or extension," which is "not a word but a thing meant by it," the outward impetus of the word, what it points to, its designation of "the concrete things coming under it."

Yet "definition" rapidly turns out to be typically more dynamic and multiple. It is, in the first place, "expression," active expres-

11. "The Image and the Word, I," 115. See also MacKenzie's suggestion (*Hopkins*, 83) that Hopkins may have been familiar with F. W. Farrar's *Chapters on Language* (1865), which explores the Greek analogical theory that names are actual, not arbitrary, reflections and visible echoes of objects.

sion: the idea inwardly or outwardly spoken, the "*uttering* of the idea in the mind," the "vocal expression or other utterance." Second, the idea expressed turns out not only to be an abstract conception but also to involve the physical and even visceral and instinctive images it may call up, "of sight or sound or *scapes* of the other senses." To these the energy of the individual mind paradoxically lends such private and perhaps so many shapes that the image-idea is inwardly concrete but objectively "inchoate": an overlap with "prepossession" seems apparent here. And finally, any word may be multiple, "may be considered as the contraction or coinciding-point of its definition*s*" (italics mine), a possibility that Hopkins will carry to its furthest extreme in the notorious and splendid use of *Buckle*, but which appears in less extreme form everywhere in his poetry.

The importance of this embryonic theory lies in its attempt to reconcile a word's potentially dense, multiple, and even private suggestiveness with its essential fidelity to a precise and objective reality, precisely apprehended but not narrowly comprehended. In theory as in later poetic practice, in both as in religious faith, Hopkins viewed the "moments" of the word, and of the world, as one moment, rich, mysterious, of infinite variety, offering free play to the mind, yet precise, and precisely governed. He had little tolerance for mere suggestiveness, explicitly objecting to the separation of a word's connotation from its precise meaning (*JP* 126)—a warning here of the discipline as well as the response to richness his poems will expect of readers. At the same time, however, he could tolerate and exploit to their fullest the complexities of word and world because there was for him metaphysical as well as metaphorical unity underlying both.

The theory of language outlined in this essay blends rapidly and inevitably into a theory of what a work of art asks of us if we are to grasp both its wholeness and its diversity. Especially important to a way of reading Hopkins' own later poetry is the emphasis on simultaneous apprehension of parts and wholes, progression and unity:

> . . . even in the successive arts as music, for full enjoyment, the synthesis of the succession should give, unlock, the contemplative enjoyment of the unity of the whole . . . .
> The more intellectual, less physical, the spell of contemplation the more complex must be the object, the more close and elaborate must be the comparison the mind has to keep making between the whole and the parts, the parts and the whole. For this

reference or comparison is what the sense of unity means; mere sense that such a thing is one and not two has no interest or value except accidentally . . . .

The further in anything, as a work of art, the organisation is carried out, the deeper the form penetrates, the prepossession flushes the matter, the more effort will be required in apprehension, the more power of comparison, the more capacity for receiving that synthesis of (either successive or spatially distinct) impressions which gives us the unity with the prepossession conveyed by it. (*JP* 126)

Any reader of Hopkins' poems is aware of the powerful resistance they offer to merely "spatial," "successive," or linear reading, and of how extremely "close and elaborate must be the comparison the mind has to keep making" between parts and whole, whole and parts. While this may be a challenge posed to some extent by any complex literary work, especially by any lyric poem, it is surely a particularly acute difficulty—or pleasure—for the reader of Hopkins. His poems not only develop idea, feeling, imagery dramatically and in a linear way, but they usually require that at every point we "receive the synthesis of the succession" both horizontally and vertically, apprehending many meanings, dimensions, levels of insight, in one moment of perception. They demand of readers what Hopkins felt nature and God demanded of him, the capacity for complex simultaneity of apprehension, and especially for recognition of complex, not obvious, unity.

The best poems, therefore, are constructed somewhat like a set of superimposed transparencies, or in Cotter's phrasing in a different context, like "multiple exposures."[12] When we see that the individual levels are distinctively there, yet patterned one above the other so as to create out of many dimensions one whole, and one whole that is also in motion, then and only then the poem flashes like a hologram into the shape, color, focus of the full and positive picture. This complex multiple unity results specifically from the fact that even the least of the poems tend to involve what Hopkins commented on in Greek tragic lyrics: an "overthought," clear and susceptible to paraphrase, and an "underthought, conveyed chiefly in the choice of metaphors etc used and often only half-realised by the poet himself," but "usually having a connection," "commonly an echo or shadow of the overthought" (to Baillie, January 14,

12. *Inscape*, 323n2, on the interweaving of allusions to the Gospels in "The Candle Indoors": "This feat of multiple exposures of scriptural verses has long been explored by Christian preachers and artists."

1883, *FL* 252–53). In Hopkins' major poems, the numerous "underthoughts," metaphors intricately echoing both the "overthought" and each other (and more than "half-realized" by the poet, in my view), create the characteristic though logical density of idea and structure.

Such a poetic method may, of course, lead to some seeming extravagance, even some absurdity, on the part of the critic of the poems; Yvor Winters' disgusted comment on criticism too tolerant of multiplicity does give one pause: "This kind of thing, whether in theory or in practice, represents one of the ultimate stages of Romantic disintegration."[13] Nevertheless, if this be treason against critical discipline we must risk making the most of it, since unless one strains to oversimplify the poems, tolerance of multiple "underthoughts" is usually required by the nature of Hopkins' vision and style.

In critical theory, however, as in spiritual vision and poetic practice, Hopkins' respect for complexity and mystery was balanced by an equal respect for clarity and "formulation." Without initial precision of observation, without intensive and minute study of the world's variety, the observer cannot do justice to either its richness or its underlying laws, and the poet cannot create a style adequate to his simultaneous sense of mystery and formulated pattern. As he wrote of his own early and meticulous account of the Devon waves, "This is mechanical reflection and is the same as optical; indeed all nature is mechanical, but then it is not seen that mechanics contain that which is beyond mechanics" (August 13, 1874, *JP* 252). This study of "mechanics" in order to find what is within and beyond them, an approach nourished specifically by Ruskinian and generally by post-Darwinian thought, is one that gathered steadily to a greatness in Hopkins' early journals, finally finding its full justification and expression in mature sacramental theory and poetic practice.

In spite of the many jotted experiments in poetic phrasing that fill the early journals, the tenacious and sometimes successful attempts at fresh and precise imagery,[14] the general impression of these journals is initially somewhat disappointing. They reflect an immensely meticulous and curious mind, but one that seems con-

---

13. "The Poetry of Gerard Manley Hopkins, II," 93.

14. For example: "the dented primrose" (54); "Moonlight hanging or dropping on treetops like blue cobweb" (23); "stars like gold tufts.

    —— —— golden bees.

    —— —— golden rowels" (46).

tent with mere exactitude of observation, an almost mechanical imitation of Ruskin's method, and in a style of a curious hardness as well as sharpness. Nevertheless, those aspects of the world that most concerned the young Hopkins, and the terms in which he described them, do suggest an essentially, or at least potentially, metaphysical view of mechanics. From the earliest diary (1863–1864), he was interested in aspects of motion and force, in animals, in water, in clouds, leaves, skies; he was fascinated by the relations among masses, planes, angles, colors, and with the effects of "pie-ing" in general, often as these were affected by motion and shifting light; he elaborately described textures—smoothness, roughness, "crispness" especially. Above all, he sought and described patterns of all kinds, especially noting all manner of sharp outlines, edgings, pencilings, tracery, ridgings, networks; in describing such patterns, his language tends to emphasize a strand of imagery that will remain characteristic, imagery of lines, spokes, radiations: "spearlike rays" of the sunrise (17), "lashes" of honeysuckle (167), "vertical stemming" of tree-covered hills (169), "spokes" of light on cloud (65), "radiation" of oak-boughs, beech trees, the hairs of barley ears (144). Inevitably in the early poems also this sense of veining and patterning, embodied in imagery of spokes, rays, wheels, lines, is central, waiting its full significance and ordering by a vision of more than Mermaids.

The first and obvious point to be made about all this observation is that it reflects Hopkins' characteristic combination of meticulousness and wonder in response to the physical world, a view that saw the universe as full of large and small miracles, demanding, and rewarding, not only notice but analysis; the ice on cedar needles (193), the feeling of bluebells rubbed together (209), the "laws" of candlesmoke (204) deserve and get from him as much attention as the grandeur of mountains, clouds, stars. Equally obvious is that persistent search for pattern, order, distinctness, but also linkage of lines of being already discussed. But a further characteristic of the journals' method is somewhat less self-evident, and also more crucial to this study's thesis.

In spite of their meticulous and even finicky detail, the journals' descriptions rarely conjure up a recognizable and solid picture of their subjects. Because Hopkins was always trying to penetrate to inscape, even before he coined the word, he seldom dealt with the obvious and familiar aspects of mountain, stream, tree, flower, and the result is that nature undergoes an odd process of diffusion; a strangeness as well as vividness attaches to most descriptions, and we watch the very process of the Coleridgean imagination dissolving, diffusing, dissipating in order to re-create. Closely related to this process is a dual view of nature's combined stability and mobility, and a doubleness of descriptive method. This method combines what Hopkins called "stalling" (*JP* 194, 196, 211)—arresting nature in such a way that it seems almost static in the moment of apprehension—with a simultaneous emphasis on its vibrant charge of motion. There is an important early caveat on this: "Observe that motion multiplies inscape only when inscape is discovered, otherwise it disfigures" (May 14, 1870, *JP* 199). This remark can also be applied to the method and relative success of some of the poems, but the ideal seems clearly to be a vision of vibrancy that is not static, and of stasis that is not dead: already the ideal of "immortal diamond."

Also related to this ideal, and to inscape as "the form speaking" and audibly in motion, is Hopkins' later method of composition—one not unique to him among poets, but apparently habitual with him. He began by composing in his head, perhaps aloud, but anyway "away from paper" (May 12, 1887, *FL* 379; December 22, 1880, *LD* 42). This initial stage would presumably have involved the mental inscaping of whatever was to be the whole poem's subject and probably the establishment of central imagery, some sound patterns, and certainly meter; as drafts of the poems indicate, it often also produced the final version of the opening line. At this point, however, the heard inscape had to become captured and made visible, and he "put it down with repugnance" (*FL* 379). At this point also, attention to "mechanics" powerfully entered the process, and through laborious revisions he arrived at the complexity and unity of imagery and sound that create the full "inscape of speech for the inscape's sake." In spite of his aversion to revision (doubtless shared by most of us), and his anxiety about its effects—"one's first verjuice flattens into slobber and sweet syllabub" (*LB* 146)—without that "repugnant" process most of his poems could not have approached what they now are, either technically or thematically and emotionally. His revisions are almost always improvements and intensifications of original versions of lines and whole poems, working toward the complex unity, music, and multidimensional qualities of language that create the voice of "incomprehensible certainty."

That voice and vision were latent from the beginning in the young Hopkins' double attention to the mobility of facts and to their power, if closely studied, to speak of what lies within and beyond them. But it was when "the meet of lines" that "may be" Beauty (102) occurred, when God came to be fully perceived and received as the center and source of both flux and law, motion and stability, when natural laws could be understood as resulting from supernatural law, that Hopkins' response to fact and the elusiveness of fact could be translated into coherent theory. That theory, philosophical and poetic, with its combined respect for mystery and passion for precision, is epitomized in what may serve as summary of this whole point: two comments on fellow artists who exemplified for him the extremes of realism without splendor and of mysticism without sense. Of Hunt's painting *Shadow of Death* he severely remarks, "No inscape of composition whatever—not known and if it had been known it could scarcely bear up against such realism" (1874, *JP* 248); of a Swinburnian sunset, "Either in fact he does not see nature at all or else he overlays the landscape with such phantasmata, secondary images, and what not of a delirium-tremendous imagination that the result is a kind of bloody broth: you know what I mean. At any rate there is no picture" (January 1, 1885, *LB* 202).

This last comment also leads to a second major aspect of Hopkins' poetic theory, its emphasis on "Emphasis," or "heightening." He could not admire a delirium-tremendous imagination, but no more could he admire mere accuracy and flat precision. There is a great difference between poetry that produces a "bloody broth" and poetry that shows the world as Hopkins saw it, "mounted in the scarlet," and his theories consistently advocate a style that combines accuracy and intensity. This is ideally a style that, in all its aspects, reflects with fidelity the world's "native colours," but that heightens them, sets them in motion while retaining pattern, intensifies them by all possible devices of emphasis while respecting their intrinsic nature.

The importance of emphasis is inescapable in Hopkins' critical writings from their very beginning. The early essay on "Poetic Diction" insists, in opposition to Wordsworth, that poetry must involve "an emphasis of structure" and "an emphasis of expression" stronger than those of prose, and that both must serve "an emphasis of thought stronger than that of common thought" (1865, *JP* 85). His later comments reiterate the same point in all areas of poetic practice: of diction he demands not "tameness" but "nerve and flow" (*LD* 65, 66), not "meagreness" but "flush and fusedness" (*LD* 55); of any poem's inner temper and movement he demands a vital pulse of action, objecting to anything that is merely "a pointless photograph of still life"—a comment on a passage in the opening of *The Ring and the Book*—or merely "minute upholstery description"—a comment on Balzac (*LD* 74). Of drama specifically he demands an emphatic attack on the reader's attention, requiring "a nameless quality which is of the first importance both in oratory and drama: I sometimes call it *bidding*. I mean the art or virtue of saying everything right *to* or *at* the hearer, interesting him, holding him in the attitude of correspondent or addressed or at least concerned" (November 4, 1882, *LB* 160).

That he considered "bidding" crucial not only to drama and oratory but also to his own kind of poetry, which partakes of both, is demonstrated everywhere in his poetic practice. Earlier discussion has touched on the simultaneously inward and outward, private and dramatic, aspects of the poems, the results of Hopkins' Christian form of Keatsian "camelionism," intensified in specific ways by the dramatic aspects of Ignatian meditation technique.[15] But the poems also demonstrate more than a generally dramatic method in evoking scene, circumstance, inner and outer action and dialogue, and more than "bidding's" attack on the reader's attention. Though we do feel in many poems that we are intensely "in the attitude of correspondent or addressed or at least concerned," in most Hopkins does not literally address the reader at all, but instead speaks rhetorically to the elements of which he writes: the windhover, the nun, the "blue March day," Oxford and Earth and Peace and Despair, his own heart repeatedly, and, above all, Christ and God. It would be possible, perhaps, to speculate on primarily psychological reasons for this practice. It may, and probably does, betray a deep loneliness, for example; having no one with whom to speak fully, no human correspondents who could wholly share his thoughts, feelings, faith, he perhaps tried to escape isolation by turning to a world of natural or inner or unseen correspondents. Such speculation, however, even if valid, is not altogether helpful in getting us closer to the poems, and I would think that the obvious is probably the major explanation: that Hopkins' assumption of active, responsive, potentially eloquent life in all things resulted from his belief that the world is charged in all its aspects with the energy and eloquence of God.

Because of this belief, his dramatic apostrophes or questions to

15. See especially "The Composition of Place," *Spiritual Exercises*, 35–36. For further discussion of the aims and methods of "bidding," see Daniel A. Harris, *Inspirations Unbidden: The "Terrible Sonnets" of Gerard Manley Hopkins*, 137–39.

physical things are not equivalent to pathetic fallacy. While he always maintained intellectually the distinction between objective things and the subjective mind's impact on them, everything, inner and outer, was for him literally, not poetically or merely figuratively, instinct with divine life, divine eloquence, and could therefore appropriately be an object of dramatic address. And finally of course, behind all the various aspects of "bidding" in the poems lies the belief that the real and ultimate "listener," God, is always there, responsive to the call of the instressing mind and heart. Though this "always" will be desolately qualified in two of the later dark sonnets, the basic generalization holds: dramatic rhetoric is one of many means of expressing a heightened, but not distorted or fanciful, response to literal reality.

Among other such means are, of course, all the technical devices of poetic emphasis, which he both advocates and uses: heavily stressed rhythms, internal and partial rhyme, alliteration, assonance, consonance, the elaborate musical "chimes" of Welsh *cynghanedd*, which carry these devices to their furthest and most intricate extreme, and the tough, taut words of Anglo-Saxon rather than Romance derivation, words wiry with "the naked thew and sinew of the English language" (*LB* 267–68).[16]

Again, however, Hopkins considered these to be a means of heightening, not falsifying or abandoning, common and actual reality. Patmore, one reads without surprise, was "a little amused" by Hopkins' claim to a style representing "the extreme of popular character" (April 5, 1884, *FL* 355), but both in theory and in practice Hopkins had justification. In theory, he tirelessly opposed the use of nonpopular language—"I hold that by archaism a thing is sicklied o'er as by blight" (*LB* 218); "I look on the whole *genus* [archaic language] as vicious" (*LD* 156)—and explained the premise behind such statements in a relatively early letter to Bridges: "So also I cut myself off from the use of *ere, o'er, wellnigh, what time, say not* (for *do not say*), because, though dignified, they neither belong to nor ever cd. arise from, or be the elevation of, ordinary modern speech. For it seems to me that the poetical language of an age shd. be the current language heightened, to any degree heightened and

16. For detailed comment on the laws of *cynghanedd*, see Gardner, *Hopkins*, 2:144–58; Ll. Wyn Griffith, "The Welsh Influence," 28; McChesney, "The Meaning of 'Inscape,'" 58–60. The Anglo-Saxon influence is more puzzling, since Hopkins apparently did not seriously study Old, or even Middle, English until às late as 1882 (*LB* 156, 163), but he was a fanatical student of etymology from his early years and obviously well grounded in the basic English poetic tradition.

unlike itself, but not (I mean normally: passing freaks and graces are another thing) an obsolete one" (August 14, 1879, *LB* 89).

This theory may have sprung in part from Hopkins' whole intensified vision of the actual world as seen through the medium of faith, as well as from plain common sense, but the question inevitably arises as to whether he practiced what he preached. This question will be considered in detail in later chapters, but two basic points may be summarized here. First, Hopkins' apparent archaisms almost invariably have their roots not merely in obsolete usage but in current dialect ("wimple," "sillion," "what road," "fashed," for example), and his poems are in fact studded with colloquialisms, conversational turns of phrase, and extremely homely, mundane, "popular" images ("heartburn," "dead letters," "weeds," "that spell," "out of sight is out of mind," to cite a few). That such language is often felt not to be popular and natural at all, but odd, or that its popular immediacy is easy to overlook, is perhaps not only evidence of reader ignorance; it results also from the way in which the ordinary and familiar is constantly heightened, "to any degree heightened," in Hopkins' poems.

Second, one may often feel of Hopkins' language at its best, as of Shakespeare's, which he cites as a supreme example of "current language heightened" (*LB* 89), that while it may not be what people in fact normally use, it is the language we would use if we could, given the circumstance and feeling, and perhaps do use inwardly: not the current language of ordinary individuals, but that of high and concentrated thought and feeling, the language of the inner mind and heart. Lovers do not commonly talk like Romeo and Juliet, or Antony and Cleopatra, but love does; ordinary people, however despairing, do not talk in the language of the "terrible sonnets," but despair does. Fidelity to common truth, in short, but to a concentrated and heightened truth, marks Hopkins' critical theories of language as distinctly as it marks his spiritual vision.

In conclusion, this discussion must return, as all things Hopkinsian return, to the concept of that "One spot" and center as it is specifically related to Hopkins' theories of order and variety in poetry. All aspects of theory and method so far discussed have reflected his constant attempt to order complex variety into unity while retaining the specialness, richness, and dynamic emphasis of variety, and to relate all elements of the perceived world and the created poem to a center of intrinsic law. With a more detailed consideration of that whole attempt this introductory section, like Hopkins' thought, will come full circle.

From his undergraduate days, Hopkins held that beauty consisted of asymmetrical symmetry, asymmetrical but patterned form, as illustrated by the seven-leaved chestnut fan ("On the Origin of Beauty: A Platonic Dialogue," May 12, 1865, *JP* 87–88), and throughout his life the seven-leaved fan would remain lovelier to him than the six-leaved in all areas of perception. But insistence on law underlying apparent oddity and irregularity, on beauty as a "relation" of freedom and form, is the dominant point of the early dialogue, and becomes more dominant as the source of form in all things is seen to be not merely aesthetic, but divine. Not only the rhetorician and the poet but also the priest held that "in everything the more remote the ratio of the parts to one another or the whole the greater the unity if felt at all" (lecture notes on "Rhythm," *JP* 283), and the archetypal illustration of this pronouncement is, characteristically, the circle.

Like the "undiscoverable" ratio of the circle's circumference to its diameter discussed in these notes, the world's many aspects and relationships—and the poem's—may seem mysteriously beyond comprehension and infinitely remote from each other, utterly distinctive and "disseveral," but all are related by radii, lines of stress and energy, to and from the divine center. To this concept may be traced Hopkins' basic theories of language and their practical applications. Like the characteristic ray-radiation imagery mentioned earlier, both theory and practice show the attempt to find and reveal in language, as in the world, richness, variety, flexibility, freedom, but also to find and impose the links and boundary lines that make of disheveled or formless variety the unity of inscape. Finally, to this concept should also be traced three of Hopkins' most obvious poetic characteristics: his distinctive kind of sensuous imagery; his preference for the sonnet form; his use of sprung rhythm and associated devices.

Whenever Hopkins' use of synaesthetic imagery is traced to religious rather than to secular or mainly temperamental sources,[17] it is usually attributed, and rightly so in large part, to the fact that his mind was steeped in the premises and procedures of Ignatian meditation. In some detail, Hopkins' notes on the *Spiritual Exercises* consider the point that in meditation, to see is not enough; "videre personas" is a beginning, but it is followed by the commands

17. See Heuser, *Shaping Vision*, 10, on the influence of Newton, Ruskin, the Pre-Raphaelites; Peters, *Critical Essay*, 18–19, on the relevance of instress to this sort of imagery; Hopkins himself on the instinctive tendency of his senses to cross over into each other (*JP* 234–35).

"attendere, advertere, et contemplari"; in imagining any scene, therefore, the meditant must employ all his senses, must strive not only to visualize but also "to hear with my hearing," "*to savour and to taste*," and "*to touch* by touching" (*SD* 175). In his comments on the "Meditation on Hell," Hopkins elaborates upon the Ignatian hierarchy of the senses, a hierarchy of ascending potency: "Sight does not shock like hearing, sounds cannot so disgust as smell, smell is not so bitter as proper bitterness, which is in taste," but finally, "bitterness of taste is not so cruel as the pain that can be touched and felt. Seeing is believing but touch is the truth, the saying goes" (*SD* 243). While the poems obviously do not mechanically follow this strict hierarchy of the senses, they do reflect its emphasis, tending to employ sight only in strange and telling conjunction with the other senses, and especially tending to emphasize touch—"the truth, the saying goes."

Ignatian methodology, then, surely accounts in part for Hopkins' particular use of the senses. That the larger concept of mystery may also have prohibited the use of primarily visual imagery will be further explored in later analysis of the poems. What I would emphasize here is that Hopkins' way of pressing all the senses to bear on and in a single moment is a reflection and product of his instinct in all areas of life to forge wholeness out of multitudinousness, or rather to mirror the complex coherence that he believed inherent in the world because of the presence of God at its governing center.

Second, Hopkins' preference for the sonnet form—thirty-four of the forty-eight mature poems are Petrarchan sonnets of one kind or another—explicitly reflects his respect for complex unity and, perhaps more subliminally, his need for freedom, but freedom within a canon of law. In part, no doubt, it also resulted from less theoretical causes, such as his lack of time and energy for sustained creative effort in longer forms.[18] But there is a remarkable consistency—"the highest consistency"—in Hopkins' central choices, as man and poet, in large matters and small, which appears to show an instinctive as well as intellectual and aesthetic need for control. It is therefore perhaps hardly surprising that the rebellious, intensely individualistic, even arrogant man, who nevertheless chose to enter one of the strictest of religious orders, should also

18. "It is not possible for me to do anything, unless a sonnet, and that rarely, in poetry with a fagged mind and a continual anxiety" (August 7, 1886, *LD* 139), and the earlier, and bleaker, statement, "I have written a few sonnets: that is all I have done in poetry for some years" (June 30, 1886, *LD* 135).

have been the radically innovative poet who chose as his favorite one of the strictest of literary forms.

There is no need to linger on such relatively speculative ground, however. Hopkins' own comments on the sonnet declare his devotion to "strict laws" governing freedom and to exactitude combined with mystery. In spite of his many and radical innovations in the form, in this as in larger areas he felt that he was not rejecting tradition and rules, but honoring fundamental authority, perceiving the basic, not superficial, inscape of the sonnet form.[19] And as he saw it, that fundamental inscape exactly answered to his own vision of the world in general, and of art in particular, as asymmetrical symmetry, complex unity, variety strictly and beautifully governed by law. An ash tree in Wales, he notes, has "a single sonnet-like inscape" (*JP* 259), but such singleness, whether natural or poetic, is an intricate and subtle thing. Hence his obsession with the mathematical beauty of the Petrarchan sonnet: "The equation of the best sonnet is $(4 + 4) + (3 + 3) = 2 \cdot 4 + 2 \cdot 3 = 2(4 + 3) = 2 \cdot 7 = 14$," so that "the equation or construction is unsymmetrical in the shape $x + y = a$, where x and y are unequal in some simple ratio" (October 12, 1881, *LD* 71–72). This mathematical analysis, whether illuminating or not, obviously reflects his passion for precision, but even in anatomizing the sonnet he demonstrates also his habitual preoccupation with what is beyond precision, with the beauty not merely of asymmetry, but explicitly of mystery: "Now it seems to me that this division [into octave and sestet] is the real characteristic of the sonnet and that what is not so marked off and moreover has not the octet again divided into quatrains is not to be called a sonnet at all. For in the cipher 14 is no mystery and if one does not know nor avail oneself of the opportunities which it affords it is a pedantic encumbrance and not an advantage" (*LD* 71).

Finally, to Hopkins' search for language adequate to express both the ordering and the intensifying power of God may be traced some of his specifically technical innovations and characteristics. Sprung rhythm was, of course, the chief of these, his major means of creating a style accentuated but still natural, true to the kindred points of emphasis and ordinary reality. Just as he had insisted on accurate vision heightened, on current language heightened, so he insisted on natural rhythms heightened: "Why do I employ sprung

19. As in his justification of outrides to create longer than pentameter lines, on the grounds that the Italian sonnet is in fact longer than its English counterpart, since its thirteen-syllable line cannot be matched by normal pentameter (October 29, 1881, *LD* 86). See also Gardner, *Hopkins*, 1:82.

rhythm at all? Because it is the nearest to the rhythm of prose, that is the native and natural rhythm of speech, the least forced, the most rhetorical and emphatic of all possible rhythms, combining, as it seems to me, opposite and, one wd. have thought, incompatible excellences, markedness of rhythm—that is rhythm's self—and naturalness of expression" (August 21, 1877, *LB* 46). To this clear summary I would only add that "markedness of rhythm" or "stress," on which Hopkins constantly theorizes, was not to him merely a matter of technical emphasis limited to poetry. It too is related to his view of a world "keeping nevertheless mounted in the scarlet its own colour too," a world intensified but not falsified by the heightening of essential reality: "stress . . . is the making a thing more, or making it markedly, what it *already is*; it is the bringing out *its nature*" (November 7, 1883, *FL* 327, italics mine).

Specifically, his elaborate formulation of the laws of sprung rhythm—whether or not these laws are in any way comprehensible, helpful, or particularly observable in his own practice—obviously reflects his characteristic attempt to justify and control freedom by authoritative rules. That critics from his day to ours have struggled to elucidate his laws, and that any reader will probably be somewhat baffled by his idiosyncratic theories on ordinary scansion,[20] suggests that his dictum on mystery, "the clearer the formulation the greater the interest," does not quite apply in this area. Nevertheless, Hopkins thought he was clarifying and formulating, which is the main point. What he wrote somewhat irritably about his punctuation (also markedly idiosyncratic) applies to sprung rhythm as well: "About punctuation my mind is clear: I can give a rule for everything I write myself and even for other people, though they might not always agree with me perhaps" (*LB* 215). To him, therefore, Bridges' relaxed understanding and use of sprung rhythm apparently smacked of mental flabbiness and poetic anarchy, and he repeatedly protests that it is *not* "something informal and variable without any limit but ear and taste," *not* "a shambling business and a corruption" (*LD* 39), *not* "rhythmic prose" or "prose betwitched" like Whitman's rhythms, but "a regular and permanent principle of scansion" (*LB* 155, 157, 45). In this technical area as elsewhere, Hopkins' theory and method reflect not only a psychological need for authority but also his belief in the basic authority of God's laws behind all freedom and all variety, and his attempt to enact in the sphere of art similar laws.

20. See for example *LB* 155; *JP* 274, 281; *LD* 87.

To these fairly obvious points about sprung rhythm I would add one further thought, bearing on the odd inconsistencies in Hopkins' often interchangeable use of the terms *rising* and *falling* to describe meter, and particularly on the ease with which he could legislate that sprung rhythm is not, after all, a rising meter (December 22, 1880, *LD* 40), but a falling one ("Author's Preface," 1883, *P* 45, 47). Some of his apparently aberrant scansion of other poets may be explained in part by his explicit habit of scanning not as a prosodist but as a musician, for "convenience" not counting initial unstressed syllables (*P* 45)—as in the instance of Gray's "In vain to me the smiling mornings shine," which Hopkins considers a fine example of a trochaic line (October 29, 1881, *LD* 87). It is perhaps better explained by the deeply characteristic attempt to feel into what is essence, not surface: "In considering the character of a rhythm we must be careful to see what it really is, not the easiest or most obvious way of scanning it ('Now the hungry lion roars' is iambic though it begins with a trochee . . .)" (lecture notes on "Rhythm," *JP* 274). And possibly his interchangeable use of *rising* and *falling* may need no further explanation than the technical fact that sprung rhythm is a "mixed" and therefore flexible meter, and the slightly more complex fact that he seems to have thought of rising feet as suitable to dramatic present action, falling feet as suitable to narrative (*JP* 274), and his own poems tend to combine both modes simultaneously.

There may be a further, albeit speculative, reason. As *The Wreck of the Deutschland* constantly demonstrates, the actual effects of sprung rhythm on ear and emotions are such that technically "rising" feet may be heard and felt as "falling," and vice versa, depending on the total movement and meaning of a line or stanza, on what it "really" is. The whole of the first stanza, for example, is clearly predominantly in falling meter by a mechanical count of feet, but the feel of the stanza is not only intensely "present" but vigorously "rising" in an emotional and thematic, not technical, sense. This same suitability of a technically falling meter to high and "rising" content appears also, and persistently, in other poems and may simply be a technical achievement. Possibly, however, the inseparability of rising and falling, ascent and descent, and specifically the concept of the fall-to-rise of the Incarnation, obviously central to the poetry's content, as to the whole thought and rhythm of Hopkins' life, is also present, and is felt to be present, in the rhythm of the poems. Since stress "is the making a thing more, or making it markedly, what it already is," and since what most deeply and ubiquitously "is" in Hopkins' thought is Christ Incarnate, Christ both crucified and risen, the most marked as well as most mysterious aspect of sprung rhythm may reflect not only artistry, but faith.

Similarly and finally, Hopkins' use of sound devices, and some of his oddities in grammar, may show more than a technical concern for emphasis, and since these points cannot be stated and restated in analysis of each and every poem, I summarize them here.

(1) While Hopkins was obviously fond of words—especially monosyllabic words—beginning with hard consonants, and fond of creating an emphatic "anvil-ding" impact through alliterative play on such words, there are few lines in which the heavily battering alliteration is not combined with more muted, at least more subtle, sound effects. The result bears a close relation to his emphasis on mystery-in-precision, precision-in-mystery. Explosively alliterated words have the sound and feel of "sharp and sided hail" (9), have a solidity and cut to them, a firm outline apparently keen, obvious, and graspable. As they are combined, however, with a softer and more elusive music, especially derived from what Hopkins called "alliteration in vowels," which he considered most beautiful (November 7, 1883, FL 331), and from modulation in consonants (as in the phrase quoted above), complexity of sound joins with complexity of meaning to belie that distinctness; music as well as content compels a sense that there is something going on that is, in whole or in part, "past all grasp."

(2) All the related sound devices of alliteration, assonance, consonance, consonantal and internal rhyme, cynghanedd chime, not only add emphasis to meaning but also mirror Hopkins' basic concept of the relation between the many and the One. All involve the inevitable growth of variety from unity, of the many from the origin, but also, through repetition, echo, chime, rhyme, assume a constant return to the "one"; a few basic but endlessly creative sounds expand, proliferate, form an unbroken but varied chain of song and sense, and yet return always to their initial nature and initial source. They constitute, whether deliberately or not, a technical dramatization of Hopkins' religious view of the world's processes, and God's.[21]

(3) Finally, though I am again on speculative ground here,

21. See Miller, *Linguistic Moment*, 250–54, for a fuller and subtle discussion of theological assumptions behind technical devices, though its conclusions are far more radical than mine.

some of his persistent omissions of grammatically essential elements and connections may result from more than the need to condense and unify.[22] In part, at least, these peculiarities may embody an underlying assumption that the grammar of the world and spirit is both so complex and so clearly logical and unified that smaller connections and logicalities are unnecessary. If "All things rhyme in Christ," in Miller's fine phrase and perception,[23] perhaps also all things parse in him; if Christ is the Logos in whom all words find their origin, he is perhaps also the underlying structure of all *logoi*, of all ordered utterance.

In large and small matters, from the use of a stress or a vowel to the uses of God and humanity, Hopkins' thinking was governed by fidelity to the divine center circled and sought by the homing spirit, the "incomprehensible certainty" from which all the world emanates, and to which it must always be related. That fidelity also governs and informs all aspects of the poetry in which theory assumes flesh, finding the "authentic cadence" that is the voice of mystery.

22. Especially typical is what Bridges first identified and defended at length, "his habitual omission of the relative pronoun," because he wanted poetically telling words "to crowd out every merely grammatical colourless or toneless element" (*PB* 98). For fuller discussion of Hopkins' various ellipses see Robinson, *In Extremity*, 69–70; Peters, *Critical Essay*, 67–106; Gardner, *Hopkins*, 1:140–42, 2:121–24.
23. Miller, *Disappearance of God*, 313.

II

Orion of Light

5

The Wreck of the Deutschland
(1875–1876)

> The labour spent on this great metrical experiment must have served
> to establish the poet's prosody and perhaps his diction: therefore the
> poem stands logically as well as chronologically in the front of his
> book, like a great dragon folded in the gate to forbid all entrance, and
> confident in his strength from past success.
> —Bridges, *Poems*, 1918

THIS WELL-KNOWN if grumpy warning of the dragon's invincible
power, and the following suggestion that readers would be wise to
"attack him later in the rear,"[1] are heeded, I suspect, by all or most
teachers of Hopkins to this day. Most modern critics, however,
whether or not they otherwise distrust chronological treatment of
the poems, as I do, feel compelled for both logical and chronological reasons to arm themselves for a frontal engagement. Whatever
the merits of the early poems, whatever their hints of the later style
and thought, *The Wreck of the Deutschland* is unquestionably the
first work in which Hopkins found the "authentic cadence" for his
authentic vision, and the first in which the full scope of that vision
is apparent.

The poem is an intensely concentrated orchestration of the
themes and cadence of later works. In it sound all the central
themes of redemptive suffering; humanity's relation to God and
nature; God's mysterious nature and acts; his purposeful and powerful presence, whether recognized or not; the nature of heroism,
inner and outer; and the concept and necessity of somehow "wording" great mysteries. In it too are the central qualities of stylistic

1. Notes, *PB* 106. References to the poem, followed by stanza number only,
are to the Gardner-MacKenzie edition.

method, and though Hopkins later wrote, "There are some immaturities in it I should never be guilty of now," both the virtues and
the vices of the "firstborn," as he called it (January 26, 1881, *LB*
119), were on the whole to remain characteristic. It therefore not
only stands as a dragon in the gate but also, in Gardner's phrasing,
"stands like a great overture at the beginning of his mature work."[2]

The poem is not, however, a now declawed and tractable reluctant dragon. It remains a fierce and radical poem, whose immediate, and residual, impact, even upon those who know it well, is
surely that of Hopkins' desired "explosion." Fortunately neither
the lapse of years nor the proliferation of critical comment has
managed to reduce its obscurity to bland clarity, or to rub off the
edge of its aggressive oddity and power. Like all major works, it has
survived both time and its critics, and it will certainly survive the
following commentary.

This will not be a stanza-by-stanza explication, since that linear
procedure has been ably followed by others, and since I increasingly find the poem absolutely dragonlike in its resistance to such
linear reading, however skillfully done, and with whatever degree
of cross-referencing. Nor will I be emphasizing evaluation, either
in defence or in attack. Though Hopkins wryly hoped to "convert"
Bridges to the poem (*LB* 46), my own aim is to work as objectively
as possible within its world and spirit as I understand them, hoping
to illuminate some aspects of the relation between concept and cadence: the ways in which multiple levels, depths, weavings and in-
terweavings, chimes of meaning, metaphors, and sounds try to
reflect and partially incarnate in words the Word. Nevertheless, already implicit in such a detailed commentary is a judgment of the
poem's worth, so I will openly lash with the best word first: I think
The Wreck of the Deutschland not only a unique tour de force in poetry, but one of the great poems in the language.

One of the great *poems*, I should emphasize, for in content the
central premises may seem alien to some readers, or actually offen-
sive, and even a sympathetic reader may sense a kind of coldness,
though a fiery coldness, at its heart: a failure of human sympathy
for those who wretchedly, and by lay standards needlessly, suffered
and died, which results from the poem's and the poet's passionate
commitment to the concept of redemptive suffering. Still, it is
great as poems may be great, so intense in its own feeling, conviction, and language and so finely wrought in its own terms that a

2. Gardner, *Hopkins*, 1:153.

chameleon reader, at least, may find it wholly persuasive in those terms. It is a dramatization and affirmation of the great Christian mystery, a poem of total acceptance of that mystery, not a logical defence of it or a sympathetic dramatization of merely human tragedy; "bringing in the infinite" involves that latter hazard, as well as many strengths.

The origin and "genre" of the poem have received such thorough discussion in other commentaries that I need only summarize two points here. First, given the background discussed earlier, it is seemingly inevitable to hindsight that this first great poetic effort was generated by, and dramatizes, a fusion of physical and spiritual fact, of inner and outer event, and that it therefore embodies actuality meticulously analyzed and transmuted. As is habitually the case with Hopkins, the literal was recognized by him as metaphorical, but "metaphor" in turn reveals a higher literalness.

He explicitly emphasized to Bridges the literalness of his own experience, writing with a touch of defensive irony but clearly with deep earnestness, "I may add for your greater interest and edification that what refers to myself in the poem is all strictly and literally true and did all occur" (August 21, 1877, *LB* 47), and no factual detail of the actual wreck itself escaped his notice and interpretation.[3] With considerable understatement he wrote to Dixon that on first reading of the wreck, "I was affected by the account" (October 5, 1878, *LD* 14), and clearly every aspect of the various newspaper reports he read "affected" him in ways and for reasons both obvious and more implicit. The German origin and name of the ship, the death of the exiled Catholic nuns, the heroic stature, physical and spiritual, of the chief nun, emphasized in the newspaper accounts—"the chief sister, a gaunt woman 6 ft. high, calling out loudly and often 'O Christ, come quickly!' till the end came"[4]—obviously had a specifically Catholic meaning and appeal to him. More generally, he must have felt deeply challenged by

3. See *The Times*, December 11, 1875, and *The Illustrated London News*, December 18, 1885, quoted in *FL* 439–43. For the newspaper accounts in full, see the appendix in Norman Weyand's *Immortal Diamond: Studies in Gerard Manley Hopkins*, 353–74. The Falck laws, expelling the Catholic clergy from Germany, were part of Bismarck's "Kulturkampf" campaign to establish the supreme power of the state.

4. *The Times*, December 11, 1875, quoted in *FL* 443. This version of the nun's words, calling specifically on Christ by name, appeared in the earliest accounts and must have sparked the poem's emphasis; a later version gives her words as the more general "My God, my God, make haste, make haste!" (*The Times*, December 13, 1875).

such statements as this from *The Times* of December 9, 1875: "There is as yet no definite explanation (beyond that which the snow storm may supply) of the deviation from her course which led the ship . . . to ground on the shifting sands of Kentish Knock," and the conclusion that the loss of the *Deutschland* so soon after the loss of another German ship was "a coincidence of calamities which at present there is no reason for thinking other than fortuitous." Here was a challenge sufficient to spark more than a vindication of Catholic martyrdom, a challenge to faith itself, and the poem therefore dramatizes in detail Hopkins' conviction that nothing in this world is "fortuitous," that throned behind seas and snowstorms, "throned behind Death" itself (32), is the purposeful sovereignty of God.

More specifically and personally, he was clearly "affected" by recognition of the similarity, even the near identity, of his own most intense and "literally true" spiritual experience—which I take to have been his initiation as a Jesuit—and that of the actual ship, and particularly of the actual nun. While recognizing in her, as later in the windhover, a figure of heroism beyond his own achievement, he dramatizes here, as in the sonnet, the points of likeness, and the ultimate point of intersection. Both poet-priest and nun have been touched and tested by the pain of redemptive suffering, and the grace of it, the one inwardly, privately, and with some resistance, the other publicly, physically as well as spiritually, and with a response of total affirmation more immediate and therefore more splendid than his own, the two experiences ultimately uniting to form one triumphant testimony to God as martyr-master and martyr-savior.

Hopkins' faith that nothing in God's world is without purpose, not even—indeed not especially—suffering, converged with his habitual perception of the fusion of physical and metaphysical, literal and "metaphorical," and ignited his mind and heart both to poetry after long silence and to the special sort of poem *The Deutschland* is. Again, given his simultaneously dramatic and private impulses, and his constant search for the unifying principle underlying apparent disparity, the result now seems inevitable: a poem whose method and voice fuse the narrative, dramatic, homiletic, and lyrical modes, and whose structure and imagery insist on the superimposed inner and outer experiences of "wreckage" and salvation. "An ode and not primarily a narrative" he labeled it himself (April 2, 1878, *LB* 49), perhaps rather conventionally, though with a typical respect for the tradition, and if one needs a single label perhaps *ode* will do. What the poem "really is," however, in genre as in cadence, is something so distinctively sui generis as to have no real parallel in English poetry before or since. It is the special shape and utterance required because he had "*seen something*" (*LD* 147), the mystery and certainty of God's redemptive power.

As a final preliminary point, it is worth remarking that like the literal event of the wreck itself to Hopkins, the title of the poem points not only to literal fact, and beyond fact to symbol, but beyond symbol to something like irony, and beyond irony to single truth. From the poem's beginning, the wreck is both a fact and a spiritual, probably multiple, metaphor: for the original wreck of the Fall, the initial wreck of all mankind out of which in Hopkins' faith God brought the possibility of salvation for all; for the agonizing but saving suffering of each individual who is tested, perhaps punished, and ultimately offered redemption by the touch of grace; and, though mutedly in this poem, I think, for the punitive destruction of what opposes God's will, "man's malice" and human unbelief, individual and national.[5] The irony implicit in the title, however—though Hopkins would certainly not have called it irony or even paradox, but "plain truth" (*FL* 389)—is that *The Wreck of the Deutschland* is not essentially a poem of literal or spiritual "wrecking"; it is not an elegy for the dead, or even for the living, and in contrast to "The Loss of the *Eurydice*," it is not, as I hear it, a tight-lipped Catholic admonition to nonbelievers.[6] It is a poem of salvation, of "salvage" out of various wrecks, a poem of resurrection, a hymn of praise.

The effect, and of course I would say the intent, of the style is to reflect the complexities of that great mystery of redemptive suffering by, in, and through Christ, while making it also intensely concrete, intensely "certain." The poem as a whole is therefore a

5. In a later commentary the direct relation of "wrecking" to sin is far more explicit: "*afflictio*, affliction, properly *wrecking*, is the material side of evil ... the havoc done—or the havoc of mind answering to it"; "*confractio*, the being wrecked by the havoc or mischief of sin" (1879, *SD* 187). For a suggestion that the wreckage of language itself adds a further dimension to the poem's title, see Miller, *Linguistic Moment*, 245–48.

6. For a favorable reading, however, see Youree Watson, S.J., "*The Loss of the Eurydice*: A Critical Analysis," 307–32; for an illuminating exposition, Mariani, *Commentary*, 119–26; for useful discussion of the historical circumstances as well as the poetry, MacKenzie, *Reader's Guide*, 95–104.

kind of mysterious "cipher" (22), a sign and a "sake"[7] of divine mystery, the "form speaking."

Since the opening stanza comes close to being a microcosm of the entire poem, in both content and method, just as the poem itself comes close to being a microcosm of the entire body of Hopkins' work, the following discussion will concentrate on tracing the ways in which it leads out to and illuminates the poem as a whole. In concept, structure, stylistic detail, and total tone, this germinal stanza helps to dramatize the way in which the "circling bird" has now found both its pattern of flight and its authentic music.

The first lines announce "the dominant of my range and state," the dominant idea of Hopkins' life, and of this poem: "Thou mastering me / God!" This will be the repeated acknowledgment, refrain, exhortation, and prayer of the whole work: "Be adored among men, / God, three-numberèd form" (9); "melt him but master him still" (10); "Make mercy in all of us, out of us all / Mastery, but be adored, but be adored King" (10); "A master, her master and mine!" (19); "Thou martyr-master" (21); "the Master, / *Ipse*, the only one, Christ, King, Head" (28); "Do, deal, lord it with living and dead" (28); "I admire thee, master of the tides" (32); "our thoughts' chivalry's throng's Lord" (35). Second—and I still speak only of content in its simplest form—the stanza swiftly defines the nature of that mastering God, mighty in power over land and sea, living and dead, mighty to bless, giving the gifts of existence and physical life ("breath and bread"), mighty also in terror, in the destructive power necessary to what is in his gift also, spiritual life. Third, the last lines introduce the crucial theme of the origin, nature, and effects of grace: "and dost thou touch me afresh? / Over again I feel thy finger and find thee." That single image of God's finger probably reminds us of Michelangelo's *Creation*, though I should think with a considerable change in the scale of God and man; it certainly contains all the complex theological beliefs and definitions that underlie the whole poem. It is the Ignatian image for the creative, active agency of God, "digitus paternae dexterae" (*SD* 195), and specifically it is the image of the pressure of grace: "For grace is any action, activity, on God's part by which, in creating or after creating, he carries the creature to or towards the end of its being, which is its selfsacrifice to God and its salvation. . . . it is

7. For Hopkins' full explanation of *sake* see Chapter 7, note 5: it seems to approximate in one word a combination of instress and inscape.

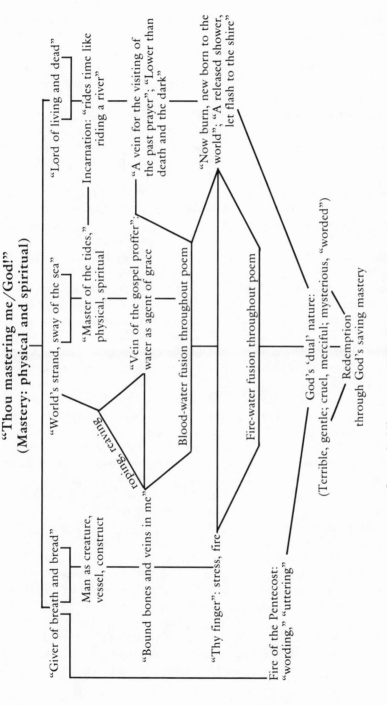

Stanza 1: Microcosm of *The Wreck of the Deutschland*

divine stress, holy spirit, and, as all is done through Christ, Christ's spirit" (*SD* 154). The image therefore points toward the theme and dramatic movement of the whole. The sources, the nature, the impact, the pain and the glory of grace form the central subjects of both parts of the poem, part I moving from its action on the poet himself to its action on all people and in all times, part II moving again from particular instances of its action—on the ship, on the nun—to a final plea that its power may be universally triumphant. And finally, while this first stanza does not explicitly announce what is perhaps the ultimate statement of the poem, "I did say yes" (2), that "yes" is surely implied in the exultant and joyous tone of the exclamatory opening: "Thou mastering me / God!"

In content alone the first stanza reveals Hopkins' way of seeing and concentrating the whole in the parts, the many in the one, the end in the beginning, a method that mirrors his faith that God is the Alpha and Omega who penetrates and unifies all wholes and all parts. Far more intricate and interesting, however, is the way in which every aspect of "cadence" embodies that faith and vision in the "heightened, to any degree heightened" language of poetry.

The first two lines themselves reflect much of Hopkins' welding of technique and thought, a welding that typically resulted from revision: the replacement of "God mastering me; / Giver of breath and bread" from manuscript A with the lines' present and final form (see Appendix A). The original version, in spite of a slight grammatical ambiguity, presents the central idea as clearly as the revision, includes the crucial and characteristic emphasis on the continuing action of God in the present participle, and reflects Hopkins' habitual manipulation of normal syntax in the service of idea: to his way of thinking, that participle of continuation made unnecessary, and indeed false, any grammatical completion of the sentence—technically, the four opening lines are a grammatical fragment.

But the revision does more, exemplifying the way in which Hopkins worked toward full "formulation" of his basic vision. Most obviously it replaces a quietly, even passively, reflective strength of beat and word order with the much more dramatic "bidding" of the anvil-ding attack, an attack essential to the triumphant tone and to the concept of joyous submission voiced in that tone. It also establishes a direct, personal, and vital relationship that has almost the effect of a confrontation. The two words "Thóu" and "mé," heavily stressed by the sprung scansion, linked by a participle that is immensely strong in meaning but unstressed,

The opening stanzas of *The Wreck of the Deutschland*, with Hopkins' revisions of Bridges' transcription, MS B (MS.Eng.poet.d.149.fol.15 recto).

or weakly stressed, in meter,[8] seem to strike sharply against each other like flint, to give off sparks, to "ring and tell" of the meaning of that relationship. The confrontation, so crucial to the entire poem, is immediately dramatized as one in which two electrically

8. On the metrical ambiguity here, perhaps one of the "immaturities" of which Hopkins was conscious, see Appendix A.

potent forces meet, in which the second, even in submission, or actually because of it, achieves its existence, identity, right to assert itself as a "me," and in which potential combat is suggested but simultaneously resolved in a whole but still strenuous harmony.[9]

The circular construction both of this single phrase, in which "me" is enclosed by "Thou" and "God," and of the whole stanza, which returns to its opening "Thou" with the final "thee," dramatizes the point that God is not only center of the world but in his "outsetting" the sovereign encloser, embracer, of all things, including especially the central, but subject and merely potential, self; he is already shown to be "the girth of it and the wharf of it and the wall" (32). In practice as in theory and faith, the emphasis is on difficult and strenuous unity: "In everything the more remote the ratio of the parts to one another or the whole the greater the unity if felt at all" (*JP* 283). In the second stanza also, in which "I" and "Thou" are again in strenuous confrontation, use of the apparently insignificant preposition *at* will especially reemphasize the same point: "I did say yes / O at lightning and lashed rod." Less automatic, less polite, than *to*, almost implying by analogy a shaking of the fist in defiance, *at* suggests a potentially dangerous, potentially rebellious, relationship, making the more impressive that it is with "yes" and not with denial that the poet responds.

One final point about these four initial words suggests a possible further dimension of their density. While I do not wholly agree with W. A. M. Peters that the first line is primarily an adjectival phrase in effect, equivalent to "past all / Grasp God" (32), since the verbal impact seems so crucial, his suggestion about the restrictive quality of the words is very persuasive: placed as they are, they serve to identify and emphasize the essence of God, the central quality, as "Thou, God, mastering me," for example, would not.[10] From the beginning, therefore, Hopkins' typical grammatical multiplicity, especially his way of mining the possibilities of grammar, works to reveal both essence and essence-in-action.

The immediately following line, "World's strand, sway of the sea," exemplifies a second basic characteristic of Hopkins'

9. Compare "For a self is an absolute which stands to the absolute of God as the infinitesimal to the infinite. It is an infinitesimal in the scale of stress. And in some sense it is an infinite, if looked on as the foredrawing of its whole being" (*SD* 153).

10. *Critical Essay*, 110, a reading also supported by Schneider, *Dragon in the Gate*, 76.

method, the use of manifold and somewhat mysterious "moments" of words:

> Thou mastering me
> God! giver of breath and bread;
> Wórld's stránd, swáy of the séa;
> Lord of living and dead . . . .

The possible association of "strand" with "rope" will become crucial and explicit as the poem develops, but even if we first take the phrase in its most natural sense as referring to land and sea, there is a curious and important effect created by syntax and diction: the line has a Janus-function, looking both ways. God is not only "giver" of land and sea, as he is "giver of breath and bread," and lord of both, but as the appositional placement and feel of the phrase imply, he *is* in some special sense what he creates, is one with his creations as well as master-maker of them, literally as well as metaphorically. "Sway," suggesting both sovereignty and motion, already evokes simultaneously the power and motion of the physical sea, over which God is lord, and the yet greater power and action that inhere in the nature of its creator-ruler. Later stanzas will elaborately develop both this and the first half of the apposition, God-as-"strand," both as stable and controlling shore (32) and as sustaining, binding rope of being (4, 12).

In the same way, "find" in the final line of this stanza has some slightly elusive and multiple vibrations: "Óver agaín I feél thy fínger and fínd thée." It clearly has its normal denotation, though in context the discovery conveyed is one that is both sudden and a regaining of something known and lost awhile. The whole line also emphasizes a meeting of separate but reciprocal, and reciprocally seeking, forces: the inescapable finger reaches down to find and touch its passive object, but the man replies with that active, answering response that makes full discovery possible. And we will remember this true finding of the true victor, true life, when Death's later bragging drumroll announces, "Some find me a sword; some / The flange and the rail; flame / Fang, or flood" (11); the poem has told us from the beginning that throned behind Death is God, and that mightier than Death's weapons, and wielding them, is the finger of grace.

As in this stanza, so throughout the poem Hopkins makes intricate use of the complex vibrations of words; as God is mysterious and manifold in his workings, yet essentially one, so are, or should be, the least of the terms by which a poet tries to word him. Bridges, predictably, objected to Hopkins' use of "grammatically ambiguous" words, to his apparent insensitivity to the "irrelevant suggestions" of homophones, and to the way in which "he will provoke further ambiguities or obscurities by straining the meaning of these unfortunate words" (*PB* 99). Examination of a few outstanding examples of this provoking practice, however, reveals neither irrelevance nor insensitivity, though much complexity, in Hopkins' manipulation of "ambiguous" words.

One readily defensible example is the word *bay* in "Yet did the dark side of the bay of thy blessing / Not vault them, the million of rounds of thy mercy not reeve even them in?" (12). Given the importance of the fact and metaphor of water in the poem, and the actual location of Kentish Knock in the mouth of the Thames, this word will probably first suggest harbor, safe anchorage, however dark—"the roads, the heaven-haven of the reward" (35). "Vault," however, immediately shifts the picture from a bay of the sea to the dark bay of a church, and probably to the arch of the sky also,[11] and finally, because of the still reverberating echoes of "only the heart, being hard at bay, / Is out with it!" (7–8), we may have a baffling impression of irreconcilable images. But if we can change our expectations and way of seeing so as not to insist on merely visual logic, the images make important sense thematically and imaginatively. Central to this stanza, and to the entire poem, is the implied contrast between the hunted heart, driven to a stand, snarling its opposition to God, and the mercy that protects, encloses, forgives, and saves even that heart. The combined water-church-sky implications give us the wholly "relevant" sense of the massively overarching and all-embracing mercy that makes of sea, storm, and land, that makes of the whole world, one great refuge, sanctuary, cathedral. Only if we are looking for a clear visual picture, or for simple cerebral clarity, will the "moments" of "bay" seem either strained or meaningless.

A similar multiplicity appears in "The sóur scýthe crínge and the bléar sháre cóme" (11), technically a spectacularly typical line in its use of the monosyllabic foot and elaborate assonance and alliteration, but typical also in its attention to rich yet coherent sense. As Gardner was the first to suggest, "cringe" carries its root meaning and original "prepossession" of "fall" (Anglo-Saxon "crincgan") as well as its common denotation, so that it evokes

11. See "opposite bays of the sky," and the sky as "vaulted in very regular ribs with fretting between" (*JP* 193, 207).

both the descent of Death's inevitable scythe and simultaneously the wincing response of the shrinking victim.[12] "Sour," though slightly less defensible perhaps, does legitimately mean both "bitter" and "cold and wet," but seems especially chosen for two effects beyond denotation: the oblique appeal to the senses of taste and touch as well as sight and, above all, the reminder that as God's action in us can be "sour or sweet" (8) depending on our response, so too can death be either. Finally, "blear," typical of Hopkins' fondness for adjectives that are also verbs, means "gray," making visible the bleak metallic color of the scythe, but again also carries the sense of its effect on the victim: dimming of sight. That it especially means "dim with water," and that the line in which it appears immediately precedes the stanza on the *Deutschland*'s departure to destruction at sea, seems not accidental.

Finally, among many such examples of multiple meaning inherent in a single word is the coinage *unchancelling*: "Thy unchancelling poising palms were weighing the worth, / Thou martyr-master" (21). God's seeming duality, his apparently paradoxical nature and actions, is here suggested and resolved in the fusion of one word's "moments." The dominant meaning in context is that God himself drove the nuns from the safety of the chancel to suffering and glory at sea, but even this sense probably involves the latent meaning of "liberating, setting free," inherent in the Latin root of "crossbars, lattices." Beyond this, and reinforced by the next words, "poising" and "weighing," is the possible meaning suggested by Peters, "unwavering, steady," and allied with it "not influenced by chance" (French "chanceler," or plain English "chance").[13] Even beyond these, though to my mind slightly less probably, there may be the vibration suggested by Philip M. Martin, that God reveals himself to his worshipers by removing the barrier of the chancel screen.[14] God, in a word, is both destroyer and preserver, banisher and savior, hunter and healer, firm of purpose, redemptive in action.

The words and phrases cited so far are complex in meaning whether one hears or reads them; there remain the homophones,

12. *Hopkins*, 1:117. Compare the similar later use of "wince" in "No worst, there is none" (65).

13. *Critical Essay*, 186.

14. *Mastery and Mercy: A Study of Two Religious Poems*, 48. This meaning would nicely anticipate the revealed appearance of Christ (28), though I am dubious about a present participle of revelation in a stanza emphasizing the still-veiled purpose of the God "above" and God's own, not human, sight.

particularly important since Hopkins composed orally to start with and wanted all his poems to be recited aloud, heard, not merely read. If one does hear the poem, if not literally at least with the inner ear, not only will some of the more debatable rhymes lose their oddity ("to leeward" / "night drew her" / "*Dead*" [14]), but some important and proliferating meanings and metaphors begin to break surface. The major and most-discussed example in this poem is that of "A prophetess towered in the tumult, a virginal tongue *told*" (17, italics mine). Reading aloud, we can hardly help hearing the ear-rhyme "tolled," especially in conjunction with "tongue" and perhaps even "towered," and this suggestion of a pealing bell becomes explicit and important in a later stanza:

> . . . lovely felicitous Providence
> Fínger of a ténder of, O of a feáthery délicacy, the bréast of the
> Maiden could obey so, be a bell to, ring of it, and
> Startle the poor sheep back! (31)

That Hopkins wanted to emphasize the bell image is evident in the revision from the original "swing with, be musical of it" (A) to the present version, and the result is that the early homophone has initiated and contained the central idea, argued first and persuasively by Robert Boyle, that the nun calls both the faithful and "the comfortless unconfessed of them" (31) to confession in all its senses, to the Mass, and therefore to salvation.[15] We are probably also to make a connection retroactively to the very early "I can tell" (3), though the phrase seems merely colloquial and the telling is still wholly private there, to "tower" (3), to "truer than tongue" (2), and to "past telling of tongue" (9): the whole line of metaphor and thought of "wording" God is implicit in the homophone *told*. This, and other lines of meaning similarly inherent in lesser examples of homophones ("heart"/hart; "wrung"/rung and "wring"/ring; "wrack"/rack; "ark"/arc; possibly though more dubiously "peeled"/pealed), will be discussed later, but the main point here is that those homophonic ear-chimes that have meaning are sooner or later shown by Hopkins to have it; we are not awash in a beaconless sea of punning sound and meaning.

These few examples of special qualities of diction all serve to illustrate the same point: the multiple but not anarchical or nonsensical functioning of the "moments" and meanings of words. We must perceive and respond to multiplicity, but within the limits

15. *Metaphor*, 10–15. Mariani suggests a musical pun not only on "told" but also on "virginal" (*Commentary*, 60).

and guidelines of grammatical, metaphorical, and thematic context, and with attention to dominant grammatical meaning. We are not free to attach to words and phrases any and all associations they may happen to have for us: at least in my view, context and sense exclude the meaning of "reddish-brown" for "bay," for example, and of "portion" for "share"; similarly, homophones that may fancifully tempt us but have no other support in the poem are to be rejected ("pane"/pain, "altar"/alter, "made"/maid, "vein"/vane, for example). In practice as in theory, the function of individual words reveals how Hopkins used these smallest poetic units to embody both the complexity and the ultimately purposeful and coherent unity not only of the poem but of the God behind the poem.

Second, among the general characteristics of Hopkins' method revealed in the first stanza is the extraordinarily visceral sense of pressure conveyed by both imagery and meter, especially those of the last four lines:

> Thou hast bóund bónes and véins in me, fástened me flésh,
> And after it álmost únmade, what with dread,
>   Thy doing: and dost thou touch me afresh?
> Óver agáin I féel thy fínger and fínd thée.

These lines vividly dramatize that central comment on the most potent of the five senses, "Seeing is believing but touch is the truth, the saying goes" (*SD* 243). The mysterious certainty of spiritual experience is not to be adequately conveyed by merely visual and therefore too precise and readily graspable means or, at the other extreme, by misty and mystical means; it requires images that, without being wholly visible, or even wholly tangible, are potently, even painfully, felt in the deep heart's core. We therefore feel, without seeing, the physicality of the self and of God's massive creative power, heavily emphasized by stress and alliteration in the first line quoted above, as well as the enormous uncreating power of that probing, searching finger's pressure described in the last lines.

This sort of imagery is characteristic of the entire poem, giving us a constant sense of physical impact, physical strain, which is yet not wholly physical, often a sense of a twisting, racklike wrenching, always a feeling of energy at tension, of the spirit stretched and tested to its highest pitch by usually unseen but always massive forces. Hence such lines as: "And the midriff astrain with leaning of, laced with fire of stress" (2); "Wring thy rebel, dogged in den" (9); "Father and fondler of heart thou hast wrung" (9); "With an anvil-ding / And with fire in him forge thy will" (10). Hence the importance of the latent reminders of this imagery in the homophones *ring* and *rung*. Hence also the more obviously twisting, battering imagery of the physical wreck, "wrack" (31), and such odd (and to my mind overly ingenious) syntactical imitations of crushing physical speed and impact as:

> They fought with God's cold—
> And they could not and fell to the deck
> (Crushed them) or water (and drowned them) . . . . (17)

Related to this strenuously visceral imagery of pressure is that of motion and electrical stress that allows nothing to remain static or merely visible; again, the central vision requires words that heighten its distinct reality but resists any attempt to arrest or freeze it. The dominant strand of fire-lightning-flame imagery throughout the poem is of course partially, and powerfully, visual: the whole work flashes with flame and star, with scarlet and rose and the blaze of "a crimson-cresseted east" (35), with God's "fall-gold mercies" and "all-fire glances" (23), with his lightning and "dooms-day dazzle" (34) as well as with his starlight and saving "shower" of grace's gentler fire (34). But the residual effect of this imagery is not of something seen, but of something felt and heard, "electrical horror" (27), and electrical splendor and beauty. The poem is "laced with fire of stress" more than with visible fire, and not with the eyes mainly, but in some inward way, we respond to its crackling voltage.

Even the most apparently visual images are usually associated with something that sets them in motion, or at least calls into activity senses other than, or in addition to, sight. The stars, distant but patterned so that each is distinctively visible, rapidly become a single inscape-in-motion, "starlight," which is both active itself and fused with, responsive to, human action, and which probably also carries an association with sweet scent: "I kiss my hand / To the stars, lovely asunder / Starlight, wafting him out of it" (5).[16] The vivid descriptions of the storm itself swirl and spin with the motion of "whirlwind-swivellèd snow" (13), and the sea's power beats upon our sense of touch more than on our eyes: "And the sea flint-flake, black-backed" (13), "the rash smart sloggering brine" (19). Even images specifically involving color are usually associated with movement also, by implication or by statement. The "dappled-with-damson west" (5) shimmers with the stippled color and

16. See Appendix A on the revision from "calling him out of them."

changeableness conveyed by Hopkins' favorite word, "dappled"; snow is not merely white, but "Wiry and white-fiery" (13); the "crimson-cresseted east" (35) flames with the motion as well as the color of torches; that brilliant little image of "the jay-blue heavens" (26) evokes not only color but, by association, a flash of color in motion, possibly combined with other relevant connotations (spring, birdsong, growth, joy). In that same stanza, the phrases "blue-beating and hoary-glow height" and "or night, still higher, / With belled fire and the moth-soft Milky Way" synaesthetically combine sight, sound and pulsation, touch; "pied and *peeled* May" (italics mine) evokes a combination of shining freshness revealed to the eyes, as the gray fog-cover is stripped away, and an almost tactile feeling of the smooth sleekness of that freshness. Just possibly there may also be some anticipatory vibration of the bell sound and image of the following lines if one hears the homophone; possibly also, like "wafting," the word may have carried for Hopkins some associations with scent, if he remembered consciously or unconsciously a moment recorded in an early journal: "At Skinner's Weir yesterday they were peeling osiers which gave out a sweet smell" (May 4, 1866, *JP* 134).

I might add that the worst image in the poem, in my view, the famous "lush-kept plush-capped sloe" (8), is so largely because it is too insistently and lushly sensuous, lacking that interpenetration by the nonphysical, or at least the vibrations of multiphysical appeal, that lends the images discussed so far a complexity beyond lushness. The image does of course succeed in making intensely concrete the mystery of God's revelation in man, and the choice of the wild plum does intensely convey the "sour or sweet" aspects of that mystery—"sweet" if man's answer is "yes," the "best word," "sour" if it is "no," the "worst." It nevertheless seems to call too much attention to itself rather than to its idea, and as it is developed in the following lines, is too obvious in its Keatsian mouth-watering qualities, all of which is compounded by a rather self-conscious technical virtuosity in adaptation of the "*cynghanedd* traverse."[17] It strikes me as a rich but static image, in short, one of the exceptions and "immaturities" in this poem of usually consistent emphasis on a charge of more than physical energy.

17. The true "traverse" allows the midsection of a line to be passed over but requires that the first and last parts alliterate exactly. "*W*arm-*l*aid *g*rave (of a) *w*omb-*l*ife *g*rey" (7) thus follows the rules as strictly as English allows, while the line in question introduces the small license of additional unalliterated consonants: "(H)ow a *l*ush-*k*ept, (p)*l*ush-*c*apped (s)*l*oe" (Gardner, *Hopkins*, 2:149–50).

That charge of vital motion is also, and perhaps most obviously, sustained by Hopkins' habitual reliance on verbs and verbal forms. Again, stanza 1 is microcosmic in its illustration of this point: while wholly lacking any purely adjectival forms, it depends heavily on active verbs ("bound," "fastened," "unmade," "touch," "feel," "find"), on the already discussed present participle "mastering," on nouns implying their verbal source or association ("giver," "living," "sway," "dread"), on the active gerund "thy doing." And this verbal emphasis, while potent, is relatively restrained compared to the powerful, often brutally powerful, verbs that prevail as the poem continues; if we leave it with some sense of having been battered, electrically shocked, "almost unmade," it is partly because of the relentless recurrence of such repeated verbs, and their participial counterparts, as "lash," "flash," "spring," "swing," "forge," "beat," "burn."

Supporting this same charge of stress, even adjectives and nouns tend to be verbal in form, or at least in implication. As in the case of "mastering," present participles constantly replace adjectives and emphasize in the same way essential and continuing action: "the widow-making unchilding unfathering deeps" (13), "the hurling and horrible airs" (15), "a lingering-out sweet skill" (10), "Thy unchancelling poising palms" (21), to cite only a few instances. As in the case of "thy doing," gerunds with a heavily verbal quality consistently replace mere nouns: "leaning of . . . fire of stress" (2); "his going in Galilee," "its swelling to be" (7); "for feeling the combating keen" (25); "Time's tasking . . . that asking for ease," "the appealing of the Passion," "The jading and jar of the cart" (27), and so forth. And the persistent use of actual nouns that are also verbs allows Hopkins to "mean things," to stabilize motion momentarily in an object, while avoiding any complete arrest or freezing of motion, object, or experience: like the function of "*sway* of the sea" (1) is that of "The *swoon* of a heart that the *sweep* and the *hurl* of thee trod / Hard down" (2), "the *hurtle* of hell" (3), "a *fling* of the heart" (3), "I am soft *sift*" (4), "the *combs* of a *smother* of sand" (14), "*buck* and the *flood* of the *wave*" (16), "*beat* of endragonèd seas" (27), among many other examples (italics mine).

Somewhat more intricate are two other instances of the noun-verb, both of which have generated much critical discussion because of their coinciding "moments." In the line "Has one fetch in her" (19), "fetch" may carry its main verbal implication, but even as a noun it has at least four meanings that function appropriately in context: (1) in ordinary usage, "plan, device," a sense in which

Hopkins uses it quite naturally and casually in prose (May 14, 1881, *FL* 247, for example), and the allied "far reaching effort"; (2) in dialect, "deep painful breath or inspiration";[18] (3) in nautical usage, which cannot have escaped Hopkins' notice, since he uses the verb in a partially nautical sense in stanza 33, "the act of tacking"; (4) and perhaps above all, a genuine sight as opposed to a subjective vision: "I suppose the vision of the pregnant woman to have been no mere vision but the real fetching, presentment, or 'adduction' of the persons, Christ and Mary, themselves" (*SD* 200).

Second, there is the much-debated "spell": "I whirled out wings that spell / And fled with a fling of the heart to the heart of the Host" (3). The dominant meaning is surely that of a period of time, and probably specifically of a period of duty, but this sense only becomes clear, and comes perhaps with a small shock of surprise, when we discover that the word we have initially taken to be a verb lacks an object. It may well be that Hopkins intended this ambiguity, or sublime double take, so as to suggest this early in the poem the implications of the verb: these wings do visually "spell" the cross, as Boyle first suggested.[19] While I cannot see that the word can grammatically make sense as a verb in this immediate context, the verbal (in both senses) implications will emerge powerfully and clearly later in the poem's development of the concept of "wording, uttering."

If satisfactory verbal forms are not available, Hopkins transforms the grammatical function of existing words in some way, or if necessary creates the appropriate word. A word that is both a verb and a noun may be pressed into service, somewhat awkwardly, I think, as an adjective: "Read the unshapeable *shock* night" (29). More successfully, a preposition may function as an active present participle, even as a verb: "O unteachably *after* evil" (18), in which the incorrigibly fallen heart has as its entire and constant activity the deliberate, even eagerly excited, pursuit of evil. This is "current language"—as in the cry "After him!" (*P* 260n)—concentrated and heightened. And finally, if a combined noun-verb does not exist at all, Hopkins coins it, the major and lovely example in this poem being "Let him easter in us" (35). The occasion, and all it implies of spiritual resurrection, not only becomes an action but also

18. Pick, *Priest and Poet*, 46.
19. "The Thought Structure of *The Wreck of the Deutschland*," 335, a verbal reading also urged by Devlin, *SD* 305n195.4. For the argument that under any interpretation the word is simply clumsy and dictated mainly by rhyme, see Schneider, *Dragon in the Gate*, 110.

promises, through the emphasis on its root *east*, that bright rising of new radiance made explicit in the following parallel phrases: "Let him easter in us, be a dayspring to the dimness of us, be a crimson-cresseted east."

The opening stanza, then, out of which this discussion has somewhat deviously grown, introduces in its content the crucial ideas of the poem and reflects in its style, even in this relatively straightforward set of lines, some of the complicatedly multiple and active qualities of diction and syntax that characterize Hopkins' method in this and later poems. In both larger and more specific ways also it is a microcosm of the whole, introducing most of the key metaphors, and hence key concepts, that will develop, intertwine, echo, answer to one another throughout the poem.

Most obvious, of course, are the images, soon to become complex symbols, of sea and land. The sea, in fact, is not only spoken of but may perhaps be felt in the rhythm and the irregular line lengths of this stanza, and of the whole poem. One is always on dangerous ground and running the risk of downright silliness in attributing too much metaphorical or metaphysical import to such technical elements, but here I think their importance can be sanely argued from their effect: the battering but controlled power of the meter combined with the surge and swell of the lines as they eventually crest in the long grandeur of the final line already give us, not a picture, but the feel of the sea. We are already caught up in the grip and the tides of the storm, in "wind's burly and beat of endragonèd seas" (27), and so are at least subliminally prepared for, even living in, one of the poem's governing metaphors. That the stanza pattern also controls motion, is the "girth of it and the wharf of it and the wall," and that the rhyme scheme at last, and somewhat surprisingly, returns to close the circle with the "A" rhyme, is characteristic and significant in ways that perhaps now need no further comment.

Even if we do not feel in the stanza form both sea-surge and mastery imposed on it, the explicit introduction of those central concepts is obvious. They will be developed in complex figurative ways, but as in most of Hopkins' best poems, complexity does not derive from mere "interesting uncertainty," from concealment of central metaphors and symbols, but from the inherent and proliferating mystery of what seems initially distinct, evident, and "certain." In this case, just as "Lord of living and dead" is not merely a commonplace general phrase but one that specifically foreshadows God's mastery of the dead who drowned in the wreck, and of the living—poet and world—who survived, so "Woŕld's stránd, swáy of the séa" pointedly establishes his control of the two physical elements that converged in the literal wreck. Since the wreck itself is not only a literal event, however, but also a metaphor for higher "plain truth," so also shore and sea, sand and water, are more than physical elements and are soon developed in rather elaborately metaphorical ways.

In two major cases, they pass from a physical to a spiritual-figurative "moment" almost simultaneously, while having in addition complicated links with other aspects of the poem. The result is a constant intersection of literal and metaphorical and of metaphor and metaphor, all adding up to the single grand metaphor—which is also to Hopkins literal truth—of the poem as a whole.

I have been suggesting so far that in the beginning is also the end of this poem; in order to show that the reverse is true as well, I begin this particular discussion with an example from near the end of the poem. "I admire thee, master of the tides," is the quiet opening of stanza 32, a line that derives its loveliness of sound from beautifully controlled assonance and alliteration, and its restrained but reverent and moving power from that simple word *admire*, whose root sense of wonder we are to remember and feel. This line reminds us, of course, of "sway of the sea," and of all God's physical power and spiritual purpose as demonstrated in the wreck. The following lines carry that reminder further, carry the meaning far beyond acknowledgment of redemptive mastery displayed in a specific present instance:

> I admire thee, master of the tides,
> Of the Yore-flood, of the year's fall;
> The recurb and the recovery of the gulf's sides,
> The girth of it and the wharf of it and the wall;
> Stanching, quenching ocean of a motionable mind;
> Ground of being, and granite of it: pást áll
> Grásp Gód . . . .

Everything we have seen of God's spiritual use of physical water in a specific case is now related to "its spring in eternity," to the Deluge, with all its implications of sin and promise of salvation. God's mastery of all "tides" in all times, and of all "falls" also, seasonal but also by implication moral, is emphasized by that perfectly balanced second line, balanced in meaning as in sound. That God is "world's strand," source and sustainer of all *physical* permanence in the midst of flux, all-embracing "wharf and wall" that gives to the formless and the shifting form, limit, existence, is then clearly developed in the following lines. Again, however, as in the case of "fall," the "*gulf's* sides" has some complex vibrations: the word fuses, like "world's strand, sway of the sea," like "Yore-flood . . . year's fall," the central elements of land and water (sea bay, land chasm), but it also perhaps implies some deeper than physical abyss. In any case, rapidly and without comment, the spiritual implications of all the preceding lines break surface completely in the fifth line, as God's mastery is applied to all inner oceans; the human mind too requires divine ordering of its tides, shoring of its shifting sands, a point the poet's own experience has already dramatized.

Specifically, that somewhat difficult and congested line, "Stanching, quenching ocean of a motionable mind," has two further complications worth pausing on, one basically syntactical, the other a matter of multiple meanings. The slant rhyme of "stanching, quenching" and the internal rhyme of "ocean"/"motion" seem designed to dramatize in sound a strenuous harmony imposed on fluctuation and are perhaps linked also to a yet larger "rhyme," one that emerges from the oddity of syntax. One's probable initial sense that this whole line is in apposition to "master of the tides," that God himself is therefore paradoxically the ocean that restrains and "quenches" all other oceans, may not be a wholly mistaken one; as in "sway of the sea," Hopkins may have intended to remind us that God encompasses both motion and permanence, that he controls and in some sense *is* both "ocean" and "granite," is immanent in, as well as transcendently above, the elements he masters and uses as redemptive agents.

Second, the choice of "Stanching, quenching" would seem to reflect more than a fondness for consonantal rhyme and difficult harmony, since all the "moments" of both words are functional here. In the case of "stanch," these are: the dialectical "quell"; the adjectival and appropriately nautical "watertight," hence "firm," and hence as a verb, "make firm" (see also *P 72*); and the common medical meaning of the verb. In light of the total meaning of the poem, and the weaving of metaphor in it, I should suppose that Hopkins intended that last meaning especially, to suggest that Christ's wounds, Christ's blood, "paradoxically" heal man's spiritual wounds, stanch the loss of spiritual lifeblood. In the same way, "quench" means not only to "subdue, suppress, extinguish" (the latter meaning particularly relevant to God's dual nature as, and dual mastery of, fire and water) but also to satisfy, as thirst is satisfied by water. The relevance of this last meaning, and indeed of all the meanings of both words, to the underthought and overthought of the whole poem need not be further labored.

The ideas and the phrasing of this late stanza lead the mind not only forward to the crucial stanza on "a mercy that outrides / The all of water," the "all" of life and death, and of sin, and of heresy (33), but also inevitably back to such phrases as "it rides time like riding a river" (6) and "though in high flood yet" (7) and above all to stanza 4, whose images and phrasing will expand during the course of the poem until they culminate in stanza 32's quietly triumphal assertions.

In stanza 4, the two central images of hourglass and well involve again the key literal elements of sand and water, and again employ them to make a metaphorical statement that seems to have little to do with the actual wreck but does in fact have a most intimate relationship. The images make the point that natural man without God—a self that knows and serves only the Time-spirit, in Carlyle's phrase—is simply "soft sift / In an hourglass," simply shifting sand, externally seemingly firm, "at the wall / Fast," but "mined with a motion, a drift, / And it crowds and it combs to the fall." (Anticipating stanza 32's "the year's fall," "motionable mind," "the wharf of it and the wall.")[20] At the self's deep center the undermining trickle goes on, not of his transient physical life only, but of his arid spiritual life as well. And if he remains mere sand within, and a mere vessel of time, not eternity, he, like the *Deutschland*, will find the seeming safety and solidity of land to be his destruction, will find not "Ground of being" (32) but a fatal grounding, will be wrecked on "the combs of a smother of sand" (14), on the Kentish Knock of his own shifting inner reefs.

The same point is made, with a very slight shift in imagery, at the beginning of part II. It is significant that although the first stanza Hopkins wrote in composing the poem was apparently the relatively factual, almost journalistic, narrative stanza 12 (*LB* 44), this was not where he chose to begin either the poem as a whole or its second and seemingly "narrative" section. The purpose of

20. For a different interpretation of the entire stanza, see Schneider, *Dragon in the Gate*, 21–22. Hopkins' own prose in an earlier letter may be the most useful gloss on the hourglass: commenting on his younger sister's "grownupdom," he says, with slightly forced playfulness, "As for me ... I have prescribed myself twenty four hourglasses a day (which I take even during sleep, such is the force of habit) and ... even this does not stop the ravages of time" (April 25, 1871, *FL* 114–15).

stanza 11, like that of the whole of part I, is to give us the wider spiritual meaning behind the particular wreck, in this case to warn us of the universality of death: in whatever shape it comes, violent or peaceful, it will come to all, though we in our blindness will not acknowledge our own mortality. The point of the hourglass image is therefore repeated here in more dramatic form, in the explosively sardonic irony of "But wé dream we are roóted in eárth—Dúst!" Again, to place one's hopes in the shifting "land" of life, in the world of time only, is to trust that which, like the sand in the hourglass, will always fall, is to forget the Death-scythe which, in its descent, ends all other falling:

> Flesh falls within sight of us, we, though our flower the same,
>> Wave with the meadow, forget that there must
> The sóur scýthe crínge, and the bléar sháre cóme.

On the other hand, with God's grace humanity is more than sand and dust, and Death is servant, not king. Death's savage power and majesty are brilliantly dramatized as outwardly strong but inwardly empty puffery in the monosyllabic words but windy sounds of the opening of stanza 11: "'Some find me a sword; some / The flange and the rail; flame, / Fang, or Flood' goes Death on drum, / And storms bugle his fame." Before the saving majesty of God such windy bravado must give way, and it is God's fame, not Death's, that both "stars and storms deliver" (6); it is he who is the mighty chivalric leader of the greater army and whose bugle summons humanity to its ranks (35); it is he who is "throned behind / Death with a sovereignty that heeds but hides, bodes but abides" (32).

Therefore in the early stanza 4, the metaphor for man sustained by God is not earth but water, and moreover, water fed by water, by streams of grace from the massive uplands; the same element that seems to be wholly destructive, but is not, in the rest of the poem is thus shown this early to be the agent and symbol of redemption:

> I steady as a water in a well, to a poise, to a pane,
>> But roped with, always, all the way down from the tall
> Fells or flanks of the voel, a vein
>> Of the gospel proffer, a pressure, a principle, Christ's gift.

Hopkins may have had in mind here a specific allusion to the Sermon on the Mount, which he would later refer to as "that river of divine wisdom, which rising on Christ's lips flows from that mountain down all time" (September 7, 1879, SD 21); almost certainly we are to take the voel as Calvary, as Sister Mary Adorita Hart has persuasively argued.[21] What is certainly clear, and utterly characteristic, is that the lines transform literal and in part visible fact (the long thin lines of the mountain streams of Wales, the actual mountain, Voel, Foel, or Moel, near St. Beuno's)[22] to metaphorical meaning without losing the vividness of the literal. The life-giving, life-sustaining "vein" of the Gospel's promise and offer of redemption, the "pressure" of God's stress, the pressure of grace and of challenge, the fundamental "principle" of Christian truth, and specifically of the Ignatian "First Principle and Foundation," are spiritually felt the more intensely because they are in part physically seen and felt.

The nature of this stanza's images, as well as its emphasis on human thinghood but God's sustaining grace, leads back once more to stanza 1. The seemingly unrelated images of hourglass and well are linked not only by their relationship to the central sand-water, shore-sea metaphors of the rest of the poem but also by their similarity to each other: they are vessels, containers, constructs, the central image of the mortal self already introduced in stanza 1. That self is a mere construct of bones, veins, and flesh into which God must breathe life and grace and full being, a construct infinitely frail in contrast to the mighty swayer of land and sea, so frail that one touch of the creating finger can almost unmake it. "Thou hast bóund bónes and véins in me, fástened me flésh" especially emphasizes the fact that he is a scaffolding, a skeletal structure overlaid with substance, a structure, need one say it, not unlike a ship. The second stanza then swiftly and dramatically develops the fusion of man-and-ship in storm, the fusion of the two wrecks, the two tempests, spiritual and physical: "lightning and lashed rod"— both the spiritual lightning of grace and rod of punishment and the physical lightning and lashing of the ship's spars in storm; "the sweep and the hurl of thee" and "the midriff astrain with leaning of, laced with fire of stress"—both the man, helplessly whelmed and struggling in spiritual anguish, and the ship, astrain and helpless in the battering seas.

For the sake of this emphasis on the fusion of man and ship, grace and storm, Hopkins sacrificed in revision another, and soon to be central, image and fusion: the original version was "The

---

21. "The Christocentric Theme in Gerard Manley Hopkins's 'The Wreck of the Deutschland,'" 73.

22. September 8, 1874, *JP* 258; Gardner, *Hopkins*, 1:55; *PB* 106.

swoon of a heart that the swoop and the hurl of thee trod. . . ." He will later develop the image of the Holy Ghost as falcon, bird of prey as well as dove, but apparently chose at this point not only to avoid the perhaps too obvious "swoon"/"swoop" chime but to achieve immediately and emphatically the central fusion that is essential to the coherence of the whole poem. He probably also saw the effectiveness of anticipating through ironic repetition the opening of stanza 13, "Into the snow she sweeps, / Hurling the haven behind"—again suggesting a confrontation of human and divine powers, but this time emphasizing the contrast between human presumptions and divine omnipotence.

From the first two stanzas, then, it is clear that both human beings and their creations are frail and fragile constructs, "the prey of the gales" (24), inner and outer. Without God, that is all they are, and all they will be seen to be in the late desolate sonnets: without God, the self is a merely physical and disgusting thing— "Bones built in me, flesh filled, blood brimmed the curse," or a "scaffold of score brittle & bones." But the later sense of loss is bitter exactly because Hopkins had once known, and could still imagine, what it was to have that physical vessel touched and filled by God's grace. Implicit in the opening stanza of *The Wreck of the Deutschland*, explicit in those immediately following it, and developed in the rest of the poem are the possibilities of mere human things if they are so blessed by grace. On this point I must again pursue a circuitous course, tracing an intricately linked chain of words and metaphors.

The somewhat curious syntax of "fastened me flesh" has the effect of suggesting that the completed "me" is only, and permanently, flesh, that there is no "me" apart from physical substance and its underlying skeleton. But the word *veins* in this same line will prove to be charged with the possibilities of human beings when God touches them to more than physical being, and its implications will proliferate and expand throughout the rest of the poem. Readers will already have noted not only that stanza 4 develops the vessel-construct image of the first stanza but that the word *vein* functions there importantly and figuratively. "A vein of the gospel proffer" makes the water of grace lifeblood also, Christ's blood, shed from the pierced side at the crucifixion: "and forthwith came there out blood and water" (John 19:34). It is this that laces the merely physical veins of the world and humanity with life and meaning, as it laces the poem: later stanzas, through various modulations, develop that fused vein-blood-water metaphor.[23]

In stanza 18, as Hopkins imagines the nun's first appearance in the storm, God's touch, the "touch" again of stanza 1, pierces the armored bone-cage of his heart, freeing the sources of life, of sorrow that is also joy, of poetry:

> Ah, touched in your bower of bone,
>   Are you! turned for an exquisite smart,
> Have you! make words break from me here all alone,
>   Do you!—mother of being in me, heart.
> O unteachably after evil, but uttering truth,
> Why, tears! is it? tears; such a melting, a madrigal start!
>   Never-eldering revel and river of youth . . . .

Tears of joy then turn temporarily to tears, and blood, of bitter sorrow—"Heart, go and bleed at a bitterer vein for the / Comfortless unconfessed of them" (31)—but finally, tears modulate again into life-giving water, blood of sorrow into blood of salvation, in stanza 33's triumphal confession of faith. The storm-waters of life and death are swept to their furthest and plumbed to their deepest seamark, and both are laced with love; Christ's blood offers both the living and all those drowning in purgatorial darkness the streams of grace that have earlier flowed from Calvary's heights to the individual poet:

> With a mercy that outrides
>   The all of water, an ark
> For the listener; for the lingerer with a love glides
>   Lower than death and the dark;
> A vein for the visiting of the past-prayer, pent in prison,
> The-last-breath penitent spirits—the uttermost mark
>   Our passion-plungèd giant risen
> The Christ of the Father compassionate, fetched in the storm of his strides.

Since critical explications of the details of this stanza tend to diminish its imaginative power and clarity while immensely increasing its obscurity, for the moment let it simply be "left in the memory," speaking for itself and allowing a reader to "like some without exhausting all" (*LB* 50). At this point, I will turn instead to something illustrated by the presence in this stanza of both the

23. On the whole of stanza 4, and for the best stanza-by-stanza reading of the entire poem, see Peter Milward, S.J., *A Commentary on G. M. Hopkins' The Wreck of the Deutschland.*

mighty "fetched in the storm of his strides" and the gentle "glides":
the latter sends us back to a second major group of metaphors,
closely related to those of vein-water, the softer metaphors of
"melting"; the gentler side of God's stress takes this form, has this
effect.

If God comes to man not as the anvil-master but "stealing as
Spring / Through him," he will "melt him but master him still"
(10), moving the impervious heart, as seen, to "a melting, a madrigal start" (18), delivering in stars as well as storms the stress that
"hearts are flushed by and melt" (6), offering to us the meaning
and the challenge of the Passion, which "Will, mouthed to flesh-
burst, / Gush!—flush the man, the being with it, sour or sweet, /
Brim, in a flash, full!" (8). In the last two instances, the play on
"flush" needs particular notice: the effect of God's touch and presence is not only man's spiritual purgation but also the kindling of
new warmth, fervidness, spiritual "color."[24]

The latent—or perhaps evident—sexuality in this line of imagery will be touched on later, but the dominant overthought in
Hopkins' own mind would seem to have been what he discusses in
some detail in prose, with particular application to the soul in and
out of grace. Of the latter, he states that "freezing is the earthly
blockish insensible condition of a soul which may indeed be melted
by warm breath but must first be so melted before it can sway to it"
(SD 208),[25] a point personally dramatized in stanza 18. In all cases
of the appearance of this metaphor, it is linked either explicitly or
implicitly both to the heart-vein-fluid imagery and to that central
image of the vessel emptied and inexhaustibly filled again "to a
poise, to a pane."

Linked also to the imagery of veining/lacing, and like the word
veins itself, introduced as an apparently purely physical term in
stanza 1, a second metaphor implied in that stanza develops
through many modulations until it carries the full force of spiritual
meaning: "roping" or "reeving" imagery, like that of "vein-water,"

24. Compare Hopkins' comment on the cured leper: "not the skin only and
the outer man looked handsomely, but the heart and spirit in God's eyes flushed
and with that far fresher and lovelier colours" (SD 20).

25. In context, Hopkins is pursuing the Ignatian metaphor of "tepidity" or
"lukewarmness" of soul. He concludes that the fervent soul in grace is "on the
boil" and "ready to pass, by evaporation, into a wholly spiritual condition"; the
tepid soul lies between this and the other extreme of the "blockish" and frozen soul
out of grace (SD 208).

twists through the poem and, like it, emphasizes the way in which God's stress laces the world and holds it in being.

In a somewhat subliminal way, at least on first reading, "world's strand" first introduces the image of God as lifeline of the universe, and the metaphor then becomes slightly more apparent, though still not fully explicit, in "Thou has bound bones and veins in me, fastened me flesh," with its suggestion of the connecting, threading together, lacing of skeletal parts. The image is developed, still implicitly, in "laced with fire of stress" (2), with its dual implications of painful lightning-shock and sustaining instress, and finally becomes explicit in stanza 4. "But roped with, always . . . a vein of the gospel proffer" overtly confirms for the first time the fusion of vein and rope imagery that we may have been sensing and that will continue to intertwine throughout the poem; more importantly, these lines make us feel as from within the sensation of well-water interpenetrated, crisscrossed, roped both round and through, by the streams and strands of grace.

Most crucially, the same metaphor reappears in stanza 12: "Yet did the dark side of the bay of thy blessing / Not vault them, the million of rounds of thy mercy not reeve even them in?" In both its senses—the nautical one of "fasten, surround by rope" and perhaps the closely related dialectical "gather in"—"reeve" condenses and emphasizes the central point: the "million of rounds," the infinite coils, of God's encircling mercy surround, hold fast, control the fragile and destruction-bound vessel, the vessel that is not only the *Deutschland* but every person aboard (and not aboard) her. "I say that we are wound / With mercy round and round / As if with air," Hopkins will write again much later (60). That firm, twisted strand of divine love and energy controls all the seemingly opposed energies in motion that would appear to "untwist" the world: those of the "whirlwind-swivellèd snow" (13), of the "inboard seas swirling and hawling" (19), of the "hurling and horrible" winds that make of the physical ropes and rigging .ʼ false and fatal refuge (15), of the heaving waves that cut both the brave sailor's life-rope and his body's "braids of thew" (16). All these apparently counter energies, sometimes even apparently demonic and hellish energies, as of "fiery" snow and "endragonèd seas," are to Hopkins agents of the sovereign hand that holds, binds, laces, makes firm all the world's forces, all its "motionable" oceans, physical and spiritual.

Through yet another circling return to stanza 1, it is now possible to consider without oversimplification what is perhaps the most obvious idea of that stanza, and of the poem as a whole: in content and in imagery, Hopkins explores the apparently paradoxical nature of God. Up to this point, I have resorted to hedging the word *paradoxical* with various qualifications to suggest its only partial adequacy; I would now emphasize that if we use the terms *paradoxical* and *paradox* at all in treating Hopkins' vision and method, it needs to be with a clear recognition of the distinction between merely witty, or at best cerebral, illogical logic, contradictory truth, and religious paradox. "Yet after all there is nothing like the plain truth," Hopkins wrote to Patmore; "paradox persisted in is not the plain truth and ought not to satisfy a reader" (May 6, 1888, *FL* 389), a statement that seems startling coming from a writer not notable for "plain" expression, who himself persisted in use of paradoxical methodology, and whose very religion is based on what seems to a layperson very like sublime paradox. But what Hopkins was objecting to is clarified in part earlier in the same letter: "The use of a paradox is to awake the hearer's attention; then, when it has served that end, if, as mostly happens, it is not only unexpected but properly speaking untrue, it can be, expressly or silently, waived or dropped" (388). The objection is similar to his opposition to Bridges' concept of "mystery," an objection to what merely intrigues, interests, startles, is merely clever and superficially revealing, but does not penetrate to or demonstrate underlying "plain truth." He demanded, and practiced, expression of what was to him "properly speaking" wholly true, including divine coherence beneath all seeming contradictions.

On a related point, he would also have agreed, I suspect, with Rainier Maria Rilke's advice to the young poet, "Seek the depths of things: thither irony never descends."[26] Though this idea is no longer fashionable, and perhaps not even valid, and though Hopkins himself is perfectly capable of irony in his letters, the basic position is one that an unashamed moralist and a convinced believer in divine truth is likely to adopt. It is certainly one that Hopkins' poetic practice demonstrates; whenever he employs anything approaching irony, as in the title of the poem itself, as in stanza 11, it is in order to emphasize the literal "truth" behind it.

One rare example of apparent dramatic irony in the poem may serve as proof of this point:

26. *Letters to a Young Poet*, trans. M. D. Herter Norton (New York: W. W. Norton, 1954), 24.

Into the snow she sweeps,
Hurling the haven behind,
The Deutschland, on Sunday . . . . (13)

Heavy emphasis is thrown by periodic sentence structure, by punctuation, and by stress on the final phrase, "on Sunday," and it seems at first bitterly ironic that the ship should sweep to her destruction, so confidently, even so gaily, on the Lord's day, the day of rest. Hopkins' point, however, would seem to be the "plain truth" that in spite of ignorant human expectation and presumption, it was indeed and appropriately on the Lord's day, and by the Lord's doing, and that it is not from "rest" (such as his own in stanza 24) but from storm that salvation comes.

Nevertheless, Hopkins does employ the terms, the imagery, the methodology of paradox as a means of expressing his ultimately nonparadoxical vision, a means of demonstrating both the way in which God's acts may appear to divided man and the reality of God's actual unity of nature and purpose. The first stanza emphasizes God's apparent duality: he is maker and unmaker, lord of life, lord of terror. As the immediately following stanzas make clear, however, and as the entire poem will fully demonstrate, the massive finger unmakes only to make anew, and while it may be terrible and painful, it may also be "Finger of a tender of, O of a feathery delicacy" (31). It is for human beings to choose, by their response, the degree of pressure and pain it will inflict, but whatever their responses, the nature of God is constant: known or unknown, answered with "yes" or "no," he is master and redeemer, his wings are mighty but sheltering, and the world, knowing it or not, is always "under thy feathers" (12).

Between the first stanza's statement in the present tense, "Over again I feel thy finger and find thee," and stanza 9's "I found it" in the past tense, comes first a dramatization of personal experience (2–3), then a more general consideration of the sources and meaning of that experience (4–8), which justify the series of summarizing paradoxes in stanza 9: "Thou art lightning and love, I found it, a winter and warm; / Father and fondler of heart thou hast wrung: / Hast thy dark descending and most art merciful then." The poet's first harrowing "finding" of God in the past and the repeated touch of terror and grace in the present ("afrésh," "óver agáin"), inflicted by the news of the wreck, fuse into one renewed experience of discovery, of fresh insight into the true nature of that seemingly paradoxical God.

Behind the paradoxical ideas and imagery of stanzas 1–3 lie some of Hopkins' most specifically doctrinal beliefs, as well as at least one specifically scriptural allusion; the stanzas are therefore major examples of Hopkins' transmutation of learning and doctrine into poetry. Behind stanza 1's description of skeletal man, for example, and specifically behind stanza 2's "Thou knowest the walls, altar and hour and night," is almost certainly an allusion to Ezekiel, as well as one direct quotation from it: "Son of Man, dost thou think these bones shall live? And I answered, O Lord God, thou knowest" (37:3). This verse is immediately followed by a passage surely reflected in the wording, as well as the ideas, of stanza 1: "Thus saith the Lord God to these bones: Behold, I shall send spirit into you, and you shall live. And I will lay sinews upon you, and will cover you with skin: and I will give you spirit and you shall live, and you shall know that I am the Lord" (37:5–6). These echoes, while not essential to an understanding of the meaning, do widen the "landscape," the implications, even the mission, of the personal confrontation.

Yet more important to a reading of these stanzas is knowledge of some of the theology they translate into poetry. This is a point at which ignorance is not bliss, a "close reading" of the text alone not adequate, and external knowledge really essential to an understanding of what the poet meant, because the poetry's vivid shorthand seems already to be expressing what later prose commentaries will intricately explore and develop. In "I did say yes," for example, and in the development of this whole concept in the poem, is condensed much of Hopkins' detailed thought about the nature and freedom of the human will in relation to God's mastery. The first stanza has clearly made the point that the tiny construct, man, is not free to escape the touch of the probing finger, but the opening of stanza 2 makes equally clear that he is then free to respond to it in various ways, two points that Hopkins summarizes in prose as follows: "Ordinarily when grace is given we feel first the necessary or constrained act and after that the free act on our own part, of consent or refusal as the case may be" ("On Personality, Grace and Free Will," *SD* 149). The same idea underlies the later reference to one of God's great acts of grace, the conversion of Paul: "Whether at once, as once at a crásh Pául" (10). We are to understand what a later prose commentary insists upon, that this "crash" was not actually "a violence done to his will," for he was still free afterward to choose denial of the offered light (*SD* 156). Stanza 8 has already emphasized the point that we may will to refuse the offer of grace, and may do so even to the final extremity—"We lash with the best or worst / Word last!"—but whatever the individual response, God will be master in Christ:

> Hither then, last or first,
> To hero of Calvary, Christ,'s feet—
> Never ask if meaning it, wanting it, warned of it—men go.

A warning is obviously implied here—woe to the person who comes to judgment with "no" on his lips—but the emphasis is not on the threat of damnation; as in stanzas 2–5, it is on the idea that only in consent do man's true freedom and glory lie, only in "correspondence" to grace: "this is the *arbitrium*, the verdict on God's side, the saying Yes, the 'doing-agree' (to speak barbarously)" (*SD* 154).

Implicit in the poem, and explicit in the later prose, are two further "formulations": first, the subdivision of the will into the *arbitrium*, the elective will, the conscious faculty that decides action (*SD* 142) and may choose either for good or for ill (149), and the *voluntas*, the affective will, which seems to be more spontaneous and instinctive and which is determined by God to lean always toward the good, while the elective must be changed by God's grace (151); and second, the further anatomization of each will according to its responses at each stage of choice.[27]

The central issue emerging from this intricate theorizing, beyond the ancient problems of free will and predestination, is the distinction Hopkins finds in both Ignatius and Scotus between "the act of commission and the act of consent" (*SD* 144), so that full guilt attaches only to consent to sin, and full merit only to absolute consent to God ("for to consent implies no degree, it is pure Yes or No" [*SD* 145]). The ideal therefore is not merely obedient consent, but loving consent, a response of "fainness" by both wills, a response essentially of both deliberate and desirous choice. The possible distinction between these responses is one that comes to be critical and painful for Hopkins in later years, but in this poem the two wills are one. Though the poet struggled in the grip of his storm before coming to loving submission, his "yes" is ultimately not only of the head but of the heart also. In part II, the nun's in-

27. Before action, the *arbitrium* decides choice; at the time of it, gives its "consent, willingness"; after it, gives "avowal, ratification." The *voluntas* responds with desire, "fainness," before the act; delight at the time of it; "gaudium," joy, after it (*SD* 142). Ideally therefore, the two wills would meet in a response of joyous avowal to a rightly made choice.

stant response with both wills will be viewed as her supreme and greater glory: instantly "reading" the meaning of the storm, instantly knowing "the who and the why" (29), her "yes" is the spontaneous and joyous cry of consent, "O Christ, Christ, come quickly" (24).

In the early stanzas in question this "yes," and the consequent transformation of the bone-vessel self without grace, is dramatized in vividly compressed and paradoxical imagery. The physical, earthbound construct, appalled by the high divinity that, in demanding that his creature rise to the heights, first crushes him to the depths—"trod / Hard down with a horror of height" (2)—the heart in panicky and desperate flight from both grim height and grim depth—"The frown of his face / Before me, the hurtle of hell / Behind, where, where was a, where was a place?" (3)—becomes suddenly, by an assent to grace, a soaring, towering, spiritual being. The terrible "finger," which has almost become in stanza 2's "trod" the massive foot, the "lionlimb," of a later poem, now becomes implicitly the wings, the sheltering feathers, of the Holy Ghost. Above all, because of both these transformations dramatized in the imagery, the man becomes almost one with God, one with the divine and towering dove-falcon:

> I whirled out wings that spell
> And fled with a fling of the heart to the heart of the Host.
> My heart, but you were dovewinged, I can tell,
> Carrier-witted, I am bold to boast,
> To flash from the flame to the flame then, tower from the grace to the grace. (3)

The final line here, and indeed the whole of part I, condenses some details of doctrine to which the prose may again serve as a clarifying gloss. Most generally, the lines dramatize that touch of grace which affects the free *arbitrium*, which does not determine man's choice but changes it: "it is a lifting him from one self to another self, which is a most marvellous display of divine power" (*SD* 151). More specifically, the last line seems to assume two of the three terms in Hopkins' later formulation of the threefold nature of grace: first, corrective, redeeming grace, "Christ's grace," which especially touches the mature mind and the elective will and which is, above all, "a purifying and a mortifying grace, bringing the victim to the altar and sacrificing it" ("Thou knowest the walls, altar and hour and night"); second, elevating grace, the grace granted especially at the Pentecost, the grace of the Holy Ghost, "which lifts the receiver from one cleave of being to another and to a vital act in Christ: this is truly God's finger touching the very vein of personality, which nothing else can reach and man can respond to by no play whatever, by bare acknowledgment only, the counter stress which God alone can feel . . . ["Thou heardst me truer than tongue confess"], the aspiration in answer to his inspiration" (*SD* 158).[28]

Soaring then from the flame of torment to become one with the flame of Christ's redemptive fire, towering, dove-and-falcon-like, from the pain of corrective grace to and through the glory of elevating grace, the heart's depths become heights, its defeats victory, its retreating "flights" from pain ("fled with a fling of the heart") true rising flight and soaring conquest. Again, Hopkins probably intended and saw no paradox here, but "plain truth": as in an early diary he sees no major difference between the words *flee* and *fly* in their original senses (1863, *JP* 11), so here *fled* conveys a literal, not paradoxical, dual meaning.

This seemingly paradoxical tension between height and depth, conquest and defeat, and this resolution are of course central to the poem because they are central to the concept of the Incarnation. That Christ descended to undergo a birth into death, "Warm-laid grave of a womb-life grey" (7), and to turn death to victory, was his glory, and mankind's, and the poem therefore develops the paradox and reconciliation of height and depth first personally, then more generally, and finally universally. The "horror of height" and the "hurtle of hell" experienced first by the poet, then by the ship and its passengers, are triumphantly opposed and conquered not only by the touch of grace on the inner heart but by the whole being of the nun herself as she, like Hopkins' heart earlier, but more grandly, "towered in the tumult" (17), both spiritually and physically. Above all, that all people are, or may be, saved by "Our passion-plungèd giant risen" (33) is the great message of the poem's conclusion.

Stanza 33 is intensely difficult in detail, while being intensely strong and even clear in total meaning and impact. In order to avoid what students often testily feel all analysis must necessarily do and be—a myopic and ruinous dissection—I consign to notes

28. The first form, "quickening" grace, which especially "belongs to God the Father" (*SD* 158), is not an issue in the poem, since it is especially the grace of innocence. "Corrective" grace, however, Christ's grace, accounts for his emphatic introduction in this stanza—"Thy terror, O Christ, O God"—to be followed by imagery introducing the third person of the Trinity, and source of the third form of grace, the Holy Ghost.

some comments on the more minutely vexed particulars, but one matter of syntax and three of meaning must be explored here. One may hope that ultimately, even in mere criticism, "the clearer the formulation the greater the interest."

Like most critics, I assume the omission, a fairly natural and typically Hopkinsian omission, of the relative pronoun in the third line: "with a love [that] glides." The logical syntax of the opening lines, though involving the gigantic chiasmus effected by the juxtaposition of the two "for" phrases, does seem essentially parallel, "with a mercy that outrides" / "with a love [that] glides," exactly as in the last line of stanza 32 from which these lines directly follow: "with a sovereignty that heeds but hides."[29] The combination of this parallelism with the in-folding, enclasping effect of that chiasmus has a characteristic relation to meaning: the three central qualities of God are strongly emphasized through parallelism— "sovereignty," "mercy," "love"—and they enclose, enclasp, encircle, their human objects.

Those objects, "the listener" and "the lingerer," I take to be types respectively of those who, in this life, have listened or may still listen to the peal of the summons to grace ("the comfortless unconfessed of them," for example, who have not as yet said an irrevocable "no") and of those who continue to withhold or delay assent, in this life or after—especially after, given the full statement that God's love for them "glides / Lower than death and the dark" and the following elaboration of the souls in purgatory.[30]

Especially crucial to this stanza's impact, and to its reconciliation of height and depth, and breadth, and timelessness, are two of the rhyme words, "ark" and "mark," emphasized both by the very fact that they are stressed rhyme words and by their allusive density of meaning. The seeming contrast between the ark, safe refuge above the waters of now as of "Yore," and the love that descends

29. The main alternative reading of the stanza's opening lines assumes a grammatical shift from *for* as preposition plus object ("for the listener") to *for* as conjunction ("because") plus subject and verb: "for the lingerer . . . glides." The lingerer is then Christ, who hesitates to damn even after death, who "bodes but abides." Though this reading makes perfect sense, that sort of shift in grammatical construction is not typical of Hopkins, while omission of the relative pronoun emphatically is (see again *PB* 98).

30. The "past-prayer, pent in prison" (purgatory or limbo) cannot now pray for themselves and would be past all hope were it not for Christ; these especially include those who have repented in their last moments of life. The reference also seems specifically to be to the Harrowing of Hell, after the crucifixion and before the Resurrection. On these lines, see especially Milward, *Commentary*, 149.

even into those waters' lowest depths to continue its priestly ministry ("visiting") emphasizes the actual oneness of the Old and New
Testament God; as in stanza 6, they are one from all time and in all
time, with a mercy that is infinite, in life and after. And if, as I suspect, a reverent pun on the homophone *arc* is hinted at, we are also
reminded of the rainbow-covenant that promised what the whole
poem has tried to show—a promise kept, an act of grace that does
not destroy, that actually seeks to save, by water.

Since I hear the whole of this stanza as periodic in structure and
rising in tone, I take "mark" to be a noun, the object of the main
and climactic verb "fetched," both words functioning primarily,
though not only, in their nautical senses. "Mark" would therefore
reconcile in its own "moments" breadth and depth, signifying both
the boundary, frontier, farthest limit of the sea and the measure-
ment of its depth, as well as such possible, though lesser, implications as "object to guide the sailor" and "target." An echo of
Othello may possibly have been in Hopkins' mind—"Here is my
journey's end, here is my butt / And very sea-mark of my utmost
sail" (5.2.267–68)—but in any case that meaning, if not that allusion, seems clearly here. "Fetch" I would think functions both in its
normal sense, "pursue, go in search of, gather in," and in its nautical sense, "to reach, arrive at, come up with."[31]

As a result, God's power through Christ is again shown to "ride
time like riding a river," since the Yore-flood and the ark and the
Incarnation and possibly the Harrowing of Hell are made simultaneously past and present.[32] In addition and above all, the dimensions of immense height—"throned behind / Death"—of immense depth—"lower than death and the dark," "passion-
plungèd"—and of vast breadth—"the storm of his strides"—fuse
in "the uttermost mark" to emphasize a power that sweeps all the
world's limits, and all eternity's as well.

The final stanza of the poem epitomizes for a final time these
same seeming polarities, and their resolution. In subject matter, it
begins with the depths—of death, of human sin and England's
guilt—and its tone is one of somber though restrained and rever-

31. For alternative readings of the stanza's conclusion see Appendix A.
32. This helps account for the past tense of *fetched*. While context would logically call for present tense, parallel to "outrides" and "glides," meter requires and
Hopkins' theology allowed the monosyllabic past tense: Yore-flood, ark, and
Christ's walking the Sea of Galilee are as present as the present wreck, and the Harrowing of Hell, like the Passion (4), both was and is, happened and continues to
happen.

ent sorrow: "Dáme, at oúr dóor / Drówned, and among oúr shoáls, / Remémber us." But the stanza rises steadily in content and in tone through all the blaze of Easter-sunrise imagery, through the crescendo of epithets for Christ-God, to the exultant climax that dramatizes what it prays for, the heroic workings of the high and flaming God among the lowly "hearths" and hearts and minds of his human soldiers:

> More brightening her, rare-dear Britain, as his reign rolls,
> Pride, rose, prince, hero of us, high-priest,
> Our heárts' charity's heárth's fíre, our thoúghts' chivalry's thróng's Lórd.

Almost indissolubly entwined with the already intricately linked height-depth-flight-combat imagery of stanzas 3–4 is a second major strand of paradoxical imagery, and hence of seemingly paradoxical thought, that of God the hunter and lover. The concept of God as hunter, though deleted in the revision of stanza 2's original "swoop," has been implied in stanza 3's dramatization of the heart in desperate flight from its pursuer, but in that stanza the hunted became one with the hunter, and the hunter himself became neither lion-limbed predator nor falcon but dove of the Holy Ghost. Later stanzas develop the hunting metaphor both more grimly and ultimately more triumphantly.

That the heart can never escape the divine hunter and, more important, that the heart opposed to God is no towering bird but at best a "hart," if the homophone holds, or more probably a snarling, lashing animal, is the point of "only the heart, being hard at bay, / Is out with it! Oh, / We lash with the best or worst / Word last! (7–8), a point reiterated in "Wring thy rebel, dogged in den" (9), "dogged" picking up one implication of "hard" and redramatizing both animalism and intransigent stubbornness in evil. The *Deutschland* herself, in arrogant ignorance of the power and purpose of God's "sweep and hurl," goes forth like a bird, like a hunting falcon—"Into the snow she sweeps" (13)—to become the prey of "endragonèd seas" (26) and "roar[ing]" night (17). The nuns, hunted from their homeland by all the forces unleashed and symbolized by Luther, "beast of the waste wood" (20), become victims of the natural "hunters" but triumphant counterparts of the royal Hunter: "Surf, snow, river and earth / Gnashed" (21), but to oppose their savagery and conquer it, "a lioness arose breasting the babble, / A prophetess towered in the tumult, a virginal tongue told" (17). This whole line of thought and imagery is then summed up, and its seeming paradoxes resolved, in one of the great phrases in Hopkins' poetry, perhaps in any poetry: "but thou art above, thou Orion of light" (21). The God who has hunted down the poet, and the ship, and the nuns, who relentlessly pursues all hearts to bring them "hard at bay," is also, and always, celestial hunter, lord of light, shining and merciful redeemer of his prey, "heart's light" (30) as well as heart's pursuer.

Complementing and not contradicting the hunting metaphor, therefore, is that of God as lover and human beings as lovers in response. Already latent in "the swoon of a heart" (2), the proper response to God's power and love is developed more fully in stanza 5: "I kiss my hand / To the stars, lovely-asunder / Starlight . . . / Kiss my hand to the dappled-with-damson west." Man must not only respond but "correspond," and he therefore now makes the physical gesture of love and greeting and acknowledgment that puts into outer action the earlier inward gesture, "yes":

> Since, tho' he is under the world's splendour and wonder,
>> His mystery must be instressed, stressed;
> For I greet him the days I meet him, and bless when I understand.

As the near rhyme of the earlier "asunder" with "is under" helps suggest, and as these lines make explicit, God is always there, recognized or not, felt as distant or as near. Nonetheless, human beings must do more than take that mysterious reality for granted. They must, if they can, when they can, not only make it intensely actual within themselves, feel it on their pulses, turn perception to full spiritual recognition through a "greeting of the spirit" ("instress"), but must also "stress," demonstrate, emphasize that inner recognition to themselves, to others, to God, by the total physical-spiritual response of the lover's greeting. In short, humanity dares not assume as its right God's presence and love, like a spoiled child (or lover, or wife) who blindly and arrogantly assumes its father's (or lover's, or husband's) care and tenderness, though God in all these roles is both demanding and tender. At the end of part I, in a phrase made possible by the poet's preceding experience and his correspondence to it, that last concept is summarized: "Father and fondler of heart thou hast wrung" (9).

In part II this love theme, this music of a spiritual *liebestod*, gathers to a fully orchestrated greatness. The curiously Herbertian stanzas 22 and 23 are important to the poem in several ways, tonally and thematically. They are needed for their change in tone and level of physical intensity after what has preceded; we need to shift briefly to "madrigal" (18) song after brass and percussion. They are needed also for Hopkins' purposes to prove the point that nothing occurs, and certainly did not occur in this case, by mere accident; given both his basic faith and his habitual way of seeing in literal fact its spiritual meaning, he could not possibly have passed over without comment the facts that it "happened" to be Germany, Luther's land, that exiled the nuns and that there "happened" to be five of them on the ship, nuns of the Franciscan order at that. Hence the exclamatory recognition of the significance of the number, "Five! the finding and sake / And cipher of suffering Christ" (22), and the following elaboration on the theme of the stigmata.

Above all, these stanzas lyrically develop the theme of Christ as lover and bridegroom. The suggestion of a wedding ceremonial begins in the last line of stanza 21, in which the flinty storm flakes of earlier stanzas are transformed into the strewn flowers of a joyous ritual: "Storm flakes were scroll-leaved flowers, lily showers— sweet heaven was astrew in them." This transformation is then developed and completed in stanza 22's concentrated fusion of the stigmata, the "rose-flake," and the rose ("cinquefoil token")— symbol of suffering and martyrdom, symbol also of passion and love.[33] More explicitly, the nuns, like Saint Francis, like all Christ's chosen, are marked by the stigmata as "his own bespoken" (22), marked by the marriage seal of his "Lovescape crucified" (23), and like new and inviolate Danaës, are also "sealed in wild waters, / To bathe in his fall-gold mercies, to breathe in his all-fire glances" (23).

The betrothal of Christ and nuns is then glanced at again in the tentative question as to the chief nun's motive in calling on him— "Is it love in her of the being as her lover had been?" (25)—and the theme culminates finally in the lyrical stanza 30, a stanza in which Hopkins again presses meaning out of literal fact, this time the fact that the wreck occurred on December 7, the day before the Feast of the Immaculate Conception:

> Jesu, heart's light,
> Jesu, maid's son,
> What was the feast followed the night
> Thou hadst glory of this nun?—
> Feast of the one woman without stain.
> For so conceivèd, so to conceive thee is done;
> But here was heart-throe, birth of a brain,

33. On the rose emblem, and specifically on the significance of its five leaves, see the earlier poem "Rosa Mystica" (27).

Word, that heard and kept thee and uttered thee outright.

It is difficult to touch upon this whole line of metaphor without falling on the one hand into pedantic comment on its use by Saint John of the Cross, Saint Theresa, and other mystical poets, not to mention Donne, or on the other into the reductiveness of merely sexual language. Hopkins was treading a fine line, and somehow our responses need to do likewise if it is the poetry we wish to read. Without underestimating the sexual impact of "Thou hadst glory of this nun," or of the same idea implicit in stanza 2's "swoon of a heart" under the stress of the hunter-lover, and in the whole line of imagery of melting, we are asked by Hopkins to feel both the intensity and the intense spirituality of this love and, in this stanza, of this great consummation and birth. That it is a spiritual consummation, conception, birth, is of course explicitly emphasized here by that "But" in the second to last line, which insists on the contrast, as well as the similarity, between the nun and the Virgin; elsewhere the same point is implicit. What the language intends and, "if we know how to touch it," conveys is a powerful instressing of the nature of the divine lover, and of love for him. He is the eternal creator, as Father-begetter, as Son-bridegroom, as "arch and original Breath" of the Holy Spirit; full love of him requires not only a swoon of the heart, a kissing of the hand, a surrender of self, but an actual heart-and-brain throe of spirit that, having conceived Christ in purity, also gives him a new birth by "uttering" him in the midst of the pangs of pain and death.

This new incarnation, the new advent of Christ made possible whenever an individual understands and responds to his stress, is triumphantly announced and acclaimed in the penultimate stanza:

> Now burn, new born to the world,
> Double-naturèd name,
> The heaven-flung, heart-fleshed, maiden-furled
> Miracle-in-Mary-of-flame. (34)

These lines, somewhat too frenetically compounded perhaps to the eye, though not to the ear, complete the development of the lover-hunter metaphor through their dramatization of both the terror and the gentleness of the Incarnate God, and they emphasize again the transformation of a human vessel when God deigns to touch and enter it. ("Maiden-furled" vies with "Orion of light," I think, as one of the great religious compressions in this poem, and in poetry.) The lines also assume a typical fusion of time schemes: the compressed imagery not only speaks of the original Incarnation in time, and of Mary, original mother, but clearly suggests that in all times Christ may be "new born," and in all who will receive him may be "heart-fleshed," making each heart potentially Mary's equivalent, "mother of being in me" (18) both of personal existence and of Christ. The same rather complex, and daring, assertion about the nature and "time" of the Incarnation lies behind the early and difficult stanzas 6–7, to which I now briefly return.

Stanza 1 has already made the point that the God of all time and eternity may choose to reach down through time to touch directly and personally any given individual, and the point that he is always both present in time and above it. Stanza 4 has emphasized the "always"-sustaining, ever-flowing, blood-streams of grace; Calvary is now, not merely a past place and event in time. Stanzas 6–7 then offer a condensed sermon on that first entry of God into time, considering the entry's origin and impact in vivid, though also obscure, detail:

> Not out of his bliss
> Springs the stress felt
> Nor first from heaven (and few know this)
> Swings the stroke dealt—
> Stroke and a stress that stars and storms deliver,
> That guilt is hushed by, hearts are flushed by and melt—
> But it rides time like riding a river
> (And here the faithful waver, the faithless fable and miss).
>
> It dates from day
> Of his going in Galilee;
> Warm-laid grave of a womb-life grey . . . .

Taken together with the rest of stanza 7, two points are internally clear here: that it was Christ's Incarnation and Passion that first fully revealed God in earthly time, and still do so; that this entrance into time is the crucial, almost incomprehensible, event upon which salvation depends, but upon which both faith and faithlessness may founder. A third point may also be relatively clear—that it is upon recognition of the Incarnation that any understanding of the "stroke and stress" delivered by nature must depend—but this point introduces the necessity of invoking external textual evidence. Since the first version of "Nor first from heaven" was "Nor first from Paradise" (A), Hopkins cannot have intended two of the interpretations offered by his critics: that "heaven" refers merely to the natural heavens (stars, storms, sunsets), or that the "stroke" refers to human evil, originating in man's rebellion and fall in Eden and necessitating the Incarnation.[34]

About what he does mean, however, we may well fable and miss unless we invoke what he and Scotus "knew" but otherwise "few know": his concept of the origin of the Incarnation. Following and developing Scotus, Hopkins' view was that Christ existed as wholly God in "eternal" time, in "the heaven of the Godhead"; he existed also in "angelic" time, "that heaven or aeon of Mary in which he had lived and been manifested to the angels" (*SD* 177), manifested through the taking of flesh (*ensarkosis*), though not yet human flesh and form (*SD* 171); finally he entered earthly time as fully man at the Incarnation. Second, Hopkins believed with Scotus that the Incarnation was planned even before the creation of man, let alone his Fall, as an act of love, and not primarily as an act of redemption: with the Fall it became both, and Christ entered historic time as suffering God Incarnate.[35]

This not altogether orthodox theology is what the stanzas in question seem to be saying in compressed form: the potent stress of God, the "stress and stroke" delivered directly by grace and mediately by the natural world, originated neither in nature (agent but not source) nor, in a specific sense, in heavenly or angelic time ("his bliss," "heaven"); though intended from those times, "It dates from day / Of his going in Galilee," his full incarnation as man in historic time and place. Simultaneously, however, "it rides time like riding a river," and the point made by the contrast between that precise, temporal, calendar word *dates* and the much more difficult and dimensionless river simile is that the Incarnation occurred *in* historic time but is superior to it, *and* has been inherent in, planned from and for, all times, eternal, angelic, historic. It not only rides and survives the river of mortal time that destroys all other things (see stanzas 4, 11), but has been borne on, part of, the current of eternity also. Like God himself, the principle of the Incarnation has always been, will always be, "master of the tides."[36]

34. On the first point, see Boyle, "Thought Structure," 348, and Downes, *Ignatian Spirit*, 60; on the second, Gardner, *Hopkins*, 1:58–60, and Pick, *Priest and Poet*, 45.

35. See also *SD* 181 and Devlin's comments and notes, *SD* 109, 114, 290n138.1, 296n170.3.

36. As Devlin points out (*SD* 306n196.1), a much later meditation may clarify the river image: "Time has 3 dimensions and one positive pitch or direction. It is therefore not so much like any river or any sea as like the Sea of Galilee, which has the Jordan running through it and giving a current to the whole" (*SD* 196). God entering linear time remains the eternal "current" and source of direction.

At that critical "date," however, at a shattering moment in history that to Hopkins should be the fulcrum of all human life and thought, God chose to penetrate mortal time, absorbing and transforming its shifting currents, making of them the "high flood" of salvation. Though the nature and stress of God, the whole principle of the Incarnation, may have been "felt before" (7)—by the patriarchs and prophets perhaps, by the "elect" such as Abraham, and even by such great "heathens" as Plato (SD 196, 37)[37] —and though this stress continues to be at the height of its potent flood tide, the crucifixion was the overflowing and absolute revelation of God in time: "Thence the discharge of it, there its swelling to be" (7). As Hopkins later wrote in contemplating the piercing of Christ's side, "The sacred body and the sacred heart seemed waiting for an opportunity of discharging themselves and testifying their total devotion of themselves to the cause of man" (March 21, 1884, SD 255).

As the entire poem makes clear, however, Hopkins believed that the Passion brought humanity an offer not only of redemption but of suffering, and of choice. The heart, "hard at bay," can no longer rest in ignorance, or in a dimly sensed ethic of sacrifice "felt before"; it must now make the absolute choice between "yes" and "no" in response to absolute fact. This is the choice described in stanza 8, in which the challenge of the Passion is "discharged" again in each individual, and later it will be the nun's choice for "yes" that allows her to give Christ a new Incarnation in time. That all may do so, that God is paradoxically in time and above it, in humanity and above it, eternal but ever-returning, is the point of that late stanza 34 which gave rise to this discussion, and it is a point which, like all others, has been introduced at the opening of the poem.

Two final circling returns to the first stanza will complete the circle of this chapter, though each will involve some pursuit of smaller radii that extend in various ways from the center, while also meeting at that center.

The dominant "fire of stress" imagery, already discussed in relation to Hopkins' vision of God's electric mystery and mastery, is crucial also to his dramatization of God's seeming duality but actual unity, and indeed it subsumes all the seemingly paradoxical

---

37. These lines may also compress, or at least foreshadow, Hopkins' later view that since the Incarnation was planned from the beginning, the prophecies of the Passion "are like histories written beforehand and are in nature after the event they tell of" (SD 162).

imagery so far considered. That it works most obviously to express "Thy terror, O Christ, O God" (2), to reveal God as terrible king of "the thunder-throne" (34), wielder of lightning, hurler and master of "electrical horror" (27), needs no further comment or demonstration. But in its modulations into other forms of flame, light, shining, and even water, it is also a means of supporting concretely the statement, "Thou are lightning and love, I found it, a winter and warm" (9), a fire that laces the world not only with terror but with love.

The change from terrible flame to flame of grace and glory begins in stanza 3 ("to flash from the flame to the flame then"); that flame then becomes the gentle beauty of starlight (5), and the warmth of spring (10), and the light of Orion, the hunter-redeemer (21), and the sweetness of "his fall-gold mercies . . . his all-fire glances" (23); finally it becomes the mighty fire of the conclusion, which is yet so gentle that it can be "maiden-furled" and which comes to man not in darkness, and not in terrible force, but in the radiance of love:

> Mid-numberèd he in three of the thunder-throne!
> Not a dooms-day dazzle in his coming nor dark as he came;
> Kind, but royally reclaiming his own;
> A released shower, let flash to the shire, not a lightning of fire
> hard-hurled. (34)

The last line's transformation of terrible fire not only into kindlier and more gracious shining but also into life-giving water draws together all the imagery of the waters of grace that rope and vein the world, and of the fire that charges it. "The sweep and the hurl of thee" (2) initiates this fire-water fusion by combining the pressure of "fire of stress" with the surge and hurl of stormy seas, and "*laced* with fire of stress" not only leads out to the blood-water fusion already treated but adds to those fused elements the third of flame. As the dual nature of God's stress is further defined, "springs" (6) would seem designed to hint at that same fusion, and explicitly in this stanza the stroke and stress of lightning swinging from the thunder-throne become what "hearts are flushed by and melt," and what the whole strand of "melting" imagery has shown and will show, "a lingering-out sweet skill" whose fluid and gentle warmth can be equal to the terrible fire-and-anvil stress in power (10). Christ's Passion itself, his own submission to the fire of stress, is described in terms that would seem nearly incomprehensible out of this metaphorical context: "The dense and the driven Passion, and frightful sweat" (7). While those alliterated adjectives can with some straining be read as logical modifiers, or at least reminders, of the events of the Passion itself,[38] their main sense lies in the metaphorical fusion of Christ's physical and spiritual "storm" of suffering and the impenetrable storm of wind and driven snow and driving water that swept upon the *Deutschland*. Moreover, "the frightful sweat" again fuses fire, water, and blood. It flowed because of the fire of stress and torment inflicted on Christ in Gethsemane and at the crucifixion and, more generally, because of God's whole "stress of selving": "It is as if the blissful agony or stress of selving in God had forced out drops of sweat or blood, which drops were the world" (November 8, 1881, *SD* 197), a suggestion, deeply relevant to this poem, that the whole world is not only sustained by the water-and-blood of grace but is so laced by it that it is in some sense one with that grace.

As in Christ, so for the nuns later, fire and water fuse, and both are gracious. There is a sense of lovely relaxation and release, almost a holiday (as well as holy day) feeling in the statement that "these thy daughters . . . Are sisterly sealed in wild waters, / To bathe in his fall-gold mercies, to breathe in his all-fire glances" (23). Fire, water, and air, lightning and sunlight and starlight, and storm and "black-about air" (24) become here one all-encircling, all-gracious element in which humankind may live, breathe, be bathed in light and washed clean, and above all, die to live.

The fusion of fire and water reaches its culmination in the last stanza of the poem. The Lord of the thunder-throne comes now not as consuming fire, but as that life-giving "shower" of radiance (34), an outpouring of the waters of grace that is also a flashing explosion of the fire of stress. In the final stanza, "Let him easter in us, be a dayspring to the dimness of us, be a crimson-cresseted east" completes this strand of imagery, completes the poem. "A crimson-cresseted east" not only summarizes the crucial colors of the rest of the poem, not only reminds us of nature's sacramental function, "wafting him out of it," but sets the whole world's rim blazing with the torches of God's gracious fire; "dayspring"—a simple word transformed by plumbing the literal meaning to its depths—sums up the fusion of God's brilliant fire of flame, his gentler fire of

38. "Dense": rich in meaning, especially mysterious meaning, and its events crowded, compacted, in time. "Driven": a reminder of the lashing of Christ through the city to Golgotha, and perhaps of the hurried events and the haste of judgment.

light, and his sustaining, ever-flowing, eternally rising waters of grace.

Finally, there is the crucial interweaving and fusion of the fire of God's stress and grace with the specific fire of the Pentecost, with the whole concept of the gift of tongues in its widest sense. Like all other major themes, this has been introduced in stanza 1, in what seems there merely a concise summary of God as source of physical life: "Giver of breath and bread." But "breath," essential not only to physical survival but specifically to speech, also initiates the entire motif of expression, "wording," figurative as well as literal inspiration, which develops into one of the major strands of thought and imagery in the poem.

In stanza 2, this motif is already very closely related to the fire imagery already discussed. Elevating grace, as seen, is especially the grace of the Pentecost, so that when Hopkins writes "Thou heardst me truer than tongue confess / Thy terror, O Christ, O God," he is making two almost contradictory points. The obvious assertion is of his own intense sincerity of response, too deep for words—though not for tears—and audible to God, the response almost demanded by a God who is by his very nature "Beyond saying sweet, past telling of tongue" (9). But there is also perhaps a hinted suggestion that the speaker-poet has not, yet, fully received the gift of tongues that descended in fire on the apostles and was essential to their ministry. That crucial inner word *yes* is of course basically sufficient, and in a sense subsumes all other words, but the poem goes on to explore rather elaborately the speaker's developing gift of utterance, as he responds first to his own experience—meditating on the choice between "the best or worst word"—and, most important, as he responds to the nun who "read" and "uttered" God so accurately.

The nun's first impact on the speaker is such that her words strike out, call forth, answering words, and music, from him: "A virginal tongue told" (17) evokes his heart's equally spontaneous response—"make words break from me here all alone, / Do you!"—and leads to the recognition that even the incorrigible and as it were illiterate heart is capable of "uttering truth" (18). Hopkins' revision of this stanza's third line illustrates rather dramatically the direction of his thinking on this point. The original phrase, "make words break *for* me here all alone" (A, italics mine), emphasizes the poet's imaginative process, the freeing of his poetic voice, but at the same time, curiously, makes him the more or less passive receiver, the object on which the nun's words beat, like the seas, producing in the midst of his lonely silence an inner, an imagined, but not an *uttered* response. The final version in B emphasizes the finally more crucial points: he must actively "utter God outright" as well as in his heart, but must do so not for himself, nor in order to be a "poet," but in order to be a spokesman of God's truth.

The following stanzas proceed to utter many truths about the nature of God, the significance of "five," and the glory of suffering, but the poet remains baffled by the true meaning of the nun's crucial appeal to Christ. He perceives that her wording sacramentally names, blesses, and transforms her seeming destruction: "The cross to her she calls Christ to her, *christens* her wild-worst Best" (24, italics mine), a phrase in which the dual meaning of "*calls* Christ to her" is also important ("names," "characterizes," but also "invokes," "calls for"). But he still must question "what did she mean?" (25) and must beg the original sources of "breath" (1) to give him the power of understanding and utterance: "Breathe, arch and original Breath" (God as the Holy Ghost), "Breathe, body of lovely Death" (Christ Incarnate and crucified) (25).

His groping search for her real meaning and motive allows Hopkins to suggest the impulses that might have moved a lesser person than the inspired nun, and thus to make the more emphatic the discovery of true revelation. Two such motives are suggested in stanza 25, developed in stanza 26, and rejected, with some sad irony, in stanza 27. The first of these might have been that of a faithful bride of Christ and the Church, of a devoted but not necessarily visionary believer: "Is it love in her of the being as her lover had been?" (25), suffering and dying as Christ suffered and died and, perhaps specifically, remaining firm in the midst of a seastorm that terrifies others (Matthew 8:23–26). The second possibility is that natural motive of anyone exhausted by any sort of battle, a longing for rest and reward after struggle: "Or is it that she cried for the crown then, / The keener to come at the comfort for feeling the combating keen?" (25). Stanza 26 goes on to dramatize metaphorically what it is like to achieve whatever one's imagined "crown" after combat may be, and in doing so, skillfully raises our eyes, and our aspirations, higher and higher. The imagery moves from the "down-dugged ground-hugged grey" to the "jay-blue" skies of spring to the heights of heaven and its stars and, finally, through scriptural allusion (1 Cor. 2:9), to a "treasure" altogether beyond the senses, beyond nature; we are thus prepared for stanza 27's rejection of both of these possible, reasonable, but limited motives.

In rejecting the second of these, in stating that it is not in the midst of immediate and terrible danger that the heart longs for mere ease, Hopkins uses imagery that will remain sadly persistent throughout his life and poetry, but that is here closely related to the pervasive ideas and images of this particular poem; it describes what unredeemed humanity is—a physical animal (drudging or snarling, still animal)—and what the heart sunk in its sorrow is, un-"wrung" and unsustained by the fresh waters of grace:

> The jading and jar of the cart,
> Time's tasking, it is fathers that asking for ease
> Of the sodden-with-its-sorrowing heart,
> Not danger, electrical horror . . . .

Perhaps recognizing in these lines and in himself some tinge of self-pity, Hopkins turns swiftly, in rejecting the first motive, to an ironic comment on himself and on all whose love of suffering may be a bit sentimental until put to the test; those who, in perfect safety, may revere and rejoice in the Passion (stanzas 7, 24), but who would find its demands considerably less attractive should they be applied to themselves: "then further it finds / The appealing of the Passion is tenderer in prayer apart," he writes tersely.

For the nun then, and for the poet—again the two crucial experiences are fused—motivation, understanding, revelation do not spring from rational reasons, natural impulses, even religious beliefs: their source is direct spiritual vision, literally direct in her case, imaginatively so in his. All the rather excessively panting and broken lines beginning stanza 28 are designed, not wholly successfully, I think, to dramatize the shattering and immediate impact of that overwhelming sight, as well as the poet's inability to "word" it immediately:

> But how shall I . . . make me room there:
> Reach me a . . . Fancy, come faster—
> Strike you the sight of it? look at it loom there,
> Thing that she . . . There then! the Master,
> *Ipse*, the only one, Christ, King, Head . . . .

This is one of the rare instances in Hopkins' poetry in which his language disintegrates at a moment of revelation into these obvious devices of excited incoherence; usually his style retains, even at such moments, its "sharp and sided" quality, because his faith made religious experience inscrutable often, but not incommunicable or incoherent. Perhaps the explanation here is indeed

Schneider's, already mentioned—his desire to avoid too explicit an announcement of a miracle—but an alternative to deliberate obfuscation at so crucial a moment would simply be that Hopkins slightly overdid an attempt to make it not obscure at all, but absolutely clear and dramatically real. In spite of self-conscious technique it does seem to have that effect: we and the poet are there, as he seeks "room" at the rail amid the mass of desperate passengers, as he, and we, staring seaward, see first only an unidentifiable shape, an "it," a "thing," vast, even ominous and terrifying— "Look at it loom there"—before the dramatic recognition of "There then!" and the astounding revelation.[39] He is trying, in short, to re-create through the poetic imagination the spiritual imagination, inspiration, of the nun, while explicitly recognizing how far his "Fancy" lags behind her immediate sight.

Unlike him, she instantly recognized and worded the great Logos of the world, "*Ipse*, the only one, Christ, King, Head," a recognition and utterance toward which he has had to grope through blurred vision and verbal incoherence, an utterance equivalent to "In the beginning was the Word and the Word was with God, and the Word was God" (John 1:1). Physically but never spiritually blinded by "the rash smart sloggering brine" (19), the nun both correctly "read" the seemingly chaotic text of the storm and named its—and the world's—master and author: "Wording it how but by him that present and past, / Heaven and earth are word of, worded by?" (29).[40]

It will be evident that I read stanza 28 dramatically, in the sense that I assume a deliberate distinction not only between the "I" and the nun but also between both and the poet; I understand Hopkins-the-poet to be consciously dramatizing the failure of any merely poetic language to capture divinity, or even fully to speak for the vessel of that divinity, the nun. In contrast both to this reading and to Schneider's, Miller's more intricately theoretical explanation of the stanza emphasizes Hopkins' own failure to find the

39. Robinson's similar though more complicated reading (*In Extremity*, 117–18) makes a further important point: Hopkins does not claim that the miraculous vision was seen by any passenger other than the nun (118). He therefore did not need to shroud in stylistic obscurity what he does not say happened, a public miracle. See also, however, MacKenzie's rejection of any physical appearance of Christ, even to the nun herself (*Reader's Guide*, 50–51).

40. "God's utterance of himself in himself is God the Word, outside himself is this world. This world then is word, expression, news of God" (December 19, 1879, *SD* 129).

single word for Christ. Miller allows that the nun does see and read "the unitary presence of God in the storm," but "this insight must be expressed by the poet in multiple language" and, further, what she says "must be interpreted: 'the majesty! What did she mean?' (line 193). Ultimately her word must be moved back into the babble, the confusion of tongues introduced by Babel and confirmed as well as repaired by the gift of tongues at Pentecost."[41] The argument so far, including the perception that Hopkins has not allowed "*Ipse*" to stand alone as in fact "the only one," the only word, I find entirely persuasive and brilliantly phrased. Persuasive also is the argument that in both stanzas 28 and 22 there is "the implicit recognition . . . that there is no way of speaking of this theological mystery except in a cascade of metaphors whose proliferation confesses to the fact that there is no literal word for the Word."[42] It is only with the conclusion of this line of perception—the conclusion that the inadequacy of language also shows the inadequacy of God, or of the poet's faith, or both—that I will later find myself wholly disagreeing.

Hopkins goes on to show that in uttering God, the nun said more than "yes," did more than kiss her hand to stars and storms, showed more than recognition and response. She had the full gift of tongues, the ability to give Christ a new birth in that "Word, that heard and kept thee and uttered thee outright" (30), the capacity, as Boyle points out, to "be a bell to" Christ (31) at her highest pitch of selving and self-annihilation.[43] She therefore becomes not only bride-mother but also one with God's fire of the Pentecost, with its strength, and with its swift and speaking brightness: "The Simon Peter of a soul! to the blast / Tarpeïan fast, but a blown beacon of light" (29). She is the spiritual beacon more than compensating in Hopkins' mind for the physical beacon the *Deutschland* never saw; she is the speaking light of God to all who will see and hear.[44]

41. *Linguistic Moment*, 258.
42. Ibid., 261.
43. *Metaphor*, 10. See also MacKenzie on the basic image as neither church bell nor sheep bell but the bell buoy, a suggestion arising from the intriguing fact that buoys of what were called the "tall nun" type were used on Kentish Knock (*Reader's Guide*, 53).
44. A lay reader may see a puzzling double suggestion of betrayal in the allusions to Peter and the Tarpeïan rock, but almost certainly the emphasis is on both "rocks" as foundations of the church. Conceivably they also imply that human beings are too often traitors to God but with consent to grace can become both his rock and his fire.

It is appropriate therefore that the final stanza appeals to her to speak not only to but for all humanity, to be the intercessor for all before the judgment-throne. Having worded God in her lifetime, having now reached safe anchorage beyond the storm, she may now forgive those who were at least partially responsible for her death,[45] and she may also speak for the rest of us who are still inarticulate, still on the open seas:

> Dáme, at oúr dóor
> Drówned, and among oúr shoáls,
> Remémber us in the roáds, the heaven-háven of the rewárd:
> Our Kíng back, Oh, upon Énglish soúls!

Omitting as it does the expected "Send" or "Bring" or "Urge" or perhaps even "Re-enthrone," the odd syntax of that last line avoids any explicit suggestion that it is wholly within the nun's power to effect this great restoration—the choice is up to the living, and to God—while making of the prayer a kind of general *cri du coeur* to the nun, to England, and to God himself. Alternatively, or really simultaneously, an even more complex prayer, and a very complex time scheme, may be implicit here, if one reads "Our King back" not merely as exhortation but also as a modifying phrase of accomplished fact ("Our King having come back," "With our King restored to us, and once more upon his throne"). In this case, the nun is asked to "remember" what is still in the future, to see us as we might be but are not yet, to see as God sees. In either case, the oddity of "upon," which would seem to belong more logically above, "upon our shoals," suggests the identity of the two rhyme words and the possible transformation of the second: "English souls" may be the reef upon which faith founders, but might also be the throne upon which God rules.

The nun, then, is a specific embodiment of the centrality of the "word" as well as the Word, to this poem, to Hopkins' faith. More generally, the poem not only stresses through repetition and capitalization the essentially synonymous terms for God—Christ, King, Head, Sacrificed, Life, Best, Master, Breath, *Ipse*, Lord—but is rich in "messengers" that carry word of him—expressive objects, events, emblems, images: the wings that in one sense "spell" the cross and salvation, the "gospel proffer" itself, the heavens that "deliver" God's stress, and the starlight "wafting him out of it," the

45. The stressing of these lines in both manuscripts places heavy emphasis on England's responsibility (see Appendix A).

storm that the nun "reads," and the "scroll-leaved flowers" of the storm-waves, the stigmata that are "cipher" and "lettering" of Christ. These concretely manifest Hopkins' concept of the articulateness of all things if one has the "single eye" (29) to read them aright, the ear to hear their speech, the spiritual insight to decode them. Mysterious and inscrutable though God is, he sends humanity the messengers—natural, human, spiritual, divine—to speak of his nature, purpose, and "certainty" and to give humanity the power to speak in response.

The poem therefore appropriately concludes with its famous mustering of crucial words, crucial concepts:

> Pride, rose, prince, hero of us, high-priest,
> Our heárts' charity's heárth's fire, our thoúghts' chivalry's thróng's Lórd.

Much may be objected to, and even mocked, in the final spectacularly eccentric line: it is ostentatious in syntax, awkward in stressing, hopelessly clogged in sound, and almost impossible to read aloud without stumbling. Practically everything, in short, seems to be poetically wrong with it. Yet even in cold blood one can recognize what it does accomplish: its jammed possessives, its imagery, and its movement do inextricably link major themes, recapitulating one last time the central reconciliations of depth and height, humility and royalty, heart and mind, diversity and unity, mystery and clarity. Above all, out of its difficult oppositions and juxtapositions, out of its muffled and awkward drumroll of sound, does emerge with ringing clarity the final cymbal-crash of "Lórd."

For me, at least, there is also more to the line than can be accounted for in such a cerebral summary, a residual splendor and resonance, an imaginative and emotional rightness that survives all comment and all mockery. And this power, I suspect, derives in large part from the final point just touched on, from the very ungainliness and intransigence of syntax and sound. The difficulty of this line's utterance, unlike the effect of the partially similar but far smoother conclusion to part I—"but be adored, but be adored King" —places us under intense and nearly muscular strain; we struggle and heave our way through the resistant line, and the relief and revelation are therefore enormous when we win our way up to the sudden and blazing clarity of the last word, when we unclench our minds, as it were, and can say simply, and with awe and triumph, "Lord." In short, the line forces us, both intellectually and emotionally, and almost physically, to enact ourselves the struggle that to Hopkins' mind everyone must undertake, the struggle to read and penetrate the seemingly "unshapeable," to win beyond stammering inarticulateness to speech, and it grants us vicariously at the end the right to say the word that contains all other words in this poem, *Lord.*

In spite of this emphasis on the word and concept of "word," however, *The Wreck of the Deutschland* is not in my view a typical Romantic, or modern, poem about the mysteries and process of poetry, not a personal, Keatsian poem about the birth agonies of a poet, not a semiotic poem about language. While these issues are subthemes in it, the poem is about the mysteries of God, about the birth agonies of both God and man, and about the power of any truly literate heart not only to read those mysteries insofar as they can be read but to utter them in ways that may not capture, but do reflect, in words the Word. According to this poem, creatures though we are, a human being—any human being—may be the bell to ring and tell of God's grace, may be in some small way a kind of mortal trinity, "the Utterer, Utterèd, Uttering" (145, l. 31). Because Hopkins was not only man, but poet, his own "uttering," his poem, is both an acknowledgment of human and linguistic limitation before God and itself a complicated "cipher," a complex pattern and code of words, but all designed to culminate in the one word, which is not *self*, or *poet*, but *Lord*. As the nun read the storm, as Hopkins read both her experience and his own, so we are asked to read the complexities of this intricate "lettering" of mystery, which both "utters God outright" and shows him to be also ultimately "past telling of tongue."

It is Hopkins' recognition and acceptance, here and elsewhere, of the fact that God is indeed "past telling of tongue" that governs my readings of this and other poems, placing these readings in opposition to that tendency in modern criticism already alluded to: the line of interpretation that not only sees the modern obsession with language as Hopkins' central preoccupation, but derives from this, in varying degrees, a diminution, even an undoing, of Hopkins' commitment to God. With this approach to Hopkins, even as it is impressively and thoughtfully exemplified by Hillis Miller, I wholly disagree.

While Miller is far more tactful than some of his followers in recognizing that *The Wreck of the Deutschland* "is, *in part at least*, about poetry" (italics mine),[46] and not wholly about it, linguistic

---

46. *Linguistic Moment*, 256. For a more extreme, though in some of its details brilliant, pursuit of this argument, see Sprinker, "*Counterpoint*," chap. 4. Character-

theory is for him the linchpin on which depends not only Hopkins' poetry but his whole vision of the world and of God: "since everything else, his vision of nature and of the self in their relations to God, hangs on the question of the nature of language and of the adequacy of the linguistic metaphor [of Christ as Logos, and the source of all unity, all rhyme]." This statement already goes far toward reversal of Hopkins' own emphasis, but it is mainly with the extensions of it and conclusions from it that I take issue: "The theme of language in 'The Wreck' moves toward the ambiguous vision of a God who is single but who can express himself in language and in his creation only in the multiple"; "Hopkins' linguistic underthought undoes his Christian overthought."[47] While it is not always clear whether Miller attributes these views to Hopkins himself or is merely arguing that what Hopkins attempted was impossible and doomed, it is surely important to remember that Hopkins' own emphasis, in this poem and elsewhere, is precisely the reverse. He does not find deficiency in God because human language is deficient, nor transfer his own poetic inadequacy so that God becomes inadequately whole or insufficiently articulate. For Hopkins, God is past telling of human tongue exactly because he is God; a poet's attempts to word him must always partially fail, because a poet is not God, and never will be. Perhaps linguistic theory can sadly "undo" much for modern critics, whose faith may be in language, but Hopkins recognized from the beginning, and certainly in *The Wreck of the Deutschland*, the distinction between art and morality, poetry and God, and knew quite clearly which was the more powerful and worthy of total commitment.

The Wreck of the Deutschland embodies, in thought and language, that concept of divine mystery which directly recognizes, accepts, and to an extent resolves exactly the sorts of conflicts some contemporary criticism finds insoluble. Paul L. Mariani has pointed out that God is literally the Alpha and Omega of this poem, its first word, "Thou," and its last, "Lord."[48] The poem as a whole is also in itself a kind of poetic alpha and omega, a first and also consummately finished expression of Hopkins' faith and

---

istic statements include: "This stanza [22] presents directly . . . the central theme of Hopkins's works, the meaning, significance, and ontological status of language and of sign systems" (101). Hopkins' possible response to such assertions provokes speculation; perhaps merely what he wrote crisply to Bridges on another matter: "It is plainly not true. . . . Go to" (*LB* 300).

47. *Linguistic Moment*, 250, 258, 265.
48. *Commentary*, 51.

voice. "Incomprehensible certainty" finds here its adequate and necessary style: distinct, precise, concrete, almost intolerably intense and tactile and immediate in pressure; at the same time, complex and mysterious in its multidimensional and mainly nonvisual diction, its lacing and interlacing of metaphor, its superimposed structure and layers of meaning; above all, intricately unified, its complexities and varieties returning always to the same center, "*Ipse*, the only one." This "authentic cadence," though indeed discovered relatively "late," now fully matches that vision of a world "mounted in the scarlet," and of the mysterious swayer of that world who is both potently present in it and "past all / Grasp God."

III

As the Circling Bird
(1877–1889)

6

"To Glean Our Saviour"
Nature, Humanity, God

OUT OF THE *Wreck of the Deutschland* "springs the stress felt" both in the nearly contemporary poems of 1877 and in later poems. In that first major work are concentrated four central though intersecting themes that Hopkins would continue to circle and recircle, expand on or compress, widen or deepen: (1) the theme of nature's sacramental function and humanity's response to it, of "lovely-asunder starlight wafting him out of it," but also of "man's malice," his abuse of nature and God, and possible separation from both; (2) the closely related theme of "mortal beauty," both in the natural world, full of "splendour and wonder" but also bearing news of its own and human mortality, and in human beings themselves, "arch-especial" in selfhood, "carrier-witted" when in harmony with God, but also spiritually and physically frail, and often dangerously indifferent to beauties higher than mortal; (3) related to both of these, the theme of the value, possibilities, failures of ordinary plodding man, of "Jack-self," possibly splendid in self-sacrifice, even in drudgery, possibly merely the construct and creature of bones and flesh; (4) finally, the great theme of suffering, of desolation, of the "dark descending" of God's terror, of God as "Orion of Light."

In grouping the poems thematically rather than chronologically in this and the next two chapters, I am sacrificing immediate clarity and the reader's immediate convenience to what I hope is a larger end; for the obvious and perhaps irritating disadvantages of the approach, I must simply ask forbearance, and the diligent use of the index. While the great majority of critics who treat the body of Hopkins' poetry follow chronology, usually a tripartite chronology that groups the poems into three variously classified periods,

123

many of them also recognize the awkward omissions and Procrustean-bed wrenchings this requires. It has therefore seemed best to me to abandon chronological groupings almost entirely and to attempt something closer to Hopkins' own habitual way of thinking. Since that was not mainly horizontal but simultaneously circular and vertical, since "synthesis" as well as "succession" was always crucial to him, I am allowing his tendencies to govern my approach not only to individual poems but to the body of the poetry as a whole. In neither case is "succession" a wholly sequential matter, ringing down the grooves of change on a straight course or in marked stages. While there are some shifts in emphasis, Hopkins' development consisted more of circular arcs, spiraling out from one center, revolving with various extensions, returns, descents, and risings around that center—the movement of the circling bird of the early poem.

In the following discussion, therefore, chronology will be significant only insofar as it demonstrates the intersection of major themes in all periods of Hopkins' mature writing, the constants as well as some new modulations in thought and cadence, and the consistent presence in the poems of a creative tension—or *poise* is perhaps the better word—between the poles of hope and desolation. From the beginning to the end of his Jesuit life Hopkins' vision was dual, though not ambivalent, and his overall development was that of a repeated movement from complex affirmation through despair to a yet more complex reaffirmation, "from the grace to the grace."

From his first year at St. Beuno's in 1874, when he wrote to his mother that the Welsh landscape "gives me a rise of the heart" (September 20, 1874, *FL* 127), to the end of his life when he returned there on holiday, Hopkins felt that "Wild Wales breathes poetry" (September 30, 1886, *LD* 142). His joyous response to the beauties of Wales, combined with a spiritual fervor intensified by his approaching ordination, produced the great outpouring of major sonnets in the early part of 1877. These sonnets, however, express more than a "never-eldering revel" in the glories of nature and God. Even in his personally happiest year, his vision encompassed both glory and ugliness, permanence and transience, nature's creativity, mankind's destructiveness.

Three of the best known, and probably also three of the best, sonnets of 1877 are indeed poems of affirmation. "God's Grandeur" (31), "The Starlight Night" (32), and "Hurrahing in Harvest" (38) all give voice to "a rise of the heart," though in none of them is the ground and earth of present life forgotten. Specifically, they express the Ignatian concept of sacramental nature, "of the Holy Ghost sent to us through creatures" and "shewn 'in operibus', the works of God's finger," a concept Hopkins then vividly summarizes in typical language: "All things therefore are charged with love, are charged with God and if we know how to touch them give off sparks and take fire, yield drops and flow, ring and tell of him" (*SD* 195). That his own "hand within the mind the imagination" did know how to touch nature to sacramental eloquence these three sonnets brilliantly demonstrate.

"God's Grandeur" acquired its final title only in the revised version in Manuscript B (see Appendix B), but the opening line remains unchanged in all extant drafts, with counterpoint marked in all but one of them:

The world is charged with the grandeur of God.

This announcement of divine instress is the keynote, the "changeless note," of this and later poems; stated here in a single short declarative sentence, it demands no continuation, allows no qualification. In the beginning is also the end of this poem, with "World . . . God" of the first line mirrored in "World . . . wings" of the last. Potentially flat finality of statement in the opening line, however, is itself charged with vibrant energy, a sense of voltage and even high tension, by movement, meter, and sound. The monosyllables march strongly toward the arresting and emphatic shift of the third and fourth counterpointed feet,[1] where counterpoint resists the easy anapestic lilt of the alternative natural reading, and the emphasis on the climactic and alliteratively stressed final phrase is the stronger because of the preceding tension. This is a case in which Hopkins' manipulation of meter unfortunately requires the eccentricity of the counterpoint marks (and once heard as indicated, never forgotten), so that stressing becomes almost as important as meaning to the impact of "charged." In contrast, both in effect and in degree of naturalness, is the use of counterpoint in the grindingly heavy monotony of

Generations have trod, have trod, have trod.

1. For Hopkins' full and remarkably clear explanation of counterpoint see "Author's Preface," *P* 46.

"God's Grandeur," autograph of early version
(MS.Eng.poet.c.48.fol.29 recto).

Here, initial counterpoint marks merely emphasize what is inherent in the word's normal stressing, an awkward and heavily descending movement, further reinforced by the dragging repetition of the rest of the line—an effect achieved after revision of the softer

"God's Grandeur," final version, MS B (MS.Eng.poet.d.149.fol.8 recto). Counterpoint marks referred to in the text are not visible in this reproduction.

"have passed and have hard trod" (February) and the more breathy "have hard trod, have hard trod" (March).

A similar naturalness, as well as importance to meaning, appears in the opening of the sestet, where Hopkins apparently considered the counterpointing so clear as to require no marks in any draft: "And fŏr all thĭs, náturĕ ĭs névĕr spént" seems the natural and necessary scansion. This places special metrical emphasis on "And," calling attention to the fact that the word *is* "and," not the more expectable "but," or the "yet" he did use in the first draft. This apparently tiny revision seems typical of his attention to meaning as well as sound. The sestet does not in fact constitute a real Petrarchan *volte*, is not in contrast to the ideas, both explicit and implicit, of the octave, but is a full bringing out of what was already latent there. "And" therefore properly emphasizes the underlying logic and unity of the poem, of the world.

An even more crucial manipulation of meter and line movement as well as imagery appears in "It gathers to a greatness, like the ooze of oil / Crushed." Here there is a kind of more-than-metrical counterpoint, an apparently strong contrapuntal contrast between the actual meaning of the lines and their movement and feeling. The triumphant tone, flashing imagery, and rising movement of the two opening lines are maintained at the beginning of the third, only to meet a muted reversal in the rather ugly, certainly unflashing "ooze of oil," followed by a seemingly total reversal, a sudden downward thud, as enjambment falls heavily onto that stressed and pivotal and surprising "Crúshed." This movement appears to negate the whole point of the whole statement, but seeming contradiction here is actual paradox, a compression of the meaning of the entire octave, of the entire poem. Only seemingly is God's energy fallen, crushed, debased in this world, a seeming imitated in the movement of the lines; in fact, that undiminished energy cohesively resists all destructive pressures, and does so not merely in spite of crushing but because of it—the principle of the Incarnation, the "trod hard down" motif of *The Deutschland*, is rarely absent from Hopkins' poems. It is that fact which the statement declares with absolute decisiveness.

A similar manipulation of enjambment, not merely to support or imitate meaning but almost to create it, appears in the sestet. When God's fire appears in its own true terms, when it "springs" like *The Deutschland*'s "dayspring" in the lightening east, bringing with it the same flame-water of life, the line movement both exactly dramatizes its speed and invincible energy and assumes and asserts its never-absent brightness:

> And though the last lights off the black West went
> Oh, morning, at the brown brink eastward, springs— . . .

The first line's somewhat halting monosyllables and tongue-twisting sounds reflect the somber, perhaps reluctant, anyway inevitable vanishing of what I take to be the fading sunset (though it might be fading stars), but the swiftness with which the line as a whole surges without pause to "morning" makes the dawn rise with dramatic suddenness, allowing us no awareness of the intervening night. God's world is never truly dark, in short: upon the heels of "the last lights" comes the instantaneous resurgence of a sunrise that spreads its splendor until it culminates in the radiance of the great "bright wings."

That technique *is* meaning is of course more obviously demonstrated in the choice and handling of imagery that graphically demonstrates exactly how deeply and how permanently "The world is charged with the grandeur of God," in spite of all mankind has done and is doing to pollute and pervert and tread out its radiance.

Like the whole of the first line, the "shook foil" image remains constant in all drafts, supporting the truth of Hopkins' statement to Bridges that he was not "driven" to the use of it, but that "with more truth might it be said that my sonnet might have been written expressly for the image's sake" (January 4, 1883, *LB* 168). The image may, of course, evoke the possibly confusing (though not necessarily irrelevant) picture of a flashing sword or, worse yet, the meaning of "set-off"—the sense in which Bridges took it—and if it evokes these only its ambiguity is a flaw in the poem. It is encouraging, however, to find that many students, without benefit of Hopkins' helpfully explicit explanation of the image, have come close to his meaning simply from reading the poem—perhaps because they live in and recognize the industrial world of which he is writing. Recently, after lengthy discussion of "sword" and "contrast" and so on, a student said, "This may be crazy, but what I saw was Reynold's Wrap, aluminum foil." Close enough, though the implied color of gold, and Hopkins' particular associations of foil with not one but two sorts of lightning, does require the gloss of his comment: "I do not mean by foil set-off at all; I mean foil in its sense of leaf or tinsel, and no other word whatever will give the effect I want. Shaken goldfoil gives off broad glares like sheet lightning and also, and this is true of nothing else, owing to its zigzag dints and creasings and network of small many cornered facets, a sort of fork lightning too" (*LB* 169).[2] Yet Hopkins cannot have expected the detailed associations stressed here to be commonly

2. And see the comment on a field reflecting the sun, "like a square of pale goldleaf . . . catching the light" (July 23, 1874, *JP* 249). If he also knew of Faraday's electrical experiments involving goldfoil, as Boyle suggests (*Metaphor*, 26), a double "charge" of electricity was associated with it in his mind.

shared by most readers, even though after the fact of the gloss those associations do vividly suggest both the breadth and the sudden flashing depth of God's power. Indeed, the explanation as a whole seems only partially adequate as a justification of the choice and centrality of this image. Without going so far as Yvor Winters, who saw in "shook foil" the picture of a madman "brandishing a metal bouquet" and found both this image and that of the oil "grotesquely trivial,"[3] many readers may well feel on first reading that however lightning-*like* goldfoil may be in its effects, it is an image too small, too metallic, and too inert (even when "shook") to embody a world vibrant with the power habitually represented by Hopkins, explicitly and not merely implicitly, as lightning or fire. In fact, in Manuscript B he did consider the explicit use of the word *lightning* in place of "shining," but crossed out that revision and returned to the original.

This decision may have been dictated simply by the more satisfying musical chime of the "shining"/"shook" alliteration, as compared to the more obvious "like lightning" chime; more likely, or in addition, it may have been dictated by the wish to introduce early in the poem a word suggesting in sound and meaning God's gentler, softer, more gracious and steady light, a word that anticipates the "warm breast" and "bright wings" of the ending. Yet more important is a possible further reason for this emphasis on the metallic image, and for the subordination at this point of the natural image of lightning: the choice seems most deliberately designed to direct our attention to the salient common feature of the octave's imagery for the power of God and the world he acts on, and hence to the central idea of the poem. The electricity implicit in "charged," the goldfoil, and the "ooze of oil" (in one—perhaps the most obvious—of its senses) are urban, industrial, nonnatural images drawn from the mechanical-industrial world the sonnet goes on to describe and denounce, though associated with them, latent and suspended in them, are natural and divine forces that will finally "flame out" in the sestet. The imagery therefore, wholly informed by the principle of the Incarnation, exactly dramatizes the point that while God's splendor is seemingly deadened, contaminated, debased by the industrial world, it nevertheless triumphantly maintains and asserts its true nature, even in that world's own terms. Though man perverts God's life-sustaining fire to the factory fires of industry that leave a land "seared" to barrenness,

3. "The Poetry of Gerard Manley Hopkins, II," 62.

though he perverts the natural, and perhaps holy, oil of God into merely industrial oil, and thus creates a world "bleared, smeared" and "smudge[d]" with ugliness, and reeking with the literal odor of his physical body and physical works, God's grandeur, uncorrupted, underlies all human corruptions, transforming the very elements into which it has apparently been debased. Electricity therefore flames out as both splendid and gentle divine fire, metallic goldfoil contains and gives off lightnings, and the oil not only of the olive press but also perhaps of divine unction[4] will always gather to a greatness.

The octave ends, however, with heavy and dismal emphasis on the polluted world, reinforced both by sound devices and by the ironic play on clothing and nakedness. The self-proliferation and seemingly unending spread of mankind's linked perversions is oozily dramatized in the alliteration and assonance and internal rhyming of "seared"—"bleared"—"smeared"—"smudge"— "smell," which then modulate through "vowelling off"[5] into the "wears"—"shares"—"bare" chiming. Though the bitterly ironic wit involved in these last linkings seems to have come late in revision (early versions have "the soil is barren"), Hopkins clearly did decide to conclude with the irony that we clothe the world only in ugliness, in what really strips it naked, while our own sophisticated trappings not only suggest our animalism ("shod") but cut us off from what is natural and should be holy; Cotter's suggested allusion to God's command to Moses seems altogether right as a gloss on this line: "Take off your shoes, for the place on which you stand is holy ground" (Exod. 3:5).[6]

With the sestet comes the full assertion, reassertion, revelation of holy power, and grim irony is replaced by genuine paradox. Though God's grandeur has deigned to take on human form, to appear and speak in the terms of the industrial world, and to suffer both rejection and debasement there, it is now revealed as fully and

---

4. Boyle, *Metaphor*, 40, a valuable discussion that also suggests an allusion to the Agony in the Garden, "Gethsemane" meaning literally "oil press" (32). See also MacKenzie, *Reader's Guide*, 64–65, for a reading that rejects the image of industrial oil while also noting a reference I had previously missed to "coal and rockoil" as among the gifts provided by God (*SD* 90).

5. In lecture notes on "Rhythm," Hopkins terms assonance "vowelling on," while a more elaborate modulation of vowels "down some scale" is "vowelling off" (*JP* 284).

6. *Inscape*, 171.

invincibly divine, speaking in its own natural, sacramental, and finally scriptural language:

> And for all this, nature is never spent;
>   There lives the dearest freshness deep down things;
> And though the last lights off the black West went
>   Oh, morning, at the brown brink eastward, springs—
> Because the Holy Ghost over the bent
>   World broods with warm breast and with ah! bright wings.

There is probably a dying echo of the commercial world in "spent," an echo which implies that neither nature nor God can be bought and sold on the world's market or in the world's coinage, while the dominant "moment" of the word makes the major point that nature is not in fact stripped and exhausted; beneath the burn-scars of man-made desolation there lives unquenchable health, and the deep wellsprings of life are eternally fed, as in *The Deutschland*, by the high God of creative fire.

Similarly, as there was aridity but now freshness, as there was sunset but now present sunrise, so as there was death and perversion now there is hope for birth to a new life in harmony with God. The massive power of God that has been flame and potential "rod" of chastisement is now transformed, or truly seen, as that of the Holy Ghost, the dove, who exercises mighty but gentle guardianship over the world. As the main implications of "bent" suggest, it is a guardianship that will both restore to proper shape the distorted world presented in the octave and warm that world to life as the curved egg is warmed in the nest, "under thy feathers." A further possible "moment" of this image for Hopkins is implicit in a tentative early version and revision of this line. The February draft has "Because the Holy Ghost on our ~~bow~~ bay-bent / World . . ."; here as in *The Deutschland*, "bow" evokes the divine Hunter, and "bay" the image of the curving vault of this world which is, or should be, God's cathedral, holy temple as well as "holy ground." The reverberations of this rejected version may well have been still in his mind when he wrote the final version, and perhaps should be in ours.

That final exclamation, "ah! bright wings," may seem excessive and self-conscious to some readers, but for others it will have the effect Hopkins must have intended, making us feel that this radiance is suddenly and immediately before the poet's lifted eyes, and hence before our own. That vision catches at the heart, at the spirit, and must therefore inevitably evoke the spontaneous, awestruck, almost sighing reverence of that long-drawn "ah!," that catching of the breath in wonder.

Whether or not the exclamation works, the final image of the bright wings brilliantly effects the final transmutation, revelation, of the grandeur of God, crystallizing the major images and ideas of the entire sonnet. It reminds us of the electric and potentially punitive fire of God, while dramatizing that fire's essential and creative tenderness, its gentle "shining." It tells us that no march of shod generations can grind down the power that looms so far and so soaringly, as well as so lovingly, above the world. It clothes and clasps the ugly and naked world in a divine embrace, perfectly dramatized in the enclosing circle of sounds ("*W*orld *br*oods," "*w*arm *br*east," "*br*ight *w*ings") of the last line. It recapitulates the large point that though God's grandeur is infinitely mightier and huger than its creations, it is nevertheless manifest in this world, intimately available to it, deigning to enter, charge, and sustain it, to take on its forms, to embrace it from the heights and to penetrate its depths.

Like *The Wreck of the Deutschland*, though in miniature, this is a poem whose "yes" arises from and surmounts a clear and painful awareness of human failures, human distortions, and one whose method again incarnates the "incomprehensible certainty" at the center of Hopkins' world. All the technical resources of poetry fuse to dramatize the mysterious but electrically tangible activity of God, his power and Real Presence in a world that seems to have denied him many more than three times, but that he nevertheless continues to sustain and redeem.

"The Starlight Night," evidently begun the day after "God's Grandeur,"[7] is intimately related to it in theme as in time, though it omits the denunciation of human corruptions, concentrates on God's grandeur as it is delivered by "lovely-asunder starlight," and in method involves a still more complex, though perhaps less clearly successful, use of metaphor. It is curious that this sonnet has appeared to anthologists (beginning with Bridges), and to numerous critics, to be one of Hopkins' more readily accessible poems, since everything after the first line is far from easily comprehensible. The method of fusing the natural and spiritual, the precise and

7. As indicated by the first drafts of each: "God's Grandeur" dated "Feb. 23 1877"; "The Starlight Night" dated "Feb. 24 1877. St. Beuno's." These are among the many poems Hopkins dated according to the time of original conception rather than final completion. See Appendix B on the drafts and on abbreviations used hereafter in the text.

mysterious, and above all the literal and metaphorical, makes it a major example of his entire vision, a vision that tended to make the "metaphorical" more tangible, more real, than the merely mechanically literal.

In all five extant drafts of the poem the first line, like that of "God's Grandeur," remains unchanged: "Look at the stars! look, look up at the skies!"; that strong dramatic gesture and exclamatory "bidding" direct our eyes and minds to what I take to be the one literal element in the poem. The octave then proceeds to inscape the stars and the night sky in general in a series of metaphors that become more and more difficult to identify as metaphors rather than as literal descriptions.

In the second and third lines, the imagery is relatively clear in intent and effect, and the metaphors are quite evidently metaphors; reversing the effect of the imagery in "God's Grandeur," they not only personify the stars but also transfer and so elevate (in all senses) human qualities, imaginings, cities, citadels, to the heavens:

> O look at all the fire-folk sitting in the air!
> The bright boroughs, the circle-citadels there!

The revisions of the third line, which focus on the adjective for "citadels," suggest that for once Hopkins was compelled to choose between two relevant ideas and images and could not devise a means of fusing them in a single word or phrase; what he finally chose is the one with the greater metaphorical significance. Characteristically, he wanted on the one hand to convey the shimmer and quiver of movement in the stars, to set those "citadels" in motion; hence, with a brief pass at the conventional though alliterative "silver" (Feb.$_1$), he tries "quivering" (Feb.$_1$), revises to "glimmering" (Feb.$_2$ and March), and returns to "quivering" (A). The final choice, on the other hand, the revision in B to "circle," indicates a quite different but important line of thought in light of the whole poem's meaning: what he seems to have wanted most, beyond motion, and certainly beyond alliteration (which "silver" could also have provided), was a word not only descriptive of the patterns of the constellations, but one that could also suggest embracing wholeness; the sestet will make clear that the whole of nature, not merely its star-patterns, is a "circle-citadel" enclosing the inner mysteries of God.

From the fourth line on, however, the octave's imagery becomes extremely complex:

Down in dim woods the diamond delves! the elves'-eyes!
The grey lawns cold where gold, where quickgold lies!
   Wind-beat whitebeam! airy abeles set on a flare!
   Flake-doves sent floating forth at a farmyard scare!—
Ah well! it is all a purchase, all is a prize.

The effect, and I would argue the deliberate effect, is to create an uncertainty in our minds as to whether we can still distinguish between human and heavenly perspective, between literal and metaphorical description. If we "look up" are we then to look "down" again at actual things of earth, actual woods, lawns, whitebeam and poplar leaves, doves, or are these things still metaphors? Even if the "flake-doves" are not actual doves, but a metaphor, are they simply a metaphor for the leaves or cottony seed-down of an actual tree, or somehow for those of star-trees? That these questions arise at all suggests either that Hopkins is merely confused and confusing here, or that he is up to something to which the doubleness of the imagery is essential; while not being fully convinced that it works, I think the latter is what he intended. That the lines can be sensibly read simply as a description of the aspect earth wears when bathed in starlight is evidence of the vivid actuality and seeming literalness with which Hopkins frequently endows his metaphors; that one feels uneasy at reading them so points to the larger attempt. Suggested initially perhaps by the fact that the title is not "The Star*lit* Night" but "The Star*light* Night," that attempt seems to be a use of metaphor to let the beauties of heaven and earth remain in part distinctively themselves, while also fusing them into one metaphorical inscape, not merely mirror images of each other, but one image.

Because of this complex fusion, and the resulting double perspective, "*Down* in dim woods the diamond delves! the elves'-eyes" develops and does not conflict with the opening command, "look, look *up* at the skies!" (italics mine). Having obeyed that initial command, and having sensed the lessening distance between earth and heaven in lines 2–3, we ourselves are no longer earthbound, but "there," looking down the vast stretch of skyscape from the vantage point of the heavenly citadels. From the bright boroughs and citadels of stars we look out on the "dim woods" of dark night skies around us; from them we see the other star-cities, like deep wells ("delves") of light, liquid in rippling movement yet diamond-sharp, seemingly bored into the darkness, and magically shining like the eyes of fairy-folk, fire-folk.[8] In the same way, "The grey

8. This reading of the "up/down" effect lies buried in my dissertation ("'Au-

lawns cold where gold, where quickgold lies" fuses the "lawns" of heaven and earth, its brilliant coinage "quickgold," based of course on "quicksilver," compressing in one word the volatile, shimmering, vitally active and shining water-dews of earth and star-dews of sky. (This final superb compression appears only in B's two revisions; earlier versions had uniformly employed "gold-dew," variously modified by such unfortunate adjectives as "quaking" and "jaunting.") Finally, the fusion of earthly and heavenly landscape culminates in the description of sparkling, flickering starlight (and perhaps moonlight) in terms of the shimmer of aspen or poplar leaves "set on a flare" of silver whiteness by the wind, and in the double metaphor of "Flake-doves": the sky's woods now flash with star-leaves, flakes of winged light, like doves in flight.[9]

The play on the "up" and "down" perspective seems not to have been intended at the poem's inception. The manuscript versions present initially a wholly earthbound though upward-straining viewer, looking at and describing what stars and star-woods and star-lawns look like—or can be imagined to look like—from down here; the perspective only gradually becomes more complex after many laborious revisions, and one inspired one ("down"). What the drafts clearly show, however, is the more important point that there was no intent to shift in lines 4–5 from a view of the stars to a literal view of literal earth. The original version of the fourth line was "Look, the elf-rings; look at the out round eager eyes!" (Feb.₁), in which the images are clearly parallel to, in apposition to, "stars," "fire-folk," "bright boroughs," "circle-citadels there." So also are the images in the alternative lines jotted at the bottom of the page, where the new appositional "dim woods" and "diamond wells" make their first appearance:

ˣ { The dim woods quick with diamond wells; the elf-eyes!
{ The diamond wells through dim woods quick, the elf-eyes!

It is not until the final draft in B, after a series of further revisions, that "Down in dim woods" acquires its prominence at the beginning of a line, and hence its misleading suggestion that we are no

thentic Cadence': The Sacramental Method of Gerard Manley Hopkins," 162–64) but has been independently proposed by Mariani, *Commentary*, 98. For an alternative interpretation, persuasively arguing the case for the more literal reading, see Schneider, *Dragon in the Gate*, 121–23.

9. See Hopkins' early remarks on the "Gliding and winding of white-poplar sprays in the wind" (July 4, 1866, *JP* 143) and on the whitebeam's leaves, "the underside being white" (July 24, 1866, *JP* 147).

longer looking starward, but down at literal woods, lawns, and so on. My sense of Hopkins' procedure from these drafts, in short, is that there was an initial, persistent, and dominant attempt to raise earth and earthbound viewer to the heavens, fusing earth and heavens by raising the first, and a later perception that he could dramatically play on the shift from "up" to "down" without losing that dominant effect.

Up to this point, then, the poem has demonstrated what happens if one "looks, looks" long enough at any merely physical object: the literal seems to dissolve—or to be intensified to the point of dissolution—and then to reassemble itself as an inscape, an inscape that in this case encompasses almost a cosmos. Man and nature, cities and woods and lawns, citadels and trees and birds, fairy-folk and farm-fowl are all there, are all one. Fire and water, flame and coldness, radiance and dimness, gold and whiteness, solidity and motion, height and depth, fact and metaphor become one experience, one insight.

Or almost one insight. If there is something not wholly and deeply satisfying here, something with almost a whiff of "Stilton and high game," it is because the unity achieved remains a unity created by intense, ingenious, and relentlessly exclamatory language, an almost merely fanciful and certainly merely secular language, whose ingenuities are beautiful but self-conscious. There is the want of "a canon by which to harmonise and round them in," though this time *not* "e.g. one of feeling" (1866, *JP* 135). This time feeling has done, even overdone, all it can, and it is Christ who must provide, who is, the canon. Dwelling in and behind nature, in its highest and homeliest things, star-citadels and earthly farmyards, and in the human minds that see the stars and imagine the elf-folk, it is he who fully transforms all these aspects of the world, literal and figurative, fact and imagined, through what Cotter calls "the transmuting realism of the revealed Word."[10] The sestet will make clear that while the powers of human insight are splendid, they cannot wholly reach or penetrate or unify the mysteries of the dark expanses, and that the magic of nature and the mind's imaginings are less wonderful than the higher "magic" of God and his saints.

The extremely colloquial image and phrasing of "a farmyard scare" and the strange following line, "Ah well! it is all a purchase,

10. *Inscape*, 172, a reading that finds no fusion between the octave's two worlds, viewed as those of reality and of "make-believe."

all is a prize," effect that turn in thought to the sestet. "Farmyard" is the pivotal intermediary word initiating the transformation of those high and glorious citadels into what is still glorious but also intimately recognizable and homely, the "barn" of this world. The final line, seemingly so casually shrugging and so thoroughly monetary, the one nonexclamatory line in the entire octave, relinquishes the high imaginative vision and style and analytically introduces the sestet's central point. "God's Grandeur" had already implied that neither nature nor God is to be bought in the world's coinage; we are now explicitly told in what coin they can be "purchased," by what offerings they can be understood. It is not enough, it now turns out, to gaze long and lovingly upon the physical world. However intensely and imaginatively one has perceived its inscape, and even raised that inscape to instressed metaphor, inscape that remains metaphor is not enough; there is still the "plain truth" to be seen and stated.

Therefore, as Gardner nicely phrases it, Hopkins becomes an "apostolic auctioneer" crying the value of "the lot under consideration,"[11] a lot whose price is sacrifice and devotion, whose "prize" is to be won by giving more than ecstatic admiration. Echoing the opening line yet more insistently, but ending in the quietness of calm affirmation, the sestet demands that we "look" yet deeper and higher, and thereby perhaps comments a little ironically on that initial ecstasy at nature's merely physical beauty, and the mind's merely imaginative powers:

> Buy then! bid then!—What?—Prayer, patience, alms, vows.
> Look, look: a May-mess, like on orchard boughs!
>   Look! March-bloom, like on mealed-with-yellow sallows!
> These are indeed the barn; withindoors house
> The shocks. This piece-bright paling shuts the spouse
>   Christ home, Christ and his mother and all his hallows.

The sestet's deliberate attempt at analysis and interpretation is reflected in the fact that the new metaphors for the stars, and the swirl of blossoms of "May-mess" and the crisper "March-bloom," are now carefully explicated and linked to earth by the repeated literal, not figurative, "like on" phrases. More important, the movement from spring, late and early, to harvest brings us to the spiritual harvest also, the explicit statement of final truth: the glory of physical nature, and specifically of the heavens, eloquent as it is

11. Gardner, *Hopkins*, 2:235.

of God, is merely the external and visible housing of ultimate divinity, of that total and fulfilled sanctity which is not granted to the world's human sheaves.

The final metaphor for the natural heavens, "this piece-bright paling," is a complex summary of the poem. First, and perhaps most obviously, it develops and transforms the octave's fire-earth, citadel-farm, and concluding monetary imagery: the bright citadels of the stars are bright still, and they shine "piece-bright" like money, but we know that it is not in their coin alone that Christ is to be purchased, and they have ceased to be glorious and distant bastions, becoming instead the homely, and much more fragile and impermanent, fence (or even chancel) latticings.

Second, it is the very fragility of the image that is most crucial; this chancel-barrier between man and God is one that, like Hopkins' style, both conceals and reveals. It "shuts the spouse / Christ home," cuts us off from those high mysteries throned behind heaven and earth, yet this concealing barrier is both an eloquently revealing one, as the whole poem demonstrates, and a slim one, pierceable at least in part by "Prayer, patience, alms, vows" and humble spiritual insight. (That Hopkins wished to make this second point is supported by the variants of "piece-bright" in Feb.$_1$: "day-shot" and "pierced-well.") This final metaphor, in short, conveys the nonmetaphorical "plain truth": God is both immanent and transcendent, hidden behind nature but manifest in it, and we, while we are mortal, are outcasts from the immortal world, yet capable of reading in part the sacramental metaphors of the natural world that bespeak God even while they hide him.

Third, among the poems of 1877 that focus on nature and that fall on the side of affirmation, however tinged they may be with sadder recognitions, is September's truly exuberant "Hurrahing in Harvest." The title alone indicates not only that in this particular autumn Hopkins found no painful reminders of mortality, but also that he chose to express no deep fear of the spiritual harvest perhaps alluded to in the opening statement's echo of Jeremiah: "The harvest is past, the summer is ended, and we are not saved" (8:20).[12] Instead, in this harvesttime the poet himself becomes the harvester, or at least the gleaner, and gleans not death or thoughts of death, but an almost mystical union with Christ, with life. Indeed, the whole sonnet is perhaps based on a different scriptural passage, which Hopkins was later to use as the text of a sermon: "I

12. Cited by Gardner, ibid., 2:253.

tell you, lift up your eyes and see how the country is already white to harvest" (John 4:35–36). The point of Christ's parable of spiritual harvest as Hopkins interprets it is also the point of this sonnet, not a grim warning, but a promise of joy: "but Christ gives the saying a happier turn, for in this case sower and reaper both would gain and both rejoice together" (December 17, 1880, *SD* 94).

As is often the case in Hopkins' poems, the opening statement has a finality to it: "Summer ends now" (a phrasing that fortunately replaced the flatly prosaic "It is harvest" of the original version).[13] But in this case the ending is only a beginning. Through a beautiful use of rhetorical anadiplosis, the "now" of ending is instantly transformed into the "now" of a new beauty, a new and potent rising:

> Summer ends now; now, bárbarous in beáuty, the stóoks ríse
> Aroúnd, . . .

The eye is then speedily led yet higher:

> up above, what wind-walks! what lovely behaviour
> Of silk-sack clouds! has wilder, wilful-wavier
> Meal-drift moulded ever and melted across skies?
>   (Stressing mine, outride marks from B)

Nature is now apparently not sacramental, but brazenly and flauntingly pagan, though splendid, in its beauty; savagely rough in its appearance; and, given one of the root meanings of the heavily stressed "barbarous," uncivilized and rough in its speech.[14] But the poem as a whole will "lift up" not only the poet's eyes but the nature of what he sees: barbarous beauty is indeed both "wild" and impermanent, yet seen and heard rightly it is inherently ordered and sacramentally eloquent of its creator.

The revisions of the opening quatrain show Hopkins' concentration from the start on two images that emphasize potential disintegration of physical beauty, while also being linked with the central harvest-grain metaphor: both the "meal-drift" that molds and melts and the "silk-sack clouds" are present in all versions,

13. From the draft dated "Vale of Clwyd ~~Aug~~ Sept. 1 1877," where the title is "Sonnet in Harvest," corrected to "Heart's Hurrahing in Harvest." See Appendix B.

14. Gardner suggests, and others subsequently assume, a hidden pun in "barbarous" on "barb" (beard) (*Hopkins*, 2:253–54). If some association with "Barbary" is likewise lurking here, the word also contains a hint of the later stallion simile and the subsequent metaphor of the winged horse.

both creating a picture of haphazard and fragilely impermanent loveliness while implying the results of some more-than-earthly, some potentially eucharistic, harvest. The "Wilder, wilful-wavier" phrase, however, was arrived at only in B; all earlier versions, with various minor readjustments, employ the phrase "swan-wing-whiter or wavier." I conjecture that this image and its rejection reflect, first, Hopkins' initial sheer delight in the pure whiteness of flying clouds, together with a wish to link the "rise" of the stooks with the flight of winged cloud-forms, and second, his considered decision to concentrate on the more grainy whiteness of milled and spilling grain and on the haphazard, and potentially disintegrating, beauty of the physical skies.[15]

On the other hand, this impression of "wild" disorderliness is in strange and strong contrast to the implications of "what lovely *behaviour*"—such a demure and civilized word, suggesting polite and graceful deportment. In conjunction with "wind-walks," and perhaps the elegance of "silk," "behaviour" conjures an impression of a courtly, gracious, restrained promenade until that "wilder, wilful-wavier" phrase suddenly breaks upon and scatters these suggestions of order. While Hopkins was consistently fond of the word *behavior* in a somewhat idiosyncratic sense,[16] and may simply have used it instinctively (or for the sake of rhyme), this juxtaposition of the barbarically wild and the potentially ordered does already suggest that behind the physical, seemingly pagan, seemingly haphazardly mobile world there is the principle of Christian order.

In the second quatrain Hopkins discovers and announces that underlying principle which turns the barbarous to the sacramental. When he raises both physical eyes and spiritual heart to search for Christ, the splendid but superficially messy and merely visible scene acquires the ordered but also passionate power of speech, becomes eloquently articulate of its meaning:

15. Although Hopkins makes special use of the meal-harvest connection in this sonnet, it should be noted that he habitually used both "meal" and "mealy" to describe clouds from his earliest diaries: "Mealy clouds in circles over the sky with a moon" (1865); "Mealy clouds with a not brilliant moon" (1866); "the clouds meal-white" (1871) (*JP* 67, 72, 207–8).

16. In describing the flag flower in opening, for example, he puts the word in quotation marks as though acknowledging an idiosyncratic usage: "each term you can distinguish is beautiful in itself and of course if the whole 'behaviour' were gathered up and so stalled it would have a beauty of all the higher degree" (June 13, 1871, *JP* 211). Even here, however, the word seems to have something to do with the ordering and ordered principle of the whole.

I wálk, I líft up, Í lift úp heart, eýes,
Down all that glory in the heavens to glean our Saviour;
And, eýes, héart, what looks, what lips yet gáve you a
Rapturous love's greeting of realer, of rounder replies?
                              (Metrical markings from B, here and hereafter)

The stressing here is as crucial as the phrasing to dramatize the lifting of the heart, of the poet's whole being, from earth to sky, from
the physical to the spiritual, while fusing both. The accent on
"wálk" reminds us of the "wind-walks" of line 2—they are now the
plodding poet's highway as well as the wind's. The stress on "líft"
between the two unstressed words emphasizes the energy and effort of the act rather than of its doer, but the new stressing of "Í lift
úp" brings out both the importance of the individual beholder's response and the point that he can now rise like the rest of nature,
like the stooks, like the clouds, and actually rise infinitely higher
than they; there is a surprised and joyous wonder implied by the
stressing here. The juxtaposition of "Í lift úp" and "Down all that
glory in the heavens" has the same effect as the similar juxtaposition in "The Starlight Night": the very movement of the eyes and
heart raises the poet, and the reader, to the heavens; once there, he
is the spiritual gleaner, moving, gazing down the long skyfields,
and rewarded by the harvest of Christ's resonant response of love.
As was not the case in "The Starlight Night," this effect seems to
have been designed almost from the poem's inception: the important "Down" already replaced "From" in the September draft, as
did *"in* the heavens" for *"of* the heavens" (italics mine), both revisions stressing the actual presence there of both beholder and
reward.

The sestet's general idea is clear enough, as is its central feeling.
Like the preceding quatrain, it is a translation into poetry of the
theory of instress, of the "greeting of the Spirit" essential if physical
is to become spiritual harvest, sight to become insight, and it vi-
brantly conveys the joy of that greeting. The details, however, are
somewhat complex, since the imagery depends on partially submerged, though not at all illogical, connections:

And the azurous hung hills are his world-wielding shoulder
Majestic—as a stallion stalwart, very-violet-sweet!—
These things, these things were here and but the beholder
Wánting; whích two whén they once méet,
The heart rears wings bold and bolder
And hurls for him, O half hurls earth for him off under his
    feet.

The first line maintains the fusion of earth and heaven: the actual hills of earth, clothed, "hung," in blue light, and also "hung from" the sky, are reminders of the high-suspended "wilful-wavier" hills of cloud. There may even have been a more specific connection, subconscious or even conscious, in Hopkins' mind between the "meal-drift" of the octave and the "azurous" of the sestet, as in "A blue bloom, a sort of meal, seemed to have spread upon the distant south" (September 6, 1874, *JP* 258). Though this connection can hardly be expected to function for the reader, it provides some external support for the point that Hopkins intended the fusion of earth-hills and sky-hills, as do the revisions from "strong hills" to "grand hills" (Sept.) and from "grand hills" to "hung hills" (B).

The stallion simile that follows intensifies that fusion, though it has given many readers considerable and startled pause. While "world-wielding" goes far to aggrandize the image,[17] it has seemed to at least one critic (Bridges) an instance of tastelessness, and to others at best a too-sudden shift in imagery. Previous images have raised us far above the earth and the merely physical; now, so the argument goes, the simile descends to an animal, and one that, if related to harvest at all, is associated with it only in the most drudging, or most sexual, way.

Nevertheless, Hopkins from first to last draft liked and wanted this image. It stands in all versions without revision of any kind, a fact suggesting that it was for him, and is for us, the crux of the poem, not an incidental but a summarizing image. Since the entire poem has hinged upon the translation of the "barbarous" to the sacramental, the stallion is first of all a culminating symbol of everything wild, uncontrolled, physical, barbarically beautiful and potent that both reveals and is divine beauty when rightly seen, specifically when it is seen to embody both the power and the sweet delicacy of Christ. Like the ash tree and the bluebell, though far more powerful, the stallion is a thing "of strength and grace" through which "I know the beauty of our Lord" (*JP* 199).[18] Sec-

17. This word involves a deliberate, though private, inversion, since Satan is called the "Worldwielder" throughout the commentaries and spiritual writings. Hopkins may have been stressing, at least quietly to himself, that it is in fact God, not the Devil, who is the greater wielder of the world and reaper of its harvests.

18. The apparent pantheism in the equation of the hills with Christ's shoulder is helpfully accounted for by Cotter, *Inscape*, 186, and by Hopkins' own commentary on God's simultaneous presence and transcendence: "a being so intimately present as God is to other things would be identified with them were it not for God's infinity or were it not for God's infinity he could not be so intimately present to things" (*SD* 128).

ond, though simile after metaphor retains a slight distinction, we probably now actually see, even feel, in the mighty sky-hills the figure of a massive horse, so that the entire landscape-skyscape is vibrant with power and ready to take off in some form of explosive action. We may even sense already the nature and direction of that action. Riding and flying were so closely associated in Hopkins' mind, as in "The Windhover," and Saint Paul so closely identified with the true Bellerophon ("St. Thecla," 136), that he was probably initiating in the stallion simile the implicit image of Pegasus that ends the poem.[19] This image fuses man and cosmic "stallion," summing up the whole rising-to-union motif, and the result is that humanity and nature, humanity and divinity, do in fact "meet," not only in statement but in concrete dramatization.

It is this image that both accounts for and is created by "rears" in "The heart rears wings bold and bolder" (not "whirled out wings" as in *The Deutschland*'s similar moment) and generates "hurls" in the final line. Above all, it is this image that lends both imaginative and intellectual point to the apparent ambiguity of the final line's pronouns: "And hurls for him, O half hurls earth for him off under his feet." Since Hopkins was grammatically daring but rarely simply lax and careless, I understand the reference of the overlapping pronouns to be exactly and grammatically correct, to be not to Christ or stallion, or "beholder," or "heart," but to the closest logical active antecedent, "which two," in which are met and almost completely fused the divine wingèd horse and newly winged heart-rider. In this reading, the first "him" refers mainly to Christ, the primary meaning of "for" being "toward," though the secondary meanings are latent; the second "for him" retains that primary sense, but begins to bring out the fusion of Christ-stallion and heart-beholder, the "for" still meaning "toward," but now more strongly suggesting also agency-in-behalf-of (the heart's response does this "for," on behalf of, the poet, and also "for," in the service of, for the sake of, Christ); the final possessive, "his feet," which cannot easily refer to the same "him" of the preceding phrases if their antecedent is solely Christ, maintains the fusion of man and wingèd horse, man and Christ, spurning the ground

19. In the fragment "St. Thecla," Saint Paul is both compared and contrasted with the mythical rider of Pegasus: "Paul is Tarsus' true Bellerophon" (l. 10) because rather than aspiring to heaven with disastrous results, his fall from horseback on the Damascus road was the moment and sign of his conversion. The Pegasus image is argued by Ellis, "Authentic Cadence," 170; Robinson, *In Extremity*, 42; Mariani, *Commentary*, 117.

together, wingèd and one, while also reminding us of their difference.

Both this phrase and the careful qualification "*half* hurls earth for him" remember that the mortal heart is still partly of earth, is not all wings. In an exact reversal of the order and emphasis of line 5, the poem ends with emphasis on the point that we must still "walk" with feet on and of the ground, even while the spirit "lifts up," spurning and turning up the earth in its rising. Here as elsewhere Hopkins makes no claims to full mystical union with Christ, complete severance from the physical world; he remembers the difference between the fatal hubris of the mythical Bellerophon and the humility of the "true Bellerophon," Saint Paul. We are therefore left with an image that suggests both a soaring with Christ, leaving earth behind under our own feet, and a reminder that we are always, like Paul, thrown from that Pegasus, under Christ's feet, not wholly able to follow the upward flight.

In short, a metaphor that seems to claim too much must, by Hopkins, be qualified. Another poet might rest content with imaginative metaphor, to be understood by the reader as exactly and only that. Hopkins must not only convey the ecstatic truth of the metaphor but also indicate the distinct line, even within metaphor, between the literal and the figurative, the reality and the aspiration, the God-created and the word-created.

These three sonnets of 1877 "say yes" wholeheartedly to the resources and richness of natural beauty as it bespeaks and is sustained by divine beauty. Their sadder undertones, their recognition of what man does to corrupt nature, his possible distance and alienation from nature and God, the inevitable reaping and judgment of his soul at the end, are held well under the tonal surface. Three other poems of the same year, however, indicate that Hopkins from the beginning saw in nature more than eternal freshness or news of God, and in humanity a blindness and corruption too deep perhaps for even God to choose to heal.

"Spring" (33), written in May 1877, though both an earlier poem than "Hurrahing in Harvest" and about an earlier season, is in a curious way the poem of sad harvest that the explicitly autumn poem was not. Exultation in "all this juice and all this joy" leads not to soaring near union with God but to thoughts of humanity's Fall and abdication of that joy. All the sparkling vitality of natural innocence, condensed in the octave in a highly characteristic rush of active, aural, tactile imagery, leads not to a triumphant statement that its "dearest freshness" can never be exhausted but to fears for the transience of its spiritual counterpart, and to a prayer, not an assertion, that God may preserve untainted in the young the purity of the inner Spring.

The relative simplicity of method in this poem is also indicative of the fact that Hopkins' overall stylistic development was not that suggested by some critics, a movement from complex obscurity to greater simplicity. Even here, however, complexities are not altogether lacking. The octave is more than an exuberantly impressionistic evocation of natural vitality and richness; its imagery specifically emphasizes the unity of the pure world, the meeting of reciprocal energies, lines, threads of being. "Weeds in wheels" shooting forth their leaves initiate the larger circularity developed in the following images of purity answering to purity, nature to God. The blue thrush eggs are tiny heavens on earth; the thrush's song partakes of the power of the heavens, the power specifically of God ("it strikes like lightnings to hear him sing"), even combining his spiritual lightnings with the waters and pressure of grace ("rinse and wring"); the shining trees rise to meet the shining heavens that descend to meet them—"They brush / The descending blue." This is a description, in short, both of the ideal relationship between nature and God and of that between humanity and God.

In the sestet it becomes clear how far we may be from sharing in that relationship, how distinct we are from nature, how separated we may be from God. Nature's elements will eternally fulfill their function—"what they can *they always do*" (*SD* 239); its skies will be blue, its surge of juice and joy pure, rich, sweet to all the senses, and it will always sing to human ears that echoing sweet "strain" of original innocence in Eden garden. But since mankind is now forever east of Eden, our inner skies may "cloud," our juices of spiritual sweetness "sour with sinning," unless Christ arrests the movement of the inner seasons, unless he preserves in fallen man a fragile spiritual spring.

The fragility of innocence in actual youth, of "innocent mind and Mayday in girl and boy," was to become a major, and for Hopkins an infinitely poignant, theme (47, 48, 157 especially). More important, the separation between humanity and nature, humanity and God, and the strain of mortality as well as innocence in nature's song, will come to be treated not only with sorrow ("Spring and Fall") but also with something close to bitterness ("Thou art indeed just, Lord"). Ultimately, the inevitable return to God the center will evolve from that very separation a triumphal hymn to God's power and the salvation of man even while "nature's bonfire burns on" (72). The presence of these themes in an early poem, though relatively muted here, supports the view that Hopkins' development in thought was a matter of deepening and widening circles, rather than one of linear progress toward greater somberness, or even toward greater profundity.

Two other poems of May 1877, whose method need not be discussed but whose content needs brief mention, are far grimmer than "Spring," and one is grimmer than "God's Grandeur," in treatment of human separation from nature and God, human destructiveness and blindness. Nature does all it can "In the Valley of the Elwy" (34) to create a lovely world eloquent of spiritual meaning, and it is clothed not in "man's smudge" but in full beauty. Nevertheless, in spite of the one kind household, human beings can remain blind to nature's loveliness and deaf to its eloquence; unlike the poet in "Hurrahing in Harvest," here "the inmate does not correspond." In "The Sea and the Skylark" (35) the ominous themes latent in the affirmative poems, explicit in "Spring" and "In the Valley of the Elwy," are concentrated. In spite of some self-consciously clever aspects of method that make this poem in part more obscure than mysterious, its emphatic contrast between the pure and eternal sounds of nature, sea and bird, and humanity's shoddy, arrogant, though essentially transient corruption could not be more explicitly stated. Its conclusion goes yet further, flatly denying both the hope still present in "Spring" that God will preserve man's spiritual Eden and the exultant upward movement of statement and imagery with which "God's Grandeur" concluded; here we have the reversal of evolution, spiritual and physical, a reversal unhindered by God's intervening finger:

> We, life's pride and cared-for crown,
> Have lost that cheer and charm of earth's past prime;
> Our make and making break, are breaking, down
> To man's last dust, drain fast towards man's first slime.[20]

Later poems circle and develop the themes of these early sonnets. In 1879 "Binsey Poplars" (43) laments elegiacally man's destruction of nature's "sweet especial scene," now "unselve[d]," no longer invincibly sustained by God's grandeur. "Inversnaid" (56) of 1881 treats the same theme in a more affirmative mood, concentrates on description of wild natural beauty, and betrays Hopkins'

20. Compare Hopkins' comment in the early essay on Parmenides: "Men, he thought, had sprung from slime" (1868, *JP* 130).

fear of human destructiveness only in the final stanza. In contrast, "Ribblesdale" (58), written in 1882, returns emphatically to the grim contrast between mankind and nature, specifically between nature's dumb but constant beauties and man's potential spiritual power but actual destructiveness and blindness. This last poem is something of an oddity among Hopkins' works because it comes close to relying heavily on pathetic fallacy, even while denying it (Earth has "no tongue to plead, no heart to feel" except as man speaks and feels for her). The result is that the sonnet has a special tenderness of tone, a special kind of pathos, but it is not of the kind Hopkins achieved at his best. In "Spring and Fall" (55), however, written in September 1880, Hopkins succeeded in compressing and intensifying the comments of both earlier and later poems on humanity's relation to nature, and in doing so with the intellectual rigor and astringent pathos of his best work.

The poem is first mentioned toward the end of a long letter to Bridges, September 5–13, 1880: "I enclose a little piece composed since I began this letter, not founded on any real incident. I am not well satisfied with it and do not copy it on paper of the size you like" (September 10); a postscript of September 11 then adds that he has now copied it again, "improved and on paper of the size you like" (*LB* 109). This "little piece" is unusual among Hopkins' finished poems not only because it is not of the poetic "size" or shape Hopkins himself usually liked, that of the sonnet, but because of the point he pauses to emphasize here, that it was "not founded on any real incident." Yet it emerged, I speculate, from several important present and past realities, if not incidents: one technical, perhaps accounting for its form; one more a matter of personal and literary association, accounting not only for "Goldengrove" but for the particular imagined situation it dramatizes; the third thematic, accounting for its severe and haunting beauty.

In the letter to Bridges, technical matters, and particularly the scansion of a poem by Wyatt,[21] are the chief topics. Especially relevant to "Spring and Fall" are two issues arising from the debate on Wyatt and discussed at length. The first concerns the nature and qualities of "the verse called doggrel," which Hopkins thinks must not have been of popular origin, but "the corruption or degeneration of something literary," and whose characteristics he specifies as the couplet's double, never triple, rhyme, the caesura on which

---

21. Probably "The Lover Seeking for his Lost Heart" (Abbott, *LB* 107*n1*). For the full letter, see *LB* 104–9.

the line turns, and a variable number of stresses and feet, from four to six (*LB* 108). The second issue is the possibility that Wyatt was writing a kind of systematized doggerel, though still with considerable liberty, permitting himself extra syllables to the line, and optional stresses or slacks at the beginning of both halves of it, from which "he gets an effect of sprung rhythm, which however from the weakness of his stresses is slight" (*LB* 109).

With these thoughts in his mind, and in his ear what seemed to him the failures as well as the possibilities of Wyatt's meter, Hopkins may have decided to create an example of what that "something literary" from which doggerel took its origin might have been like. Knowing that his ear was "haunted" by rhythms, that his mind was offended by license without sufficient law, and that "Spring and Fall" was "composed since I began this letter," one can without too much fancifulness imagine the actual circumstances. At his desk laboring late over the letter to Bridges, Hopkins returns to the Wyatt poem, listens, counts, and probably fastidiously tsk-tsks as he beats out such lines as "Help me to seek! for I lost it there; / And if ye have found it, ye that be here, / And seek to convey it secretly, / Handle it soft, and treat it tenderly." He has already created in his mind as he walked from Lydiate (*LD* 42) a new possibility, and poem, and now beats out, perhaps actually with his hand on the desk, a crisper and tougher four-beat rhythm. It is also not impossible to trace to this technical discussion both the uncharacteristic choice of couplets for the verse form and the one startling and crucial triple rhyme for the pivot of his own sophisticated tour de force in "doggrel."

A complicated cluster of both immediate and remembered facts and associations may have generated the poem's imaginative use of the term *Goldengrove* and, more important, its imagined catechism of a child. Presumably Hopkins knew of Goldengrove Farm near St. Beuno's, as suggested by several critics,[22] though this is not provable from any direct evidence so far as I know. Equally unprovable, but at least as likely, I think, are the two suggestions made by Schneider: that he knew of Golden Grove in South Wales, birthplace of the poet Vaughan, a probability supported at least by indirect evidence (*LD* 23–24), and that he knew or knew of Jeremy Taylor's *The Golden Grove* (1654), composed at the Vaughan estate

22. Gardner, *Hopkins*, 2:309; Milward, *Landscape and Inscape: Vision and Inspiration in Hopkins's Poetry*, 70–71; MacKenzie, *Reader's Guide*, 143. Mariani suggests an alternative Goldengrove near Lydiate, *Commentary*, 176.

and named for it.[23] Even more to the point of the poem's content perhaps is the fact that this religious manual of daily prayers is an expanded version of Taylor's earlier "Catechism for Children." Though *The Golden Grove*'s strongly anti-Catholic preface may automatically have excluded it from any serious place in Hopkins' reading, it is at least conceivable that he knew not only of the title but also of the subtitle's emphasis on "younger persons."[24] It is also of some speculative interest that in one of Taylor's best-known works, *The Rule and Exercises of Holy Dying* (1651), childhood is explicitly a "prologue to the tragedy" of life, "nature calls us to meditate of death," and "Nature hath given us one harvest every year, but death hath two; and the spring and the autumn send throngs of men and women to charnel-houses . . . . Thus death reigns in all the portions of our time."[25]

Far more important than any possible external sources is the fact that the poem distills, concentrates, and dramatizes the themes that had haunted Hopkins and his poetry for many years. He must now have been ready to see and say that "Spring and Death" (4) were no longer subjects and sources of merely melancholy pathos, or wholly in contrast with each other, and that "Spring" and "Harvest" could no longer be separated, but could and must confront each other. From this confrontation comes one sad awareness of unity, not difference: the child in her fresh spring, the poet in his autumn, glean from nature in their different ways not "our Saviour," but grief for human mortality, grief for the larger Fall that marks them both for death. In method also the poem is a remarkably compressed example of Hopkins at his best, adapting form and meter to subject, fusing simplicity and complexity, and above all combining sympathetic tenderness with an almost implacable intellectual honesty and somber finality of tone.

The sprung couplets of this sublime "doggrel" combine something that sounds like a nursery-rhyme lilt and a direct clarity of rhyme—appropriate in an address to a child—with the grimmer

23. *Dragon in the Gate*, 216n7. As she points out, the letter (February 27, 1879), proves that he knew an edition and memoir of Vaughan's poems and life in which the place name figures prominently.

24. Jeremy Taylor, *The Golden Grove, A Choice Manuel: . . . . Composed for the use of the Devout, especially of younger persons* (1655). Since Taylor had been granted asylum and hospitality by Richard Vaughan, earl of Carbery, after the defeat of the Royalists, both this manual and the earlier *Sermons Preached at Golden-Grove* (1653) pay tribute in their titles to their patron and place of origin.

25. *The Works of Jeremy Taylor*, ed. Rev. T. S. Hughes, 5:365, 366.

strokes provided by the strong and consistent four stresses to the line and a rhyme that reinforces the sad harmonies in meaning on which the poem is based:

> Márgarét, áre you gríeving
> Óver Góldengróve unléaving?
> (Stressing from *LB* 120; see Appendix B)

Even in this quiet opening couplet, under the lilt is the heavy beat of sadness and finality that will culminate in the last couplet's answer to that opening question, an answer totally simple and totally final in sound, thought, and grim "irony" of rhyme:

> It ís the blíght mán was bórn for,
> It is Margaret you mourn for.
> (Stressing from *LD* 174, here and hereafter)

Apparent prosodic simplicity and deeper actual complexity are matched by the same combination in diction and imagery. Whatever the external origins of the term *Goldengrove* may have been, in the poem it speaks to most readers with lovely lucidity as a charming and beautifully childlike personification of the autumn woods. Its capitalization in context reflects the fact that the speaker is addressing a child, trying to understand how she thinks and feels, since children do seem to assume in inanimate things something answering to their own humanity, something to be named like a person, something not yet distinct from "the things of man." At the same time, the word seems so consciously an adult's attempt to speak a child's language, and to imply so sadly to adult minds a reminder of Eden, that other and now permanently lost "golden grove" and golden time, that it emphasizes both the speaker's rather poignant attempt to meet the child on her own grounds, even perhaps to regain her innocence by regaining her vocabulary, and his actual, irreversible distance from her.

Similarly, the word *unleaving* may have been designed not only to correct the rhyme ("unleafing" in A and D)—something Hopkins was not likely to have been exercised about if the "incorrect" rhyme were more significant—but also to add the dual implication. In revising he probably realized that he could compress in one word both the initial point that the leaves are falling and a sad secondary point, known too well to the adult, but not to the child: while the natural seasons in their turning will bring a new spring, while Goldengrove will remain and be leaved again, human seasons will bring only a final departure and final "fall."

The tone of both the opening couplet and the following—
"Leáves, líke the thíngs of mán, you / With your fresh thoughts care
for, can you?"—reinforces the implications of the imagery. The
tone of reflective and sad wonder, of sympathy and tenderness
combined with the slightest possible undertone of mild rebuke (especially suggested by the strong alliteration of "care for, can
you?"), reminds us that he is beyond the spring, that he cannot forget his autumn vision of human life, his knowledge that "the things
of man" are more important and infinitely more melancholy than
falling leaves. This reflectiveness of tone, helped by the falling gentleness of the feminine endings, results from a crucial revision, and
from Hopkins' persistence in preferring that revision in spite of
Bridges' advice: the original was the flatly lumptious "Leaves you
with your fresh thoughts can / Feel for like the things of man" (*LB*
119). The only merit I can see in this is the phrase "feel for"; it perhaps makes clearer than "care for" that in "things of man" he does
not mean merely manmade toys, dolls, picture books, as Gardner
suggests, but all the *lacrimae rerum* of human life.[26]

The tone and implications of both opening couplets introduce
the crucial distinctions that the following lines develop, between
adult and child, between man and nature, between conscious and
intuitive knowledge, as well as their sad similarities:

> Áh! ás the heart grows ólder
> It will come to such sights colder
> By and by, nor spare a sigh
> Though worlds of wanwood leafmeal lie;
> And yet you *will* weep and know why.

The revision in B from "though forests low and leaf-meal lie" to the
present version of that line emphatically intensifies the whole
poem's distinction between the two responses to nature's autumn,
the child's tears for one grove of trees, the adult's indifference to
whole worlds of merely natural death. The characteristic coinages
"leafmeal" ("piecemeal") and "wanwood" ("wan" carrying both
its Anglo-Saxon meanings) are both sophisticated and vividly simple in their evocation of rotting disintegration, a damply molder-
ing and dark "meal-drift" that here has no beauty of substance or
association, the pallor of illness and exhaustion, and in their striking contrast with the still lovely gold of the present grove and the
healthy freshness of Margaret's instinctive response to it.

26. Gardner, *Hopkins*, 2:309. For the *lacrimae rerum* allusion I am indebted to
Howard Nemerov.

The seemingly sudden turn in thought in the last of the lines just quoted is triply emphasized: by the heavy stress on *"will,"* indicated by Hopkins' underlining (A); by the break in verse form from couplets to this single triplet; by the shift from the melancholy gentleness of feminine rhymes to the sternness of masculine and monosyllabic rhyme. But the point of all three emphatic devices is that there is no contradiction in thought here, simply an inevitable and logical development. Hopkins is not making the facile and sentimental point that as we grow old we lose the fresh sensitivities and responsiveness of childhood, though that is the instinctive first reading of many new readers and some critical ones. The much subtler and much sadder point is that sorrow does not cease with age, though its sources are differently and more deeply understood, that adulthood will bring an end to grief for nature's autumns, but will not bring an end to tears. This seems to me quite simply the reason for the much-debated stress on *"will"*;[27] it tersely cancels any facile hope for later easy painlessness, but it is immediately followed, without punctuation break, by the one wan consolation—if it is one—granted the adult: "and know why."

The final lines then briefly and elegiacally summarize the poem's meaning. "Spring's" intuition, "fall's" knowledge, recognize the same archetypal source of sorrow:

> Now no matter, child, the name:
> Sórrow's spríngs aŕe the sáme.
> Nor mouth had, no nor mind, expressed
> What héart heárd of, ghóst guéssed:
> It iś the blíght mán was bórn for,
> It is Margaret you mourn for.

The speaker has in fact "named" for the child the immediate and partially inadequate symbol of her sorrow's source, and the poet has named it for us in the title; like us, Margaret will later name it not "Goldengrove" but "the Fall." In her "spring" of life she has instinctively recognized that there are other springs, sources of death and grief, not life. Above all, without the capacity to articulate or interpret intellectually what her heart "heard" in nature's silent eloquence of death, her spirit intuitively "guessed"

27. See among others I. A. Richards, *Practical Criticism: A Study of Literary Judgment*, 83 (she wills to weep, persists in weeping); Empson, who finds it an example of his fourth type of ambiguity (she both insists on weeping, and will weep in the future), *Seven Types*, 187–88; Pick, ed., *A Hopkins Reader*, "grammatically futuritive, rhythmically volitional" (417*n*).

and understood.[28] Though differing in their ways of understanding the true source of all grief, all falling, child and man are therefore one in their recognition of a shared mortality.

Hopkins has played upon all the "moments" of his key words *spring* and *fall*, and on all the implications of his consistently natural imagery, to dramatize some very somber distinctions and similarities. On the one hand he has shown both the sad similarity between humanity and nature and the difference between them: both are subject to the fall, but in nature's seasons spring will come again. On the other, starting from the title itself, which seems to suggest contrast, confrontation, of two states, but in which the real meaning resides in the linking "and," he has shown the distinction between adult and child, and their yet sadder similarity. Both distinctions, both likenesses, make the point that spiritually there is no spring of innocence, and has not been since the first lost golden grove of Eden; "Fall" has been our only season from birth, and will remain so until the final fall of death.

In the final couplet especially—one of the most perfect things written by Hopkins or any other poet, I think—everything works to emphasize this eternal fall: the dying fall of the fading prepositions and the reintroduced feminine rhymes, most obviously; the handling of tenses, so that "is," "was," "born for"—present, past, implication of future—are one and are blighted, the hope of "born for" negated from the very beginning of the line and of all human time. Even the slight shift in the stressing of "Margaret" noted by Mariani, with its lesser stress on the diminutive "-et" compared to the opening line, may hint at her actual adulthood of spirit and fate.[29] In this "nursery rhyme," in short, "Once upon a time" and "By and by" become the same thing, the beginning and the end of the story.

"Spring and Fall" is both one of Hopkins' most compassionate poems and one of his grimmest, a poem in which feeling and thought are disciplined by that element of the "terrible crystal" (*LD* 80) in him which here prevents any lapse into mawkishness about childhood or melancholy about age. Though one of Richards' undergraduates bluntly offered as his final judgment on

28. A's original, corrected in B, with that revision confirmed in a letter to Dixon (April 6, 1881, *LD* 49), is generally more confusing than the final version but is clearer on the one point that what is being "heard" and "guessed" is specifically the source of sorrow, the preceding antecedent: "Nor mouth it, no nor mind, expressed, / But ghost heard of, heart guessed."

29. Mariani, *Commentary*, 176.

the poem, "Sentamental,"[30] what Hopkins has actually done here is to turn a potentially trite and saccharine subject into something so tough in thought, and so strangely brooding and almost sardonically tender in tone, that whatever possible adverse labels might be attached to the poem the very last of them should be "sentamental." The poem's apparent simplicity, its actual tenderness and beauty, should not blind us to the fact that in this tiny dramatic vignette he has compressed the large and terrible themes of the apparent absence of God, of human mortality, and even of human damnation, which will reach their crisis in the final poems.

Among these late poems, "Thou art indeed just, Lord" (74), March 1889, written only three months before his death, is a complex reexamination of the particular theme under discussion in this chapter, and an apparently wholly despairing one. Though nature is not now a victim of man's destructiveness, and though it is not even viewed as transient, or as news of human mortality, but the reverse, the separation between the speaker and nature, and between him and God, now seems complete. Instead of "gleaning our Saviour" from the physical world's beauty, Hopkins now sees only that world's bitter contrast with his own sterility, a sterility not only unalleviated, but apparently inflicted, by God. Yet even this poem comes full circle, comes back to God, the only possible center and source of life. No longer confident of spiritual harvest, no longer able to assert that he is not mere arid sand but "steady as a water in a well," no longer sure that if "there lives the dearest freshness deep down things" those things include himself, Hopkins nevertheless still knows that if not from God, then from nowhere, can come the waters of grace and the spiritual harvest of creativity. The poem therefore ends with a line that echoes the cadence and even bleakly the thought of the early "Love, O my God, to call Thee Love and Love" (19), with that powerful and heart-wrenching prayer that still acknowledges God's sovereignty: "Mine, O thou lord of life, send my roots rain."

The central source of desolation in this poem, the sense of creative, scholarly, and priestly impotence, of hopeless spiritual barrenness, and the imagery of sterility in which it is expressed, do not appear for the first time in Hopkins' last years and late works (see for example, 17, 18, 127), but from 1885 onward this anguish

---

30. Richards, *Practical Criticism*, 88. For a radically different reading of the poem, as a dramatization of Hopkins' own fall into "solipsism" and "corruption of vision," see Harris, *Inspirations Unbidden*, 28.

and this imagery become increasingly insistent and desperate in his letters, as in his poems: "There is a point with me in matters of any size when I must absolutely have encouragement as much as crops rain" (May 17, 1885, *LB* 218–19); "if I could but get on, if I could but produce work I should not mind its being buried, silenced, and going no further; but it kills me to be time's eunuch and never to beget" (September 1, 1885, *LB* 222); "All my undertakings miscarry: I am like a straining eunuch," and in this desolation of "loathing and hopelessness . . . I could therefore do no more than repeat *Justus es, Domine* . . . and the like" (Retreat notes, January 1888, *SD* 262). Even in such comments, however, as in the poem, there is one shred of faith and hope left: "All impulse fails me: I can give myself no sufficient reason for going on. Nothing comes: I am a eunuch—but it is for the kingdom of heaven's sake" (January 12, 1888, *LB* 270). Also, as in the poem, there is one prayer: "O my God, look down on me" (January 1888, *SD* 262). Out of this painfully complex tension of despair and faith comes the complex pain and tone and statement of "Thou art indeed just, Lord."

"*Justus es, Domine* . . . and the like" now becomes more than a mechanically recited anodyne for the hopeless soul; it becomes the beginning and source of a dramatic argument with God, though it is perhaps typical of Hopkins that this most direct and personal complaint takes not only its basic idea but also much of its wording in the octave from scriptural authority. That authority he was at pains to transcribe in part in both the original and the final drafts (Appendix B): "Justus quidem tu es, Domine, si disputem tecum; verumtamen justa loquar ad te; Quare via impiorum prosperatur? etc. Jer. xx.1."

> Thou art indeed just, Lord, if I contend
> With thee; but, sir, so what I plead is just.
> Why do sinners' ways prosper? and why must
> Disappointment all I endeavour end?

It was surely more than Hopkins' meticulous translation of his text, however, which produced in these lines their curious hovering between humility and self-assertion. "Indeed," for example, is not only an emphatic, affirmative word but also carries strong overtones of merely mechanical agreement—a sort of official, formal acknowledgment of what the debating speaker feels to be actually untrue, or that he will at least go on to qualify. Second, though the drafts show some uncertainty as to the translation of the subjunctive "disputem" ("should I contend"; "would I contend"; "were I to contend"; "if I contend"), and though he is careful to maintain the word's hypothetical mood in all versions, the apparently final choice, "if I contend," is the least hypothetical in effect of all these possibilities. As a result, the argument remains grammatically suppositional, the overt assertion about God's justice humbly affirmative, but whether it is actually so remains deliberately ambiguous. Third, attention to more than literal translation is evident in the final version's revision from "speak" ("loquar") to "plead"— "so what I plead is just." The word emphasizes the formal judicial situation of a law court, of an advocate-witness pleading before the High Judge, and carries also the common meaning of humble and helpless begging, so that his plea is both a legally rational and "just" one and a kind of *cri du coeur* that acknowledges his helpless need.

The nuances of that repeated "just" in the opening lines, though present in the original ("justus . . . justa"), are stressed by Hopkins' placement of the second "just" in the emphatic final position in line 2. The fine and semi-ironic distinction made is between "fair, righteous" as applied to God, and "having sound reason, validity" as applied to the speaker's plea, and there is thus an opening confrontation quite different from that between "Thou" and "I" in *The Wreck of the Deutschland*. This is a confrontation between divine and mortal justice, a justice the speaker hopes may be one in fact as in word form, but as Hopkins plays upon the nuances of the word there is surely a muted sting, an emphasis on the probably inevitable disparity.

A similar ironic sting may be heard in the insertion of the word "sir," and in its deliberately ambiguous tone—a tone of grudging, almost insolent, respect, or respectful insolence. Overtly it is the address of respect of witness to judge, servant to master, priest to superior, soldier to officer, even schoolboy to headmaster. Already underlying its humility, however, is what its later repetition in line 9 brings out: heavily emphasized there by position and stress, it conveys the teeth-clenched respect of someone who knows his place and hastily remembers to express and acknowledge it, but who cannot fully accept its justice.

Much more explicit than these latent ironies in the first quatrain are the sad and bitter, reverent and rebellious ironies of the second quatrain and the beginning of the sestet:

> Wert thou my enemy, O thou my friend,
> How wouldst thou worse, I wonder, than thou dost
> Defeat, thwart me? Oh, the sots and thralls of lust
> Do in spare hours more thrive than I that spend,
>
> Sir, life upon thy cause.

Like the opening lines of the sonnet, in which acceptance is assumed in spite of hypothetical rebellion, these lines overtly deny the blasphemous conditional possibility, "Wert thou my enemy" (in which there is probably an echo of Donne, and a grim play on the traditional term for Satan), while allowing that possibility to remain implicitly conceivable and true. Hopkins' revision of the original line's unqualified "that art my friend," which had appeared in three of the drafts, seems designed to strengthen this grim implication, while also making the appeal more movingly direct and personal. Helpless but bitter irony is also emphasized by the placement in midline of the interjected "I wonder," which conveys not only genuine bafflement but the Socratic irony of a speaker not baffled at all but speaking with pointed, and in this case accusing, intent.

The rest of the poem then explicitly presents, through grim contrast, the full complaint. Initially the contrast is that derived from Jeremiah, between the prosperous unrighteous and the afflicted righteous man, emphasized by the balanced juxtaposition of "*spare hours*," brief, inactive, but profitable, and "*spend . . . life*," prolonged, active, but fruitless (italics mine).[31] It then develops into the more personal, more concrete contrast between sterile speaker and fecund nature, and the delicate modulations in imagery make the development seem inevitable. "Thy cause" reminds us of the judicial setting and terminology of the opening, while "See, banks and brakes / Now, leavèd how thick!" turns our eyes from the courtroom to the world outside; it is as though Hopkins has realized that he no longer has any real standing in that original courtroom, no more evidence to offer there, and must turn to the evidence of the larger world for new justification. Second, while the phrases "thralls of lust" and "thrive," and possibly an ironic sexual implication in "spend," lead with obvious logic to the bitter fecundity-sterility contrast of the sestet, there may also be another more latent reason for the apparently sudden shift in midline from abstract pleading and questioning to the dramatic gesture at na-

---

31. Both this juxtaposition and the effects of the interjected "sir" resulted from revision of the original "than I that bend / Ever to bear thy yoke" (H₁a).

ture; a kind of stream-of-consciousness transition is implied here. Having stated that he has spent his "life" in God's cause, the natural next thought would seem to be, "But what is 'life'? it is not in me, nor from me; it is out there, in all that riot of fecundity," and hence the turn in direction and thought.

The many revisions indicate how laboriously Hopkins worked to compress the following description of nature in a few lines (see Appendix B), but it is clear that from the beginning he wanted to emphasize the four elements that are present in the final version: nature's thick abundance; its energy and motion; its coherent patterning ("laced," that favorite word, replaces the earlier "broidered," but the intent is the same); and finally, the one particular element, "fretty chervil." This last specific image, present in all drafts, is surely deliberately ironic in intent: "chervil" means "the rejoicing leaf,"[32] and thus in a sense epitomizes all the "juice and joy" of that Eden from which Hopkins is now personally—not merely as fallen man—somehow unfairly excluded.

The final lines then sum up the poem, and in part sum up Hopkins' thoughts on the relation between humanity and nature in general, and between himself and God in particular:

> . . . birds build—but not I build; no, but strain,
> Time's eunuch, and not breed one work that wakes.
> Mine, O thou lord of life, send my roots rain.

Wholly separated now from the natural world from which he had once gleaned Christ, denied the right to creativity granted even to the lowliest aspects of nature, seeing in the birds no hint of God's "bright wings," nor even of sacramental windhover, skylark, stormfowl, totally barren, merely "time's eunuch" and apparently not even "for the kingdom of heaven's sake," he yet returns to the only possible source of life, presenting himself as potentially one with nature's fecundity *if* God wills it.

It is important that in this final plea potential irony, present from the beginning in this most ironic of Hopkins' poems, becomes desperate sincerity. "O thou lord of life" is not to be taken as bitter irony but as literal and passionately believed truth; at the end, "Domine" is no longer resented "sir," but truly "lord." Even latent claims to rights and righteousness were meticulously excised in revision of an original alternative that appears in three of the drafts: "Then send, thou lord of life, these roots *their* rain" (italics

32. Boyle, *Metaphor*, 166.

mine). How mild a hint this is that his cause is just, that he is as worthy of life as the rest of nature, yet finally even this is severely and humbly abandoned. And while that splendidly emphatic "Mine" at the opening of the last line, together with the strength of the final heavily stressed monosyllables, asserts not only his desperation but his sense of significant selfhood, it is no longer that of the resentful though servile rebel of the rest of the poem. In the end, as in the opening of *The Deutschland*, this new self acquires its existence, its importance, its right to "plead" in any sense, only in admitting with true humility its submission to God, only in praying that what is "mine" is not only self, but "lord."

This sonnet, one of Hopkins' most complex in "moments" of tone though not of vocabulary, closes one of the circles around a central theme, and closes it with a somber but reverent return within itself to the one center of life and hope. However mysterious, however apparently unjust, God's workings may seem, without him there is no life at all, no "rain" for nature, or for man. Just as God's springs of fire had been the only source of life-giving water in the seared world of "God's Grandeur," so they remain now the only source of grace for the seared and barren inner world of the poet-priest.

7

"Mortal Beauty"
Selfhood, Variety, Mortality

INTERSECTING WITH THE concept of sacramental nature is the second major theme of mortal beauty in nature and humanity, its loveliness, its splendid selfhood, its transience, its possible danger. Hopkins explored this subject in all periods of his writing, and again with a dual response from the beginning: in each stage of creativity poems of affirmation are answered by poems of more ominous, more fearful awarenesses. Again, however, this duality of vision need not indicate—in my view does not indicate—a deep ambivalence or division of thought, but simply the range, intelligent flexibility, and vital tension of a mind "poised, but on the quiver."

"Pied Beauty" (37) of 1877, whose statement is really the "changeless note" of this chapter, is probably Hopkins' best-known poem, certainly one of the most discussed.[1] I will therefore comment only on the way in which its handling of "asymmetrical symmetry," and so its shape and direction of thought and eye, exactly dramatizes concept, specifically that concept of God not only as center but as enclosing "circumference," the canon that rounds in all the world's variety. While lacking the wholly satisfying proportions of a full sonnet, it does employ its own "counter, original, spare, strange" form to make its own point and special order, and does so with a combination of such sheer joy and verve and reverence that it deserves its popular fame.

Symmetrically and typically, the poem begins and ends with praise of God, the beginning and the closing of the circle, though

1. For especially fine detailed commentaries, see Miller, *Disappearance of God*, 298–305, and Sulloway, *Victorian Temper*, 105–7; for a perceptive brief analysis, Harris, *Inspirations Unbidden*, 42.

even this near-perfect balance gains power from variation: from the contrast between the literally longer but faster-paced and almost colloquially joyous opening phrase—"Glóry be to God"—and the grand solemnity of the coda's brief, but long-held and long-reverberating organ tones—"Práise hím." Asymmetrically, the poem's numerical proportions as a curtal sonnet are 6 to $4\frac{1}{5}$, already, to both eye and ear, running "counter" to the traditional form. More important—though perhaps only the most finicky Hopkinsian will forgive this mathematical laboriousness—its content ratio is $8\frac{2}{5}$ to $1\frac{4}{5}$: eight full lines and the end of the first line are devoted to the world of "dappled things," meticulously observed and delighted in, while only one full line, plus the opening statement and its final powerful antiphonal echo, are given to that world's source. In this asymmetry resides and is dramatized the sonnet's point: the world of idiosyncratic and changeful beauty is given central attention and full freedom, but what contains and shapes that varied world, without constricting it, dominates both statement and structure. God is the Alpha and Omega of the poem, as of the world, and is so absolute that he requires only such brief yet all-enclosing and unqualified honor.

In both overall and specific movement also the poem dramatizes divine order around and within apparently random "dapple." Overall, the movement is from the keynote, the "one," down to the beauty and variety and changefulness of the many, and back to the unity and constancy of the Creator who is "past change." Specifically, our eyes follow the typical Hopkinsian arc from up, to down, and again up, not only in the large design but in each detail in the dappled world itself. However flashingly and sharply individual they are, while simultaneously changing and fusing, the concrete examples direct us purposefully from an initial fusion of sky and earth, down to earth and beneath its water, back to its surface, where "Fresh-firecoal chestnut-falls" perhaps fuses elements of the skies and the waters, upward further to what is both of the earth and of the lower heavens ("finches' wings"), and finally to a panoramic view from above of earth's landscape and qualities, natural, human, and abstract, both generalized and concretely specified. Having followed this movement, which allows us to inscape the world as a whole while also admiring its distinctive oddities, we are logically and imaginatively prepared for that final raising of the eyes, and spirit, to the God above all dappled things who does "know how" this variety came to be, and to be ordered.

In this same year, 1877, however, Hopkins wrote a fine though lower-keyed poem that concentrates specifically on the transience of human beauty, the fickleness of human contact and concern, in contrast to the constancy of the God behind and above human change and loss. While in "Pied Beauty" Hopkins' eye ranged freely, triumphantly penetrating and grasping the vividly available beauties of earth and man, in "The Lantern out of Doors" (40) he strains rather wistfully in lonely darkness to follow an occasional and vanishing light, to identify and hold it as it passes:

> Sometimes a lantern moves along the night,
> That interests our eyes. And who goes there?
> I think; where from and bound, I wonder, where,
> With, all down darkness wide, his wading light?

This lantern may suggest "a little touch of Diogenes in the night," in Gardner's charming phrase,[2] but if so, there is a reversal at work; Hopkins himself is a lanternless Diogenes seeking the truth and light of others by the light of his own mind only. Isolated, able only to speculate on the origin and destination of unseen, unknown fellow beings, he is, as he was in "The Windhover," a watcher "in hiding" and, as he will be later, a sidelined soldier, "but by where wars are rife" (66). Here, he is specifically like a lonely sentinel, remote from the actual movement of armies, questioning "who goes there?" but without either the energy or the authority to demand an answer, and receiving no answering human password. In the end, he will conclude that only the world's lantern and world's general, Christ, is capable of lighting all the travelers who move through darkness, and of replying to the challenge of all sentinels, "Friend":

> Christ minds: Christ's interest, what to avow or amend
> There, eyes them, heart wánts, care haúnts, foot
> fóllows kínd,
> Their ránsom, théir rescue, ańd first, fást, last fríend.

The certainty of statement in this poem, however, is lent some poetic "interest," even some resonance of mystery, by a rather subtle manipulation of tone and imagery. The initial tone is relatively casual, offhand, languid even: there is no intensity immediately apparent in the phrase "that interests our eyes," only a momentary curiosity, and the colloquial speech rhythms, thought rhythms, of "I think; where from and bound, I wonder," emphasize the idly

---

2. *Hopkins*, 2:241. Punctuation and stressing in quotations are from B's corrected version of A.

speculative movement of the questioner's mind. But in the last line
of the first quatrain the tone changes somewhat as the quality of
perception changes, as the literal darkness acquires a frightening
endlessness stretching to infinity and a clogging thickness of tex-
ture, and as the Keatsian chameleonism of "wading" makes the
straining viewer seem one with his obscure and struggling object.
Here, water is clearly not God's dayprings or veins of grace, but
merely part of the dark world's murk and mire and sloughs of
Despond.

An attempt to find some light in this darkness, to transform
this imagery, leads ultimately only to greater somberness, as the
next quatrain generalizes from the particular experience of the
first:

> Men go by me, whom either beauty bright
>   In mould or mind or what not else makes rare:
>   They rain against our much-thick and marsh air
> Rich beams, till death or distance buys them quite.

In spite of the initial sadness of "Men go by me," until the final
phrase of the last line, in which "by" is grimly echoed in "buys,"
there is also an attempt at hope here. The imagery now assumes
that darkness cannot quench the fire of bright human "lanterns,"
that indeed the radiance of fine human beings so far conquers the
drowning and murky night as to turn its very elements to light:
"They *rain* . . . rich *beams*" (italics mine). But ingenious poetic
imagery cannot change fact: the turn occurs swiftly in the sad
final phrase, and the beginning of the sestet acknowledges not
only the fragility of those lanterns themselves but also Hopkins'
own inability to catch and hold their passing brightness, even in
memory:

> Death or distance soon consumes them: wind,
>   What most I may eye after, be in at the end
>   I cannot, and out of sight is out of mind.

The poet's straining thread of vision, trying to trace its shifting,
vanishing object and ultimately unable to do so, his resultant
fickleness of interest, is then immediately contrasted with the only
true source of permanence and light: the constancy and power of
the Christ who "eyes" all men, whatever the darknesses in which
they struggle, and follows their passing lights not only with eyes
but with heart's love and actual redeeming presence.

The imagery of the sestet illustrates Hopkins' attention both

to the "moments" of individual words and to thematic and metaphorical layers beneath layers, links between links, in every part of
the poem. That rapid turn from the rather callous, utterly colloquial cliché "out of sight is out of *mind*" to "Christ *minds*" (italics
mine) is typical of his way of turning wordplay to crucial theological meaning, the static to the active, the colloquial to the spiritual.
(A similar, though infinitely sadder, instance of this practice will
appear in the much later "At God knows when to God knows
what" of sonnet 69.) Second, the word *interest* is quietly but intricately related to the rest of the poem. The earlier "buys them
quite" of line 8 seems to involve on first reading an illogically
startling shift from the darkness-light-water imagery that overtly
governs the octave; one probably expects something more like
"drowns them quite." As usual, however, the shift is not really
sudden: the second line has quietly planted the word *interests*,
though we doubtless take it there only at its surface value; the second quatrain has stressed the priceless rarity of some human lives,
which then turn out to be on Death's market after all; finally
Christ's constancy and power are expressed in imagery that combines the monetary and the soldierly, implying the Redeemer who
is also Prince of armies. Not only is his "interest," his concern, infinitely greater than the casual interest of poet and readers in the
beginning, but the word surely implies also at what cost he opposed and will oppose Death's bidding for mankind. As the last
line's summation of the poem makes clear, Christ the redeemer
literally "buys back" from darkness the souls of humanity, offers
himself as "ransom" and "rescue" for his soldiers—including perhaps the lonely sentinel-poet—and is first and last constant both
in heroism and in love.

This poem then, like "Pied Beauty," asserts the constancy of
the God "past change," but unlike the better-known sonnet it begins to concentrate on the transience of mortal pied beauty and
bright selfhood and to emphasize their vulnerability to darkness—
both the darkness of human forgetfulness and the final dark of
death itself. In the years following 1877, Hopkins pursued these
questions in a number of major poems, and again the vision is dual.
In 1879, "Henry Purcell" (45) returns to and deepens the theme of
"Pied Beauty," exploring and exulting in the value of human individuality. In 1879 also, however, "The Handsome Heart" (47) and
"The Bugler's First Communion" (48) not only rejoice in human
purity but are haunted by an anxious sense of its fragility, and "The
Candle Indoors" (46) shows one of the directions Hopkins' later

thought would take, toward self-castigating examination of his own sins.[3] Among the poems of 1880–1882, "Felix Randal" (53) laments the actual death of a once massively splendid, seemingly invincible man, while "As kingfishers catch fire" (57) and "The Leaden Echo and the Golden Echo" (59) return to affirmation of mortal beauty and selfhood as these are understood in relation to God. (On the problems of dating the last two poems see Appendix C.)

Though I may myself be "listed to a heresy here," the famous "Henry Purcell" sonnet seems to me one of Hopkins' less successful poems, in spite of its rousing sestet and its major statement about the true nature and glory of "abrupt self." The almost impenetrable obscurity of the octave strikes me as mainly syntactical, exactly as it struck Bridges, lacking the deeper mystery and ultimate "explosion" of the best poetry. The whole also seems somewhat at odds with itself, perhaps because there was an actual "priest-poet conflict" underlying its subject matter. Hopkins is straining to effect with his own hands, with his poetry, the redemption of a heretic from fallen angel to angel of genius worthy of wonder and even reverence, to make of that choice for Anglican heresy a *felix culpa*, a fair fall; perhaps uneasy in the attempt, he strains too hard. Perhaps also the Scotist reconciliation of individual specialness, in this case genius, with general and universal meaning beyond the particular self was a philosophical problem not susceptible to clear treatment in condensed poetic form. In any case, the sonnet's difficulty, and the extent of its failure to speak in its own poetic terms, is reflected in the fact that this is the one instance in which Hopkins succumbed to the necessity of a prose paraphrase at the head of a poem.

Privately, however, he considered it to be among his finest works. Though he was endlessly patient in writing explanations of its meaning to Bridges (Appendix C), he also commented in typically puzzled surprise, "It is somewhat dismaying to find I am so unintelligible though, especially in one of my very best pieces" (January 4, 1883, *LB* 171). Perversely also, while considering that the octave was relatively clear, he remarked, "The sestet of the Purcell sonnet is not so clearly worked out as I could wish" (May 26, 1879, *LB* 83), whereas to most readers this is where Hopkins

---

3. Explicitly the "companion" to "The Lantern out of Doors" (B), and exemplifying Hopkins' meticulously self-correcting instincts, this poem balances reliance on Christ's love with a stern rebuke to blind complacency.

breaks beyond obscurity of syntax and idea to some quite splendid poetry.

In spite of the poem's tendency to remain merely cerebrally obscure, however, its intricate lacing of imagery and dimensions of meaning does create some vibration of mystery in areas beyond those of Scotist thought and involuted syntax. The unifying effect of appropriate musical language is perhaps relatively obvious— "rehearsal," "abrupt" (which Hopkins uses primarily in its musical sense of "distinct"),[4] "air of angels," and perhaps even "lay." Yet more crucial are the unifying metaphors that suggest rising and falling, making us feel the surge and fall of the music, while carrying also more important implications. At least a general sense of these may be gleaned from the opening lines:

> Have fáir fállen, O faír, fáir have fállen, so déar
> To me, so arch-especial a spirit as heaves in Henry Purcell.
> (Markings from B, here and hereafter)

Though these lines may leave us quite hopelessly at sea as to exact meaning, they are beautiful in sheer sound and at least suggestive in content. The Alexandrine line length, the manipulation of sprung rhythm's heavy beats, the repetition of words, especially the long-drawn modulations in repeated vowel sounds, immediately give us the sense of a prayer designed to be, like Purcell's music, both majestic and intense, trumpet-throated in strength and beauty. Moreover, even if we are not, like Hopkins, so grammatically learned as to recognize in "Have" "the singular imperative (or optative if you like) of the past" (*LB* 174), or the Shakespearean echoes in the first line (see Appendix C), even if we misunderstand the line (perhaps especially if we misunderstand it), some sort of initial fall-to-rise, or rising in falling, is suggested: the prayer sounds as though it were saying, somewhat heretically, "Though he has fallen, may it have been well, may it have been splendidly." As it turns out, Hopkins intended to play upon a contrast in the word *fallen*, the contrast between "may fair have befallen" his soul after death and the feared "fall" of that soul to damnation. The end of the quatrain makes this relatively clear:

4. As in the sharp transitions of the diatonic scale in contrast to the chromatic (*JP* 76, 104), though the more common "sudden, boldly separate" meanings are not irrelevant. For Hopkins' exploration of the nature of "self" see especially *SD* 146–48, and on the Scotist hierarchy of degrees of selfhood, Christopher Devlin, S.J., "Hopkins and Duns Scotus," 13.

with the reversal
Of the outward sentence low lays him, listed to a heresy, here.

As in the misreading of the line, the intended reading emphasizes a
rising from the depths.

In the second line, the suggestion of a fallen angel who may
nevertheless still be, or rise to be, an archangel is implicit in "so
arch-especial a spirit" and becomes fully explicit in

Let him oh! with his air of angels then lift me, lay me!

The fallen genius, the light-bringer, now becomes again almost
fully angel; the reversal of the sentence is reflected in the reversed
reference and meaning of "lay," and his music's rise and fall, like
his spirit's, becomes both a potent and a soothing swayer of the
poet-listener's mind and soul. This sense of rising and falling is also
suggested in the startling verb "*heaves* in Henry Purcell" (italics
mine). In contrast to the weakish terms Hopkins used in his prose
paraphrase for Bridges, "breathes or stirs," and to the pretty little
words applied to the music of lesser musicians ("sweet notes,"
"nursle"), "heaves" not only supplies an alliterative chime but also
emphasizes the surging, perhaps imprisoned, but potentially massive, sealike, and soaring strength of that spirit.

Finally, freed in the sestet from the oddly chosen challenge to
find three credible rhymes for Purcell's difficult name, Hopkins
moves to some splendid music of his own, and in the image of the
majestic stormfowl, "walking his while" but preparing for flight,
completes the attempt to raise the fallen angel, if not quite to the
heavens again, at least close to them. It is characteristic of Hopkins'
honesty, his fidelity both to Catholic doctrine and to the quality of
Purcell's music, that he does not transform him into a soaring bird,
does not fully restore to this Lucifer the power to bring divine
light, does not allow him the "bright wings" of the Holy Ghost. He
does, however, grant to the music and the soul, while still earthbound, a massive potential power of flight, and above all the power
of radiant revelation:

so some great stormfowl, whenever he has walked his while

The thunder-purple seabeach, plumèd purple-of-thunder,
If a wuthering of his palmy snow-pinions scatter a colossal smile
Off him, but meaning motion fans fresh our wits with wonder.

Quietly but steadily Hopkins has been working toward this
simile throughout the poem, in the opening quatrain's rise-fall,

archangel-heretic motifs, in "heaves," in "his air of angels," and finally in

only I'll

Have an eye to the sakes of him, quaint moonmarks, to his pelted
   plumage under
Wings: . . .

That inscaping "eye," looking up from below as it were, sees first distinctive markings, "sakes"[5] of plumage that eloquently speak of the inner self, and that seem already to fuse angel, man, bird. "Quaint moonmarks" not only describes the distinctive "crescent shaped markings on the quill-feathers" (*LB* 83) but also evokes a pure whiteness that allies Purcell, and bird, with a beauty superior to earth and storm; "pelted" looks back to the man's genius, storm-beaten because not only heretical but simply human, though still mighty, and forward to the stormfowl's wind-buffeted but powerful wings. These specific and partial images then lead directly to the full inscaping of Purcell's genius, the full final vision, which lowers the angel to earth again, but grants him splendor there.

Darkly, majestically one with the surge and storm of its ominously beautiful elements—"The thunder-purple seabeach, plumèd purple-of-thunder"—the stormfowl yet reveals in motion and sound its grand superiority to darkness, its splendid bright purity of selfhood. Like the stallion-hills of "Hurrahing in Harvest," this seabird is a cosmic creature, of this world, not wholly of this world. Those earlier "quaint moonmarks," small individual crescents, now expand not just to the powerful and lovely "palmy snow pinions" but to that "colossal smile" whose crescent embraces the whole earth; in "wuthering" we feel and hear the mighty rushing sound, surge, beat of the bird's wings, of Purcell's music, which overcome the wind that beats upon them and the potential sounds of storm.

While not glaringly apparent without Hopkins' gloss, the final line's summary of the poem's point does justify his wry comment that the sonnet means "Purcell's music is none of your d___d subjective rot" (*LB* 84). Firmly stamped as Purcell's "own abrupt self"

---

5. "*Sake* is a word I find it convenient to use . . . . I mean by it the being a thing has outside itself, as a voice by its echo, a face by its reflection, a body by its shadow, a man by his name, fame, or memory, *and also* that in the thing by virtue of which especially it has this being abroad, and that is something distinctive, marked, specifically or individually speaking . . . . In this case it is, as the sonnet says, distinctive quality in genius" (May 26, 1879, *LB* 83).

is on the music, so sharply distinctive in shape and so powerful that it seems "forgèd," that self is nevertheless not a mere ego expressing itself, its personal "meaning" or "mood," in sound. Following Scotus, Hopkins is trying to show that display of any person's essential selfhood-in-action ultimately reveals the God-derived splendor of selfhood in humanity in general, the basic and general laws of life and their divine source.[6] Therefore the "wonder" of that final line springs from a sudden insight into essential, God-created reality. Just as Purcell's personally intended meaning was not the only source of his music's greatness, just as he (and, Hopkins may imply, any artist, any poet) intended only a particular music but gave more, so that stormbird, intending, "meaning," only the motion of flight, reveals more, reveals the special being of its kind, and so the beat of its wings fans our minds to insight, reverence, revelation.

In more overtly theological but less opaque terms, "As kingfishers catch fire" elaborates upon this concept, asserting not only the point that all true selves-in-action are splendidly fulfilling their God-given function but also the yet more crucial idea that the human self, responsive to the touch of the Holy Ghost, who "lives a million lives in every age," may become "another Christ, an AfterChrist" (May 15, 1881, *SD* 100). Unlike "Henry Purcell," however, this sonnet presents its complicated theological-philosophical theories in deceptively direct poetic terms; simplicity, not obscurity, is what we need to penetrate here.

Without knowing anything about Hopkins' theories of instress, let alone about Scotist theories of selfhood, any reader can generally understand the octave's explicitly stated point: "Each mortal thing does one thing and the same: . . . / Selves—goes its self; *myself* it speaks and spells, / Crying *What I do is me: for that I came*." And any reader can respond imaginatively without special knowledge to the initial illustrations of this idea:

> As kingfishers catch fire, dragonflies draw flame;
> As tumbled over rim in roundy wells
> Stones ring; like each tucked string tells, each hung bell's
> Bow swung finds tongue to fling out broad its name.

The octave's language, however, and its sound devices dramatize more than the evident statement about articulate selfhood-in-

6. On the difficulties involved in this concept and poem see Miller, *Disappearance of God*, 333, and Patricia A. Wolfe, "The Paradox of Self: A Study of Hopkins' Spiritual Conflict in the 'Terrible' Sonnets," 87–90.

action, and certainly more than a "do your own thing" credo. First and most crucially, the opening line's serious wordplay assumes and implies the higher origin of all this fire and selfhood, relating physical brightness to its metaphysical source. The pun on the nearly dead metaphor "catch fire" brings out the verb's literal and transitive meaning and is paralleled in the primarily literal senses of "draw" (receive, attract, elicit); the line therefore announces that it is from God's instress—Son-light and not merely sunlight—that these bright creatures derive their iridescent fire. Having stressed what was to Hopkins *the* basic literal fact, the verbs also probably "say more." *Catch* may very well play on the bird's nature as hunter, as the same verb does in the opening of "The Windhover," and so may swiftly evoke both the flash of its flight and the flash of its scale-bright prey. *Draw* may carry something of its artistic meaning (the wings in motion paint a shimmer of flames in air), but it is the water-related "draw up" that seems to function most naturally here, acting subliminally as a quiet anticipation of the "wells" of the next line and making the point that God's flame is in and drawn from both heights and depths.[7] The words therefore "play"—not quite in "ten thousand places" but in many—to multiply our sense of motion and connection and, especially, to work like similar paradoxes in *The Deutschland*, "The Windhover," "God's Grandeur," and elsewhere: from and in water is fire, from and in descent is rising flame, and in all and from all is God-derived splendor.

Second, all this vitality, flash of motion and color, ringing of sounds both tiny and sonorous, demonstrates what "Pied Beauty" has also praised: the play of individuality within a larger scheme of unity, which is here a system of action and echo, pressure and response, that will be crucial to the point of the sestet. The kingfishers and dragonflies not only give off their God-derived flame in selving but give it off in a reciprocal, perhaps simultaneous, way: fire thus answers instantly to fire, flight to flight, and, in the mind's eye, flash of brilliant blue to brilliant blue. And since alliteratively both creatures share the sound, as well as the image, of flame, the kinship seems especially emphasized ("As king*f*ishers catch *f*ire, dragon*f*lies draw *f*lame": a sound reechoed at the end of this quatrain, and emphatically again in the final line of the poem).

7. For a more specifically theological interpretation of the opening lines as alluding to the victory of Christ ("kingfisher") over Satan ("dragon"), and of the "roundy wells" as baptismal fonts, see Harris, *Inspirations Unbidden*, 43.

The same sense of reciprocity and the same intricate system of secret, and not so secret, alliances in sound are maintained in the following images, as stones, violin, and bell ring out their respective selves, small or sweet or grand, in response to the touch that sets them in motion.

That the ultimate toucher is *The Deutschland*'s finger of God seems to be remembered even in the small word "tucked" in line 3. Arrived at only after elimination of the more comprehensible variants "sweet string tells" and "string taxed tells," it carries not only echoes of the logical "plucked" but also its various meanings of "to shorten or tighten," "to press," and possibly the Scottish "beat." In sound and meaning therefore it conveys a typically strenuous, not easy, nor easily arrived at, harmony from almost painful pressure. Finally in the octave, and again as in *The Deutschland*, the alliterative chiming of "speaks and spells" makes what might logically be two separate acts seem one. The total utterance and the careful act of spelling out a word, a being, letter by letter, are fused into one triumphantly instinctive moment of speech. Alliteration may be required to carry too heavy a burden of meaning here (strict logic might demand that "spells" precede "speaks," parts precede wholeness). Nevertheless, whether necessitated simply by the demands of rhyme or dictated by a conscious philosophical choice, the line's literal and audible meaning and imaginative effect is a fusion of all acts of consciousness and language into one, quickly reinforced by the still more emphatically "uttered outright" present participle and statement: "Crying *What I do is me: for that I came.*"

This central Scotist-Hopkinsian concept of God-derived selfhood-in-action, at its highest pitch and therefore articulate, is what "might be expressed, if it were good English, *the doing* be, *the doing* choose, *the doing* so-and-so" (*SD* 151). As dramatized here, it also reflects in two ways the point of that comment already cited in relation to "God's Grandeur": "All things therefore are charged . . . with God and if we know how to touch them give off sparks and take fire, yield drops and flow, ring and tell of him." The poet's mind here touches these aspects of the world to eloquence, but they are also themselves part of a system of ultimately divine pressure and response, action and echo, act and reflection—a world in which selves in their full play and intensity are both distinct and linked because "Christ plays in ten thousand places."

The stressing that opens the sestet, "Í say more," emphasizes that now the human poet speaks in his own particular voice, after the generalized quotation of what all "mortal things," all mortal

"I's," announce in their various ways. This human, and priestly, "I" sees and "says more" because he looks beyond the splendor of selfhood-in-action to its source, because he knows that a man's higher and special splendor derives from his capacity and choice to identify and respond to the touch of Christ:

> Í say more: the just man justices;
> Keeps gráce: thát keeps all his goings graces;
> Ácts in God's eye what in God's eye he is—
> Chríst. For Christ plays in ten thousand places,
> Lovely in limbs, and lovely in eyes not his
> To the Father through the features of men's faces.

The meaning of the terse statement "the just man justices" would seem to be that while kingfishers express kingfisherhood, stones stonehood, bells bellhood, the just man expresses in action not only manhood, but "justicehood." And the wordplay of "Keeps grace: that keeps all his goings graces" not only emphasizes the relation between inward spiritual commitment and outward "doing" but at least implicitly suggests the effort of will an individual must make if his ways are to be steadfastly the ways of grace, an effort that distinguishes him from physical and inanimate nature: it is the *arbitrium*, the elective will that makes the loving choice for God, that "places him on a level of individuality in some sense with God" (September 5, 1883, *SD* 139). Consciously, therefore, this "I," this "he," who is "in some sense" God-like, "*Acts* in God's eye what in God's eye he is," not only "taking action," doing well, but "playing a role," as it were, a part the person (or poet) may think or fear is only a role, but which turns out to be triumphant reality: anyone who chooses for God and perfectly expresses that choice in action is in fact and not in fantasy one with God.

That this can be so is possible only because Christ too seems to play a role, indeed many roles on many stages. Yet to Hopkins this too is literal fact, not fiction; Christ is literally Man, God Incarnate, and he is moreover literally all individuals when his spirit enters his human creatures, when his touch of grace calls forth the answering response of affirmation. When that occurs, when the great Actor, in every sense, inspires in and evokes from his cast of human characters his own art and nature, "It is as if a man said: That is Christ playing at me and me playing at Christ, only that it is no play but truth; That is Christ *being me* and me being Christ" (*SD* 154). Therefore, as had been the case in a lesser way with all the nonhuman things uttering their lines and beings in the octave, from all the selves of earth responsive to his touch, Christ's beauty, Christ's loveliness, looks back to the creating Father. The purpose of playing here is to hold the mirror up to God.

Finally, the purpose of "playing" as Hopkins seriously plays upon the metaphor also takes us full circle to the sonnet's opening. The ending not only returns to and brings out the motif of reflection-response implicit there but also develops the swift flashing of fire-light-water with which the poem began. Like the play of light on any object (and perhaps like the play of water, "Fons vivus, ignis," *SD* 195), Christ's radiance plays vitally over and *in* the created world and is thus the high and deep source of all the fire mortal beauty may flash off in selving. As in so many of Hopkins' poems, implicit in this sonnet's opening is its conclusion, but also as in so many, the full implications of an opening line will only "explode" after the various lines and layers of meaning and imagery unfold, returning us finally—as the circling bird—to the beginning.

"The Leaden Echo and the Golden Echo" of 1881–1882, designed to be a choral song in the unfinished drama *St. Winefred's Well*, is a tour de force in oral poetry, well summarized in Hopkins' statement, "I never did anything more musical" (October 23, 1886, *LD* 149). Because its intricate choral qualities need performance, need singing even, they cannot be adequately discussed here, and I cite the poem only briefly as a deliberately dual statement of Hopkins' ponderings on mortal beauty. Through its confrontation of the two voices, the one despairing because there is no way of preserving physical beauty, the other triumphant because God, "beauty's self and beauty's giver," preserves true spiritual beauty, the poem dramatizes the two themes that have echoed through Hopkins' poetry from the beginning, and will continue to do so: sorrow for mortal beauty's transience, ever in danger in this world ("treacherous the tainting of the earth's air"), and hope for permanent beauty through trust in the God who loves it here and will eternally preserve it "Yonder." In this poem, the Golden Echo conquers, though fadingly, and the final statement, like those of "Henry Purcell" and "As kingfishers catch fire," is affirmative and deeply faithful.

In contrast, three earlier poems have stressed the strain of sorrow in this song, its fears for the fragility of mortal beauty, both physical and spiritual: "The Handsome Heart" and "The Bugler's First Communion," both written in 1879, and "Felix Randal" of 1880. They are among the so-called priestly poems, those that grew out of actual incidents in Hopkins' work among his congregations. While these do not indicate, I think, that the main line of his development was from concern with God and nature to a sudden concern with humanity, they do embody a new attempt to deal with the significance of actual people not himself, and with experiences that are not private ones between himself and God. These poems therefore raise a question on which critics and readers are divided, the question of Hopkins' capacity or incapacity for deeply human sympathy, compassion. Few readers, I suppose, will deny to Hopkins' poems a passionate intensity, but the issue now is the one already touched on in connection with *The Wreck of the Deutschland* and suggested by a distinction Hopkins himself made in commenting on "the Swinburnian kind" of poetry: "I do not think that kind goes far: it expresses passion but not feeling" (April 22, 1879, *LB* 79).

My own sense of all but one of the "priestly" poems ("Felix Randal"), and of Hopkins' work in general, is that there is in fact something lacking in the way of human empathy. Although he clearly did feel an intense and anxious tenderness for the children and soldiers and bugler boys of this world, there is a touch of chilliness to the "terrible crystal's" poetic intensity. At its best, when it is not simply mawkish ("The Bugler," "Brothers"), the flame seems indeed a hard and gemlike one, lacking the living warmth that would result from a deep involvement with ordinary humanity, a deep understanding of it. Nevertheless, what keeps Hopkins' poems from being among the greatest in humanity of vision is also what makes so many of them great in their kind, a view of mortal existence that prevented him from seeing it as the be-all and end-all. He certainly did not lack that abiding sense of "the tragedy that is kneaded up in human life" for which he praised Dixon (*LD* 155), and the dark sonnets of 1885 will come close to being truly tragic drama; nonetheless, as emphasized earlier, he regarded human life and human sorrow, including his own, from a perspective that insisted on "bringing in the infinite," seeing individual human tragedies as aspects of the much larger tragedy of the Fall, the "chief-woe, world sorrow." Ultimately, that tragedy was in turn overcome for him by his faith in the great answering "tragic" act, Christ's sacrifice, which forever thereafter cancels out the possibility of true tragedy for a man of Christian belief. As a result, most of the poems founded on "real incidents," unlike "Spring and Fall," tend to express priestly compassion, carried to an extreme in one case, but to lack the full intensity of the best poems. Hopkins was not Wordsworth, nor was meant to be.

The actual incident that inspired "The Handsome Heart" (see *LB* 86) apparently so moved Hopkins that he worked tirelessly on drafts and revisions, but it did not move him all the way to fine poetry. Unlike its metaphors, of birds and soaring muse, the poem as a whole scarcely begins to get off the ground, and though there is nothing one can strongly object to in it, there is also little to rouse response or praise. With the exception of the characteristic and strong metaphor of the homing heart ("which, like carriers let fly— / Doff darkness, homing nature knows the rest"), this is essentially a neutral poem, lacking the dimensions and complexities of the sacramental style, and interesting mainly as an expression of Hopkins' growing sense of the fragility of fine and pure selfhood.

"The Bugler's First Communion," on the other hand, which explores an identical theme, is marred not by flatness but by an almost sickly sweet pathos. Though it contains what seems to me one splendid stanza (the fifth), and one particularly fine line ("Dress his days to a dexterous and starlight order"), the poem drips with a pervasive coyness of diction and tone, felt in such phrases as "This very very day," "To his youngster take his treat," "Christ's darling," "Yields tender as a pushed peach," "such slips of soldiery." This sweet sort of phrasing, and all the "bloom-fruit" imagery, does emphasize the point that the boy's purity is both beautiful and frail, that his external "regimental red" may not suffice, without Christ's help, to make him a true soldier of God, as of England, but it evokes at least an aesthetic uneasiness and, in some critics, a suspicion or certainty of some form of homosexuality in the poet.

Except as it is suggested in a few parts of some poems, as here, this whole issue of homosexuality is probably tangential, even wholly irrelevant, to strict "literary" criticism. Nevertheless, it should be confronted briefly if we are seeking a just view of the whole man behind the poems, and of some of the conflicts and feelings in them. Though the biographical facts of the Dublin years remain incomplete, my own conviction from available evidence is that the fastidiously ascetic, self-disciplined, God-centered, notoriously overscrupulous Hopkins was not homosexual in any narrow or actual physical sense. It is possible that such inclinations were part of his makeup, and may especially have contributed to his sense of "helpless loathing" that recurs in the Retreat notes of 1888. I do not think, however, that a simplifying label adds much to our real understanding of a very complex nature, a temperament that often seems totally and toughly "masculine," in the letters to Bridges especially, but was very possibly androgynous in the Coleridgean and Woolfian sense, an emotional makeup capable of intense love and of intense sublimation of that love. Unless and until indisputable evidence shows otherwise, I therefore accept quite literally Hopkins' statement that the only person he was in love with was Christ (LB 66) and conjecture that both his human limitations and his spiritual and poetic greatness derive from that fact.[8]

The subjects of both "The Handsome Heart" and "The Bugler's First Communion" lacked the full mystery that could rouse Hopkins to fine work, while appealing to those religious and human instincts he was least able to translate into powerful, unsentimental poetry. In "Felix Randal," however, in which the subject is again mortality, this time dramatized by the actual death of a man at the seeming height of his powers, Hopkins found a strength and depth of style to equal strength and depth of theme. The relative flatness of "The Handsome Heart" is here replaced by the power of true simplicity, and the sentimentality of "The Bugler's First Communion" by an initial detachment of tone, far more moving than overt pathos, which modulates into a restrained tenderness, and finally into something approaching triumph. It is through its complex tone that the poem may best be approached.

The octave emphasizes the physical and mental vulnerability of mortal man to sickness, in contrast to the spiritually healing power of the sacraments, but also seems at pains to imply in the poet-speaker a priestly resignation, an almost casual unconcern:

Félix Rándal, the fárrier, O is he déad then? my dúty all énded,
Who have watched his mould of man, bigboned and hardy-handsome
Pining, pining, till time when reason rambled in it, and some
Fatal four disorders, fleshed there, all contended?

Sickness broke him. Impatient he cursed at first, but mended
Being anointed and all; though a heavenlier heart began some
Mónths eárlier, since Í had our swéet repríeve and ránsom
Téndered to him. Áh well, God rést him áll road éver he
    offénded!

(Markings and punctuation from revised B)

8. For a fine detailed discussion of the limitations of Hopkins' responses to human beings, see Robinson, In Extremity, 89–103, though the comments there on the homosexual issue need considerable qualification in my view. For just such qualification see Bernard Bergonzi, Gerard Manley Hopkins, 14–15; Paddy Kitchen, Gerard Manley Hopkins, 62–63; Gardner, Hopkins, 2:84–85.

There is an apparent coolness, even callousness, in that opening reaction, "O is he dead then?," and even in the following thought, "my *duty* all ended" (italics mine). A strange indifference, not only toward the dead man but toward the sacraments themselves, can be heard in the very colloquial "Being anointed and all," made still more unfeeling by a seemingly self-congratulatory note in the stress on "Í" in line 7. Finally, there is an apparently resigned and dismissive shrug of the priestly shoulders implied in "Ah well, God rest him." Even the rhymes throughout, forced as these may look to the eye, require an unforced, conversational reading that emphasizes a detached, casual, far from elegiac response to the event. In short, the surface tone conveys merely the resigned reactions of the priest to death: he has seen much of it, he has done what he can, has performed his duty, and there is an end of it; the rest is in the hands of God.

Rereadings of the octave, however, especially oral readings, can and do bring out something more, something deeper. Beneath the detachment proper to a priest, who sees death as both inevitable and nonfinal, is a deeper pain, and the apparent coolness and feebleness of language are an exact dramatization of human reaction, often seemingly stupid and numbed reaction, to loss and shock; this is the response of someone who feels not too little, but too much and too personally, the death of this one man and all it represents. Hints at such a deeper feeling appear first in the full stressing and sound of that seemingly offhand opening: "O is he *dead* then?" is very different indeed from a conversational "Óh, ís he deád, thén?" Hopkins' stressing, strictly obeyed, is in fact "the making a thing more, or making it markedly, what it already is; it is the bringing out its nature." A brief and natural attempt to deflect pain and find some consolation—"my duty all ended"—then immediately gives way to regret for what has really ended, to the sadly admiring memory of what the blacksmith was in life, the epitome of manly strength and beauty, a well-ordered and mighty physical construct. Then comes a movement inward, toward feeling with the dying man, in the keening sound of pain and lamentation, "Pining, pining," and in the visceral diction of "fleshed there," in which Hopkins seems to have taken the farrier's disease into himself, feeling as from within how it fastens on, into, the reluctant flesh. Finally, there is an attempt at priestly acceptance, distance, withdrawal, but not a complete one. Certainly the priest sighs, accepts the inevitable, and utters a nearly conventional final blessing, but the Lancashire idiom "all road" ("in whatever way") adds a special vibration to tone and thought. To some ears it may of course merely add a touch of dramatic authenticity, as the priest responds colloquially to the local who brought him the news; to mine it does more, hinting at a sadly wry attempt to retain some sense and sound of the farrier as he was in life, even some sense of his soul's presence, through the adoption of his dialect.[9]

The result is that beneath the octave's deceptively detached tone there is a strong underfeeling of real sorrow, carefully and deliberately controlled. That it is a control deliberately imposed is further suggested, rather touchingly and dramatically, by the fact that line 11 originally concluded not with "child, Felix, poor Felix Randal," but with "child, Felix, *my* Felix Randal" (canceled draft in B, italics mine).

The opening of the sestet makes explicit the tenderness underlying the octave, emphasizing the mutual relationship between priest and parishioner, almost mutual salvation:

This seéing the síck endeárs them tó us, us tóo it endéars.
My tongue had taught thee comfort, touch had quenched thy tears,
Thy tears that touched my heart, child, Felix, poor Felix Randal.

The priest has not only administered the comforting and saving power of the last sacraments, a power at which he may well wonder (this wonder I take to be the real reason for that stressed "Í" in line 7), but is himself ennobled by those to whom he ministers, becoming both more loving and more worthy of love. The mutual relationship, interaction, already stressed in the repetition of "endears," is further developed in the beautifully simple chiasmic exchange of touch and response, of "touch" and "tears," in the following lines. Finally, in the last phrase of these three lines, all the tenderness of priest and man for the pain and needs of all human "children," the tenderness so poorly expressed in the two poems previously discussed, finds a hauntingly beautiful, quietly mourning voice: "child, Felix, poor Felix Randal."

Since I am unable, even unwilling, to put a heavy critical finger on the sources of that phrase's extraordinary emotional rightness, I will comment only on one cerebral point, which looks toward the

9. While preaching in the North Country, Hopkins had of course learned the local idiom his congregations could understand, and he used *road* in its local sense in at least two sermons (December 14, 1879, and April 25, 1880, *SD* 47, 73), though in the poem it may have the additional implications suggested. Mariani suggests yet a further implication, of the metaphor of the spiritual journey, *Commentary*, 170.

poem's ending; Hopkins is typically bringing out the full meaning of the literal first name, emphasizing through juxtaposition of "poor" and "Felix" the sad irony. In the final lines of the poem, however, a yet more strange and splendid "irony" restores to the name *Felix* its literal, not ironic, meaning. Though the ending comments also on the more obvious irony, that of human blindness to inevitable death, human faith in mere physical strength, youth, happiness, it is the effect of the final line's superb image that makes of this an ending truly *felix*, to the life, to the poem:

> How far from then forethought_of, all thy more boisterous years,
> When thou at the random grim forge, powerful amidst peers,
> Didst fettle for the great grey drayhorse his bright and battering sandal!

In these lines an inscaping first occurs that seems to blend the massive strength of the man, forge, and drayhorse, a fusion that is obviously not to the spiritual honor of the farrier. It emphasizes that his strength, however mighty, was as ponderous as anvil and horse; that his gaiety, however bright and hearty in contrast to the "grim forge," was as roughly crude and disordered as its stones, as disordered as his own body will become in illness and death; and that his energetic "boisterousness" was as mindless as the mute patience of the horse.[10] Taken only so far, the conclusion seems merely that of a now not indifferent, but almost mean-spirited, priest waving an exclamatorily moralistic finger.

Yet surely this is not the way the ending feels, not what it truly leaves us feeling. Instead of the dourness of a pursed priestly mouth and spirit, something seems grandly to open and rise here; in combination with mighty strength, we sense a lightness, brightness, perhaps some underthought but overimage of Pegasus, of Hermes, and we hear a tone of real, not ironic, and certainly not spitefully moralistic, triumph.

If this is so, it is mainly because of that final splendid image and final word, which reverse the effect of "shod" in "God's Grandeur" and transform the great horse not merely to a Pegasean image of winged steed but even to a kind of swift and winged Hermes, messenger of gods, and guide of the souls of the dead. But even before

10. For clarity I have adopted A's punctuation of line 13, though B's elimination of the commas setting off "powerful amidst peers" may intentionally emphasize the fusion of elements. On meanings of "grim" (both "grimy," as I take it, but also "cruel, fierce") see MacKenzie, *Reader's Guide*, 138; on "fettle" (to grind or file a piece of metal) and on "sandal" (once a term for a kind of horseshoe), ibid., 139.

that ending, it is to the somewhat strange word *fettle* that the line owes much of its new effect of lightness. The word's various denotations are of course perfectly appropriate ("prepare," "make," "set in order," and, in dialect, "beat," "attend to animals; groom or harness horses," and "file a piece of metal"), but it is the sound of the word that is both most significant and unexpected; we surely expect some heavier, Anglo-Saxon, "anvil-ding" verb, and instead come suddenly upon *fettle*'s lightness, lift, grace, almost delicacy. The grace of the blacksmith's art then seems to pass to and change the massively heavy "great grey drayhorse" in midline, and finally, in "his bright and battering sandal," brightness, enormous power, and delicate lightness are fused. Suddenly somehow both farrier and farmhorse cease to be mere earthbound animals of heavily ponderous strength; "sheer plod" breaks into fire, and into flight, in an image so powerful that it cannot be taken as a merely ironic and moral reminder that all apparent mortal strength is actually fragile.

Nevertheless, the beauty of the final image should not blind us to the actual statement of the final lines, nor to the fact that this splendid image literally describes the splendid past, not the splendid future. What Hopkins manages to do here is something only poetry can do, and perhaps something only his own poetry can do: he expresses in one dimension of meaning his serious warning against hubris, against faith in actually transient powers; in another dimension, through imagery, he dramatizes before our eyes the translation of mortal splendor, and mortal drudgery, into the radiance of a higher glory. This, of course, is the transformation both priest and poet look for in the Resurrection, the transformation the farrier has—if Hopkins' prayers are answered—already undergone, the transformation offered to all the Felix Randals of the world. The full power of these lines, in short, as of the whole poem, derives not merely from sheer vividness of imagery but from an extraordinarily complex fusion of levels of meaning, time, and tone. The poem as a whole and its conclusion in particular are among the great examples of Hopkins' precise but mysterious incarnation of mystery.

Five years later, in 1885, also the year of the "terrible sonnets," Hopkins wrote two further poems that embody his dual vision of the value and the transience of mortal things: "Spelt from Sibyl's Leaves" (61), 1884–1885, and "To what serves Mortal Beauty?" (62), August 23, 1885.[11] Both assert the superiority of "God's bet-

11. Neither the date of inception nor that of completion of "Spelt from Sibyl's

ter beauty, grace" to the beauty of man or nature, but they are markedly different in tone and ultimate statement, the second affirmative, in part almost exuberant, the first grimly austere, though stylistically almost the reverse is true.

"To what serves Mortal Beauty?" strikes me as being somewhat arid as poetry, its method ingenious and "dexterous" but sounding a little tired, a little mechanical, reworking both ideas and devices of earlier sonnets. Its major points of interest lie in its reassertion of a consistent idea—"Self flashes off frame and face" and points toward God and God's realities—and its newly phrased, though somewhat wavering, final assertion that there is no contradiction between a love of seemingly "dangerous" mortal beauty and a love of the higher beauties of God. Summarized in the last line's "have-one's-cake-and-eat-it" qualification of the preceding asceticism, this point ends the sonnet with a dying fall curiously at odds with the poem's seeming decisiveness of affirmation:

> What do then? how meet beauty? ∣ Merely meet it; own,
> Home at heart, heaven's sweet gift; ∣ then leave, let that
>   alone.
> Yea, wish that though, wish all, ∣ God's better beauty, grace.

What seems of greatest interest here is what the manuscripts make startlingly visible. A complete though canceled draft of this sonnet immediately precedes, on the same page, in the same ink and handwriting, the first extant draft of "(Carrion Comfort)," a juxtaposition that emphatically reveals the discipline and flexibility of mind that could simultaneously work on both poems. If at the same time this juxtaposition reinforces one's sense of a difference —between the somewhat tired poetry and will of "Mortal Beauty" and the dark sonnet's poetic and ultimately spiritual intensity—it nevertheless allows us a sharp insight into Hopkins' habitual response to his central concepts and conflicts. Here, as throughout his life, he was dialectically able to take and express quite different perspectives and tones at the same chronological time of writing.

"Spelt from Sibyl's Leaves" is both infinitely more austere in statement and infinitely more complex in method than "To what serves Mortal Beauty?" It takes a most severe view of the value of mortal beauty, though that beauty does still "serve" a purpose beyond itself, while in style it is much fuller and more moving in its

---

Leaves" is indicated in B's final version, but other evidence narrows the possible time limit to 1884–1886 and strongly supports the assumption that late 1884–early 1885 was the period of concentrated work on it. See Appendix C.

description of earthly loveliness than its affirmative counterpart. Those disposed to find a priest-poet conflict everywhere in Hopkins can of course find it here: he will renounce the world's beauties, but not before reveling in them. In my view, however, Hopkins is not merely expressing his own love of dappled things, his own sorrow at their passing. He is evoking these same feelings in the reader as strongly as possible in order to make the more sharply this poem's whole point: if we go through life, through this world, as we may go through the octave, blind to its warnings, seeing only its beauty, regretting only that beauty's transience, we will come wholly unprepared to the final Judgment and the eternal rack of torment. "Life is too short for *Spelt from Sibyl's Leaves*" wrote one reviewer in 1919;[12] Hopkins' point is that life is too short to ignore it.

Hopkins called this sonnet "the longest ... ever made" (though it is not the longest he was ever to make), "longest by its own proper length, namely by the length of its lines" (December 11, 1886, *LB* 246), and the sonorously heavy majesty of the eight-stressed sprung lines does solemnly match the dark grandeur and capacious scope of the poem's vision. That vision is one that, like the "Dies Irae" hymn, combines pagan and Christian witness to the terrors of the Day of Judgment,[13] though its outcome for Hopkins is of course wholly Christian. The spinner spins, the thread is wound off, but onto Christian spools, "black, white; right, wrong." Though the winding may go on, on the rack, as for the sufferers in Tartarus, it is no arbitrary Atropos who cuts the thread of life in the end, but the righteous God of judgment who has given full warning of possible damnation.

Hopkins emphasizes the Christian's responsibility for his own final destiny through two major departures from his main source (*The Aeneid*, book 6). The title suggests that the whole world is the equivalent of the Sibyl's leaves, seemingly random like the world of "Hurrahing in Harvest" but, like it, eloquently prophetic to one who can read it. It also tells us that modern seekers of truth must make out the oracle as best they can on their own; unlike Aeneas, we are not granted the request that the Sibyl speak her prophecy openly instead of committing it as usual to leaves (6.74–76). Second, "Only the beakleaved boughs dragonish" confront Hopkins

12. *The Ave Maria* (April 1919), quoted by Gardner, *Hopkins*, 1:215.
13. Boyle, *Metaphor*, 129. For a detailed discussion of the meter's intricate *"tempo rubato"* see Walter J. Ong, S.J., "Hopkins' Sprung Rhythm and the Life of English Poetry," 123–25.

at the beginning of the sestet; he has no golden bough to guarantee safe conduct to and from Avernus, and indeed, as the poem ends, in a sense he does not return. The whole poem is in part a demonstration of the Sibyl's famous warning that the way to Avernus is easy, that the doors of death yawn open always, but to find the way leading back to light is a harder task (6.126–29). On the other hand, it does offer the hope that if we will but read the world rightly, we may see the ways to light, as well as the grim warnings of Avernus to come, constantly writ large in a universe that constantly "speaks and spells" them. In content and dramatic procedure, this is a poem of "unleaving" in every sense.

As a whole, therefore, the sonnet is not a subjective expression of regret for the loss of dappled things, nor a poem of renunciation of them, with varying degrees of resignation, doubt, faith, and certainly not an urgent warning that we should hang on to the remnants of day, refuse to unbind the self as earth is doing, resist the triumph of darkness, and the reduction of life to moral absolutes.[14] The poem nowhere offers the faintest possibility that we can choose either to sacrifice or to preserve dappled things; they will pass with a fated inevitability, and our only, and critical, choice is between the morally absolute colors into which life's "skeined stained veined variety" will inevitably resolve itself. It is Loyola's choice, the Jesuit soldier's choice, between "The Two Standards."

This is the point emphasized by the poem's complicated color scheme. The contrast is not simply that of the sestet, between black (wrong) and white (right), but one between both of these morally absolute colors and "dappled" colors. Night is not "wrong" in the octave, and therefore to be resisted; it simply is, and is inevitable. Nor is it all "black" but offers, in its black-white juxtapositions, emblems of our final choice. We cannot choose to cling to pied beauty, but we can and must choose between night's two colors, which will become, in the final night of death, either the darkness of hell or the light of heaven.

The inevitability of the coming of "night" in all its senses is dramatized in the effortful but implacable movement of the opening lines:

> Earnest, earthless, equal, attuneable, ǀ vaulty, voluminous,
> . . . stupendous

14. For the first view see Richards, "Gerard Hopkins," 200, and Leavis, *New Bearings*, 184–86; for the second, Boyle, *Metaphor*, 140–41, and Storey, *Hopkins*, 35.

Evening strains to be tíme's vást, ˈ womb-of-all, home-of-all,
hearse-of-all night.

The mere piling up of increasingly sonorous adjectives, cresting
after a brief suspenseful pause in "stupendous," then falling heavily
and swiftly into "Evening," together with the slow but inevitable
"vowelling off" of the first four words, evokes a general sense of
straining but majestic power. Within that larger wave two secondary ones occur, the first reaching a minor crest at the caesura after
"attuneable," the second at the elliptical rest before "stupendous,"
doubly emphasizing the strain to birth. The first four words, relatively quiet and restrained in tone, though somber in meaning,
focus mainly on the leveled and leveling qualities of evening; at the
main caesura, it is as though both poet and evening pause for a moment, gather new strength, and then rise to further heaving effort
in words that now stress even more strongly evening's massive en-
gulfing power as the huge dome of death settles upon the world, as
the birth-to-death is completed.

These two lines present a happy hunting ground for the "sound
for sound's sake" critics, but as even the brief preceding remarks
hope to suggest, here as elsewhere in Hopkins' best poems meaning matters, supported by sound, not replaced by it, and the variant
versions of the lines offer further evidence of meticulous attention
to meaning (see Appendix C). Originally, Hopkins considered supporting the grave and doggedly purposeful implications of "Earnest," and probably those of "attuneable," through the phrases
"dronedark" and "time's drone," which add an audible image of
the deep reverberations of evening's music, its sustained, ominously bass monotone. That *drone* was entirely eliminated reflects
Hopkins' sensitivity to the wrong, as well as to the right, multiple
connotations of a word. Since it carries implications that flatly contradict all we are otherwise made to feel about the huge majesty of
evening—implications of beelike smallness, lightness, idleness,
lazy lack of effort—*drone* is sacrificed to the less specific, but more
meaningful, *vast*.

The second word of the poem, "earthless," making the point
that evening is both unbound to earth and potently capable of
obliterating it, also has moral-religious implications that lead to
the complexity of time scheme in the second line and to the full
meaning of the poem. These implications are those on which
Hopkins had earlier commented in recording his first sight of the
Northern Lights: "This busy working of nature wholly indepen-

dent of the earth and seeming to go on in a strain of time not reckoned by our reckoning of days and years but simpler and as if correcting the preoccupation of the world by being preoccupied with and appealing to and dated to the day of judgment was like a new witness to God and filled me with delightful fear" (September 24, 1870, *JP* 200).

As indicated by the variant versions of line 2, all but two of which include the final "womb-of-all, home-of-all, hearse-of-all" phrase, Hopkins worked from the poem's inception to stress and clarify, first, that sense of "a strain of time not reckoned by our reckoning" by characterizing evening and night as time's emblems of a larger eternal scheme and, second, the ironic birth-into-death metaphor already implicit in the straining movement of the opening line and almost explicit in "strains" and "vaulty." Again the variants are evidence of his refinement of imagery in this attempt. At an intermediate stage in revision he considered a whole series of words emphasizing the apparently sheltering though actually ominous depths of the "womb" of night: "hush," "harbour," "world's haven," "dock," "world's den," as well as "pit," "well," and "delf." Eventually, I speculate, he saw, first, that the ironic prepossession of deep safety was quite sufficiently carried by the original "womb-of-all, home-of-all, hearse-of-all" phrase, a reminder that death will be a grim return to the primal darkness of the sheltering womb; second, that too specifically earthbound images could be replaced by something both larger and "simpler," something implying a more immeasurable and eternal scheme of things; and third, that the ominous and enclosing yet infinite depths could therefore be compressed in that single stark but suggestive nounadjective, *vast*. The result of this meticulous revision, whatever his thought processes in making it, is that the whole life span of human beings according to this world's time scheme, and their final destiny in eternity's larger scheme, is condensed in one swift compound metaphor.[15]

Night's triumph and night's particular splendors are then enthroned before Hopkins turns to any statements of regret for the ending of earth's dapple. Warm and variegated daylight color ends indeed, but light does not end: the vaulted blackness is royally

15. In the image of the hearse, Norman E. White persuasively finds an allusion to the Holy Week service Tenebrae, during which candles placed in a triangular frame, "hearse," are extinguished one by one, symbolizing the descent and spread of darkness during the Crucifixion ("'Hearse' in Hopkins' 'Spelt from Sibyl's Leaves'").

adorned with new lights—possibly of the moon, certainly of princely stars—fires of a new kind to replace the lost sun (ll. 3–5). That the "fond yellow hornlight wound to the west" is the setting sun, not the moon, seems to me clearly supported by internal as well as external evidence. The "yellow . . . west" collocation alone almost inevitably evokes sunset, and it is in this connection—specifically emphasizing the clouded corona of the sun's rays in setting—that Hopkins repeatedly uses *horn* in the journals,[16] though in the poem we are probably to do more than merely see: we are also to hear the dying echoes of evening's music in the other "moment" of the "horn . . . wound" juxtaposition.

What the "wild hollow hoarlight" may be is much more problematic, uncomfortably so to a critic of my leanings. The image is open to wholly opposed readings, is not ultimately clarified by other elements "in" the poem, and is therefore an "interesting uncertainty" of the sort I have argued Hopkins does not indulge in. There is evidence—thematic, textual, extratextual, and more or less scientific—that it is the sickle moon, specifically the waxing crescent moon, which becomes visible in the west after sunset and sets shortly thereafter (Appendix C). There is also what I have come to find more compelling evidence that this new light is larger, more coldly blank, less specific. Both the persuasive arguments of some major critics and Hopkins' own prose suggest that it is the chill, empty, suspended light of dusk.[17] "Hung"—and no longer "azurously" hung—like a curtain, or shroud, to the sky's vault, literally suspended for a moment by the surprising "height/Waste" enjambment, it as well as the preceding sunset "fade," to be replaced in turn by other lights. In the momentarily undefined and perhaps skull-like void,[18] the first stars gradually define themselves and become steadily more brilliant, an effect created by the growing strength and preciseness of "her earliest stars, earl stars, stárs principal."

16. See especially: "clouds behind which the sun put out his shaded horns very clearly and a longish way" (*JP* 141–42) and "My eye was caught by beams of light and dark very like the crown of horny rays the sun makes behind a cloud . . . . They rose slightly radiating thrown out from the earthline" (*JP* 200, the same entry that goes on to the comment on the Northern Lights quoted earlier).

17. Gardner, *Hopkins*, 2:313; Schneider, *Dragon in the Gate*, 165; Cotter, *Inscape*, 217; MacKenzie, *Reader's Guide*, 161, among others.

18. In an early etymological note on "hollow," Hopkins associates it with "skull" and derives "caelum" from the Greek word for skull (*JP* 12), so that the whole curvature of the blank heavens may here be imagined as such a blanched and bony emptiness.

Only after he has established what are to become the emblematic colors of moral choice, only after they are writ large in the universe and looming over us, does Hopkins turn to momentary regret for the loss of dappled things, for the vanished hornlight, for all the vanished selves:

> For eárth ˈ her béing has unbóund; her dápple is at an énd, astray or aswarm, all throughther, in throngs; ˈ self ín self
>   stéepèd and páshed—qúite
> Disremembering, dismembering ˈ all now.

At this point in the poem, "dapple" and "being" seem synonymous to Hopkins. Though ultimately they are not, here "horror prepossesses the mind" (*JP* 211), and he sees a total disintegration of selfhood, all memory of it, as well as its fact, swallowed in a vast obliteration and oblivion.[19] Dramatizing these ideas is a series of somewhat eccentric but mostly effective devices: the syncope and blurred sound of the Scottish "throughther"; the violence of the Shakespearean-dialectical "pashed"; the Irish "disremembering," which Hopkins had recently used jokingly in a letter to his sister,[20] but which here is so much more mournful in sound and meaning than "forgetting"; the rather less effective hyphenation of "as- / tray"—a too self-conscious mannerism, to the eye at least, though presumably designed and perhaps working to dramatize the idea by leaving both the concept and the reader hanging, astray, at the end of the line.

Triggered perhaps by "disremembering," the thought-change then occurs in midline: the heart, "carrier-witted" as it so often is, "recognising the good or the evil first by some eye of its own" (DN, Appendix C), does not disremember or fail to see the real implications of what the poet has just seen, just seemingly lost. Though it gives only a whispered reminder, that obsolete "round" carries also a prepossession of stern counsel (as in "roundly rebuked, advised me"), and the heart's warning is, in the final version, one of absolute finality.[21] The octave, which had begun with a kind of awe-

19. See Chapter 3, note 27, for the full context of the quotation and a companion statement on the effects of illness on perception. Seeming collapse of inscape was usually for Hopkins the result of the subjective mind's creation of "false instress," as here.

20. "But for ivery word I delineate I disremember two, and thats how ut is with me" (to Kate Hopkins, December 9, 1884, *FL* 165).

21. The canceled variant in earlier drafts is the more uncertain and rhetorically speculative "when will it end us?" (DN₂).

some birth, though into death, thus ends with a totally final death into death, ends with ending:

> Heart, you round me right
> With: Oúr évening is óver us; oúr night ˡ whélms, whélms, aňd
> will eňd us.

The sestet begins with a brief metaphorical summary of all that now remains to us; nature's emblems speak with savage clarity of our choices:

> Only the beakleaved boughs dragonish ˡ damask the tool-smooth
>   bleak light; black,
> Ever so black on it. Oúr tale, O oúr oracle!

Earth and sky, separated in the octave, the first replaced by the second, now become one inscape, one warning. Earth's elements have not been obliterated but have resolved themselves to the cutting outlines of the black boughs; heaven's elements, beautiful and splendid in the octave, however lacking in the warmth of earth's colors, have become now the metallically implacable and cold sword-light on which the boughs etch their terrible patterns.[22] Both earth and sky, in short, attack the mind with one sharp, ominous, and cuttingly savage warning. If that warning is not heeded, if we do not now respond to the moral absolutes to which all the color of the cosmos has been reduced, has always been tending, beak and sword will become the eternal engines of inner torment; the mind, "sheathe- and shelterless," will be its own sword of judgment and punishment.

In the face of this terror—which is not, as in the journal entry quoted earlier, a "delightful fear"—Hopkins responds as he has in other poems, as he almost always does, with "yes":

> Lét life, wáned, ah lét life wínd
> Off hér once skéined stained véined varíety upon, ˡ áll on twó spools;
>   párt, pen, páck
> Now her áll in twó flocks, twó folds—bláck, white; ˡ ríght, wrong;
>   réckon but, réck but, mínd
> But thése two; . . .

22. That Hopkins could sacrifice a favorite word when necessary is illustrated by deletion of "crisp" and "crispèd" as modifiers for the dragon-boughs (DN₂). Presumably he recognized that most readers would not share his private associations of firm, distinct, even steely outline, but would think instead of freshness, sweetness, smallness.

The two stressed "léts" in the first line here express more than merely resigned acceptance to my ear, more than the response of the elective will to the inevitable. Whether the lines are still part of the heart's advice to a somehow separate "me" or are, as I take them, the expression of the whole man's realization and response, I hear in them something close to the full "yes" of the affective will. If there is such affirmation here, it may derive in part from the complex relation Hopkins now sees between his present awareness and his view of earth as described in the octave. There, earth's inscape had seemed to disintegrate entirely; her dapple once "waned," her sunlight once "wound" to western darkness, no self, no order, no being at all, seemed to survive. Now, however, it appears that beneath both the dapple and the apparent unbinding, unwinding, of it, the deeper colors were firmly there, and another new and purposeful "winding" was, and is, going on to counteract that seemingly destructive untwisting. Earth's being is not "unbound" after all, but clarified; the instress of God still sustains; the inherent morality and meaning of all things are still there beneath apparently formless disorder.

Order emerging, at whatever cost, from disorder and chaos and the will that it do so are specifically and heavily emphasized in both obvious and subtle ways: by the repeatedly stressed "two," sharply emerging in meaning and sound from shapelessness; by the absolute clarity of the allied "two spools" and sheep-goats metaphors; and by the *non*stressing of "spools," "flocks," "folds"—a typically Hopkinsian subtlety in stressing, implying that these same images have previously been there in some way, but in a different, in this case multiple, number.[23] This implication is what several key words in the octave have mutedly anticipated: "astray or aswarm," "throngs," and above all "unbound," which suggests not only the haphazard unwinding of many threads and patterns but, implicitly, the sense explicit in a rejected variant, "unpenned."[24] This word may have had a special appeal to Hopkins because one meaning —"set free of enclosure"—neatly anticipates the sestet's "flocks," while a second—"un-do, erase, the order of words, the coherence of language"—relates it to the governing metaphor of the title. His final choice of "unbound," however, shows attention both to mul-

23. To compare majestic things to small, it is the difference in natural inflection and meaning between "I have only *two* cats now (since I gave away their kittens)" and "I have only *two cats* now (since the children left for college)."

24. "For earth unpenned her being" revised to "her being has unpenned" in DN$_2$.

tiple and to sensible meanings. He suspends the first connotation beneath the more comprehensible allusion to unweaving, unraveling; saves the word itself for later, more logical use in the flocks-fold metaphor ("part, pen, pack"); and sacrifices the "language" connotation, since that will become sufficiently explicit in "Our tale, O our oracle," in which it is clear that the world's "leaves" are indelibly articulate.

Certainly Hopkins' own language becomes increasingly crisp in articulation, nearly staccato in sound, as the sestet continues. In contrast to the blurred and blurring sounds and meanings of "all throughther, in throngs," "Disremembering, dismembering," we now have the sharply monosyllabic and enunciated "wáre of a wórld where bút these twó tell, eách off the óther." Where there was formlessness, there is now cuttingly meaningful distinctness, in sound as in image.

The warning is therefore grimly clear, and the choice critically absolute between the two distinct elements of the new order, "black, white; right, wrong." Although the chiasmus here has been read as an indication that Hopkins himself cannot quite distinguish between the absolutes,[25] such an interpretation seems to me more ingenious than true, ignoring as it does the clarity of the whole poem's warning, or at least turning its absoluteness into something very like dogmatic hypocrisy. Hopkins' revision of the more logical "black, white; wrong, right" (A) was dictated, I think, not by a desire to create an "interesting uncertainty" at this crucial point in the poem, but more probably by a decision to avoid the jingling rhyme, and especially by an awareness of the effect the revision does in fact have: by thrusting into the center of the phrase the words that "rhyme" in moral meaning as in sound, it focuses our attention exactly where it must be morally riveted, relegating to the periphery the words of moral and auditory nonrhyme, disharmony.

Finally, the poem concludes with its dire vision of the hell awaiting those who have failed to make the critical choice for right,

> of a ráck
> Where, selfwrung, selfstrung, sheathe- and shelterless, ǀ
> thóughts agaínst thoughts ín groans grínd.

Conscious, like Satan, of its loss of God, and of all it did to lose him, the mind is its own place, its own hell and torturer. Having failed to see in life the winding-off of dappled things onto two

---

25. Gardner, *Hopkins*, 2:314; Leavis, *New Bearings*, 186.

spools only, the mind is now itself wrung, wound on the rack of its own making, and is the self-wringer. Having remained unpierced by the beakleaved boughs and sword-light of earth, it now itself contains the eternal swords of punishment, and its thoughts of remorse and loss grate on each other like naked blades, eternally.

The physical impact of these last lines is almost intolerable, brilliantly conveyed by both meter and imagery. Especially in the final phrase, sprung rhythm's radically sprung effect mirrors meaning through the brutal beat and painful wrenching of the meter from its normal movement; the images convey not only horrors of touch, strain, wounding, but also shrieking horrors of sound in the grinding of steel on steel. Here in eternal death-pains is something far more terrible than the pangs of the birth into death with which the poem began. It should be emphasized again, however, that this physicality in describing mental pain is more than a poet's literary means of embodying the intangible, that the metaphors are not metaphors, but "plain truth," with specific Ignatian authority behind them.

In commenting on the "Meditation on Hell," Hopkins made an observation about Loyola's method that applies to his own also, and for the same reason: "he mingles without reserve or remark physical and figurative things, like brimstone and tears (which the disembodied soul cannot shed) and the worm of conscience," because he is demonstrating that the lost suffer these torments "by the imagination . . . and that as intensely as by the senses or it may be more so." As the lost suffer in hell, with the "intellectual imagination" (*SD* 136), so Hopkins suffered—and rejoiced—in life and in poetry, expressing the unity of physical and spiritual experience, of the literal and the figurative, expressing the tangible actuality of mystery while retaining its sometimes terrible, always "no-man-fathomed," strangeness.

Although the austere statement of "Spelt from Sibyl's Leaves" was not Hopkins' final word on "mortal beauty," it may serve as a conclusion to discussion of this particular theme. This poem seems to show how far his thought has traveled, and how grimly, from the early exuberance of "Pied Beauty," yet the recognitions of this late sonnet have been there from the beginning: behind the world's dapple is a God "past change"; merely dappled things are potentially dangerous, if loved as absolutes, are certainly transient, however loved, and must always be allowed to lead us back and up to their unchanging source. "Spelt from Sibyl's Leaves" presents these awarenesses with increased severity of statement, but Hopkins has not abandoned either the vision or the attempt of his earlier poems. He is still seeking to decipher the oracle, to read and hear and spell out the moral eloquence in the scattered leaves of nature and humanity, and to make of his own poetry a Christian oracle, a sacramental "Word, that heard and kept thee and uttered thee outright."

8

"Sheer Plod"
Creaturehood, Drudgery, Glory

OFTEN INHERENT IN the poetry already discussed, though distinguishable as a third major thematic strand, is the subject of ordinary mortal creaturehood. Poems on this theme explore the possibilities and failures of drudging humanity, earthbound and bone-bound physical constructs, poor Jackselves plodding through life, galled by the jading and jar of the cart, perhaps capable of glory with God's help, perhaps remaining merely a "scaffold of score brittle bones."

Paradoxically dramatizing "sheer plod" through creatures not of earth but of air, two sonnets of 1877 especially reflect Hopkins' dialectical vision. The most famous of these, "The Windhover" (36), triumphantly affirms the glory a human being may aspire to, and even achieve, through lowly drudgery and high sacrifice; the second, "The Caged Skylark" (39), concentrates on the imprisonment of the human spirit in its physical "bone-house," on the uselessness of present "drudgery, day-labouring-out life's age," and offers the hope of beatified glory only in the afterworld.

After years of hoping to discover or be persuaded that "The Windhover" is actually a straightforward poem that has been extravagantly overread and misread by most critics and teachers, including myself, I have always been forced to return, and return now, to the conviction that it is in fact as complex as it seems to be. It is an intensely concentrated example of Hopkins' intensely concentrated method, a poem in which "the truth you are to rest in [is] the most pointed putting of the difficulty" (*LB* 187). It is richly mysterious, though neither ambiguous nor incoherent.

Because its layers of meaning are not only multiple but seemingly contradictory, it does offer almost insuperable problems to

194

linear criticism, but the inadequacy of the critical process is not a fault in the poem. The sonnet simply requires a different sort of apprehension, one that "receives the synthesis of the succession," the fusion of multiple dimensions, which criticism can comment on and even illuminate, but cannot duplicate. The poem is a poem, in short, though possibly it carries poetry's form of utterance to an almost intolerable extreme of dense unity and resistance to critical explication; certainly it may be said to "go on in another strain of time not reckoned by our [critical] reckoning."

It will be clear that I take multiple layers and dimensions to be there, and to be deliberately and successfully there. It is on the acceptance or rejection of this assumption that one may first "part, pen, pack" into two flocks, two folds, the various and legion critical commentaries. In one fold stand those who equate multiplicity with merely confused ambiguity—with psychological division or simple mental sloppiness in the poet if he put or allowed it there, or with silliness, illogic, or modishness in the critic who finds it there. From this large fold issue two sorts of commentaries: those that see a crippling uncertainty and confusion in poet or poem or both,[1] and those that defend both Hopkins' sense and clarity and a general sanity of critical method, taking their stand firmly for a single interpretation, having no truck with ingenious ambiguities, multiplicities, reconciliations.[2]

In the other fold are those who may agree in principle with a position that opposes critical anarchy, but who argue that in the case of Hopkins, and particularly of this poem, multiple levels and meanings are designedly there, not to be "read into" but read out of the work itself. This group believes that its critical procedure is "the making a thing . . . what it already is; it is the bringing out its nature" (*FL* 327).

The following commentary is of this second fold, for several reasons. I cannot bring myself to believe, in the first place, that a poet so passionately and tirelessly interested, from his undergradu-

1. As in Empson's conclusion that "Buckle" reveals "a fundamental division in the writer's mind" that the reader, but not the writer, recognizes as an irreconcilable division (*Seven Types*, 244, 286), or in Bergonzi's argument that the word is a "disabling ambiguity" in the poem, though not evidence of uncertainty in Hopkins himself (*Hopkins*, 182).

2. Well exemplified in Schneider's persuasive discussion of significant as opposed to meaningless ambiguity, with its unambiguous reading of "Buckle" (*Dragon in the Gate*, 145–51), and in Raymond V. Schoder's "What Does *The Windhover* Mean?," 283.

ate days and throughout his life, in working out the most elaborate and often farfetched etymologies of words, deriving from them every possible connotation, likely and unlikely,[3] can have failed to be as conscious as his critics of the multiple meanings of so pivotal a word as *Buckle*. Nor can I believe that a writer who was elsewhere and everywhere deeply conscious of the strenuous but ultimately clear and unified paradoxes inherent in his faith and subjects could have ignored them here, particularly in a poem with which he was so satisfied—"the best thing I ever wrote" (*LB* 85). Nor can I persuade myself that superimposed poetic images and meanings would have seemed in any way odd to him, given his view of simultaneous though distinguishable mental and physical images: "It is not in reality harder for the mind to have ken at the same time of what the eye sees and also of the belonging images of our thoughts without ever or almost ever confounding them than it is for it to multiply the pictures brought by the two eyes into one without ever or almost ever separating them" (*JP* 194). Finally, though perhaps tangentially, my reading is influenced by repeated experience in teaching the poem. Almost invariably individual students, while their minds are still uncluttered by critical notes and theories, have understood "Buckle" quite instinctively, intelligently, and determinedly, in *one* sense and *one* grammatical mood, though without agreement among themselves as to what this is. In every attempt at explication, defense, and pursuit through the whole poem of each possibility, I have entertained a wild surmise that one of them will prove absolutely convincing and irrefutable to all of us, including myself. Such has never been the case. I return to the conclusion that a poem which so consistently and persistently resists single and simple interpretation is in fact not single or simple, but a most elaborate example of the method of "incomprehensible certainty."

What seems most crucial about the poem as a whole, a key to the more specific questions it raises, is its falling crescendo, its fall to rise, both in imagery and in tone. Here as elsewhere, that basic religious belief and principle are not merely stated but dramatized, so that any interpretation must somehow fully account for the movement from the heights of air to falling embers, from falcon to plow, from mastery and exuberance to drudgery and pain, and from high exaltation of tone to a lowered voice and a much quieter affirmation.

3. For examples, see *JP* 7–16 (1863), *FL* 257–73 (1886–1887), and Peters' finely reasoned analysis of Hopkins' notes on Homer (*Critical Essay*, 148–49).

Second, any interpretation must tackle both the many specific questions the poem raises and the larger one in which they converge. The former include questions about the meaning, mood, reference, not only of the notorious "Buckle" but of other words and phrases, especially in the sestet; about the importance or unimportance of the dedication, added six years after the poem was written (see Appendix D); about whether the falcon is bird, or "analogue," or "emblem," or "symbol." The single large question was identified best, and I believe first, by Herbert Marshall McLuhan: what is the meaning of the various complex similarities and contrasts among falcon, man, and Christ?[4] On the one hand, bird and man are partially similar, both beings of the natural order, the one possessing, the other aspiring to possess, the highest qualities of that order alone. On the other, the falcon, at least initially, seems to the poet to possess qualities of the divine order also, to be more similar to Christ—prince, knight, and hero—than to himself, earthbound and timidly inglorious. Third, as the very inscaping of the falcon as prince-hero in the octave demonstrates, the man, however unheroic himself, can still "say more" than the literal bird, can spiritually interpret its activity in a way that elevates both it and himself, and, finally, can understand both what it is and what it is not. Ultimately, in my reading, the poem resolves these complex relationships by dramatizing a convergence of the partial ideals in the single, total ideal, Christ, a convergence only possible through acceptance of sacrifice and fall.

> I caught this morning morning's minion, king-
>   dom of daylight's dauphin, dapple-dáwn-drawn Falcon, in his riding
>   Of the rólling level únderneath him steady aír, and stríding
> High there, how he rung upon the rein of a wimpling wing
> In his ecstacy! then off, off forth on swing,
>   As a skate's heel sweeps smooth on a bow-bend: the hurl and gliding
>   Rebuffed the big wind. My heart in hiding
> Stirred for a bird,—the achieve of, the mastery of the thing!
>   (Markings from B)

The one point on which critics and other readers agree is that the octave is a dramatically exuberant celebration of the falcon's heroic, knightly, perfectly disciplined, perfectly royal energy in action. From this follows a second unarguable fact: the central qualities of the falcon—its metaphorical royalty and chivalric mastery, its literal nature as a hunter—are consistently the qualities of

4. "The Analogical Mirrors," 326.

Christ in Hopkins' thought and writing. Christ is not only royal Son of God, heir and prince of God's kingdom, but leader of chivalric armies, whose committed followers "are *equites* (remark the word), knights, follow the profession of arms and having been knighted are bound by allegiance, fealty, loyalty, chivalry, *knighthood* in a word, to live up to a standard of courage above the civilian and even above the private soldier" ("De Regno Christi," *SD* 163).[5] 163).[5] Christ is also divine Hunter, "Thou Orion of light" of *The Deutschland*, and the terrible lion-limbed but saving hunter of "(Carrion Comfort)." Clearly, therefore, some relationship, *some* degree of alliance and kinship, between kestrel and Christ is suggested in the imagery and, as students are quick to point out, in the capitalization of "Falcon" also. That the two are not equated, however, seems equally clear from internal as well as external evidence.

Though there are further implications to the octave's concluding "stirred for a bird," its first effect is likely to be a reminder that the falcon is in fact merely a natural bird, a point emphasized both by stress and by that dangerously obvious, even close to ludicrously Poe-like, internal rhyme; this is an almost heavy-handed reduction of royal prince to small natural creature—though admirable and splendid still, it is after all, a "thing." The sestet then opens with a similar reminder, "*Brute* beauty and valour and act" (italics mine), again emphasizing what has been implicit in the imagery from the beginning: the falcon is a prince of the natural world, heir of "daylight's" kingdom, favorite of the natural morning, a flier-master of the natural winds, not the divine prince or true Master or wind of the Holy Ghost, though it is a creature that is indeed "a thing of beauty," a splendid reality that points toward its divine creator. Here as elsewhere in Hopkins' work an aspect of the natural world is not best termed or viewed as "symbol"; it is "news of God," a splendid partial revelation of him, pointing beyond itself to its source, sacramental—which is more than and other than literarily "symbolic"—in that it bespeaks, and is informed by, but does not wholly contain, divinity. It is a visible sign of a higher, invisible grace. No human eye can see Christ in full glory—"ah my dear" will remind us of the rest of Herbert's line, "I cannot look on

5. A commentary that goes on to speak of "the warfare of the Christian life," of the "recreant knight" who refuses the call to Christ's standard, and of "the disgrace of putting the hand to the plough and looking back" (163). See also such statements in the sermons as "[Christ] is the general we are to obey" and "Our Lord Jesus Christ, my brethren, is our hero. . . . He is a warrior and a conqueror . . . . He is a king" (*SD* 17, 34).

thee"—but the falcon is one of his many messengers, and as in falconry, it is one of the agents of the royal Hunter.[6]

So far, so obvious, perhaps: the falcon is both like and unlike
Christ, a partial but not total revelation of its maker. It is also both
partially like the watching poet-priest, but mainly unlike him: like
in that the priest *should* be a knightly rider following his princely
lord; unlike in the flamboyant and splendid heroism that masters
"the big wind" and contrasts so sharply with the timorous inactivity of "my heart in hiding," the sidelined malingering of the recreant knight.

As soon as we move beyond the relatively obvious, however,
complexities come not single spies but in battalions, and that
movement occurs at the moment of serious attention to the first
two words of the poem. "I caught" means more than "I caught
sight of," at the colloquial end of its spectrum, and more than its
specialized Hopkinsian meaning—"I instressed, caught, 'stalled'
the object at its greatest intensity of pitch"[7]—at the other. It also
initiates one of the poem's governing metaphors that will have crucial relevance to at least one of the meanings of "Buckle" ("come to
grips with, engage the enemy"). Since the octave begins with "I
caught" and ends with "My heart in hiding / Stirred for a bird," it
seems probable that Hopkins is again playing upon the "hunter-
hunted" metaphor so central to *The Wreck of the Deutschland*, a relationship initially paradoxical, but ultimately no such thing. As
the poem opens, the poet is a hunter, and a successful one; he has
imaginatively, mentally, captured his elusive, splendid object. But
the falcon too is a hunter, a bird of prey, beneath whose intense
scrutiny potential victims may be expected to hide, at least to
freeze. The conclusion to the octave therefore contains an apparent
double irony: the hunter-poet is now not only the hunter (in a
"hide," in a blind)[8] but also the furtive prey; unlike the potential
victims of the literal bird, he does not freeze in concealment but

6. The allusion to Herbert's "Love," first suggested by Gardner (*Hopkins*,
1:184), seems incontestable. A direct quotation from one of the best-known poems
by one of Hopkins' most admired poets cannot have been unconscious. On
Hopkins' knowledge of Herbert, see *LB* 88; *LD* 23–24, 95, 98.

7. On the connections among "catching," "stalling," "inscaping," see *JP* 211
(1871), 227 (1872), 241–42 (1874); for a detailed and fine discussion of this
point, Robinson, *In Extremity*, 47–49.

8. Possibly also an allusion to a "priest's hide" or "priest's hole." If so,
Hopkins emphasizes that unlike his Jesuit predecessors, forced to serve in secrecy
and danger under the Tudors, he is choosing secrecy and safety in a time when he is
both free and obliged to serve openly, even militantly.

"stirs," breaks cover, asks as it were to be seen and captured, in effect courts some sort of death. Again, both likeness and unlikeness between man and falcon are suggested, but even more important, and soon to be seen dominating this line of metaphor, is the point mentioned earlier: in falconry, the hawk was royalty's instrument of pursuit and capture. So it is used, and so it is, in this poem.

"Stirred for a bird" probably has one additional implication. Though it reminds both poet and reader that the falcon is a natural creature only, it may also convey almost the opposite: a joyous expression of genuine wonder that this one small natural creature could have so wondrous an effect. In this case, the "stirred"/"bird" chime is not ironically emphasizing discrepancy between effect and cause, but a legitimate and appropriate chiming. This is consistent with Hopkins' usual practice of using assonance and rhyme to indicate ultimate, or at least potential, similarity and harmony, rather than conflict. It is also consistent with this poem's way of merging seeming contrasts, and specifically with its recognition that the falcon is both worthy of wonder and not worthy of the highest wonder.

That recognition appears also in the further terms and "moments" of terms that describe the falcon in the octave, since they raise the bird above the natural order, sustaining its splendor as royal prince and master of the fields of air, while also implying that the falcon is still a natural bird, and a small one, subject as well as master of forces larger, higher, than itself. The elegant French words "minion" and "dauphin" obviously emphasize the courtly qualities of what is actually a fairly common sight in England, certainly in Wales, and so elevate the bird qualitatively to the height it is described as holding physically. At the same time, they not only assume the existence of a higher sovereign but have in their lightness of sounds as well as meaning a somewhat diminutive effect. In addition, if the kestrel is functioning here as heraldic emblem of the servant, as Ronald Bates first suggested,[9] "minion" may simultaneously diminish (to servant in the king's court) and implicitly exalt (to willing server of the King's purposes), just as Christ "annihilated himself, taking the form of servant . . . behaved only as God's slave, as his creature, as man, which also he was" (February 3, 1883, *LB* 175).

In the same way, the characteristic compound "dapple-dawn-

9. "The Windhover," also cited and emphasized by Cotter, *Inscape*, 183, and Mariani, *Commentary*, 113n52.

drawn" conveys in only three words three points that again stress the bird's mastery while suggesting implicitly its inferiority to a still higher ideal. The falcon is not only drawn by the light, drawn out, summoned forth by the dawn to command of its kingdom, but is painted in the dawn's colors, one with them: "dapple" instead of "dappled" compels us to think simultaneously "dappled-dawn," "dapple-drawn" ("drawn" in both its artistic and summoning senses), and "dappled Falcon." In light of the final line of the sonnet, where the only brilliant visual color of the whole blazes out, it is probably important that the bird, however royal, is initially associated with, and a part of, the checkered, barred, nonprimary colors of early dawn. Second, though the bird is not "drawn" as in a chariot but actually rides the dawn-winds as a knight rides his charger, there may possibly be a glance at that latent image, in which case, by an imaginative sleight of hand, the underthought doubly emphasizes the royal-riding-conquering metaphor, while perhaps suggesting that there are forces that do not originate wholly in the falcon himself. Finally, and more probably, there may be reverberations here of Hopkins' special uses of the word *foredrawn*, uses that are in themselves paradoxical. In an early essay, what is "foredrawn" is what possesses intensity and unity of being, what thoroughly exists, or is brought into such existence by the converging instress of object and beholder ("Parmenides," *JP* 127–29); later, "foredrawn" characterizes something that is only a preliminary sketch of an ideal whole, a potentiality that strives toward actuality (*SD* 153). Both senses of the word are so relevant to the poem that they may well have been in Hopkins' mind, as underthought at least: the falcon as first seen is intensely itself, though partly made so by the watcher's response of instress; it is also, as it turns out, only a preliminary sketch of a higher ideal.

The following metaphors maintain a complex fusion of literal bird, royal rider, and perhaps "striding" steed. "Wimpling," though a somewhat uncommon word, like most of those applied to the falcon, was not especially unusual in Hopkins' vocabulary, and its emphasis falls on the actual reality of the bird: implying the curve of its wing, that wing's rippling feather pattern, and perhaps its rippling rise and fall in response to the wind currents.[10] The

10. Compare the journal's references to windblown snow that "shifted and wimpled like so many silvery worms" (196) and to a glacier's horizontal waves, comparable to the "wimplings" of crosscurrents in water (175). It may be of minor interest in relation to the sonnet that this last entry ends with a comment on sycamores "falling apart like ashes."

metaphor in "rung on a rein" is an extraordinary compression that develops the bird-as-bird image while elaborating on the image of royal rider, and possibly on a rider-steed fusion. The literal falcon "rings," turning in spirals; the rider circles by straining on one rein only (there is a natural ear-pun on "wrung"); and if, as originally suggested by Richards, the technical term of the riding school is also functioning here, the bird circles like a horse at the end of a trainer's rein.[11] Although this last possibility seems somewhat dubious, reducing royal rider to obedient horse, or at best creating some logical confusion as to what is horse and what is rider-trainer-master, it is not to be categorically rejected. In light of "striding," and with the provocative though external support of Cotter's suggested allusion to Christ as "Bridle of colts untamed,"[12] it is at least conceivable that Hopkins intended here another early reminder that the bird's seeming sovereignty is less than total, that it is a natural creature with a higher master. Finally, the simile of the "skate's heel" is dual in effect: it clearly and splendidly conveys the exultation of the high sweep through air, clean, rushing, swift, perfect in balance and grace, but also in a visual sense lowers the high rider to earth, anticipating both by partial similarity and by crucial contrast the different splendor of the plow as it laboriously cuts through heavy earth.

Meter as well as imagery in the opening lines conveys simultaneously the potency of the forces the bird opposes, the surging, heaving undulations of the skyfields, and his mastery of them. Whether the opening line is to be scanned "Í caúght thĭs mórnĭng mórnĭng's mínĭŏn, kíng-" or, with stricter "falling paeonic" scansion, "Í caúght thĭs mŏrnĭ́ŋ mórnĭŋ's mínĭŏn, kíŋ-," a fall to rise is heard and felt in the combination of falling feet and rising meaning, and especially in the juxtaposition of the two "mornings"—an effect similar to that anadiplosis of the two *nows* in "Hurrahing in Harvest." The sense of a controlled rise and fall that is always resolving itself to new steady heights is then maintained by the surge of this rove-over first line—rove over in word and meter—and by the rocking effect required by Hopkins' indicated stresses in "dapple-dáwn-drawn" and especially in "Of the rólling level underneáth him steady aír." The words themselves in this line of course also effect the same transformation of fall to rise, instabil-

11. "Gerard Hopkins," 198.
12. In Clement of Alexandria's "Hymn to Christ the Savior," Cotter, *Inscape*, 177–78.

ity to steadiness: "the rolling level," in itself an oxymoronic phrase, swiftly dramatizes the falcon's control of undulation, his power to transform it instantaneously; the resolution in meaning as in meter to "steady aír" is obvious. Nevertheless, this mastery is only possible because the bird is so perfectly attuned to its surging elements; in a sense it conquers the wind currents only by a disciplined adaptation to them, a use and transformation of their power to his purposes. Such an adaptation and use of his elements the man must seek in his own sphere in the sestet.

At this moment in the poem, however, Hopkins overtly recognizes nothing less than total mastery in the falcon; the potency of both the sweep and hover, "the hurl and gliding," culminates in that predicate of unqualified conquest and heroism, "Rebuffed the big wind." In the sound of "rebuffed" alone we hear the shock of meeting of mighty wind and mightier wings, far more grandly than in the "wuthering" of the Purcell sonnet, and in meaning we already hear the awed, even abashed, admiration of the timid heart, fearful of all the world's big winds, for the royal creature who conquers them. Finally, "the achieve of" in the octave's summarizing phrase, a revision in B of A's flatter "for the mastery of the thing!," not only underscores the falcon's energy through the characteristic use of verb as noun but also adds a term and idea that will logically lead to the issues of the sestet. The falcon has not only displayed courage, mastery, conquest, which might be merely instinctive and primitive, but seems to the poet to have created in its own sphere a perfectly disciplined work of artistry, an achievement both controlled and joyous that expresses its highest selfhood. The sestet's questions are thus implicitly and even inevitably raised in the speaker's mind: What is the true nature, the true source, of mastery? What is, what should be, my own highest selfhood, my human achievement? If I compare myself to that natural hero, am I not, in my sphere, a recreant knight? Can I also in some way rise to, or summon down, those splendid qualities, that wholeness of being and doing?

Brute beauty and valour and act, oh, air, pride, plume, here
    Buckle! AND the fire that breaks from thee then, a billion
Times told lovelier, more dangerous, O my chevalier!

    No wónder of it: sheér plód makes plóugh down síllion
Shine, and blue-bleak embers, ah my dear,
    Fall, gáll themsélves, and gásh góld-vermílion.

The final version of "The Windhover," with Hopkins' revisions of Bridges' transcription and the added dedication, MS B (MS.Eng.poet. d.149.fol.10 verso). Accent marks referred to in the text are not visible in this reproduction.

As in the octave, one point at least is clear here: whatever the intricacies in mood and meaning of "here / Buckle!," the phrase brings us suddenly to the poet's present, though we may be somewhat surprised to realize that the octave's tense was the past tense, that everything seen, felt, described there *was*, and is not now. The octave has felt not only intensely active but also vividly present, and prolonged in the present, largely because of the many present participles and gerunds—two different grammatical forms, but tending to slide together in the mind because of their shared "-ing" endings. This sense of a prolonged "now" is still further enhanced if we read the lines as Hopkins apparently would have read them: "Any syllable ending in *ng*, though *ng* is only a single sound, may be made as long as you like by prolonging the nasal" (*LD* 41). In the octave there are no fewer than thirteen words allowing this prolongation, though in the sestet none. Everything in the octave, in short, functions to dramatize a literal re-calling, a calling into being again, of past experience, and a dwelling on it in a loving and wondering protraction.

With the sestet, however, the time scheme becomes both apparently clearer and actually more complex. In diurnal time, the sonnet's images implicitly move from early dawn to daytime labor to the evening fire after labor, so that metaphorically one sort of time, what we would call literal time, passes. Simultaneously, however, Hopkins emphasizes a larger, nonlinear, and to him far more literal fusion of times. As noted, "Here / Buckle!" must be present: Hopkins either says that something *does* happen, here and now, or, as I think, asks, urges, *that* something happen now. But "Breaks from thee then" involves a nearly simultaneous present and future (even if "then" means merely "therefore" it must at least imply the other meaning, "after that," and I would think the latter meaning actually the dominant one). In the final three lines, there is a similar combination of clarity and complexity in tense and time. The present tenses of "makes," "fall," "gall," "gash" obviously and clearly convey what is always so, though that in itself implies past knowledge to justify present and future certainty. But the quotation from Herbert's "Love," that sigh in the present of the heart's deep, humble, and sorrowing love for Christ, looks back in both literary and religious time, logically generating what I, with many other critics, take to be allusions to the suffering and revelations of the Crucifixion in the final line. This combination of present and past event suggests that what did happen once—the Incarnation and Passion—makes possible what always happens in the present—redemption through, and through imitation of, Christ's sacrificial suffering. Here, as in *The Deutschland* and elsewhere, all times are one time in Christ.

If this is so, it would seem logical, or at least possible, that not only times but also meanings converge and are one in "Buckle!" I will not strain credulity so far as to argue that grammatical moods converge also, as does one bolder critic.[13] Though I actually think the effect is almost of such convergence, here a choice for dominant mood must be made, and mine is for the imperative or hortatory ("or optative if you like"). To my ear, declarative meanings cannot fully account for the passionate and exclamatory intensity, simply in feeling, of the lines; nor for "here," since the falcon of course is not "here," is not doing anything except in vivid memory; nor for the appeal, the apostrophe, as to something or someone addressed, conveyed in "oh," an apostrophe both emotionally and grammatically emphasized by the comma and pause after "plume";[14] nor for the portentous "AND" and the following comparatives; nor, above all, for "then" (if he does not mean to imply something that is to come, that has not yet happened, but something that *is* happening before his mind's eye or in his heart, one would more reasonably expect "now"). I believe, in short, that Hopkins is asking, ordering, pleading that something—in fact several things—may occur that will *then* produce those further splendid results.

Among the many possible meanings, or really clusters of meanings, of "Buckle," I take the dominant and crucial one to be "descend, come down," though this subsumes some others, including specifically "plunge or stoop upon the prey." Without the presence of this meaning—whether "Buckle" is understood in indicative or imperative mood, and even with it in some declarative interpretations—it is difficult to make full sense of the last lines of the sestet, or of how the poem logically moves toward them. If Hopkins is merely saying, "Let me bring together and take on these heroic qualities," or "All these qualities come together in the bird, and/or in my mind, and that is splendid and revealing," or "Splendid selving in any sphere reveals the Creator," or so on, he could not with full logic also say "No wonder of it: sheer plod makes plough down sillion / Shine." Even under the third, most persuasive interpretation above, there would be considerable "wonder of it," a

13. Frederick L. Gwynn, "Hopkins' 'The Windhover': A New Simplification," 367: "The mood of 'Buckle' is *both* indicative and imperative."

14. Schoder's fine essay fully, and I believe first, emphasized that the comma makes the preceding nouns a series of vocatives, objects of address of an imperative verb, not the nominative subjects of an indicative one ("What Does *The Windhover* Mean?," 296). See Appendix D on the textual issue, however, and on other interpretations of "Buckle."

marked non sequitur, since the contrast is so sharply pointed between soaring bird and plodding man, high conquest and lowly service and sacrifice. Alternatively, he would have to be diminishing the significance of the latter, saying "this is not surprising, since *even* lowly service and sacrifice flash fire," whereas it is toward their elevation that the poem moves. Since I grant Hopkins a very highly developed sense of the logic and movement of a sonnet, I take the final tercet to be a development from what has preceded, not a sudden departure from it. I am even more specifically persuaded that Hopkins had a keen sense of significant parallelism in image and sentence construction, and such parallelism is marked and crucial in: "*Buckle! AND* the fire that breaks" and "*Fall*, gall themselves, *and* gash gold-vermilion." My reading of the dominant moment of "Buckle" is therefore that it is parallel in meaning to "Fall," as it is in position, and as it is in its splendid results, the outburst of divine flame.

This reading does not by any means eliminate two further meaning clusters, which seem to be functioning simultaneously with the first and actually to be subsumed by it: "come together, bring together, clasp," under which I include the meaning of "buckle on"; and "prepare for action, come to grips with, engage the enemy," which is especially assumed and subsumed by the dominant "fall, descend." The convergence of the three at this critical point in the poem occurs because of a convergence of simultaneous perceptions, all bearing on the earlier mentioned complexity of relationships among falcon, man, and Christ. (If this is so, the traditional "turn" of the Petrarchan sonnet is not merely a turn here, but a complicated summary of perceptions, and of objects of address.) The poet-speaker sees that the bird, though splendid, is a bird, a natural creature, not a spiritual prince; though "air, pride, plume" summarizes and admires the knightly qualities and bearing of the proud and crested chevalier, prince of the air, these are now more emphatically qualities of fully instressed "Brute beauty," of the falcon as splendid "thing" more than as human hero. At the same time, however, he still sees its partial, though only partial, similarities to Christ, in heroism, valor, act, mastery, royalty, and sheer beauty. Above all, he sees the great distance between both of those heroes and heroisms and himself. He therefore reacts, I take it, in two ways, which are not contradictory: he longs to attain the heroic qualities that partially reflect Christ and are necessary to his service, and he calls upon Christ's messenger to imitate its lord yet more completely through descent from high majesty and freedom to this world, through a "stooping" that is both attack and sacrifice.

The first of these reactions generates and is carried in the "bring together, buckle on" meanings. Since the opening of the sestet does in fact dramatize a "bringing together," a gathering up into one line of the bird's qualities, and since militant/chivalric imagery imbues Hopkins' thought in general and this octave in particular, it seems probable that he is saying, "Let me combine and buckle on these qualities of the heroic falcon, buckle them *'here'*"—which implies a physical and passionate gesture toward "my heart in hiding." This reading is supported not only by the passage quoted earlier on Christ's chevaliers and the "standard of courage" demanded of them but also by the likelihood that Hopkins had at the back, and possibly the forefront, of his mind the famous passage from Ephesians on the whole armor of God (6:11–17), which he at least twice chose as the text for sermons. Particularly relevant to the sonnet are his jotted notes for one of these, including "Breast plate, *cuirass* of justice—covers nearly whole man and in partic. heart," and "Martyrdom spiritual victory, not death" (October 26, 1879, *SD* 234), and a passage from the full text of a later sermon, which makes a connection between the "armor of light" and Christian penance: "The cure the Apostle gives is to put on Jesus Christ, that is the white robe of justice and God's grace or, as he says above, the armour of light. This is a robe, this is armour, that all of you either have never lost or at least can easily put on: You can go to the sacrament of penance" (November 30, 1879, *SD* 43).

If this line of allusion is indeed here, he is recognizing in the sonnet both his need for the falcon's energy, physical valor, discipline, and daring—an armor of physical light—and the fact that those qualities are only part of the full spiritual armor of God, which requires of its knight-wearer not only courage but also the self-abnegation and pain of penance. A strong "underthought" in the sestet's opening therefore may very well be: "Let me combine and take on the heroic qualities of the falcon, and then the fire that derives from 'thee' (Christ, *'my* chevalier'), but which breaks through to me from and in the falcon, will be the more beautiful, the more splendidly masterful." (I accept Boyle's suggestion that "dangerous" is to be taken in its knightly sense of "masterful,"[15]

15. Boyle, *Metaphor*, 90.

though later discussion will argue that its more common meaning is functioning also.)

That this underthought is there, and that it is one of the intended dimensions of the poem, seems probable, but that it *is* underthought, and not alone sufficient to account for the tercet's and the poem's overthought, seems more probable still. I doubt that even Hopkins would have allowed major meaning and logic of structure to be submerged in and contingent on private associations, however important these were in his mind, and however closely related to the central meaning. Moreover, this hortatory interpretation, like most interpretations based on the declarative mood, depends somewhat uneasily upon the assumption that "thee" refers to Christ, and only to Christ, and hence to an antecedent introduced only in the much later dedication, when it seems much more naturally in context to refer to the falcon. This reading also depends on the assumption of a nuance, a stress on "mý chevalier," which is not indicated by Hopkins.

This last problem can be resolved in part by assuming that he deliberately chose to leave the reference flexible and potentially dual in implication: as one might say to a child who is, for instance, playing at being a knight, "Oh, my little King Arthur," and as such a phrase would remind one of the difference between the real and the imitated king, so I suspect Hopkins is speaking here. Compare, for example, "You know how books of tales are written, that put one man before the reader and shew him off handsome for the most part and brave and call him My Hero or Our Hero. . . . But Christ, he is the hero" (sermon for November 23, 1879, *SD* 34). The windhover, "handsome and brave," has superbly acted its role as chevalier in the octave, but was not and is not the real and highest Chevalier, only a beautiful imitation, reflection, reminder of him.

Nevertheless, the difficulties inherent in this interpretation suggest that it alone is inadequate as explanation of central overthought. That main thought emerges from a conjunction of the two further linked meanings of "Buckle": "fall, descend" and, in doing so, "engage, grapple with, the enemy, capture the prey."

The second of these is so relatively rare and archaic a meaning that I do not argue for its dominance, but it seems to me suspended and very logically functioning as one dimension of meaning, a kind of thematic "outrider" beneath the primary. Following the octave, following especially from the similarity between falcon and Christ as splendid hunters, it seems quite naturally inherent in an appeal to the imagined bird to complete its flight and its nature through the stoop to earth: Hopkins asks, almost commands, the warrior-Hunter to seize upon his heart, to drag him violently from covert hiding to the strenuous life of full combat, to a kind of death to life.

It should be noted that in this reading there is no question of a command to a literal and admired creature to commit meaningless suicide—the objection Boyle very cogently argues in rejecting the "fall, descend" line of interpretation.[16] There is instead a symbolic exhortation to the remembered, newly imagined, newly instressed concept-of-falcon to become fully emblematic of the Christ it has partially prefigured and revealed, and to do so in the only way possible: it must complete its nature by abdication of the high kingdom, as Christ did; must descend, as Christ did; and in descent, in what is in every way and sense a stooping to conquer, must display yet greater mastery and heroism.

I suspect that "AND," the "enormous conjunction" William Empson compared to "shouting in an actor," and which no one can call subtle, may have had a simpler explanation than some arrived at by ingenious critics.[17] Nevertheless, Hopkins did let it stand, and as it stands its major effect anticipates "No wonder of it." It emphasizes the grand and inevitably logical, awesomely breathtaking and Pentecostal result of the imagined descent; in the tremendous plunge, the falcon's muted dappled-dawn colors burst into splendid flame, a flame that is not only more masterful but in every sense "more dangerous," not only or mainly to the falcon but to all "in hiding" who are caught up in it, caught *by* it. The hunter in descent becomes truly the Hunter, the Orion of light, and the relinquishment of high majesty is the assertion and completion of full majesty.

Thus in the opening of the sestet, at the very point at which the poet-priest sees most clearly the difference between what he has been admiring and what he should most highly admire, he sees also the actual and potential similarity of the two ideals. He can therefore simultaneously long to take on, to become one with, the falcon's heroic qualities, and can emphasize their still incomplete embodiment of the highest splendor. While the falcon of the octave has suggested the Christ of "angelic time" before the Fall, the

16. Ibid., 86–87.
17. Empson, *Seven Types*, 286. On Hopkins' correction of Bridges' ampersand here, and its possible significance, see Appendix D.

appeal of the sestet is for what then became necessary, not only the Incarnation, always intended as an act of love, but the Passion itself. There is no sudden reversal involved here, no nervous priestly rejection of the falcon's dangerous appeal, nor, conversely, a pagan abandonment to that appeal, but a logical movement of thought to complete the pattern of the life and love and sacrifice of Christ.[18] Therefore the three major meanings of "Buckle" converge at this point, and all three coincide in emphasizing a descent from the heights to enter, actually seize on, the heart and being of the human speaker.

The final lines then do make absolute logical and psychological sense if Hopkins has been thinking from the start of the sestet about a descent to true heroism and glory, though the tone now changes. There is a descent in voice and feeling, as in imagery, from ecstatic wonder to a quietly firm assertion, an assertion that does not sound to me like mere stoic acceptance, or merely sighing resignation to toil and suffering. What happens in "No wonder of it," I think, is that Hopkins simply acknowledges explicitly and firmly what he has deeply known and implied all along, though in more exclamatory terms: the relationship between the seemingly drudging servitude of Christ and the true Christian soldier and heroic sacrifice in imitation of Christ. That connection is perfectly clear and repeatedly explicit in his prose: "Poor was his station, laborious his life, bitter his ending: through poverty, through labour, through crucifixion his majesty of nature more shines" (November 23, 1879, SD 37). Or again, "It is therefore of precept to choose . . . what He has chosen, labour, and it is of counsel to choose as He has chosen, namely, the better part or the more laborious way of perfection" (November 1881, SD 164). Or again, using the specific traditional symbol of Christian labor also used in the poem, the self-castigating rebuke for his own partial failure to make the choice for labor willingly, "for the reserves I may have in my heart made, for the backward glances I have given with my hand upon the plough" (October 29, 1881, LD 88).[19]

This connection between laborious servitude and divine mastery, and this emphasis on the higher splendor of lowly and painful heroism, are implied in the sonnet in the submerged connection between the "armor of light" and the sacrament of penance, dra-

18. A point hinted at in Devlin's note on "the great sacrifice" (SD 290n138.1).

19. On the plow as traditional symbol of Christian labor see Boyle, Metaphor, 98–100, and as emblem of the cross, Heuser, Shaping Vision, 111n6.

matized in the partial likeness in kind, though not in movement or result, between the rushing "skate's heel" and the more splendid though laborious plowshare, and explicit in "Buckle!" and the following "enormous conjunction." By the end of the poem, however, there is no longer need for exclamatory or "enormous" effects of any sort. As in "The Starlight Night," "Hurrahing in Harvest," and "That Nature is a Heraclitean Fire," the recognition and certainty are enormous enough in themselves, and can be quietly affirmed *as* certainty.

The final image of the embers, which completes the sonnet's hierarchy of fire, carries the concept of heroic Christian labor to its final and ultimate sacrificial expression, and also goes beyond the imagined vision of the falcon's stoop to what this actually meant for Christ—"In his Passion all this strength was spent, this lissomness crippled, this beauty wrecked, this majesty beaten down" (*SD* 36)—though the sonnet in turn goes beyond that moment of debasement and agony, ending with the final flare and outpouring of love and triumph.

That this highest fire of all is embodied in the lowliest and smallest of the poem's images completes the pattern of fall to rise, specifically of fall to flame. The falcon's unfallen colors, dappled and "bluebleak," and therefore its fire in act and mastery, are less than its blaze of fire in imagined fall. The man, taking on if possible the falcon's heroic natural powers, but also accepting and living a "fall," a stooping, a life of drudging fidelity, will flash a lower yet a higher kind of fire, will shine in "sheer plod" more than the falcon "striding high there," and will make both his humble sword and the field of the world in which he toils shine also.

Finally, from the falling embers flashes the highest fire of all, the fire of total self-abasement, total heroism, and the conscious choice for these. Not only "ah my dear," and what cannot be a coincidental series of reminders of the Crucifixion in "gall" and "gash" and the final image of combined blood and fire, but also the emphasis through stressing on self-chosen pain ("gáll themsélves") clearly signal the allusion to the Passion. The sonnet ends therefore with the grandly summarizing point that Christ not only possessed the heroism, princely mastery, physical beauty of the falcon, and accepted the lowly servitude of the man, but chose to undergo and make the ultimate sacrifice of pain and death. The gold-vermilion that flames out at the end of the poem, the *only* brilliant visual color in the entire sonnet, is the color achieved only by total self-sacrifice.

"Fall, gáll themsélves, and gásh góld-vermílion" is therefore the culmination and epitome of the whole poem's thematic and tonal movement. In its falling crescendo, the sonnet reaches both its resolution of complexity and its heights of affirmation by descending steadily to what seem to be the depths of paradox, and the depths in imagery and tone. The triple possibilities of falcon, man, and Christ, partially similar, partially distinct, and the triple nature of true heroism converge in the assertion of that highest sacrifice of all, which produces the poem's final burst of flame, and its final calm but splendid rising. Though this sonnet, like any fine poem, is ultimately more than the sum of its parts, and though this one in particular resists dissection of parts, it can at least be said that all its layers and dimensions, when reimposed one upon the other, produce one complex but single meaning: all heroism is splendid, to be admired, to be sought, but the truest heroism is that of sacrifice, the greatest conquest is won by descent, the highest flight is achieved by fall. Out of apparent paradox comes one affirmation, out of complexity, mysterious certainty. The poem is dedicated "to Christ our Lord" not merely as afterthought or humble offering but because it is about what he was, what his service demands, what he still and always is to Hopkins: truly Lord, the ideal the lordly windhover partially reveals and splendidly bespeaks, the ideal to which the man aspires by aspiring first to the highest of natural qualities, and then by lowering himself to accept the high heroism of the plow, even of the cross, that his Lord demands.

"The Caged Skylark," written almost exactly contemporaneously with "The Windhover" in May 1877, takes a far different and far grimmer view of "sheer plod." Though probably influenced by Bosola's lines in *The Duchess of Malfi*, beginning "Didst thou ever see a lark in a cage? Such is the soul in the body" (4.2.121), and perhaps even immediately inspired by them,[20] the sonnet would seem to have been more than an exercise in new expression of an old conceit. It expresses one pervasive side of Hopkins' own thought, own partly deadening and drudging daily life, own sense of constricted and only "sometimes" song that will culminate in "The shepherd's brow." The windhover's daredevil panache is a thing of the past for this once "dare-gale skylark," symbol of the flesh-imprisoned soul. Unlike the falcon, it is neither royally free nor in its descent emblematic of glory; unlike the poet's spirit in "Hurrahing in Harvest," it cannot hurl, or even half hurl, earth

20. Geoffrey Grigson, "Blood or Bran," 23.

"off under his feet." The weight and bondage of earth, of the body, of man's "bone-house, mean house," is the total condition of human life here, a life in which "sheer plod" is only "drudgery, day-labouring-out life's age." The only source of hope in this poem is that the time will come when humanity, in death and resurrection, will ultimately find the flesh transformed, and therefore "no prison." At that time, the seeming paradox of the sestet's equation of "bones" and "rainbow" will become literal truth, the partial chime in sound will become a true rhyme in fact, and the "bone-house" prison of skeletal man will become as intangibly light, as radiantly ribbed and patterned, as the rainbow, while retaining (as "footing" implies) an infinitely finespun and delicate physicality. Until that time, however, humanity in this poem is sentenced to a "sheer plod" that leads to no present glory, merely marking time until freed from the body's prison and the spirit's impotence.

In two poems of a decade later Hopkins again examines the possibilities of physical and toiling human beings from opposed points of view, though the ideal, debased in one poem, achieved in the second, remains the same. Written, or in the case of the first at least begun, in the same month, September 1887, these two poems are the extremely difficult sonnets "Tom's Garland: upon the Un-employed" (70) and "Harry Ploughman" (71). Neither is explicitly religious, and indeed the determined secularism seems something of a limitation in the first, but both are generally based on the premises that have governed *The Wreck of the Deutschland* and all later poems: either man is merely a fleshly construct who rejects and debases God's grace and God's ordering, or he is an orderly construct sustained by that grace and responsive to it, whose most humble selving therefore flashes fire and glorifies God.

In commenting on these sonnets, Hopkins was rightly con-cerned about their possibly excessive ingenuity and opacity:

> I enclose two sonnets, works of infinite, of over great contriv-ance, I am afraid, to the annulling in the end of the right effect. They have also too much resemblance to each other; but they were conceived at the same time. They are of a "robustious" sort and perhaps "Tom's Garland" approaches bluster and will remind you of Mr. Podsnap with his back to the fire. They are meant for, and cannot properly be taken in without, emphatic recitation; which nevertheless is not an easy performance. (December 22, 1887, *LD* 153)

Both Dixon and Bridges were too baffled by "Tom's Garland" to be reminded of Mr. Podsnap or anything else, and most later readers probably react with the same bafflement; Hopkins' lengthy explanation of the sonnet (February 10, 1888, *LB* 272–74) is almost essential to any but the most clairvoyant reader. Tom himself (*not* exemplifying the unemployed, in spite of the misleading subtitle) does emerge from the poem's ingenious opacity as a lumptious but robustly cheerful epitome of useful "sheer plod," of literal "day-labouring" that is hard, but not (Hopkins says) soul-killing or heart-crippling. He is a figure who wears his own humble "garland" of honor, the crown of laborer, the crown of boot-nails, and he is therefore of course in clear contrast with those denied function or place or honor of any kind, the wolfish unemployed whose "packs infest the age." But on the whole Hopkins does not succeed here in his habitual attempt to make syntax and imagery function multidimensionally while still making sense. The poem seems to me an example of what happens to Hopkins' style when his theme lacks the depths and complexities of spiritual content, when he tries to write on a secular theme rather than on a subject and theme somehow related to his personal and religious experience. Although the religious premises suggested earlier are implicit here, they are so thoroughly submerged beneath the uneasily semiradical, semireactionary political point and the attempted "rollic" in tone (*LB* 266) as to be almost invisible, and it seems as though Hopkins tried in some instinctive (or deliberate) way to compensate for lack of genuine mystery in concept through sheer ingenuity and obscurity of style, through "over great contrivance."

In "Harry Ploughman," however, the subject is much more congenial to Hopkins' instinctive, though perhaps somewhat condescending, way of seeing ordinary man: archetypal, nonpolitical, "child of Amansstrength," perfectly performing whatever his humble function may be to the greater glory of God—in this case, a function specifically associated with specifically Christian labor. The title alone succinctly makes the point of the whole poem: the man is named by his function and *is* his activity—"*What I do is me: for that I came.*" Unlike the disjointed body of the commonwealth in "Tom's Garland," Harry is a massive construct who embodies in one individual the ideal whose parts work in perfect harmony to create both order and beauty, and to fulfill the purpose for which they were created.

The method of the poem reflects an ingenious, though still overly contrived, attempt to match the idea. The octave, unlike that of "The Windhover" and other poems, does not instantly grasp and express the inscape of the object, but assembles the total human construct part by part, building it carefully through imagery that emphasizes both massive solidity and fluidly graceful harmony. ("Harry" might well say to his creator, as Hopkins to his, "Thou hast bound bones and veins in me, fastened me flesh.") From the opening lines, "Hard as hurdle arms, with a broth of goldish flue / Breathed round," Harry not only has the toughness of the farm implements he both resembles and controls but is also surrounded by his own delicate kind of "garland," halo as it were, even though it is only that humble physical aureole of golden hair on the mighty arms.[21] The massive organization of power slowly assembled in the octave then produces in action this sonnet's elaborate version of the earlier, simpler, more effective phrase, "sheer plod makes plough down sillion / Shine." In the concluding lines, Harry's conquest of the cold and resistant sillions produces a characteristic fusion of flashing fire and flashing water—"With-a-fountain's shining-shot furls"—and demonstrates "the achieve of" any labor perfectly accomplished, the honor that may be "flashed off" even so humble an "exploit" as plowing. Though self-consciously ingenious in style, like "Tom's Garland," though more obscure than mysterious in syntax, diction, metrical and formal cleverness, this sonnet does at least create a residual sense of an archetypal nobility, does leave on the mind's retina an afterimage of Harry, and of simple humanity in general, as a mighty implement, even a mighty soldier, of God.

In the remaining two years of his life Hopkins wrote a finer pair of sonnets on this theme, opposite sides of the same coin, one of which honors another humble soldier of God, while the second denies man even dignity, let alone glory. "St. Alphonsus Rodriguez" (73), October 1888, is one of Hopkins' most simple and most moving affirmations of the heroism of daily drudgery, of the glory possible through inner self-conquest and outer fidelity to lowly duty. In contrast, "The shepherd's brow" (75), April 3, 1889, is so grim in its view of humanity that it makes man simply an object of disgust, or at best contempt, a death-bound animal whose trivial "sheer plod" is both ridiculous and futile. In both, Hopkins treats his own most deeply personal concerns of those years, though the first is an objective public poem, the second intensely private.

"St. Alphonsus Rodriguez" was "written to order" as a tribute to the saint on the first feast following his canonization, a circumstance that may in part account for the poem's relative simplicity:

21. Compare "Sunrise sky gracefully swept in fine hair flue" (*JP* 160).

"The sonnet (I say it snorting) aims at being intelligible" (October 3, 1888, *LB* 292, 293). But as the "terrible sonnets" indicate, Hopkins was in any case increasingly inclined to treat the theme of "the war within," the theme that links him so intimately with his subject in this poem, with a complex austerity, if not transparent simplicity, of style. Moreover, the sonnet demonstrates his ability to adapt his cadence to subject as well as to circumstance and theme: he offers to the simple laybrother and porter of the Jesuit College in Majorca a tribute Alphonsus would have understood— strong, honest, unostentatious, relatively simple though deeply suggestive in language.

As the various drafts of the sonnet indicate, Hopkins labored both to raise initial prosaic flatness to expressive simplicity and to discipline rich obscurity to rich starkness.[22] The versions of the opening line clearly illustrate the first direction of revision, as the flat "grow" is immediately replaced by "flower," and that too-soft word is in turn replaced by the important flame imagery:

		flower
Bod.$_1$a:	Honour shd. ~~grow~~ from exploit, so we say,
b:	Honour should flash from exploit, so we say,

Bod.$_2$: ⎰ Glory is a flame off exploit, so we say,
⎱ Glory should flame off exploit, so we say,

A: Honour should flash from exploit, so we say,

B: Honour is flashed off exploit, so we say,

The converse movement of revision, which chastens rich complexity to suggestive directness, is illustrated by the drafts of the sestet's opening lines. Though early versions are again relatively straightforward, Hopkins arrived in midcourse at some very characteristic compound epithets for God that he was later to sacrifice: "continent carver" (Bod.$_1$b); "mountain-mason," "mountain-quarrier," "continent-wright," "world-wright" (Bod.$_1$d); "earthsmith" (Bod.$_1$e); "continent-quarrier, earth-wright" (A). Bridges evidently objected to the A version as "cheeky," a charge Hopkins denied, somewhat snidely: "the imagery as applied to God Almighty being so familiar in the Scrip-

22. The drafts are A (*LB* 293), B, and two much-revised early drafts, abbreviated in the text Bod.$_1$ and Bod.$_2$. See Appendix D.

218 ■ Gerard Manley Hopkins and the Language of Mystery

ture and the Fathers" (*LB* 296). Yet he did finally eliminate these epithets, and though one feels some regret for their loss, Hopkins' instinct (and Bridges') was probably correct: though potent and ingenious, these compounds would have been a little too clever, and therefore a little out of place, in a poem that is otherwise simple, and dedicated to a simple and saintly man.

The ultimate success in suiting style to subject is particularly epitomized in the final lines of the poem, in which all the words, including rhyme words, are utterly ordinary; in which the simple phrase "world without event" carries both sad and triumphant echoes of "world without end"; in which "watched the door" is so totally simple and yet so moving; in which the last line's awkward rhythm and difficult juxtaposition of "a's" in midline create, in spite of ellision, a slightly awkward beauty, a slightly tense and stumbling harmony, appropriate to Saint Alphonsus himself:

> . . . while there went
> Those years and years by of world without event
> That in Majorca Alfonso watched the door.

The sonnet, in short, is a movingly direct tribute to one man whose humble work and quiet heroism won him glory, and an affirmation of all such drudgery and heroism; it was granted to Alphonsus— and one hopes to Hopkins also—that all the trumpets, silent here, sounded for him on the other side.

In apparently violent contrast to that view of "sheer plod" is the view of "The shepherd's brow," a poem that Gardner called "a work of the most downright Swiftean cynicism" and that Bridges refused a place among the finished poems in the first edition, saying that it "must have been thrown off one day in a cynical mood."[23] Far from being "thrown off," however, the sonnet resulted from laborious and concentrated effort, and its bitterness was not the expression of a passing mood but was intimately related to Hopkins' total religious vision, as well as to his far from passing sense of personal futility and his gift of self-mockery.

Very early in his life Hopkins stated, a little artily, an idea that would become painfully as well as triumphantly true for him in later years: "the *sordidness* of things, wh. one is compelled perpetually to feel, is perhaps . . . the most unmixedly painful thing one

23. Gardner, *Hopkins*, 1:155; Bridges, *PB* 123. For the many drafts and revisions, see Appendix D.

knows of: and this is (objectively) intensified and (subjectively) destroyed by Catholicism" (September 12, 1865, *FL* 226–27). It is obvious that many of his poems demonstrate and announce the power of the Catholic faith to "destroy" the sordidness of humanity and the world, to cleanse and ennoble both. On the other hand, from *The Wreck of the Deutschland* on, and exactly because of his faith, Hopkins was painfully aware of the wretched contrast between what physical, arrogantly godless humanity is and what it might be, what God created it to be.

> Man was made to give, and mean to give, God glory. . . . Does man then do it? Never mind others now nor the race of man: DO I DO IT?—If I sin I do not . . . . No, we have not answered God's purposes, we have not reached the end of our being. . . . Are we his singing bird? we will not learn to sing. Are we his pipe or harp? we are out of tune, we grate upon his ear. Are we his glass to look in? . . . we misshape his face and make God's image hideous. Are we his book? we are blotted, we are scribbled over with foulness and blasphemy. Are we his censer? we breathe stench and not sweetness. . . . If we have sinned we are all this. (ca. 1882, *SD* 239–40)

No less than the more triumphal poems, "The shepherd's brow" is a crafted, though painful, product of this faith. While it concentrates wholly on man the animal, and offers almost no hope of redemption, "cynical" describes it no better than it fully describes Swift, since the poem issues from a disgust that is evidence, not denial, of a high though defeated belief in human possibility. Maturity, an increasingly grim knowledge of himself and others, and specifically a desolate sense that "all my world is scaffolding" (October 2, 1886, *LB* 229) lend this sonnet's style and thought an almost brutal cutting edge, a satiric savagery uncharacteristic of most of Hopkins' work. Yet it is exactly because the ultimate source of that savagery is the same deep-held faith and wide vision that had informed his life and poetry from the beginning that the poem is one of Hopkins' finest.

On first reading, the opening quatrain is deceptively simple. It seems merely to present, directly and dramatically, two heroic and majestic pictures, one of awed acceptance of the power of the heavens, one of tragic rebellion against it, which will serve to emphasize by contrast the later description of puny, wholly unmajestic, wholly contemptible, man:

Early complete draft of "The shepherd's brow," with revision of lines 1–7, MS H (MS.Eng.poet.d.150.fol.44 recto), referred to in the text as H₁a and b.

> The shepherd's brow, fronting forked lightning, owns
> The horror and the havoc and the glory
> Of it. Angels fall, they are towers, from heaven—a story
> Of just, majestical, and giant groans.

"The shepherd's brow," complete draft with revisions (MS.Eng.poet.d. 150.fol.44 verso), referred to in the text as H₂a and b.

The shepherd seems to represent a somewhat Lear-like, though more primitive, and more reverent, natural man, confronting the elements' fury and glory, and heroic even in his frailty. The addition of "brow," which appears only in the last of many revisions, emphasizes both the physical fragility of the human "bone-house," the brittle "scaffolding" soon to be ridiculed, and the mental and

"The shepherd's brow," continuation of preceding revisions and final version (MS.Eng.poet.d.150.fol.45 recto), referred to in the text as H₂c and H₃.

spiritual heroism of the man: like the nun and the poet of *The Deutschland*, he reads "the unshapeable shock night" correctly, acknowledges God's terror and splendor, and says "yes."

This interpretation, while not a "misreading," is an under-reading of the full complexity here, because it ignores the logical inconsistency between the glorification of the shepherd and the later "But man—we, scaffold of score brittle bones"; the shepherd, after all, is presented as "man" also. Though such a small inconsistency might not be a fruitful matter to notice or quibble over in another poet, in Hopkins it is usually a pointer toward some larger idea, in this case an idea that emerges from the typical complexity in time scheme.

Although the tense and therefore the action throughout the sonnet are present, both the shepherd and certainly the fall of the angels seem centuries removed in time from modern humanity, the "we" of the next quatrain. Hopkins therefore seems, in the first place, to be superimposing times in order to call up simultaneously in a dramatic present the three pictures, two of them heroic, though contrasting in heroism, the third entirely unheroic. We are thus allowed and compelled simultaneously to "look on this picture and on this," and obviously "Man Jack" in general and the introspective, futilely intellectual poet in particular do not profit from the comparison. Second, the conflation of times, which has a theoretical basis in Hopkins' notions about the possible coincidence of angelic and historic time,[24] supports what seems imaginatively to happen in the first four lines: we not only see the shepherd as a figure of colossal human grandeur, even unfallen grandeur, reverence, innocence, but sense that he actually watches the fall of Lucifer and his angels as the lightning of God's anger casts them from heaven. Further conflations of both Christian and pre-Christian time may also be sensed here: as suggested by Mariani, the shepherd may be Milton's shepherd, Moses, and even the Shepherd, Christ himself, whom Moses prefigures[25] (in the latter case, he not only acknowledges God's lightning but in fact "owns," possesses it); subliminally also a picture may be evoked of the shepherds who watched and heard the radiant announcement of the Nativity, saw the counterlight to that first lightning of anger, and owned "the glory of it." Finally, and less conjecturally, the similarity between the fallen angels and the fallen Titans suggests that

24. See Hopkins on the fall of Satan's angels "from their selfraised pinnacle and tower of eminence" (*SD* 202) and Devlin's comments on the time scheme here suggested (*SD* 112–13; 309n202.1). "Forked lightning" may specifically allude to the Holy Spirit's "seven jets or currents of breath," associated by Hopkins with "the stress of God's anger which . . . called into being fire against the Devil and his angels" (*SD* 137).

25. Mariani, *Commentary*, 305–6; Cotter, *Inscape*, 237; Ellis, "Authentic Cadence," 241.

Hopkins was also trying to move beyond even this capacious but strictly biblical time scheme to encompass a vision of all falls in all times; this similarity, while not explicit here as in *Paradise Lost*, is implicit in the "giant groans" of the sonnet's final version and in the repeated "angel-giants" and "giants" of earlier drafts.

It is in relation to this vast time scheme that ordinary man should see himself, and does not—"hand to mouth he lives." It is in contrast to the stature and glory achieved by acknowledgment of God, in contrast even to the grandeur of mighty pain and fall, that Hopkins does see him:

> But man—we, scaffold of score brittle bones;
> Who breathe, from groundlong babyhood to hoary
> Age gasp; whose breath is our *memento mori*—
> What bass is *our* viol for tragic tones?

Physically fragile still, but wholly lacking now the shepherd's physical as well as spiritual heroism, fallen indeed but wholly stripped of majesty, no "tower" but a mere "scaffold," incapable of "giant groans" and able only to gasp out his contemptible "music" of mortality, man is now simply a flimsy skeletal structure, unredeemed by the Shepherd, unresponsive to the terrible and glorious stress of grace, a ghastly death-figure even in life. As "scaffold" further suggests, we are each our own hanging place, our site of shameful death, with our breath of life our death rattle, a daily reminder of the death we live now as well as of the final death to come. As Hopkins commented in his meditation "On Death," "this breathing body is my corpse and I am living in my tomb" (*SD* 245).

The echoes of Shakespeare in these lines—the compression of the "Seven Ages of Man" in "Who breathe . . . gasp," and the parallels to Macbeth's "Tomorrow" speech especially—reflect the sonnet's movement from the great supernatural "stories" of the past, biblical, classical, Miltonic, to the present story of natural man, a tale signifying nothing. The Shakespearean allusions may also offer a hint that "scaffold" carries one additional meaning, its archaic sense of "platform for performance," though even Shakespearean tragedy seems a thing of the past here, and we see instead the stage of Beckett.[26] Not towering, nor falling from gigantic

26. In "groundlong" Gardner further suggests an analogy to "groundling," inferior spectator (*Hopkins*, 1:123), a metaphor that does apply to the poet in the final lines, and to both poet and readers as we watch the dramatic scenes of the opening quatrain.

heights, man now creeps through his life-role both as literal baby
and as adult, and his lines are only the gasp and splutter of a dying
and death-bound animal. The revision from the original "lute" to
the final "viol for tragic tones?" may have been made in part for the
sake of a grim double ear-pun ("bass"/"base"; "viol"/"vile"),[27] and
the manipulation of terminal rhyme is such that "tragic tones"
must remind us of the "giant groans" that once did supply the majestic ground melody for true tragedy.

The sestet, beginning with that snorting exclamation of contempt "He!," goes on to fill out the picture of man as Yahoo, scrab-
bling for food, excreting in shame, his humanity, his proud claim
to be Man, a mere travesty:

> He! Hand to mouth he lives, and voids with shame;
> And, blazoned in however bold the name,
> Man Jack the man is, just; his mate a hussy.

From the phrase "hand to mouth" Hopkins typically extracts all
possible implications, pressing down on a clichéd metaphor until it
comes to life and yields its full significance. It obviously develops
the precariousness of human life emphasized in "scaffold of score
brittle bones"; it reminds us that man lives only in the moment,
without reference to that eternal time scheme established in the
opening lines; it underscores the idea that we live with greedy hand
literally to mouth, as baby especially, but also as adult, and can
therefore hardly speak lines or utter music of tragic resonance. In
conjunction with "and voids with shame" it sums up man's total
body, total life cycle: in eating and excretion consists his entire, and
entirely shameful, performance on the stage of life. Since "voids"
may also be connected with the dramatic metaphor underlying the
poem, there is the additional implication that both man and his
harlot-mate "void the stage" as contemptibly as they had entered
upon it, exit creeping, animalistic, without dignity. No Christ
"plays in ten thousand places" here to save us from our roles as
shabby extras in a very shabby play.

In the following lines the dramatic metaphor becomes almost
explicit; man is playing out a grotesque travesty, playing badly a
false role that cannot disguise the true face behind the makeup or
ennoble the inglorious company in which he plays. In whatever

27. "What bass can *his* lute bear to tragic tones?" (H_1a). As circumstantial evidence for Hopkins' awareness of the pun on "base," see "But how is it you cannot
judge of a melody without hearing a bass? (this is the standard spelling: *you* write
'base')" (April 27, 1881, *LB* 125).

bright colors he advertises himself as "man," however gloriously chivalric seems the part he plays, the name he takes, the pasteboard shield he bears, whatever his pretenses to the radiance of God's fire, he is still merely the clown, common, crude, ridiculous, and indeed only barely human: "Man Jack the man is, just." (We should also hear the ironic echo in this word play of "*just*, majestical, and giant groans.")

With the concluding lines comes a typically Hopkinsian turn in thought, a movement from "we" to "he" to "I," from general condemnation of humanity to examination and condemnation of himself. He presents himself as being as ignominiously petty in his spluttering pretensions as all men, at least as inferior as they to that original shepherd fronting the lightning, and at an even greater remove than they from any sort of reality:

> And I that die these deaths, that feed this flame,
> That . . . in smooth spoons spy life's masque mirrored: tame
> My tempests there, my fire and fever fussy.

Both phrases of the first line here have typically multiple meanings that synthesize what has been and is being said. "And I that die these deaths" (a phrase appearing in all drafts) condenses the points, first, that he daily dies the deaths all men die each day on the scaffold of self; second, that he dies the deaths of men, angels, giants, constantly reliving, redying those falls in himself; third, with specific comment on himself as the fussily and futilely intellectual poet, that he dies and redies these deaths because he thinks of them, envisions them, writes about and dramatizes them, instead of simply being content to gasp out his own Jack-self life like other men. Similarly, "that feed this flame" would seem to have a triple meaning: first, he strives to keep alive the little spark of life in himself (an interpretation supported by the variant "that fan this flame" in H_2a and b); second, he is fuel for what he has earlier called "nature's bonfire" (72), part of the total conflagration of the world; and perhaps above all, he is a constant target of God's "forked lightning" because he constantly provokes God's anger without even recognizing, "owning" it.

With that long hiatus in the next line comes the slow, wryly despairing admission of how far removed he is even from the grotesque masque of human life, let alone from giant tragedy, how ridiculously his finicky fire, his tempests (in a teaspoon), contrast with, pervert, the grand lightning and storm of the opening lines. The result of this recognition, and the result of elaborate revision

(Appendix D), is that the sentence itself peters out, lacks the predicate the *thats* have anticipated, simply expires, in syntax, in the fussy "f" and "s" alliteration, in the weakness of the feminine rhyme, guttering and dying in a final, feeble splutter.

In the image of the "smooth spoons" the "heart in hiding" of "The Windhover" is dramatized in a new way, one that allows no possibility of that heart being roused to life and action. The nature of the image itself indicates Hopkins' withdrawal into a small, civilized, and prissy world, a Prufrock world remote not only from storm and tempest but even from the crude activity of common life. From this safe world, safe covert, he does not even stir to see a royal windhover in action, let alone to "front" the lightning, but with peeping cowardice "spies" (and spies on) the world as it is reduced, made smooth and safe, but also distorted, in miniature. Since life has already been shown to be a puny thing, this further reduction of it debases it almost to invisibility, and of course removes the poet even further from any possibility of grandeur; since life has also been characterized as an imitation, a masque (and probably a deceptive "mask" as well), his vision of it now in mere reflection puts him at yet a third remove from even such ephemeral reality as our world possesses.

In the dramatic metaphor underlying the poem there are some sad and satiric echoes of those earlier assertions that the just man "Acts in God's eye what in God's eye he is— / Christ" and that the union between humanity and Christ is "no play, but truth." If that shepherd of the opening lines is in any way Christ, or more probably at least an "AfterChrist" because of his reverence, the ideal he embodies does not continue to hold center stage, in no way affects, in no way represents, the play or the actors of common existence. Life is now neither a splendid epic drama that is in fact splendid truth nor a grand tragedy accompanied by the deep music of tragic suffering; it is not even a courtly masque, but an antimasque of satyrs, clowns, and fools, accompanied by the absurd dissonance of gasping breath, a contemptibly comic, not even tragicomic, dance of death. In this poem, humanity in general and the poet-speaker in particular have failed the divine audition, have failed even to meet the call to it.

Late though this fine poem is, and intensely serious as it is in voicing one side of Hopkins' thought and vision, its view of life, of "sheer plod," of God's fire and nature's bonfire, was not his total view. Though the sardonically self-critical humor of the ending does imply a larger and healthier perspective, the vision of the whole is grimly reductive. Bridges' instinct was therefore right to the extent that it recognized as more deeply characteristic the sort of wider view that finds expression and synthesis in a slightly earlier but thematically more typical poem, "That Nature is a Heraclitean Fire and of the comfort of the Resurrection" (72), July 1888.

On September 25, 1888, Hopkins wrote somewhat puckishly to Bridges, "lately I sent you a sonnet, on the Heraclitean Fire, in which a great deal of early Greek philosophical thought was distilled; but the liquor of the distillation did not taste very Greek, did it?" (*LB* 291). Indeed it does not taste very Greek, but it does taste most distinctively Hopkinsian, a distillation of almost all his own philosophical and religious thought. In this sonnet, all the themes discussed in this and previous chapters find their meeting point and fusion, and we come full circle back to the themes reconciled in *The Wreck of the Deutschland*, explored—sometimes separately, sometimes together, in later poems—and now again newly reconciled: the themes of the vitality and significance of nature, but also its inferiority to higher beauties; the distinctive selfhood but mortality of human beings, foundering and wrecked on all the world's reefs; the apparent transience and futility of their "treadmire toil," but the final glory of their ultimate destiny. Like *The Deutschland*, this poem concludes that neither God's nor nature's fire will obliterate man's "firedint" completely, that God's beacon will guide all wrecked ships to haven, that "Man Jack" will not remain a scaffold of brittle bones but will be transformed to that which, produced by fire and stress, survives all fire, "immortal diamond."

For this rich distillation of pervasive themes the Petrarchan sonnet form, even as Hopkins had already stretched its limits, was not capacious enough; this sonnet is therefore in fact "the longest ever made," employing not only six-stressed Alexandrine lines but three codas. That Hopkins still felt the need of some form, however, that instead of abandoning the sonnet entirely he transformed it almost beyond recognition, while insisting that the transformation was lawful, reflects his deep-seated need and respect for justification in sanctioned tradition. He was willing to break every law in the book of the "poetic decorum" Bridges insisted on, but even in his most idiosyncratic poetry he was not willing to break what seemed to him the laws of God, the laws that give both freedom and shape to the formless. In form, therefore, as in idea, this sonnet reaches toward the limits of anarchy while demonstrating the divine order that always controls it.

The first nine lines, the "octave" and the opening of the "ses-

tet," are an inscaping of controlled anarchy understood in Heraclitean terms, an instressing of "strife" at work upon the world's elements, a process that involves the disintegration of individual
things but the constancy of process itself, the emergence of a kind
of cyclical permanence and poise from the tension of opposing
forces.[28] Thus the first two lines, which generally describe the
proud bravado of the high clouds in their roistering march and
revel, also specifically emphasize both their instability and their
masterful power and continuity:

Cloud-puffball, torn tufts, tossed pillows ∣ flaunt forth, then chevy on
an air-
built thoroughfare: heaven-roysterers, in gay-gangs ∣ they throng; they
glitter in marches.

The first three phrases alone make the point that the clouds are
constantly losing but constantly regaining their light but chubbily
round shape in different form, and the following images dramatize
the idea that "hunted" though the clouds are by the forces of Strife,
they are also themselves hunters, racing ("chevy"-ing) across the
skyfields, their gay roll and gallop emphasized by the meter's
jaunty rise and fall. Most important of all, "they glitter in
marches": though they are mere air and water, they are the basic
Heraclitean element of fire also, and with all their gaily abandoned
and unstable lightness they form an army more than sufficient to
match in power and supersede in beauty the "Squadroned" marks
left by man's futile toil. ("Marches" may also have a secondary association with the skyfields, the sky's borderlands, but the military
metaphor seems the dominant one.)
    Cloud-and-wind motion then modulates into, and in part
causes, the next picture, the one that begins the sliding, and darkening, descent to earth, which finally reaches the depths of mud,
and man:

Down roughcast, down dazzling whitewash, ∣ wherever an elm arches,
Shivelights and shadowtackle in long ∣ lashes lace, lance, and pair.
Delightfully the bright wind boisterous ∣ ropes, wrestles, beats earth bare
Of yestertempest's creases; ∣ in pool and rutpeel parches
Squandering ooze to squeezed ∣ dough, crúst, dust; stánches, stárches

28. For useful background, see Gardner on the poem's combination of
Heraclitean and Empedoclean philosophy and his demonstration of its extraordi-
nary garnering of sights and actual phrases previously recorded in the journals
(*Hopkins*, 1:162, 164).

Squadroned masks and manmarks ┃ treadmire toil there
Fóotfretted in it. Million-fuelèd, ┃ nature's bonfire burns on.

The combat remains one in which a blurring of shape occurs, as light-and-shadow patterns crisscross and interweave, and yet one in which the elements remain in part distinct ("lashes" and "lance" especially), blurring only to create a new order ("pair").[29] That both the combat and the elements engaged in it are simultaneously heedlessly joyful and ultimately purposeful, like the clouds, is stressed by the effect of "the bright wind boisterous" as it turns its power upon the earth, scouring it clean of all disfigurements, not only those of mud and storm but also those of humanity.

The "moments" of two specific phrases here warrant particular notice. "Squandering ooze," effective enough simply in onomatopoeic sound, suggests not only the liquid and messily dispersed quality of mud but also reminds us of the prodigality of "million-fuelèd" nature in general; of the gay irresponsibility and similar prodigality of the endlessly dispersed but endlessly reforming clouds; and, in conjunction with "stanches, starches," of the idea that out of disorder comes an ever-returning new order, at least in nature. Similarly, "stanches, starches" implies the natural process whereby permanence emerges from impermanence, healing and wholeness from seeming hemorrhage, a process that will be translated into spiritual terms at the sonnet's conclusion. Here, the point is simply the rather grim one that the wind dries the marks of human passage, the marks of Toms and plodding priests and Harry Ploughmen, first to a relatively hard firmness, then to a precarious and powdery stiffness that is clearly impermanent in itself but will return to the permanence of the cyclical and eternal "bonfire."

Man as man, however, has no permanence here; the marks of his "treadmire toil" (a coinage combining "treadmill" and "mire") are less permanent than the mud in which he wearily toiled, on which he impotently traced, "fretted," the laced pattern of his existence, the mud which having been dried to earth and then to dust will soon return to air and cloud, and so on around again. Man's pattern vanishes, while nature's larger pattern remains; his little orderly army of "Squadroned masks" is no match for the unruly but

29. Compare "The hangers of smaller but barky branches, seen black against the leaves from within, look like ship-tackle" (1869); "thatch casting sharp shadow on whitewash in the sun" (1874); "When the wind tossed them they [chestnut trees] plunged and crossed one another without losing their inscape" (1870) (*JP* 192, 250, 199).

powerful armies of wind and cloud. There is perhaps one tinge of hope, however, a hope central to the rest of the sonnet, latent in the word "masks": it implies that the physical marks we leave on earth, the life-masks, as it were, the molds of a physical self, are only outward, and perhaps deceptive, signs of our selfhood, are not after all the total reality—there is the spirit too to be considered. The conclusion of the sonnet will first reject this hope, then finally and triumphantly assert it.

The first nine lines are a complex example of Hopkins' method, not merely because of their extreme ingenuity, intricacy, even obscurity and overcontrivance, nor because they are a dazzling display of his powers to inscape the cosmos in a certain way, but because they ultimately feel a little cold, a little self-consciously clever. With all its boisterous vitality, nature in these lines lacks the deeper energy and resonance it acquires when it is charged to its depths with God's energy, when it is sacramentally news of God. This may of course simply reflect what happens to nature in Hopkins' poems, and to his own style, when neither is deeply informed by Christian mystery or fired imagination, when only careful craftsmanship is at work, a "hand at work now never wrong" (76), expressing with arid ingenuity a merely "rational faith" of the sort Devlin finds in the entire poem.[30] Or it may indicate that Hopkins knew exactly what he was doing: this is a picture of what nature looks like when seen only through pagan, or Darwinian, eyes—vital, powerful, mechanically intricate, but having no deeper voice to speak of God, shining only with a cold fire. When he moves on to speak of the relationship between the human soul and nature's fire, and finally to assertion of Christian resurrection, the style changes noticeably, becoming much less obscure, ingenious, involuted in syntax, and less difficult in diction, but gaining the full suggestiveness and power of true mystery.

The turn to the poem's conclusion begins with the pivotal word "bonfire." Almost certainly a grim Anglo-Saxon pun is intended ("ban"-fire, bone-fire), summarizing the inevitable physical destruction of the body's brittle scaffolding. Like the early image of "shook foil," "bonfire" seems a small, inadequate image for the cosmic conflagration it is supposed to embody, but again, as in the earlier sonnet, the seeming inadequacy is probably deliberate. However voracious and "million-fuelèd" the fire of the natural

30. "A dry wind of rational faith blows through this poem, driving odd scraps of imagery before it" ("Time's Eunuch," 312).

process is, in comparison with the redemptive fire of God and the brilliance of redeemed man it is ultimately no more than a Guy Fawkes display, and warrants no more than this small metaphor.

Before triumph, however, comes fear; that bonfire may be sufficient to destroy nature's highest and grandest fire, to destroy not only man's body, and its marks on earth, but his soul, and his "mark on mind":

> But quench her bonniest, dearest | to her, her clearest-selvèd spark
> Mán, how fást his fíredint, | his mark on mind, is gone!
> Bóth áre in an unfáthomable, all is in an enórmous dárk
> Drowned. O pity and indig | nation! Manshape, that shone
> Sheer off, disseveral, a star, | death blots black out; nor mark
> > Is ány of him at áll so stárk
> But vastness blurs and time | beats level.

That queer and even grotesque little sound-pun on "bonfire"/ "bonniest" leads to the several paradoxical ideas and metaphors in these lines. Nature, it now appears, is not boisterously and brutally indifferent to human beings. As in "Ribblesdale," she apparently loves them because they are not merely one more insignificant element in her natural cycle, to be consumed and obliterated like the rest of the things of dust, but her most splendid fire, whose "forgèd feature" is both a fire within and a "firedint" that forges its impression on the world and other minds. Human beings are what nothing in nature can equal, not kingfishers, nor windhovers, nor all the clouds and bright winds of the world, and what nothing can destroy. Even in the octave's imagery only man's humblest and most physical creations have been either literally or metaphorically a part of nature's bonfire—pillows, roads, whitewashed cottages, ship's tackle, dough, footprints. Humanity is more than these, is "Manshape," an utterly "arch-especial" inscape, which shines, like "lovely-asunder starlight," "Sheer off, disseveral, a star," distinct from all the other lights of the world.

Or it should be. That nature is not in fact capable of love has been clear in earlier poems and prose. What Hopkins is doing through the pathetic fallacy here is expressing as fact a wish that opposes his knowledge, lending to nature his own belief in splendid human selfhood and beauty. At the same time, through that conditional subjunctive "But quench," he has tacitly admitted how vulnerable that self is, and how cruel a stepmother nature may well be in fact. The concentrated ambivalence of these lines expresses Hopkins' simultaneous hope and fear, hope for what should be, fear of what may actually be.

This intentional ambivalence is emphasized by the paradoxical imagery that fuses fire and water, light and darkness. Reversing temporarily the nonparadoxical meaning of similar fusions in *The Deutschland* and elsewhere, Hopkins now sees water as the element that simply quenches fire, the dark sea in which all fires are drowned, not as the water of grace, the "vein of the gospel proffer," the blazing "shower" of salvation. The very movement and sound of the sonorous lines expressing this despair seem to swallow all hope in a monstrous and heavy wave of darkness, unordered and unslowed by the usual moment of midline rest (|), a wave cresting steadily, and descending with a final obliterating crash:

> Bóth are in an unfáthomable, all is in an enórmous dárk
> Drowned.

As in "Spelt from Sibyl's Leaves," vastness and darkness not only strain to obliterate selfhood but actually do so, and here apparently without offering any emblems of salvation: no earl-stars appear in this blackness to offer the hope of choice; no boughs etched upon light retain their distinctness and moral meaning. Nothing of man is strong, distinct, or bright enough to survive this drowning fire. Like the dust of the earth from which he came, he is leveled by "big winds" that no heroism, physical or spiritual, can rebuff.

At this point "The shepherd's brow" stopped short; little man made his small gestures at life and effort, pretended to be Manshape, but ultimately fed the great bonfire and was consumed by it. "That Nature is a Heraclitean Fire" goes on to "the comfort of the Resurrection," and to Hopkins' total vision of the relationship of nature, humanity, and God. Without wholly abandoning his previous faith in nature's sacramental function, without wholly allaying his earlier (and later) grim thoughts on our separation from nature and nature's news of our mortality, without denying the previous imagery and thought of this poem itself, Hopkins turns all these themes and metaphors to bear on the final lines, makes all their notes sound in the final trumpet peal of the codas:

> Enough! the Resurrection,
> A héart's-clarion! Awáy grief's gásping, | joyless days, dejection.
> Across my foundering deck shone
> A beacon, an eternal beam. | Flesh fade, and mortal trash
> Fáll to the residuary worm; | world's wildfire, leave but ash:
> In a flash, at a trumpet crash,
> I am all at once what Christ is, | since he was what I am, and

Thís Jack, jóke, poor pótsherd, ˺ patch, matchwood, immortal diamond,
                Is immortal diamond.

Having reached the depths, spiritually, metaphorically, literally, the poet gives that desperate upward kick that at least raises him, gasping, to the surface: "Enough! the Resurrection." There is an initial sense of exclamatory grasping at straws here, followed by a somewhat artificial rejection of despair, but these gestures are enough to bring him up from darkness to the point where he can truly see, feel, announce, the source of hope; as is the case in many of Hopkins' best and most faith-full poems, the final affirmation is quietly triumphal, profoundly assured, intense but not merely exclamatory.

The fire, water, combat imagery of the first fifteen lines, all the imagery of flux and change, is now not rejected but transformed. The natural bonfire, "world's wildfire," still burns on, and physical man is still subject to it, with Hopkins' full acceptance; his "mortal trash" and "matchwood" elements will be fit fuel for that fire, his flesh fit wormfood, returning to the endless natural cycle of decay and creation. But the Heraclitean fire is answered and transcended by the greater fire of God's stress of grace, which is presumably the ultimate source even of the lesser bonfire but is certainly the fire of spiritual salvation. The drowning dark is still there, but this *Deutschland* sees the beacon that will guide it to safety; combat and Strife are still there, but God's call to victory, the "heart's-clarion," the "trumpet crash," makes humanity mightier than all the physical armies that "glitter in marches," that threaten to obliterate the small marks of its own plodding march through life.

Above all, change, process, flux are not denied but translated into new terms that subsume the old. Creative change is no longer a question of the blurring of element into element, of shape into shape, but of a radical and sudden transformation: "In a flash, at a trumpet crash, / I am all at once what Christ is," and the new shape is gloriously impervious to all further change. Nevertheless, this radical change is in part possible because, as in nature, its potentiality was always there; as clouds and trees, earth and wind, are essentially, potentially, fire, so because of Christ human beings are essentially and potentially "immortal diamond." Because Christ deigned to take on all the ignominy of humanity and so transform it, man has always been, even in life, a strange but splendid paradox: "This Jack, joke, poor potsherd, patch, matchwood, immortal diamond." Common, ridiculous, foolish physical fragment as he is, flimsy fuel for the cosmic fire, he has nevertheless been also diamond; with the Resurrection, that quality alone remains, becoming the total actuality: "*Is* immortal diamond."

This final image triumphantly summarizes the point of the entire poem, and indeed of Hopkins' entire life, faith, poetic career. The human soul, like the diamond, is a product of the stress, pressure, fire exerted on it in life: formed, tested, tempered by that fire of stress, by the pressure of God's finger, it becomes not only sharper, firmer, brighter than nature's fairest shapes and brightest fires but impervious to all natural fire whatever. Shining with a paradoxically frozen but vital flame, its flashing and varied lights achieve an eternal permanence that has transcended, but has not lost, has not denied, the vitality and value of the mortal world.

This poem represents the end of a long journey: the Romantic search throughout the century for vital permanence and some way of understanding the intersection of actual and ideal; the late-century Aesthetic search for a life lived with the intensity of a "hard, gemlike flame"; Hopkins' personal search, expressed throughout his life and in all his poems. Because he never lost sight of the order behind the transience of life, the One "past change" behind the changing many, the actual as well as potential splendors of humanity and nature in spite of their physical mortality, he could return near the end of his life to one final major affirmation of his pervasive vision. That this sonnet is not in fact Hopkins' final poem may be a source of regret if one wants life to be as neat as art, as neat as criticism, but his last poem, "To R. B.," is a farewell to his muse, not to his faith. In life and in poetry he remained true to the one center, and in his life, as in his poetry, "a changeless note is heard." Whatever its variations, developments, experimentations, successes, failures, his "authentic cadence" remains from beginning to end an attempt to word adequately the mysterious certainty of that center: "Love, O my God, to call Thee Love and Love."

IV

Dark Descending

9

The "Terrible Sonnets"
(1885)

THE WRECK OF *the Deutschland* was an early and triumphal concentration of Hopkins' central vision, recurrent themes, "authentic cadence." The six great sonnets of desolation, six of "the terrible posthumous sonnets," as Bridges and all later critics have called them, form a second, though deeply darkened, microcosm of his response to basic mysteries.

It is a tragic microcosm indeed, born of a fiat that creates ordered darkness, not ordered light, and one so concentrated within itself that there seems to be no larger world left for it to epitomize. For the first time in Hopkins' poetry the dialogue of the mind with itself, and with itself alone, seems to have begun. For the first time, Hopkins seems cursed to dramatize unwillingly Satan's prideful claim that "The mind is its own place," and seems specifically driven to exercise with desolate results the second of Satan's boasted powers, to make "a Hell of Heav'n" (*Paradise Lost* 1.254–55). The lines quoted earlier in reference to the century as a whole, from a fragment also written in 1885, seem to describe exactly what we see and feel in reading these dark sonnets: "The times are nightfall, look, their light grows less; / The times are winter, watch, a world undone" (150).

Yet just as this fragment turns from the spectacle of total "wreck" to hope for salvage, from a "world undone" to an attempt to rebuild the "world within," so the "terrible sonnets" attempt to remember and return to some inner wholeness, and in the midst of "thy dark descending" to reach toward some hope at least for mercy, some glimpse at least of light. In spite of the many difficulties posed by any attempt to arrange all six sonnets in a provable order of composition, or even of transcription and revision, the one indisputable fact is that Hopkins placed "My own heart let me more have pity on" (69) last when transcribing fair copies of the four "unbidden" sonnets; in doing so, the poet at least, and perhaps the man, chose to emphasize a groping return not only from inner darkness to inner sight but also from a wholly internal world to the sacramental world outside the mind. Its concluding image, however contorted in syntax and complex in tone, typically fuses spiritual and physical, figurative and literal, allowing us to catch again a brief sight of the actual and beautiful world beyond the inner prison: "as skies / Betweenpie mountains—lights a lovely mile."

Numerous critics have sensed in these sonnets something new in method: a "more reserved style," a "greater directness," a "chastened severity," a less "copiously elaborated" quality, a "pitch of concentration" that may be said to constitute a "powerful new rhetoric,"[1] and to an extent a new austerity is indeed there. Except in the sprung Alexandrines of "(Carrion Comfort)," Hopkins has now returned to something approaching standard rhythm, rejecting the baroque architecture of such poems as the earlier "Henry Purcell," the partly contemporaneous "Spelt from Sibyl's Leaves," the later "Tom's Garland," "Harry Ploughman," "That Nature is a Heraclitean Fire." Yet any reader who seriously engages the language of these sonnets finds it by no means transparently direct, nor any less intricate than that of many earlier and later poems. If we are not only gripped by the grim differences in content but also sense something more astringent in the style, that sense results from the intensified density of each word and image, every grammatical and metrical nuance. This is indeed a "pitch of concentration" perhaps new in poetry, but not altogether new in Hopkins' poetry; it is "the making a thing more, or making it markedly," what it has always been, the intensely truthful language of "incomprehensible certainty."

Recently, and much more radically, Daniel Harris has found in these sonnets a contrast both to the earlier language and to the typical earlier structure "so abrupt . . . so sharp"[2] that it raises questions not only about a new style but about the very bases of

1. Bridges, *PB* 101; Murry, *Aspects of Literature*, 57; Pick, *Priest and Poet*, 144; Leavis, *New Bearings*, 187; Storey, *Hopkins*, 36.
2. *Inspirations Unbidden*, 3. Though Harris urges that his interpretations not be read as "partial biography," or as reflecting doubt of Hopkins' own statement of unwavering faith, the thrust of this searching but admittedly "bleak" reading of the sonnets (xv) is that they unwillingly express at best a radical perversion of faith, at worst its loss, and are therefore in priestly concept and vision "failures" (xiii).

Hopkins' faith. On this and other issues cogently explored by Harris fuller discussion appears in due course, but it will be evident already that I do not share his overall view of the poems as "an explicit and unalleviated psychomachia" of spiritual isolation and despair.[3] While the dark sonnets are obviously and in every sense more "terrible" than *The Wreck of the Deutschland*, while imagery, landscape, tone have radically changed, and while these poems are simultaneously more controlled and in some ways more complex in cadence, they nevertheless embody in my view both Hopkins' unchanged artistry and his most basic and consistent attempts and impulses of spirit. Like that first great poem, like Hopkins' whole life, they dramatize not only his almost ruthless integrity and honesty, artistic and spiritual, but a tragically hard-won "yes" to the lightning, and the darkness, of a God who is still the "Orion of light."

The sources of desolation that gave rise to these dark sonnets were certainly manifold and complex. There may possibly have been a specific experience, such as the January Retreat of 1885, which provided the "one touch" of the knife, the "one touch, something striking sideways and unlooked for" (March 1870), something that made steady and bearable pain suddenly unbearable.[4] More probably, the chronic physical and nervous exhaustion that had haunted his life for years, and the chronic sense, and fact, of failure—not only as poet but as priest, teacher, and scholar—now simply came to an inevitable head. I would also not underestimate how little in his daily surroundings offered release or solace for eyes or spirit; though far from intolerable to someone in a balanced state of mind and nerves, and actually better than conditions in Lancashire or Glasgow, Dublin's grayness, constriction, and poverty and the cramped rooms, and minds, his teaching faced were far in every sense from the "lovely miles" around St. Beuno's and must have contributed something to the claustrophobic inward turning that is so marked in the dark sonnets.

Yet as Hopkins' meditation notes reveal, the sources of desolation seem not to have included loss of faith in God or God's existence, but the reverse. Though one entry states, "I must ask God to

3. Ibid., 75.
4. "But neither the weight nor the stress of sorrow . . . by themselves move us or bring the tears as a sharp knife does not cut for being pressed as long as it is pressed without any shaking of the hand but there is always one touch, something striking sideways and unlooked for, which in both cases undoes resistance and pierces" (*JP* 195).

strengthen my faith or I shall never keep the particular examen"
(June 1884, *SD* 256), he is mainly tormented, as in this very entry,
by his own failure to meet that absolute God's demands, to find
consolation in all the God-given sources of it, to live up to his vocation with energy and love.[5] In the sonnets themselves, the anguish
of seeming abandonment arises from the very fact that the
abandoner is *not* dead but somehow "away" or, when present,
darkly cruel. Though some of them desperately transfer his own
failures to God, the sonnets as a group are an agonized but faithful
response to desolation, not abandoning Ignatian discipline of
thought and therefore neither mystical at one extreme nor wholly
despairing at the other. Though they clearly dramatize a "dark
night of the soul," it is not viewed as the mystic's state of blessed
darkness, "more lovely than the dawn," through which the soul
steals forth to meet its lover, Christ.[6] It is instead the Ignatian
"darkness and confusion of soul," "diffidence without hope and
without love," seeming separation from God. Nonetheless, the
sonnets and their creator remember that this darkness may be won
through by effort, perseverance, patience, submission, recognition
that God's apparent withdrawal is a probationary testing of the
soul's strength, and through hope that he will soon send consolation.[7] Without underestimating the depth of the sonnets' pain, it is
therefore well to set against despairing readings of them this reminder from MacKenzie about the struggles of this year: "What
emerges in poem after poem is his refusal to give way to his depres-
sion, or to believe that God is dead; just as in letter after letter during the same period we find his astonishing mind busying itself
with some recondite enquiry or exhilarated by some new insight.
Even in the darkest hour he orientates himself towards the dawn."[8]

Since I have already referred to the sonnets as "a group" of
some sort, and shall be treating them as a group whose dramatic
—as distinct from biographical—movement of thought has some
significance, a preliminary comment on the problems of chronol-

5. See especially the entries for September 30, 1884; January 6, 1885; March
17, 1885 (*SD* 257, 258–59, 260).

6. *The Collected Works of St. John of the Cross*, translated by Kieran Kavanaugh
and Otilio Rodriguez, 68–69.

7. *SD* 204; Loyola, *Spiritual Exercises*, 170–72. Though Harris has conclusively shown the non-Ignatian structure of the sonnets, he also accepts their essentially Ignatian, not mystical, response to desolation (*Inspirations Unbidden*,
12–14). For a contrary argument on this issue, see Downes, *Ignatian Spirit*,
138–48.

8. *Reader's Guide*, 173.

ogy and transcription they present is imperative. The two problems are related though partially separable, the latter being far more important to any reading that views the sonnets as poetic artifacts rather than as raw confessional or autobiographical evidence.

Of the actual chronology of composition very little is known. It is usually assumed that "(Carrion Comfort)" (64) and "No worst, there is none" (65) are the two sonnets Hopkins referred to in a letter of May 17, 1885: "I have after long silence written two sonnets, which I am touching: if ever anything was written in blood one of these was" (*LB* 219); controversy has centered mainly on which of the two was "written in blood." Since Hopkins never sent these sonnets to Bridges, however, and since neither appears in a completely final form in the extant manuscripts, we have no means of knowing whether these were the sonnets referred to, nor the order of their inception, nor exactly how long he worked on them, nor when he decided to stop "touching" (revising) them, nor whether he ever did consider them sufficiently finished. Nevertheless, from the nature of the extant drafts it is clear that these two sonnets were at least copied out by him in an attempt at something approaching final form at the same time: the only version of "No worst" and the closest to final version of "(Carrion Comfort)"—carried through line 9—appear on recto and verso of one page, and the pen, ink, and handwriting are identical. It is also possible to conjecture, at least, that "(Carrion Comfort)" was begun slightly earlier than "No worst" and was continuing to give him more trouble, since two drafts of it, probably to be dated on or after August 23, 1885, and many individual line revisions preceded its most "final" copying, which is literally sandwiched around the one version of "No worst." These last copies I would date well after the May letter, possibly even as late as 1886 or 1887 (see Appendix E). In any case, the two sonnets seem to have been paired in Hopkins' mind when he came to attempt fair copying and belong together in time of more or less final "touching." I shall also be arguing that their order of actual inception matters less than the grim logic with which the content of "No worst" follows from the end of "(Carrion Comfort)," though that "logic" admittedly remains a matter of interpretation, not provable fact.

The other four sonnets, 66–69, are almost certainly slightly later in inception than these two, though earlier in completion— "completion" in this case meaning only abandonment, so far as we know, of further revision. Bridges actually dated these poems as late as 1887–1888 on the basis of handwriting, but most critics

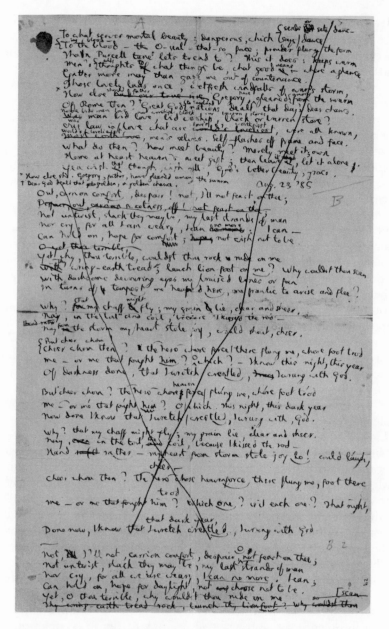

The first extant draft of "(Carrion Comfort)," canceled, with the beginning of the revised second draft (MS.Eng.poet.d.150.fol.29 recto), referred to in the text as H₁.

"(Carrion Comfort)," continuation of the second draft (fol.29 verso), referred to in the text as H₂.

"(Carrion Comfort)," lines 11 and 12, followed by canceled "early v. of Tom" and opening of "No worst, there is none" (Ms.Eng.poet.d.150.fol.31 recto).

agree in placing them among the sonnets to which Hopkins referred in September 1885: "I shall shortly have some sonnets to send you, five or more. ~~Three~~ Four [sic] of these came like inspirations unbidden and against my will. And in the life I lead now, which is one of a continually jaded and harassed mind, if in any

"No worst, there is none," continued, followed by the "final" version through line 10 of "(Carrion Comfort)" (fol.31 verso), referred to in the text as H₃.

leisure I try to do anything I make no way—nor with my work, alas! but so it must be" (September 1, 1885, *LB* 221).

Except in "To seem the stranger" (66) and "I wake and feel the fell of dark" (67) the extant versions show relatively few central revisions, temptingly suggesting an originally "inspired" quality but

The "unbidden sonnets": "To seem the stranger," followed by the octave of "I wake and feel the fell of dark" (Ms.Eng.poet.d.150.fol.35 recto).

unhappily proving nothing: some or many destroyed or lost drafts could have preceded these fair copies. More persuasive as support for this identification as the promised sonnets of September is the fact that other candidates for such a grouping of five do not readily

The "unbidden sonnets": the sestet of "I wake and feel the fell of dark," followed by "Patience, hard thing!" and "My own heart let me more have pity on" (fol.35 verso).

present themselves, while on recto and verso of the same page appear "Ashboughs" (through line 11) and the four in question. The reason for that correction from *three* to *four* must remain conjectural: perhaps the careful revisions in "To seem the stranger" and "I wake and feel" initially excluded one or the other from the "inspirations unbidden" category; or if Harris is right in taking "unbidden" to mean not merely spontaneous but "unwanted" because dangerously heterodox,[9] perhaps more than the initial "three" had to be scrupulously acknowledged as such; or perhaps this was simply a slip of the pen or memory.

Far more important than the "unbidden" identification to my reading of the group is the order in which the four finished sonnets appear: on one page, below the eleven lines of "Ashboughs," "To seem the stranger" and the octave of "I wake and feel the fell of dark," with the sestet continued on the verso; on this same verso, "Patience, hard thing!" (68) and "My own heart let me more have pity on." Whether or not Hopkins originally wrote the sonnets in exactly this order, whether or not these drafts are the first and only "inspired" versions, whatever the order of the revisions may have been, and whether or not this arrangement in any way reflects the actual, literal stages through which his thought and psyche moved, he chose to transcribe fair copies in this sequence, a sequence that I accept as his deliberate poetic ordering of chaotic actual experience. So taken, the series forms a crafted dramatic artifact, a psychodrama moving from a bitterly felt but still grimly and somewhat analytically controlled state of exile, physical and spiritual, to the depths of near damnation, to some degree of final recovery. And if, as I believe, the order of all six sonnets first devised by Bridges, and followed in the Gardner-MacKenzie edition, makes the most valid guess at an ordering that Hopkins himself would ultimately have approved, the movement of the whole spiritual drama is the more serious, complete, and of a certain magnitude: from the strenuous and hard-won affirmation of "(Carrion Comfort)," steadily downward to the depths of the cliffs of fall, and then close to the depths of hell itself, and gradually upward again through dutiful obedience to a poem that at least glimpses some light upon the mind's mountains.

It is hazardous to treat the sonnets in the sequence just summarized, or in any sequence, if one's main attempt is to argue that Hopkins the man, as distinct from Hopkins the poet, literally underwent the stages proposed, in the order proposed. The ordering I have accepted, as have many other critics, dramatizes a process from struggle to despair to some recovery, but is not to be taken as exact biographical fact. Equally suspect as biographical evidence would be three alternative orderings, all of which accept the "un-

9. *Inspirations Unbidden*, xiii.

bidden" four in order but differently place the two wild cards, as it were, the two undatable sonnets: an extremely optimistic and comforting sequence could place "No worst" first, followed by the "unbidden" four, ending with "(Carrion Comfort)," in which case "that night, that year, of now done darkness" could be made to refer to the whole dark year of 1885, now survived and triumphantly learned from; the converse order, emphasizing a wholly desolate view of Hopkins' state in that year, could place "(Carrion Comfort)" first and "No worst" last; the third possibility, equally desolate in biographical assumption, but truer to the textual pairing and probable late revision of "(Carrion Comfort)" and "No worst," would treat these two as finales concluding the "unbidden" sequence.

It is because the evidence of the manuscripts supports no absolute ordering, and no such biographical interpretation, that MacKenzie calls any such attempt "as alluring and inconclusive a pastime as the renumbering of Shakespeare's sonnets."[10] It is for this reason also that Harris argues persuasively and at length against any sequential treatment whatever, viewing the sonnets as "a mere group, in a contiguous but not patterned assemblage." Castigating the numerous critics who have followed Bridges' lead too uncritically, Harris emphasizes that "the order of the poems' transcription is wholly suspect as the basis for any interpretation— first, because the order of transcription carries no presumption concerning the order of composition; second, because 'To Seem the Stranger,' while placed first, was finished last."[11] On the point that order of transcription proves nothing about order of composition, and that neither necessarily reflects autobiographical fact, Harris's evidence is indisputable, his argument rigorous, his challenge to all critical readings based on unrecognized assumptions or conscious biases of the utmost value. With other aspects of his logic, however, and with the final conclusions, I take some issue.

First, the argument hinges upon the assumed lateness in time of the grim revisions in "To seem the stranger," a lateness by no means so plainly deducible from the manuscripts as Harris contends; though possibly late, those changes are no more demonstrably last-in-time than those in the other dark sonnets. From this posited lateness, however, Harris derives the conclusion that Hopkins was finally wholly unable to accept or assert even that

10. *Reader's Guide*, 170.
11. *Inspirations Unbidden*, 15, 7–8.

glimpse of consolation offered by the "lovely mile": "it appears that Hopkins, in the very act of transcribing what he assumed would be the fair copy of 'To Seem the Stranger,' was again overwhelmed by those gnashings of despair which 'My Own Heart'— had it truly been designed to conclude a sequence—was supposed to have ameliorated."[12] The tacit assumptions, here and later, are that time of *revision* is not only provable but is the crucial factor in interpretation and that interpretation may validly use the revisions as exactly the sort of autobiographical information that Harris has previously faulted as the practice of careless critics.

Second, while necessarily recognizing the order in which Hopkins chose to transcribe the four "unbidden" sonnets, Harris speculates that this order was a kind of pretense, a charade put on for Bridges, and in part for Hopkins himself: "The order of the series was perhaps Hopkins's mask against Bridges's disapproval and against his own recognition of an interior agony which, if it sometimes abated, also seemed endless"; in the revisions of "To seem the stranger," however, "the mask fell, leaving any intelligible notion of a self-protective series in shambles." Most critics, the argument continues, have failed to penetrate this pretense and to notice the crucial moment of self-revelation; as a result, they have seen only "the mask Hopkins wanted Bridges to see—a triumphant exhibition of God's grace—rather than the abyss Hopkins saw."[13]

This sort of argument is almost impossible to refute on demonstrable grounds: the fact that so many have failed to see behind the mask may or may not attest to the stupidity of the many, but since we are rarely privy to the inmost thoughts of writers, almost any text can be regarded as mask, not face, if the critic chooses to take that line of argument. Rather than pursuing that theoretical aspect of the issue, however, I would emphasize instead what seems to me a more important, albeit also conjectural, point, about writers in general and Hopkins in particular. This is the possibility, even acknowledged fact in some cases, that a poet, qua poet, always wears some sort of mask, at least if the poetry is to be any good; a fine poem, or sequence of poems, is not likely to be mere literal self-expression in any obvious sense. The self of a poet in the process of creation is very likely not quite the self who sharpens the pencil,

12. Ibid., 9. Immediately followed by "One does not say that Hopkins, in struggling through a new sestet, surrendered to his sorrow at the expense of his original poetic intent; rather, he discovered a deeper, more tragic vision of his own condition" (9), but I am not sure one can have it both ways.
13. Ibid., 10, 11.

worries about the fuel bill, combats chronic headaches, or even suffers anguish on the mind's mountains. In the process of revision especially, the poet-self may cast a cold eye, though an intense one, both on what he has written and on what he has been. As poet, therefore, Hopkins may very well have worked to intensify in revision the bleakness and the power of "To seem the stranger"—exactly as he worked at various stages on "(Carrion Comfort)"—without in any way feeling that he was falsifying or should abandon as false his originally chosen order. That order, whether mask or not, he did choose, an order true to his lifelong choices, to his deepest beliefs, and last but not least to his dramatist's sense of poetic power.

This difference between the "real" person and the creating poet is something that critics who are nonpoets seldom emphasize, or find suspect, but it is something that fellow poets, such as Bridges, instinctively understand. I would therefore urge the importance of the main point Bridges emphasized in the passage from which critics have lifted only the famous phrase: "Few will read the terrible posthumous sonnets without such high admiration and respect for his poetical power as must lead them to search out the rare masterly beauties that distinguish his work" (PB 101). These sonnets, even the "unbidden" sonnets, are works of art and of an artist, not direct, spontaneous cries of the heart untempered by the attention, craft, mastery, "poetical power" of the poet. They are both intensely honest expressions of the real man's anguish and works that shape anguish and chaos into wholes that simultaneously intensify and transcend the pain that inspired them. This possibly obvious point needs emphasis because these sonnets present such a special temptation to think otherwise, so compelling seems their personal voice and so immediate their anguish. The point is worth stressing also because it is both admirable and to a degree consoling that even at his most desperate, most private, most desolate, Hopkins was able to turn great pain to great art, to create, where he could not find, order, to "utter" both the horrors and mysteries of this "unshapeable night" in shape and words that still "say yes" to artistry, and still try to "say yes" to "(my God!) my God."

In summary, then, I take the dark sonnets of 1885 to be tragic artifacts: to be in part Hopkins' Christian version of ancient Dionysian myth, and, more specifically, to be his King Lear, not only in general mode but in detail. And just as one probably does not approach King Lear primarily for biographical evidence of Shakespeare's state of mind at the time, nor conclude that he failed because he was no longer writing the golden comedies, so it seems reasonable to approach these sonnets as poetic achievements of a special kind, not as unmediated psychological confessions, certainly not as evidence of artistic failure. And without wholly discounting Harris' impressively mounted argument that from Hopkins' own point of view they represent a priestly failure of will and faith, my reading will emphasize instead the clear and admirable attempt by both the poet and the priest to create a Christian ordering of tragic chaos.

"(Carrion Comfort)," Bridges' title for this sonnet, was not and would not have been Hopkins'. Exactly because he rejects the temptation to be the carrion-eater and so becomes himself the prey of that seemingly predatory hunter who is God, the speaker at last arrives, through struggle, at the grander comfort. As in *The Deutschland*, as in "The Windhover," he becomes almost one with the divine Hunter because he ultimately recognizes him as an Orion indeed, but an Orion of light. Alone among the "terrible sonnets" this one is finally almost exuberant in tone, and alone among them, it confidently asserts that the dark night is "now done."

As the poem opens, however, the will to struggle and survive, the will "to be" at all, is far weaker than Hamlet's, though "the question" is the same; the choice for life is so weary and so faint that it can find voice only in negative terms, and the kind of syntactical manipulation so central to *The Deutschland*'s opening affirmation here has exactly the opposite effect. The first quatrain is framed in, and based on, negatives—seven in four lines. Beginning with a desperate affirmative negative, as it were, it descends through increasingly heavy but lifelessly dragging monosyllables to the weakest possible affirmation through negation of negation:

> Not, I'll not, carrion comf͜ort, Despair, not feast on thee;
> Not untwist—slack they may be—these last strands of man
> In me ór, most weary, cry *I can no more*. I can;
> Can something, hope, wish day come, not choose not to be.

"I cán," stressed though only hesitantly strong in its denial of the far stronger "*I can no more*" preceding it, briefly opposes the mood and syntax of negation, but it immediately subsides in stress ("Can sómething") and idea, collapsing into those hopelessly bleak hopes of the fourth line. That truly terrible double negative, "not choose not to be," somberly compresses the wholly negative weakness of will and hope. While it literally closes the quatrain not with negation but with the affirmative words "to be," and in full statement overtly counters "*I can no more*," it ominously echoes both the feeling and the negative-positive construction generating that earlier cry and is hardly strong enough to drown out its powerful and continuing reverberations.

This mastery of sheer syntax, and the dramatic power resulting from it, did not by any means come to Hopkins spontaneously (see Appendix E). The negative weariness of the opening line resulted from several stages of revision that steadily sap the strength of the original "Out, carrion comfort, despair! not, I'll not feast on thee," and its still stronger crossed-out alternative, "Despair, *out*, carrion sweetness, off! *not* feast on thee" (H₁a). The exclamatory power and energy of these versions is deadened in the second draft by deletion of all the imperatives and the exclamation mark, and by replacement of both "out" and "off" by "not." The line was then both further weakened in feeling and clarified in meaning in a third stage of revision: weakened by excision of the too emotional "O" and the far too strong "*not*" tried in the second draft—"Not, I'll not, carrion comfort, despair, O *not* feast on thee"; clarified by the capitalization of "Despair," identifying it unambiguously as noun, not verb.

The seemingly inevitable fourth line also underwent important revision:

H₁a: Can hold on, hope for comfort; ~~hope;~~ not wish not to be.
H₂: Can hold on, hope for daylight, not ~~wis~~ choose not to be.
H₃: Can something, ~~hold, hope daylight~~
        hope, wish day come, not choose not to be

The original "hold on" is relatively flat without being sufficiently weak in sound or stress or meaning, a problem remedied by "something," but the crucial revision is the one that occurs in midthought, as it were, the revision in H₂ from "not wis[h]" to "not choose not to be." This completes the complex fusion of affirmation and negation central to the whole quatrain; there is still some faintly defiant possibility of the dignity of will and choice, however negative their object, though it is obviously a pathetically feeble possibility. Further adding to the diminishment of any real strength are the steady deletion of all the phrases of too much hope and visual brightness ("hope for comfort," "hope for daylight," "hope daylight") and the submersion and truncation of the original "*comfort*" in the final "come."

The imagery of this quatrain, strongly reminiscent of that of *The Wreck of the Deutschland*, introduces four dominant metaphors that will govern the rest of the sonnet, and whose relationship, seemingly unclear at first, will in development turn out to be one of intricate interlacing: hunting and combat; feasting, probably introducing a larger Dionysian and eucharistic theme; roping, twisting, untwisting, to become the sestet's winnowing metaphor; daylight and darkness. The first two are already clearly and intimately connected: refusing to feast on despair, to glut himself on the rotten remains of dead hope, dead life—the last self-pitying comfort apparently left a hopeless man—Hopkins simultaneously rejects the role and initiative and victory of the hunter. Though this role would obviously not be that of kingly windhover but only of scavenger-vulture, it would at least be that of the eater, not the victim, and in abandoning this role he becomes instead the "eaten," the prey of the lion-limbed tormentor's "devouring eyes."

With "Not untwist—slack they may be—these last strands of man / In me" the imagery changes,[14] but the underlying relation between this metaphor and that of the opening line is both psychologically and imagistically logical. Close though his tendons of manhood are to becoming as rotted as the carrion comfort he rejects, he still struggles to resist the total disintegration that would make him wholly like it. Frayed, raveled, nearly "unbound" though the threads of his humanity may be, almost wholly bereft though he now is of the roping-reeving stress of God that sustained his being in *The Deutschland*, and the world's in "Spelt from Sibyl's Leaves," the last shreds of manhood still distinguish him both from the carrion-eater and from the cannibalistic carrion food he would become in feasting on his own despair. This is an attempt to assert Christian will in a context of Christian tragedy: though the ancient curse of the house of Atreus seems darkly potent and remembered still, this speaker will not knowingly eat his own damnation, nor dismember his own flesh and being.

Therefore, though his choices immediately make him the prey of a dark hunter whose mere look devours, whose touch of limb and whirlwind of wings and breath are sufficient to untwist all his strands of being, he is still "man" enough to question his tormentor:

But ah, but O thou terrible, why wouldst thou rude on me
Thy wring-world right foot rock? lay a lionlimb against me? scan
With darksome devouring eyes my bruisèd bones? and fan,
O in turns of tempest, me heaped there; me frantic to avoid thee and flee?

14. I cannot quite accept Mariani's proposed transitional pun on "not"/ "knot," tempting though it is (*Commentary*, 229).

After the grim restraint of the opening quatrain, the initial out-break of feeling here seems the more powerful and dramatically in-evitable; we feel that the mouth and mind so clenched against the need to "cry *I can no more*" must need to cry somehow. In that ini-tial broken but long-drawn appeal of pain and bafflement and defi-ance they at last find outlet, and though the modulation from "ah" to "O" perhaps slightly shifts the pitch of sound—from something approaching Lear's "Howl!" to a quieter and more hopeless pain —it is pain and even anger now that generate the questions, not dead despair.[15] The pathos here, however, is deepened by the fact that the whole appeal is addressed to an apparently mindless brute-tormentor, as if it could or would answer human cries of any sort, as if it were his onetime God.

That expectation is of course to prove true, but at this point in the dramatic movement of the poem the speaker has not identified the name and nature of his torturer; its name now is simply its major and wholly cruel quality, "thou terrible," and Hopkins pre-sents himself as being wholly unable to see in this massive bird-beast the bright wings, the sheltering feathers, the warm breast of his seemingly lost God. For the moment, the finger of grace has be-come simply a "lionlimb," the radiance has become "darksome," the gigantic wings beat above his broken body and soul only to de-stroy them. On second and all further readings the reader may and should read rightly the implications of the octave's complex meta-phors, as Hopkins implies he should himself have read them, but in the poem's dramatic unfolding, they, like the God they describe, withhold their full significance. It is not until the sestet that the speaker can penetrate their meaning, can pick up and repeat, now calmly and analytically, that desperate initial "why?" and answer it with affirmation of God's purposeful and merciful stress of purga-tion. At that point he recognizes that the dark eyes intently scan his soul to detect there a hidden wish to "say yes," that the terrible wings do not destroy but turn "heaped" bones to the pure heaped grain winnowed from the chaff, but in the octave the "plain truth," though present in the metaphors, remains hidden from the poet himself.

The actual though hidden nature of God is specifically present also in three of the more crucial individual terms of the octave,

15. On the revisions of this line, and for a brilliantly original and illuminating demonstration of the truncation of Ignatian colloquy in all these sonnets, see Harris, *Inspirations Unbidden*, 77–79.

"wring-world," "rock," and "lay," terms that emphasize present cruelty but imply latent kindness. A keen ear for Hopkinsian puns may also find such a hint in the "rude"/"rood" homophone, but this should not be insisted on; the main emphasis here is on cruelty only, the adjective-turned-adverb characteristically fusing quality and activity. The other terms, however, seem more naturally dual in implication.

Although Hopkins never made a final choice between the alternatives "wring-world" and "wring-earth" (H_3), the word *wring* appears in all versions and functions doubly in all versions: initially it conveys the cruel pressure that can totally and painfully "untwist" not only the poet's last strands of selfhood but also the world's; later, the poem will assert, as *The Deutschland* asserted, that God's unmaking, "un-twisting" powers are actually those that "reeve" and sustain, in this case by wringing out, and thereby purifying, what is partially impure (and perhaps, as in *The Deutschland*, making possible a "ringing out" of affirmation).

The implications of "rock" and "lay" are similarly dual in a somewhat more complicated way: both imply a perversion of kindly, gentle, nurturing forces to destructive cruelty, a reversal that the sestet will reverse again to proper order. "Rock," functioning grammatically as a verb but carrying also its prepossessions as noun, dramatizes both the constant grinding motion of this massive foot and its crushing weight—like Margaret Clitheroe's, his sentence is "*Pressed to death*" (145). At this point in the poem, the implication of a different sort of motion, that of gentle rocking, as of a parent rocking a child, seems only to suggest the huge power of this creature whose gentlest movements can break and maul. Later the implication of loving, if stern, parenthood will prove to be literally true.

A comparable intent seems apparent in the use of "lay." Hopkins' revision from "launch . . ." (H_1a and H_2) to "lay a lion-limb against me" cannot have been dictated by alliterative considerations alone; he presumably saw that while "launch" directly suggests both purposeful and violent strength, the gentle "lay" does not diminish but in a subtler way immensely increases our sense of that terrible power. This tormentor need not even exert its full strength to crush, and may not even intend to do so, but its most casually indifferent, seemingly lightest touches (and touches not even "upon" but simply "against") are sufficient to reduce the victim to a broken ruin of shattered bones. Again, however, this casual but killing gentleness will eventually be seen as true and purposeful mercy, and the other meaning of "against" (in opposition to) will release the metaphor of saving combat. (It is conceivable that the lion statue above the main entrance of University College in Dublin affected the image here: albeit a benignly supine lion, the statue also suggests massive latent power, and it was certainly a sight Hopkins saw, passed under, daily, with what thoughts we can perhaps justifiably imagine.)

The turn in thought to the sestet is dramatically reinforced by the change of tense from present to past. The night of darkness has ended indeed, in midpoem, and we with Hopkins now look back on it with the joy, and the terrified awe, of understanding:

Why? That my chaff might fly; my grain lie, sheer and clear.
Nay in all that toil, that coil, since (seems) I kissed the rod,
Hand rather, my heart lo! lapped strength, stóle joy, would laugh, cheer.
Cheer whóm though? The hero whose heáven handling flúng me, foót tród
Me? or mé that foúght him? O whích one? is it eách one? That níght, that yeár
Of now done darkness I wretch lay wrestling with (my God!) my God.

Just as Hopkins recognizes here God's coherent purpose and true identity, the "plain truth" behind the octave's imagery, so at this point the coherence of the whole poem's imagery becomes clearer to the reader: who and what is animal, who is eater or eaten, who is antagonist or cheering supporter, but above all the reciprocity and exchange of roles in all these questions—these are the central issues embodied in the guiding and linked metaphors of the whole.

The grain-chaff metaphor, triggered mainly by a new way of understanding the fanning "turns of tempest" and "heaped bones" immediately preceding it, probably emerges also from the twisting-untwisting language of the opening and from the submerged metaphor underlying the feasting imagery of the whole of the octave. Had Hopkins chosen to be the carrion-eater he would have been eating death, not life, would have been perverting a sacrament, in a sense—a perversion that becomes fact in "I wake and feel the fell of dark." In "(Carrion Comfort)," however, as Miller argues in his fine discussion of this whole metaphor, the speaker becomes in submission both part, at least, of the food of the Eucharist himself ("grain") and partaker of it ("lapped strength"), participating in the sacrificial rite, and the death-to-life, that sacrament commemorates and embodies.[16] Against the central Dionysian and Aes-

16. *Disappearance of God*, 347. See also Hopkins' gloss to line 47 of "The Loss

chylean tragic myth of dismemberment and cannibalism, Hopkins sets his own truth of the God who dies to life, and to give life.

Certainly a gladness beyond mere acceptance of purgative suffering is at least implicit in "sheer and clear" and is clearly signaled by the somewhat unexpected "Nay" beginning line 10, which actually introduces a new and true "yes"; in contrast to the desperate "Not" of the opening line, this is a truly affirmative negative. The poem now moves on to "say more" than a passive and dutiful acceptance of chastisement, to say that even in the midst of chastisement there was a combination of pain and joy, of rebellion and instinctive humility, of animalism and heroism, and ultimately a reciprocal relation with Christ.

Hopkins arrived at the final version's condensed expression of these ideas through careful revision. Not until the last extant draft, for example, does "since (seems) I kissed the rod" appear, all earlier versions simply stating "because I kissed the rod." The revision is important not merely alliteratively but theologically. It briefly expresses the mysterious fact that even without consciously knowing or willing it, without his mind's choice, his heart was somehow "carrier-witted" in a response of love.[17] It is this response that makes theologically legitimate the full implications of that apparently semiblasphemous question, "Cheer whóm though?"— Christ? myself? both? Obviously orthodox would be the obvious meaning: that he might "cheer on" both Christ and himself, the one to exert even more strongly his purgative and saving might, the other to further struggle against despair and further effort in the saving combat. But the second meaning allowed here is that he might also "praise, applaud" himself as well as Christ: he has (seems) performed the only act for which man ever merits praise, not simply in the initial refusal to succumb to despair, but in the positive "verdict on God's side, the saying Yes, the 'doing-agree,'" a verdict that may be only a "mere wish, discernible by God's eyes" only, but that is nevertheless "the life and spirit of man" (SD 154, 155). It is this hidden wish for more than "day," the wish to "corre-

---

of the Eurydice": "'Cheer's death'=the death of cheer=the dying out of all comfort=despair" (May 30, 1878, LB 53).

17. See the much earlier "Crown Him now who can crown you then, kiss the hand that holds the dreadful rod," which is immediately preceded by "His hand created you once, now it deals out to you your being and the bread and all things that keep you alive" (Dominical Sermon on the miracle of the loaves and fishes, 1877, SD 232).

spond," that the intense scrutiny of those "darksome eyes" has detected in his soul's depths.

Moreover, that important qualification "the rod, / Hand rather," briefly contemplated but canceled in the first draft, though present in all subsequent drafts, in conjunction with "lapped," which does not make its appearance until the third revision, emphasizes man's proper understanding of God, and their proper relationship. The two phrases at first seem to work in opposite directions, but ultimately they arrive at the same dynamic relationship established in the first stanza of *The Deutschland*. The shift from "rod" to "hand" mainly dramatizes Hopkins' growing awareness and final recognition that the "lionlimb" of the octave was in fact the punitive hand of his personal God, "my God," and that God reaches down to touch humanity not in malice but in mercy. Yet at the same time, both "rod" and especially "lapped," whatever its eucharistic undertones, seem to reduce the man far beneath the status of manhood, to make him something God could scarcely choose to notice seriously, either to punish or to redeem, not a carrion-bird, to be sure, but still an animal: a kind of faithful dog that waggingly accepts both loving sustenance and punishment with endearing but mindless loyalty. Implicit in these very images, however, and even before the introduction of the wrestling metaphor, is the third point that the "last strands of man / In me" remain, and are newly strong. Though necessarily humbly inferior to God, he has not only "recked" but actively "kissed" the rod, the hand, that punishes; in doing so, he has answered with human love the touch of the finger of painful grace, has recognized Christ's gentler summons to "his own bespoken," has perhaps kissed the ring of the nun's divine Bridegroom.

As both his instinctive response of "yes" and this newly established relationship suggest, and as the wrestling metaphor further emphasizes, the implied answer to "Cheer whóm though?"—though phrased as another question ("is it eách one?")—is "both," and "both" for one obvious and one more implicit reason. Clearly both combatants deserve praise and encouragement for *different* acts and qualities, Christ for his invincible "heaven-handling," the man for his humility and submission. But the phrasing and near rhyme of "whích one . . . eách one?" and especially the tone of "or me that fought him?" imply a near equality in nature, courage, merit. Unless Hopkins has abandoned the whole thrust of the rest of the poem and is dangerously close to abandoning his faith as well—the position argued by Harris[18]—such phrasing can only be

18. *Inspirations Unbidden*, 103, a reading that finds both the queries and the

possible because, even in the midst of combat, the antagonists were alike both in their activity and in their goals, sharing a combat that makes them one. The active spirit of Christ the hero is the Paraclete, and "a Paraclete is one who comforts, who cheers, who encourages, who persuades, who exhorts, who stirs up, who urges forward, who calls on; what the spur and word of command is to a horse, what clapping of hands is to a speaker, what a trumpet is to the soldier, that a Paraclete is to the soul: *one who calls us on*." This sermon then goes on to use what Hopkins admits is a "homely" example, that of a cricketer shouting to his teammate "Come on, come on!" and says in summary, "a Paraclete is just that, something that cheers the spirit of man, with signals and with cries, all zealous that he should do something and full of assurance that if he will he can" (1880, *SD* 70). This urgent "cheering on" of holy stress, encouraging and challenging man to stand up and achieve his best, if necessary by initial combat with Christ himself, is what the sestet, indeed the whole sonnet, dramatizes. And when the intransitive "cheer" (l. 8) demands an object and finds one, when Christ's challenge to combat and redemption is answered by the poet's equally urgent response, Christ and his opponent become one in their mutual urging of each other to fight—in the fullest sense of the phrase—the good fight, the great and saving battle for the self's manhood and the soul's salvation.

In the final lines, the night of wrestling with his dark angel has explicitly ended, and the "day" wished for so weakly in the octave and in merely physical terms has broken spiritually, not merely because he has fought and survived two combats—the one against despair, won by winning, the other against the "hero," won by losing—but because he can now recognize with horror the dual nature of his previous presumption. Unlike the somewhat similar lines in "I wake and feel the fell of dark," "That níght, that yéar / Of now done darkness" does not merely or mainly make the slightly self-pitying point that his night of suffering seemed as long as a year, his year of suffering one seemingly endless night. There is horror, not just pathos, in that stressed "yéar," resulting from Hopkins' recognition that he has been too exuberant, too "cheerful," about his part in the combat. While initial struggle may be necessary, even meritorious, persistent rebellion damns, and the lines express the fear that his struggle against God may have seemed

---

approximate rhyme a rhetorical means of masking, evading, the "real import" of the questions.

not only to him, but to divine eyes also, so terribly and impenitently extended.

Hopkins of course now fully acknowledges the identity of his opponent by fully naming him. Presumably he has known, as we have known, that "the hero" was Christ, but as long as Christ remained as nameless as the initial "thou terrible" Hopkins could freely pursue, on one level of consciousness, the question of merit-through-combat, and could do so without terror. Now, however, the name must be "uttered outright," and so strikes home, bringing with it both horror at his own presumption and awed gratitude for his opponent's forbearance and forgiving love.

The stages through which this final line passed reveal both Hopkins' meticulous theological discipline and his poetic daring. The first point is demonstrated by his cancellation in the last revision of the phrase "wrung with God," some version of which appears in all preceding drafts, and its replacement with "lay wrestling with." Both phrases reflect his attention to unity of imagery and idea, but only the latter is wholly accurate as a description of the man's actual position in relation to God as the whole poem defines it. "Wrung with" would have neatly echoed "Thy wring-world right foot" and all the imagery of pressure, twisting, untwisting, crucial to the rest of the sonnet; by placing man momentarily on a par with God, it would also have reemphasized the violence of the struggle, developed the implications of "is it eách one?," and ultimately implied the major point about the human wrestler's incredible presumption. The revised version, however, is scrupulous in its reminder that whether man is the prone victim or, like Jacob, erect in heroic combat, he is always and inevitably "trod hard down" by the mighty foot of God, flung to the ground by Christ's "heaven-handling," and can only rise again when he abandons the presumptuous battle. The introduction of the present participle "wrestling" in conjunction with the past tense of "lay" may also hint at how prolonged and present the combat then seemed and still seems, and may even imply what "No worst, there is none" will make explicit: that night is not at all "now done."

The revisions also reflect Hopkins' dissatisfaction with a final line that lacked the emotional intensity sufficient to convey the magnitude of his past presumption, the magnitude of his present recognition. Through several drafts he was content to emphasize these points simply through use of "I wretch" and the "wrestled, wrung with God" phrasing. In the last draft he apparently decided that something must be done to make the contrast between "wretch" and "God" far sharper, and he tried first an even flatter line than the earlier version:

our

I wretch in wrestle wrung with ~~great~~ God.

This attempt is then heavily crossed out and followed with dramatic suddenness and dramatic effect by the final version, in which the poet's horrified recognition seems to break out spontaneously in the words of that one brief, terrified exclamation.

Some readers will find this daring attempt too melodramatic to be moving—it left Winters, for example, "quite cold."[19] Even Hopkins himself may have had momentary doubts, artistic or perhaps doctrinal, about the exclamation: something, very possibly the exclamation mark, is heavily crossed out, though then immediately replaced—"(my God*!*)." This replacement may reflect a rapid decision that its emotional daring was poetically effective, and/or a conclusion that he was not taking the Lord's name in vain, but meeting the Ignatian conditions for its use, only "with truth, necessity and reverence."[20] Alternatively, he may simply have closed the parenthesis without exclamatory punctuation and then swiftly decided to dare it. In either case, the result of this characteristic daring is that the theme, as well as the emotional intensity, of the whole poem is summarized in that brief repetition of the same words in radically different tones. The exclamation of terrified awe reminds us of all the sonnet has shown of God's massive, potentially terrible, power and man's necessary submission to it. The final phrase—in which I hear not an echo "of the agonized words of the dying Christ"[21] but rather quiet recognition, release, gratitude—reminds us that while God is indeed great in power, he is not the beast-tormentor of the octave, casually cruel, brutally destructive. He is after all a personal God, whose "rod, / Hand rather" touches humanity in love, who is for Hopkins, and he believes for each human being, personally and intimately "my God." What the nine words of "over again I feel thy finger and find thee" said in *The Deutschland*'s opening, this sonnet's ending says in two.

19. "The Poetry of Gerard Manley Hopkins, II," 84.
20. *Spiritual Exercises*, 26–27.
21. A possible echo on which two fine critics entirely disagree. Mariani, the first to note the allusion, emphasizes "the privilege of being crucified with Christ" it would convey (*Commentary*, 233); Harris, the forsakenness: "A gasped, awed recognition of past grace extended, it is also an acknowledgment of grace now lost" (*Inspirations Unbidden*, 104).

"(Carrion Comfort)," the most heavily revised of the "terrible sonnets" in extant drafts, is as a whole a kind of *Deutschland* in miniature, in both concept and imagery, and it is the only one of these sonnets in which the struggle with the divine Hunter is not only grand in ultimate result but even in its terror almost exuberant. I therefore speculate, as did Bridges, that this was the sonnet "written in blood," not because its content is "terrible," but exactly because it is not: by sheer wrenching effort, artistic, emotional, spiritual, Hopkins managed to forge out of desolation a poem of hope, to wring from despair joy, from struggle redemption. But the ominous suggestions of what has made the struggle so intense, of what has been and of what is to come, are there: in the opening quatrain's desolate isolation and desolate hope, especially; in the second quatrain's dramatization of torture at the hands of an unknown torturer; even perhaps in the final lines, whose assertion that the "year" of darkness is "now done" seems to tempt whatever gods may be to prove otherwise.

The relationship between this sonnet and "No worst, there is none" is parallel to the movement expressed in Caradoc's soliloquy, on which Hopkins was also at work in 1885:

> To hunger and not have, yét ǀ hope oń for, to storm and strive and
> Be at every assault fresh foiled, ǀ worse flung, deeper disappointed,
> The turmoil and the torment, ǀ it has, I swear, a sweetness,
> Keeps a kind of joy in it, ǀ a zest, an edge, an ecstasy,
> Next after sweet success. ǀ I am not left even this . . . .
> (152, *St. Winefred's Well*, 2.55–59)

In "No worst," Hopkins is "not left even this." This sonnet recognizes that spiritual darkness can never be assumed to be "now done" in this life, rejecting not only the strenuous "zest" and final affirmation of "(Carrion Comfort)" but even its bleak initial hopes for physical day and physical survival. The only comfort now lies in the hopes for physical night, for sleep, death's daily shadow, and ultimately for death itself. Having found in the other poem that to be "flung" to the depths could lead to a splendid rising, Hopkins now confronts only the bottomless cliffs of desolation, the "hurtle of hell" here and hereafter. Having there been redeemed by the "wring-world" stress of God, by the "turns of tempest" winnowing his soul, he is now simply wrung with endless, senseless pain and can only creep to ignominious shelter in the midst of a wholly destructive whirlwind from which no God speaks to his suffering servant. This is the sonnet that might well have been titled "Carrion Comfort." Though this poem does not quite reach the depths of the "cliffs of fall"—"I wake and feel the fell of dark" will nearly do so—the poet's precarious hold on a fragile and hopeless hope is here close to being entirely broken.

The sonnet's method demonstrates Hopkins' demanding combination of austerity and density in all its elements and particularly his power to make sheer grammar a thing of grim beauty and significance forever. Especially in the opening line, but also throughout the poem, and indeed throughout Hopkins' poetry in general, the elementary grammar of experience as of language is complicated, but precisely and spiritually eloquent.

> No worst, there is none. Pitched past pitch of grief,
> More pangs will, schooled at forepangs, wilder wring.

The first flat, grim statement, often misinterpreted because even careful readers tend to hear what they expect and wish to hear rather than what Hopkins is saying, uses the superlative only to deny even its bleak consolation: there will never be a point at which one can at least have the comfort of saying "This is the worst, nothing can be worse than this, it must get better"; one can never say and hope that the worst is "now done." Announcing the point both of the immediately following lines and of the whole sonnet, this typical manipulation of syntax again plays relentlessly upon the possibilities of multiple negatives, as in the opening of "(Carrion Comfort)"; this time, however, not even the faintest affirmative can emerge from the grammatical lockstep of the line.

Deepening still further the bleakness of this opening are the underlying allusions to *King Lear*, which parallel what I take to be the dramatic and logical movement from "(Carrion Comfort)" to this poem and perhaps account for the pairing of the two sonnets in Hopkins' drafts. The first poem has dramatized Edgar's conventional hope that the Wheel of Fortune must turn upward, that "The lamentable change is from the best, / The worst returns to laughter" (4.1.5–6); the second dramatizes his soon ensuing tragic recognition: "The worst is not / So long as we can say 'This is the worst'" (4.1.27–28).[22]

22. For the allusion to "the worst is not" I am indebted to Howard Nemerov, though others have also noted it. Gardner, while curiously omitting this particular echo, first suggested the pervasive influence of *King Lear* on the entire sonnet (*Hopkins*, 1:178–79). The relation between Edgar's two speeches and the two son-

That "the worst is not" and never will be reached is the point of the following complex metaphors. "Pitched past pitch of grief" is one of Hopkins' most typically dense phrases, complicated enough in grammatical reference, its complexity further increased by the use of "pitch"—multidimensional in itself in meaning—as both noun and verb. Originally Hopkins considered some simpler versions of the phrase: "grief past pitch of grief," above which the final alternative is jotted, and "Grief past grief" or "tops grief." His typical final choice was for the richest and most telling of his four alternatives (see Appendix E). Grammatically, the phrase modifies "pangs," and both as noun and as past participle "pitch" has mainly to do with the level, the degree, of their intensity. In Hopkins' later writings the noun *pitch* seems to replace *inscape* and especially *haecceitas* to signify the level of distinctiveness, refinement, intensity that a self may reach on its scale of possibility, as in the often-quoted statement on selving: "I find myself both as man and as myself something most determined and distinctive, at pitch, more distinctive and higher pitched than anything else I see. . . . Nothing else in nature comes near this unspeakable stress of pitch, distinctiveness, and selving, this selfbeing of my own" (1880, *SD* 122, 123).[23] In the prose, however, as in the opening lines of the sonnet, "pitch" does not necessarily imply a triumphant rising toward fulfilled goodness of selfhood; it may be "unspeakable" in a different sense, since Hopkins envisions also a scale of possible pitch that is infinite toward evil, so that there can be both infinite pain and even the possibility of the "ideal sin" (*SD* 147).

"Pitch" in this poem is also almost certainly intended to imply its musical connotations, especially that of the tightening of a string to achieve a higher and higher and finer pitch.[24] It therefore evokes a physical sense of unbearable strain, raised, tightened, to highest "stress of pitch" and then raised beyond that, endlessly. In so doing, it leads logically to "wring" (l. 2), possibly suggesting that the engine upon which the poet-speaker is tortured is not only the anvil but the rack; certainly it initiates the horrible dissonance of the rest of the poem's "music" of pain—the cries of the sufferer,

---

nets as wholes has not, I believe, been previously suggested.

23. For discussion of further complexities see *SD* 146–48, 151; Devlin's notes, 146.5 and 146.6, 293; Peters, *Critical Essay*, 23; Miller, *Disappearance of God*, 344.

24. As noted by Devlin, in treating the concept of "pitch" both Scotus and Hopkins assume the image of a violin and its tuning mechanism (*SD*, appendix 2, 343).

the shrieks of Fury, the blows of the hammer on the anvil that "wince and sing."

"Pitch" may also initiate imaginatively, though not syntactically, two further images and ideas central to the sestet: extreme height and depth (as noun, "angle of inclination," the mountain climber's term, a meaning assumed in Hopkins' discussions of scales of pitch; as verbal past participle, "hurled, flung down, cast to the depths"); possibly also the image of darkness. (Students, I find, instinctively react, and usually react first, to that connotation of blackness.) If here, these connotations are perfect examples of "underthought, conveyed chiefly in the choice of metaphors etc used . . . commonly an echo or shadow of the overthought" (1883, *FL* 252–53).

This short phrase, therefore, manages to say literally that the pangs of pain are strung to higher and higher levels of intolerable but endless intensity, levels that top and retop the seemingly highest and total pitch of "ideal" grief. By logical metaphorical association, it evokes the terrible "music" and the terrible torture to come. By implication, by underthought bypassing syntax, it suggests that the sufferer is flung ever deeper than the seemingly lowest depths of despair and calls into our minds the horrific heights and depths, and even the darkness, that the rest of the sonnet will develop.

Metrically as well as grammatically the opening line illustrates Hopkins' mastery of the essentially simple but potentially complex. He is now willing to return to something like standard meter, but he manages to enrich its possibilities with the nuances of sprung and counterpointed rhythms without making any elaborate display of them. The first line, for example, can be scanned as normal iambic pentameter, with either an initial spondaic or trochaic substitution ("Nó wořst, theře ís noñe. Pítched pašt pítch of gríef"), but the more heavily falling, more jagged, possibilities of sprung feet may also be heard beneath, or even dominating, the iambic pattern: "Nó wořst, theře ís noñe. Pítched pašt pítch ǒf gríef." In the same way, the famous ninth line may be scanned according to standard meter in one of two ways (with an initial anapest or an initial trochee), but the enjambment of "fall / Frightful" strongly suggests a more natural sprung scansion, which also places heavy and emotionally intense stress on the second "mind": "Ó thě mínd, mínd hǎs móuntaiñs; clíffs ǒf fǎll / Fríghtfǔl." The third and fourth lines seem even more resistant to standard scansion and require sprung stressing to catch the natural weighting and word units: "Cómfořtěr, whére, whére ís yoǔr cómfořtiñg? /

Márў,́ móthĕr ŏf uš, whére iš̆ yoúr rĕliéf?" The same may be said of most of the lines of the poem; the ear must and does adjust itself to the nuances of a basic sense of standard rhythm combined with sprung rhythm's flexibility and heavy beat, a combination that involves more variety, certainly greater intensity, of stressing than can be achieved by the substitution common in all good poetry.

In spite of numerous revisions in word order, all versions of the second line include *schooled*, a word not quite as grammatically and conceptually complex as *pitch*, but with its own suggestive doubleness. The residual meaning, feeling, we are likely to take from this line is that while one can stand a sudden shock of pain, repeated pain in the same area is unendurable, especially because we are "schooled" to anticipate it, knowing how bad it was before— thoughts of the dentist's drill come inevitably though perhaps trivially to mind. In short, we are likely to assume that "schooled" modifies the poet-speaker. In fact, of course, it grammatically modifies "pangs," endowing them with a vicious humanity, an ability to improve in sadism as they learn from their predecessors, a horribly perverted capacity for discipline in unrestrained savagery. In my view, however, the apparent conflict between the imaginative and grammatical meanings is most deliberate and not a conflict at all. The victim, here as later, becomes one with his pain and is perhaps himself the source of it. The question is already raised as to whether there is a torturer beyond himself; already a strange fusion is created of self, pain, and tormentor, all of which are "schooled at forepangs," all of which become more cruelly skilled with practice, and all of which are somehow within the tortured mind.

In the following futile attempt to break out of the mind's prison and torture chamber, to seek the only possible sources of remission and deliverance, the phrasing emphasizes both the assumption that those sources exist somewhere—an assumption never denied even in these sonnets—and the point that they are not available to the suffering speaker: "Cómforter, whére, whére iś your cómforting? / Máry, móther of us, whére is yoúr reliéf?" Grimly ironic repetition swiftly makes the point that the Paraclete, the Comforter, is now only the name not the act, and the metrical stresses suggested on the repeated "whére" and on "iś" underscore the hopelessness and almost desperate wailing of the question. In the next line, increased desperation, even accusation, is emphasized by the probably heavy stress on "yoúr": if the Paraclete, who has already been shown in "(Carrion Comfort)" to be a somewhat strenuous comforter, betrays its function now, surely at least Mary the divine mother should console her human child in pain.

Since the questions are met with silence, the second quatrain can only turn back to pain, can only seek a kind of "comfort" and "relief" in attempting to define further the nature, perhaps the sources, of suffering, an attempt that actually involves intensification of pain, a further tightening of the screws. Like the ending of "Spelt from Sibyl's Leaves," the quatrain reflects Hopkins' thoughts on the pains of hell, "the thought that probably the sense of the penalty of loss is what of itself begets the (sort-of self inflicted) penalty of sense or, as I have often thought, that the *pain* (grief) of loss relieves itself by pain of sense" (*SD* 141).

> My cries heave, herds-long; huddle in a main, a chief-
> woe, wórld-sorrow; on an áge-old ánvil wínce and síng—
> Then lull, then leave off. Fury had shrieked "No ling-
> ering! Let me be fèll: force I must be brief."

"Pain of sense" in these lines is both made cruelly physical through multisensuous imagery and translated into more inner psychological and mental terms. "Heave"—a revision of the original flat "come"—visually evokes the surging, sealike motion of a flock of sheep, a phenomenon on which Hopkins commented at least twice in the journals,[25] but in context that external sight and its visual distinctness are brought inward and have a muscular and auditory more than visual impact. The implication in meaning of the heaving chest itself, together with the difficult panting of the *h*-alliteration, conveys both the whole body's straining and the spasmodic gasping of his animalistic cries as they are wrung from him. The physicality of "huddle" is radically transformed into the wholly psychological by the nature of the shelter his cries seek, or to which they are driven: "a main, a chief- / woe, world-sorrow." Much more terribly now than in "Spring and Fall" Hopkins is personally doomed by "the blight man was born for," reenacts individually the original alienation from God, for the ancient universal loss suffers on an anvil that now offers none of *The Deutschland*'s

---

25. "I saw the phenomenon of the sheepflock on the downs again from Croham Hurst. It ran like the water-packets on a leaf . . . : at a gap in the hedge they were huddled and shaking open as they passed outwards they behaved as the drops would do . . . in reaching the brow of a rising and running over" (August 30, 1868, *JP* 187); "They [farmers] were marking a sea of sheep" (September 17, 1872, *JP* 227). Whether the water associations imply some underthought of tears as well as cries in the poem, and even had some effect on the choice of "main," I leave readers to consider.

confident hope that it is God who is there forging his redemptive will in man, a truly "grim forge" on which no "bright and battering sandal" is now created. There is perhaps a kind of shelter and comfort in the idea that his personal suffering results not simply from personal sin but from the sin that has marked all humanity since Adam's fall—a comfort not allowed by the later image of the mind's "cliffs of fall"—but the main force of the whole metaphor is to present a panic-stricken heart and being "hard at bay," though here without any human capacity to say either "yes" or "no."[26]

The grammatical complexity of this metaphor creates a fusion that further untwists whatever strands of man remain. Strictly speaking, the imagery of animal helplessness and number, as well as the suggestion of panic in the coinage "herds-long" ("headlong"), modifies the cries rather than the whole man, but the total implication is the one assumed above, that he is nothing but cries now, nothing but animalistic pain, no selfhood, no human voice left. The difficult syntax of the following lines emphasizes this reduction through the questions it raises: what is the subject of "wince and sing"? What exactly lies and is beaten on the anvil? Again, grammatically it is the cries that "huddle" there, "wince and sing," "lull, then leave off," but the logical and visual strangeness of the first two images not only creates the necessary nonphysical inwardness but also supports the important fusion. "Wince," while very odd as a modifier for "cries," is wholly fitting as a description of the body's flinching as it anticipates the coming blows and as the shock and sound of those blows ring through its being. The result is that while he is only cries now, his cries, his mind, are endowed with a capacity to suffer as intensely as a physical body subjected to physical pain. Similarly, "sing" is less appropriate to the sound of his cries than to the metallic ringing of the hammer blows on the anvil, the blows we have been hearing all along in the meter, and perhaps in the early homophone "wring" ("ring"), but again the point is that the terrible music of torment evokes a similar "music" from the victim; cries and blows together follow an endless process of onset, brief lull, and new onset. The total effect is to make us feel

26. The "age-old anvil" and the whole poem may owe something to the Prometheus myth, as suggested by Sister Mary Humiliata, "Hopkins and the Prometheus Myth," a suggestion pursued by MacKenzie, *Hopkins*, 92–93, and Cotter, *Inscape*, 224. Though Hopkins does not seem to me to present himself as the heroic martyr for humanity, but as a far more broken and causeless sufferer, the allusion is tempting as possible underthought.

that the poet-speaker, poet-singer, is only pain now, that he is the blows, the cries, and perhaps the torturer.

Although some subliminal associations with the classical Furies may suggest that the tormentor here is also a vengeful agent of a just though hidden and silent God, and although the past tense, "had shrieked," may hope or pretend that pain is over, the sonnet as a whole allows no such comfort.[27] This insanely savage "Fury" is either the torturer within—"My spirits were so crushed that madness seemed to be making approaches" (September 1, 1885, *LB* 222, referring to his state in the previous spring and summer)—or the sadistic agent of some wholly irrational or satanic force external to the mind, or both. In any case, its only, wholly cruel, and vividly present announcement of its nature and purpose is

> "No ling-
> ering! Let me be fèll: force I must be brief."

The idiosyncratic "ling- / ering" probably looks too self-consciously odd to the eye, but it is not so to the ear, or to the mind. The oddity dramatizes initially a pause contrary to the content of the statement, offers a taunting hope, a brief hiatus, but since it is immediately followed by a surge with renewed speed and power into the next line it dramatizes both Fury's sadism and the nature of its attacks. Reinforcing the same effect are the moments of "fèll" (that notation indicating a long hold and pause) and of "force" (denoting "perforce," connoting its obvious other meaning): in meaning and connotation these convey both the cruel might and the descent of the hammer blows, and at that heavy caesura between them we should probably feel that after an initial blow a short lull has intervened, followed by a savagely renewed assault.

The sestet's initial lines dramatize the point that there is "No worst" in this life in terms that are both less savage than those of the octave and more terrible in their bleakness:

> O the mind, mind has mountains; cliffs of fall
> Frightful, sheer, no-man-fathomed. Hold them cheap
> May who ne'er hung there. Nor does long our small
> Durance deal with that steep or deep. Here! creep,

27. Harris persuasively argues that far from offering even pretended respite, the past tense emphasizes the suffering before the poem opens and out of which it grew, prompting its futile appeal for Christian comfort, "But the attempt to superimpose Christian colloquy on pagan noise fails" (*Inspirations Unbidden*, 106).

Wretch, under a comfort serves in a whirlwind: all
Life death does end and each day dies with sleep.

The austere beauty of that first line and its truth make it one of the great lines in Hopkins' poetry. With perfect restraint and brevity it calls up the inner landscape of all human minds, the actual landscape of the spiritual life, making its grim configurations so tangible that we can almost see and even touch them, yet making them wholly inward; the perspective is such that though we initially seem to view the mind's mountains from a distance, as Hopkins draws back to comment on them, we nevertheless find ourselves, like him, on those "cliffs of fall," within that landscape which is within us. Moreover, exactly because the mountain metaphor, unlike those of the octave, allows us to turn outward for a moment to the physical world beyond the mind's prison, only to draw that world's most massive terrors into the mind again, this new embodiment of the "No worst" theme is the more telling, and perhaps the more frightening. Facing the "no-man-fathomed" depths, depths that are bottomless, or at least so deep that no man who has fathomed them survives, we may experience a spiritual vertigo that is at least as visceral in impact and as intensely inward as the tortured sense of psychological enclosure we have felt in the preceding lines. Technically also, the line is a concentrated example of Hopkins' craftsmanship at its best. Quite simply, but with powerful effect, the long *O* and long-drawn *i's*, the linking *m*-alliteration, the stresses on both *minds* work to create the haunting tone of weary reflectiveness and hopeless finality. The enjambment of "cliffs of fall / Frightful" then alters tone and tempo, dramatizing the terror of the mind's swift plunge down those sheer steeps.

Two of the special meanings of "pitch" now become grimly significant because they become synonymous. "Steep" and "deep" are now the same, both destructive, not distinguishable as the upward pitch to self-fulfillment, the downward pitch to destruction, or, if distinguishable, the first is too steep for him to scale now. Nevertheless, in this sonnet, Hopkins still clings to one precarious mind-hold above the abyss. In a sense, the very fact that the sestet is initially reflective, interpretive, rather than dramatic shows the mind's temporary return to control and dominance; there has been a sufficient lull in the torture to permit a pause for reflection and generalizaton and a brief sardonic comment on those who have never known the cost of knowing the cliffs of fall. But it is only when the speaker realizes the implication of one of his general statements that he discovers the one desolate "comfort" allowed in this poem: because of the brevity and frailty of human "durance" —a word ironically implying its root meaning, "strength, toughness," as well as simply "endurance"—we cannot, need not, struggle eternally on the mind's mountains. The grim comfort implied in Fury's "force I must be brief" becomes the one consolation now; there is no need, it seems, either to climb or to fall, only to hold on a little longer. With a full return to the dramatic method and personal present that entirely belies the temporary distance from his suffering previously achieved, the poet accepts that one desolate hope: "Here! creep, / Wretch. . . ."

The "wretch" of "(Carrion Comfort)," presumptuous though he was, had at least wrestled manfully with a powerfully present God. Now, lower than his "herds-long" cries, lower and more alone than Lear on the stormy heath, he can only creep into the ignominious shelter of hope for death, temporal and eternal. This is the last refuge left on the whirlwind-swept cliffs whose tempests do not winnow but destroy; it is the last shameful comfort suffering man can find when the Comforter is absent; it is the last covering for a child denied its mother's consolation. No God speaks to a new Job out of this whirlwind, no Holy Ghost breathes from or through it, "Mary, mother of us" does not reach down to protect and embrace, and Hopkins can therefore only wish *night* come, can only wish—not even choose—"not to be."

In strained, flat monosyllables, and with a dead finality of tone like that of the opening statement that it purports to answer with consolation, the final line plods to its weary and hopeless extinction; the dull beating of heavy sounds dies weakly into that hush which is the poor but only present substitute for final comfort: "all / Life death does end and each day dies with sleep." The exhausted quietness of this ending is to my ear wholly desolate, the more terrible because here the poet-priest, if not the priest, abandons not only the hope of heaven's afterlife but the dread of hell's.[28]

This sonnet is an intensely concentrated example of Hopkins' "authentic cadence" at its best and most powerful. A spiritual experience becomes almost unbearably physical and visceral in impact without ever becoming merely physical; the senses—sight, as usual, least of all—function with painful intensity, but only to

28. For more positive interpretations of the final lines see Mariani, *Commentary*, 227–28, and Cotter, *Inscape*, 224–25. For an even bleaker reading than mine, taking "Life" as an epithet for Christ but finding in the buried reminder "a mockery of his earlier faith," see Harris, *Inspirations Unbidden*, 108.

make cruelly tangible the inner world of spiritual torment, never to relieve us from it; superimposed layers of metaphor, grammatical reference, and associated underthought graphically embody the vivid yet bafflingly "no-man-fathomed" quality of the whole dark experience. No less than God himself, indeed because of God himself, spiritual anguish was for Hopkins a mysterious certainty that his cadence perfectly incarnates.

The first of the "unbidden" sonnets, "To seem the stranger," represents in some ways a quite different quality of desolation and even makes some attempt to grope upward, or at least outward, on the cliffs of fall. It does not dramatize from within a wholly internal and wholly nightmarish experience but is a poem of statement, recognizing an actual external world, seeking to analyze both outer and inner sources of desolation, even trying to remember sources of consolation. Ultimately, however, it descends perilously close to the depths, since heaven and hell, hardly distinguishable now, alike dictate Hopkins' total isolation from family, country, and God and his total sterility, not only as poet but also as preacher, teacher, scholar, prophet. Although I do not accept Harris' argument that it is "the last of the 'terrible sonnets' to be completed and thus in some sense Hopkins's final analysis of his torment," for the reasons discussed earlier, I am close to agreeing that its one point of detailed revision in the sestet constitutes "the most radically heterodox gesture of his poetry."[29]

Strangely, in spite of its deep pain and its terrible and brilliant conclusion, this sonnet is low-keyed, muted, even at times somewhat mechanical in cadence. It is true that so simple a line as "I am in Ireland now" is haunting in its music, carrying sad reverberations far beyond those that easily lift from the written page. It is true that the governing imagery of thwarted procreation in all areas, and the linked imagery of thwarted heroism, is dexterously handled throughout. But in this sonnet, until and even at the end, music and imagery are less central than the careful manipulation of the moments and grammatical possibilities of certain individual words and phrases.

The quiet, seemingly objective opening statement, "To seem

29. *Inspirations Unbidden*, 113, 117. This entire reading should be consulted, since its details are more intricate and illuminating than my objections to assumptions behind them convey. Of particularly provocative interest is the conclusion that the sonnet "remains a profoundly Christian poem: its primary subject is Hopkins's all but parthenogenetic effort to give rebirth to himself as a Christian" (124).

the stranger lies my lot," doubly implies a muted rebellion against the sorrow of separation that the opening quatrain overtly accepts with sad resignation. "Seem" clearly suggests that this is not, or should not be, Hopkins' true role, that he could be more if there were greater challenges or any answering recognition from any source, a source of frustration he will scrupulously analyze in later Retreat notes: "But I say to myself that I am only too willing to do God's work and help on the knowledge of the Incarnation. But this is not really true: I am not willing enough for the piece of work assigned me, the only work I am given to do, though *I could do others if they were given*. This is my work at Stephen's Green" (January 5, 1888, *SD* 263, italics mine). That meticulously honest self-correction, "But this is not really true," is a kind of keynote in the sonnets also, producing at times balanced self-reproach but at others, as in this poem, intensification of the truth of desolation. That desolation is further intensified in the first line by "lies my lot," grimly implying the fatality that decrees his exile; the Fates, perhaps, not Christ, have rolled the dice, have cast the lots, and it is this muted idea that the last lines of the sestet will painfully and radically develop.

In the second quatrain a second abdication is made, as the rejected lover (almost petulantly, one fears) asserts his independence by abandoning the suit before attempting it:

> England, whose honour O all my heart woos, wife
> To my creating thought, would neither hear
> Me, were I pleading, plead nor do I: I wear-
> y of idle a being but by where wars are rife.

As a whole, this quatrain expresses and exemplifies the linked failure of words and heroic deeds. As Harris acutely observes, the syntax itself dramatizes the inability to speak: "the speaker slides in these lines from potential apostrophe to declarative statement," enacting as well as stating the failure of words to speak *to* anyone or anything, ultimately dramatizing an abortion, even a parody, of Ignatian colloquy.[30] Simultaneously, the final phrase deftly returns to the earlier "sword and strife" imagery, a return that completes the statement of his impotence not only as teacher-lover of humanity but as soldier of God. Having accepted Christ's call to arms, to glorious sacrifice, he now finds himself denied even that pain and glory, a mere sidelined soldier, an observer "but by" (only on the

30. Ibid., 115.

periphery of) the wars—military, political, moral—in which he should but cannot be engaged.

Most noteworthy here, if slightly too obvious, are the striking oddities in the last two lines. While the enjambment of "wear- / y" seems rather more forced than similar instances in other poems, it does work, as usual, in oral recitation: musically, it creates a kind of rove-over internal rhyme ("hear/Me," "wear-/y"), satisfying to the ear; thematically and emotionally, it makes us feel the weariness by drawing out the vowel and dragging the word over into the next line, and it leads to that line's heavy movement, which reflects an exhaustion that can barely drag itself from one word to the next. Second, the extremely idiosyncratic "idle a being" does achieve an effect that normal syntax could not have produced: "weary of being idle" would imply, if only weakly, too much potential power of choice to be something else; "weary of an idle being, existence" allows a life that has some sort of shape and quality to it, again perhaps only a temporary quality that could be exchanged for another. The present version, in contrast, has three important effects: it puts full emphasis on "idle," the first word that comes to Hopkins' mind as being his essence, all he is, a condition, not an action; it allows him a bare existence, without energy or purpose or choice; it emphasizes, through use of the present participle as a noun, the futile and tedious continuation of something that ought to be life and action but is endlessly thwarted and inactive.

The sestet's conclusion expresses with bleak and powerful compression the central source of desolation as this sonnet defines it. As in *The Deutschland*, love, "heart-throe, birth of a brain," should issue in the "Word," but here that strain to birth is aborted:

> Only what word
> Wisest my heart breeds dark heaven's baffling ban
> Bars or hell's spell thwarts. This to hoard unheard,
> Heard unheeded, leaves me a lonely began.

These lines express not only the poet's frustration, though that is crucial, but also the scholar-priest's inability to complete, or contribute to, any significant work. All his planned scholarly "beginnings" of the 1880s (works on Homer, on Greek lyric art, on Irish dialect, on Saint Patrick's *Confessions*, on Roman rituals, on Pindar and the Dorian measure; Egyptian studies; endless etymological studies) issued in nothing but fragments and perhaps reflect the almost frenetic attempts of a still versatile but tired mind to drive it-

self to energy, to keep the wheels in motion, to find some meaningful warfare through "grinding at grammar," all the while crippled
further, perhaps, by a perfectionist's fear that scholarship's minu-
tiae, like poetry's beauty, could not be sufficient as acts of service
or expressions of faith. So as he wrote to Baillie after sorting his letters in April 1885, "there they lie and my old notebooks and beginnings of things, ever so many, which it seems to me might well have
been done, ruins and wrecks" (April 24, 1885, *FL* 255). A sad distance lies between this statement, and this sonnet, and his youthful
cheerfulness as he wrote to the same friend in 1864 about his many
embryonic poems: "So, though I finish nothing, I am not idle"
(July 20, 1864, *FL* 214). Moreover, as the Retreat notes make
clear, to the extent that he was a soldier at all he was an unwilling
conscript in the political warfare of Anglo-Irish politics, in which
the Catholic Church seemed to him to be mistakenly aiding Irish
rebellion: "and against my will my pains, laborious and distasteful,
like prisoners made to serve the enemies' gunners, go to help on
this cause" (1888, *SD* 262).[31]

Stylistically, the final lines are the only ones in the poem of
characteristic Hopkinsian intensity, and typically they are lines that
by no means came "unbidden," as the intricate revisions indicate
(Appendix E). The germ of his "creating thought" has now become
at least embryonic "word," and the revision from "Wisest my heart
holds" or "keeps" to "breeds" lends him for a brief moment a life-
creating energy; but that potential life is then immediately aborted,
crushed in sound as in meaning by the triply battering alliteration:
"baffling ban / Bars." The grim and radical revision from the
vaguer "some ban" to "dark heaven's ban" makes heaven as dark
and as cruel as hell, nearly indistinguishable from it in effect,
though this revision may be no more final than similar alternatives
in "(Carrion Comfort)" and "No worst," and though some slight
moral distinction is perhaps retained in the difference between
"ban" and "spell." Hopkins' scruples on this point may have joined
with alliterative considerations to account for his original tinkering
with the adjectives and the words they modify: he first revised
"dark heaven's ban" to "baffling heaven's dark ban," making the
judgment cruel but its source only mysteriously incomprehensible;
the second, perhaps final, revision sets aside any such scruples and
returns to the grimmer statement. As a result, thwarted alike by

31. See Bergonzi's full discussion of this quotation's political context,
Hopkins, 133–38.

heaven and hell, oddly bisexual, but doubly cursed to sterility, caught in the viciously unbreakable circle imitated by the chain of linked sounds, internal rhymes ("hell's spell," "dar[k]"/"bar[s]"), and the near chiasmus ("hoard unheard, / Heard unheeded"), he now not only "seems" the stranger to family and country but is in fact alienated from God himself, and what should go forth to be and to generate life is as dead as the miser's hoarded gold. He therefore now has no real "being" at all, not even a useless but present and continuing one; he is now merely "a lonely began."

Winters found this odd locution "so grotesque as to be ruinous,"[32] but it seems to me, as to numerous other critics, the one great inspiration in the poem. Though perhaps initially generated by the demands of rhyme and meter, meaning is flashed off technical necessity here, since neither the noun "beginner" nor an understood noun-plus-verb, as in Bridges' paraphrase "(one who only) began" (P 289), does what the startling coinage achieves. A verb that should imply both action and future possibility is doubly deadened—arrested as noun and frozen in the past tense; his past efforts, his past beginnings, are therefore doubly past now, stillborn at birth, irrevocably over. Unlike his poems, the text of his life cannot be revised, has no possibility of new variants: "began" can never become "accomplished, completed" because "began" itself is a desolate and unchangeable completion. While God remains somewhere the "Alpha and Omega, the beginning and the ending," the speaker here has become an aborted and grotesque fusion of the two, a mutant, solitary and, like his words, stillborn.

In spite of some fine moments, however, this poem seems to me poetically the least successful of the "terrible sonnets." Though in content it approaches the depths of the cliffs of fall, especially in the final lines, its somewhat wistful, close to self-pitying tone, its specifically personal and topical identification of the sources of desolation, its combination without fusion of extreme simplicity and extreme eccentricity, its overall lack of stylistic or dramatic density, make it a sadly moving personal sonnet, but not, to my ear, a deeply compelling one. It feels unfinished to me, psychologically and artistically, too much a "began" even in revised form, and I speculate that Hopkins' revisions show, at least in part, his own recognition of its need for further poetic intensification.

This speculation is more coldly cerebral, far less dramatic, than the one argued by Harris, but while I do not discount the despair-

32. "The Poetry of Gerard Manley Hopkins, II," 84.

ing honesty shown by the radical revisions, I cannot read those careful tinkerings with word order and word choice as the product of a mind wholly "overwhelmed by . . . gnashings of despair."[33] Nor does the evidence conclusively prove that they are a final summation, either of the sonnet series as a whole or of the year's desolate experience, since heavy revision does not automatically prove last-in-time, or last-in-thought, reconsideration. The poet's conscious mind seems to me clearly at work here to finish a poem, rather than to finish or undo a sequence, or a life.

If this is so, of course, it may reveal something almost as terrible to Hopkins himself as loss of faith: the exploitation, at least manipulation, of faith and its stages in the service of art, the very sacrilege he feared most to commit in writing poetry at all. Yet he was unquestionably by instinct and skill a poet-craftsman as well as an honest priest and man, and neither instinct nor skill deserted him as he struggled to express his seeming desertion by God. The evidence of this sonnet, and of all the dark sonnets, testifies mainly not to the priest's abandonment of faith but to the poet-priest's attempt to shape into art and insight a great darkness, a darkness that was most terrible because it issued from great faith. This, I believe, is what he painfully and consciously strove to do, and did do, with varying degrees of poetic completeness, in the sonnets of this desolate but not Godless year.

"I wake and feel the fell of dark," however, is truly almost too terrible to read or to bear. In this sonnet, "mystery" is retained in thought and method, but the depths that had seemed "no-man-fathomed" are now plumbed. Only the poem's whispered fragment of an ending, "but worse," shows that even now Hopkins will not quite say "This *is* the worst."

In the previous sonnets Hopkins had retained at least some fragile sense of the world external to the mind, some slim "life-line" not only attaching him to God, in Gardner's metaphor, but also linking him to the world of natural time and space and activity.[34] In "(Carrion Comfort)" he could "wish day come," physical day, and while deliberately blurring natural and spiritual time in "that night, that year," could conclude that the soul's night is "now done" in actual time. In "No worst, there is none" he could draw bleak consolation from the fact that life is temporal, and

33. *Inspirations Unbidden*, 9.
34. Gardner, *Hopkins*, 1:178. See also Miller's discussion of the breakdown of normal time, space, and language in the poems of Hopkins' last years, *Disappearance of God*, 353–57.

therefore temporary, and that each natural day dies with natural night. In "To seem the stranger" actual space and time are very much at the center of the poem until the final lines eliminate external space and completely reverse time's natural movement. That elimination of a world external to the suffering mind, that disjunction of space and time, becomes complete in "I wake and feel the fell of dark." Explicitly the "night" is no longer temporal or temporary but almost infinite, and there is no "space" now but the self, the inner mind and the foul body in which that mind is locked, and the unimaginably remote cosmic spaces, where perhaps a departed God "lives alas! away."

The dramatic movement of the poem is such, however, that this grim statement, while implicit in the opening quatrain, is not quite explicit:

> I wake and feel the fell of dark, not day.
> What hours, O what black hõurs we have spent
> This night! what sights you, heart, saw; ways you went!
> And more must, in yet longer light's delay.

In spite of the opening line's desolately paradoxical statement, in spite of the painful prolongation of time dramatized by the lengthening of "hours" to the disyllabic "hõurs," there is a kind of deceptive hope here. The past tenses of "spent," "saw," "went" initially suggest that at least the psychopathic nightmares are over, and even when that possibility is rejected in the fourth line there remains a faint chance that day will come, however tardily, and that this "night" is one temporal, literal night. This deceptiveness has two major effects, both central to this poem's particular kind of mysterious certainty: it obviously makes the more devastating the second quatrain's explicit statement that this is an almost infinite spiritual night; it also evokes every reader's memory of such actual nights of irrational terror, of waking from nightmare to continuing waking nightmare. The result is that we feel the horror of both the spiritual and the literal, and the nightmarish sense that time is wholly disjointed, that it is both terribly present and terribly endless.

This combination of literal and metaphorical is immediately at work in "fell," whose various implications lend spiritual experience the impact of physicality without losing the sense of metaphysical terror. Probably Hopkins uses "fell," as he had used "began," with underthoughts of its verbal sense, the past tense conveying the permanent and irreversible completion of night's falling, but it almost certainly functions mainly as the noun, "animal pelt, skin."

Hopkins' recorded memories of nightmare support this meaning: "I had a nightmare that night. I thought something or someone leapt onto me and held me quite fast"—an entry that goes on to say, "It made me think that this was how the souls in hell would be imprisoned in their bodies as in prisons" (September 18, 1873, *JP* 238). This meaning is also supported more specifically by his use of the word itself in happier days, when the "falls" of a glacier looked to him like "the skin of a white tiger or the deep fell of some other animal" (July 15, 1868, *JP* 174). The image may also owe something to Saint Ignatius ("there is no beast so wild on the face of the earth as the enemy of human nature," Satan) and conceivably to Saint John of the Cross, for whom the soul in its dark night sometimes "feels as if it were swallowed by a beast and being digested in the dark belly."[35] The full context of the nightmare entry, however, together with the sonnet's sestet, suggests that the origin of the image may have been experience of his own body's weight, and hence of a more internal and self-made "beast" of darkness: "The feeling is terrible: the body no longer swayed as a piece by the nervous and muscular instress seems to fall in and hang like a dead weight on the chest. I cried on the holy name and by degrees recovered myself" (*JP* 238). Finally, the adjectival meaning of "fell" as "cruel, ruthless," as in "No worst," may vibrate somewhere beneath the two primary moments. All senses of the word combine to convey the crushing weight and terrifyingly tactile presence of this huge and shaggy beast of darkness, a creature that is clearly not the lion-limbed savior of "(Carrion Comfort)" and may be in part the poet's own dark physicality.

The sense of helpless disorientation created by these lines is emphasized by the strange fragmentation of the speaker himself. We hear something akin to Prufrock's "Let us go then, you and I" in the wavering of the pronouns from "I" to "we" to "you, heart." Hopkins has occasionally before addressed his heart as something that is both a part of and apart from himself (28.3, 28.18, 38, for example), or it has addressed him (61), but there has always been some sense of underlying, unsplintered identity, and the heart has always been the source of instinctive insight into spiritual realities: "The heart is what rises towards good, shrinks from evil, recognising the good or the evil first by some eye of its own" (*SD* 257). Now, however, the strands of wholeness begin to untwist, and the

35. Loyola, *Spiritual Exercises*, 174; Saint John of the Cross, *Collected Works*, 337.

heart's "eye" sees not the reality of God but the reality of pathological unrealities. Disjunction is further reinforced by that painfully broken, monosyllabic line, "This night! what sights, you, heart, saw; ways you went!" Grim paradox, underscored by the "sights"/ "saw" repetition, emphasizes that darkness does not bring blessed blindness, and the heart must instead "see" only too clearly the horrors besetting its dark journeyings.

That Hopkins is already dramatizing here the horrors of hell, well before the final tercet makes the comparison explicit, seems probable, since parallels with the meditation notes on darkness as one of the punishments of hell are very close. Darkness is defined and explored as psychological and spiritual darkness, a condition of energy balked and imprisoned, of "foiled action" that should rightly strain toward God, and the notes then proceed to a very pertinent (though slightly misquoted) comment on Saint Theresa's vision of hell:

> the understanding open wide like an eye, towards truth in God, towards light, is confronted by that scape, that act of its own, which blotted out God and so put blackness in the place of light; does not see God but sees that, so giving a meaning to something I remember in St Theresa's vision of hell, to this effect: "I know not how it is, but in spite of the darkness the eye sees there all that to see is most afflicting". Against these acts of its own the lost spirit dashes itself like a caged bear and is in prison, violently in-stresses them and burns, stares into them and is the deeper darkened. ("A Meditation on Hell: 'Poenae,'" 1881, SD 137–38)

Beyond the evident parallels, it is significant in connection with "fell" that the final image of the soul staring at darkness is the "caged bear"; here as in "No worst," and in the nightmare entry previously quoted, the darkness and the torment and the tormentor are implicitly self-generated, are, in fact, the self itself.

In the second quatrain, the "I" becomes whole again, but only in order to reflect on the infinitude of its night and the central source of its desolation:

> With witness I speak this. But where I say
> Hours I mean years, mean life. And my lament
> Is cries countless, cries like dead letters sent
> To dearest him that lives alas! away.

In the opening phrase, Hopkins comments bleakly on the testimony of his own experience of past "nights" that brought no day, as this will bring none, and in the explicit translation of "hours" to "years" to "life" there is perhaps an echo of that legal "witness" imagery: the sentence is to life imprisonment, to solitary confinement in the dark prison of the self. From this prison of life's uncertain "hours" of night an earlier Advent sermon had promised the release of Christ's sudden light of Second Coming;[36] from this prison in the sonnet Hopkins can only send out his wholly futile appeals for reprieve in lines that dramatize the unbreakable circle in which he is caught. The pain of loss, the sense of abandonment by God, is the central source of his desolation, yet he can only turn for help to that lost God who, though he still exists somewhere, is already assumed to be totally absent from the poet's world, and can only appeal in cries that he knows end in some cosmically remote dead-letter office.

The simile of the "dead letters" develops, and probably subsumes, the metaphor of the stillborn "word" of "To seem the stranger": not only his cries but all his "letters"—sermons, meditations, scholarship, poetry—are so dead and so misdirected. ("Ah, Bartleby! ah humanity!") The simile itself is utterly colloquial, mundane, close to home, and at the same time frighteningly metaphysical. A more elevated simile could not make us feel and recognize the sense conveyed here of deep personal injury and loss, the loss of a once dear and intimate friend who has now moved on, without a word, without caring. On the other hand, since the context compels us to envision the endless reaches of empty space through which these "letters" travel to their final silence, the ordinary is "mounted in the scarlet," translated into spiritual terms without losing the impact of its literal actuality.

Up to this point the sonnet may possibly have come "unbidden"; only a single, almost uncorrected draft of the octave appears in H (see Appendix E). The sestet, however, underwent considerable revision before arriving at its concentrated expression of damning, and damned, and irrevocably fated, self-loathing:

> I am gall, I am heartburn. God's most deep decree
> Bitter would have me taste: my taste was me;
> Bones built in me, flesh filled, blood brimmed the curse.
>
> Selfyeast of spirit a dull dough sours. I see

36. "So then the world is again dark without him, because Christ the light of the world is gone. . . . And this night is not of so many hours, a number known beforehand; it is of quite uncertain length; and there is no dawn, no dayspring, to tell of the day coming, no morning twilight, the sunrise will be sudden, will be lightning, we are told" (First of Advent, November 30, 1879, *SD* 40).

> The lost are like this, and their scourge to be
> As I am mine, their sweating selves; but worse.

Until the last two words, Hopkins grimly follows here the letter, but not the spirit, of Ignatian law. That law requires the meditant to "ask for an interior *sense of pain* which the lost suffer," using all the senses to arrive at a proper fear of sin and hell, and ultimately at a joyous contemplation of God's mercy.[37] In the poem, Hopkins creates only a present and apparently eternal hell of self-disgust, especially dwelling, as he does also, though less brutally, in meditation notes, on taste: "*Fourth point—taste as with taste of tongue* all that is bitter there, the tears ceaselessly and fruitlessly flowing; the grief over their hopeless loss; the worm of conscience, which is the mind gnawing and feeding on its own most miserable self. It is still the same story: *they*, their sins are the bitterness, tasted sweet once, now taste most bitter" (*SD* 243).

The physicality of "gall" and "heartburn" is surely to be allowed its full literal impact: we are to "*taste as with taste of tongue*" actual bitterness, to feel the gnawing of the physical, and ignominious, burning within, to respond to these as literal facts. But these facts, together with "Bitter would have me taste: my taste was me," are also spiritual metaphors of a complex sort. Hopkins is not only inverting his own earlier joyful metaphors of the distinctive taste of self, unequaled in nature and to be tasted "but at one tankard, that of my own being" (*SD* 123), nor is he merely developing the grimmer implications he has already recognized in them—"above all my shame, my guilt, my fate are the very things in feeling, in tasting, which I most taste that selftaste which nothing in the world can match" (*SD* 125). He is also perverting religious imagery in order to dramatize his own perversion of its substance. As in "The Windhover," "gall" is a reminder of the crucifixion, but here the speaker is himself the bitter and mocking affront offered to the suffering Christ, and here no flame of "gold-vermilion" follows to promise resurrection. Grotesquely, "heartburn" follows instead. This may be more than a debasement of what the ardent human heart has always been to Hopkins, truth-sensing and truth-telling; it may also be a monstrously bizarre reminder of the Sacred Heart, the divine heart that shed the blood and flames with the fires of love and redemption and is to be worshiped as "Christ's most per-

---

37. *Spiritual Exercises*, 45, 41; *SD* 135. For a full and perceptive discussion of the imagery of bodily dissolution and disgust in these sonnets, see Harris, *Inspirations Unbidden*, 53–71.

fect character" (*SD* 103),[38] here debased, because forgotten, to mere fleshliness and its trivial pain. These individual perverted images are then developed into a larger metaphor, that of the perversion of the Eucharist itself.

In "(Carrion Comfort)" Hopkins had not only eluded the curse of the house of Atreus but had refused to pervert a sacramental rite by feasting on despair; here that "curse" is inescapably himself, and now he does pervert the great sacrament by feeding on the self that has become a debasement of its elements. The physical vessel, which in *The Deutschland* God both built and sustained in grace, is now simply a physical construct, even a kind of perverted chalice; there is nothing of Christ's vein of grace and redemptive blood in the gall and blood that fill it. In the same way, there is nothing of Christ's body in the "dull dough" of self, nothing of the leaven of Christ's spirit in the "selfyeast" that cannot raise but only sours.[39] The idea of near union with Christ's mystical body implied in "(Carrion Comfort)" is retained here in the elements of the Eucharist, but those elements are radically inverted to emphasize total alienation from God. Hopkins, like Caradoc, "With dreadful distillation of thoughts sour as blood, / Must all day long taste murder" (2.64–65).

This damnation of feeding on the self as Host is presented here as being the result of God's decree, not of the man's own choice for sin; though in the prose he stresses the self's responsibility, "that act of its own, which blotted out God" (*SD* 138), he does not do so here. There is a kind of bitter reverence perhaps in the acknowledgment that God masters him still, dictating his misery, but that he could not bring himself to say at this point "Thou art indeed just, Lord" is dramatically reflected in his revision of "God's most just decree" to "God's most deep decree." The past tenses of "was," "built," "filled," "brimmed," likewise the result of revision, also emphasize the point that he was created to be such a fleshly vessel of sin, has been so from the beginning and without his choice. The

38. Sermon on the Sacred Heart, which gives a clear exposition of Hopkins' thinking not only about the divine heart of Christ but also about human hearts (June 26, 1881).

39. See Matthew 13:33, a parable identified and discussed by Boyle, *Metaphor*, 155. Puzzlingly, he does not make the suggested connection with the Sacred Heart, though that image and doctrine are central to his discussion of Hopkins' poetry. It may be that no priest, including Hopkins, could even conceivably dare to make this sort of allusion. If so, I am guilty of more than a merely literary lapse in taste; on such points as this, the dangers of "Lucifer's song" in criticism are acute.

result of that irrevocable past action by God is his present, also irrevocable, condition: "I am gall, I am heartburn"; "a dull dough sours." Here as elsewhere metaphor states literal truth, unsoftened now by simile. Bitterness toward God, disgust toward self, is reinforced, as always, by sound: by heavy *b*-alliteration in the first three lines; by the still heavier linking of "deep decree" and "dull dough"; and in the final lines, by the scorn and scourge of *s*-sounds that finally trail off into the impotent whisper of "worse."

The final lines turn outward for a moment from the locked prison of self only to recognize the possibility of eternal damnation in selfhood. In writing them, and indeed in using night and darkness throughout these sonnets, Hopkins may have remembered with a sense of bitter loss the text of the Advent sermon cited earlier (Romans 13:11–14), from which he had evolved both a warning and a promise of hope in the Resurrection: "For though our translation says 'the night is past,' this is not to be understood as if it said the night were wholly past and day come, but rather . . . that the night has got on and day is approaching. Life then is night . . . . death will shew us daylight" (November 30, 1879, *SD* 39). In the sonnet's last line, what the heart "saw" in the octave, in a night that was indeed not "wholly past," he now "sees" more clearly still and in eternal terms, not "daylight," but the darkness of the damned which is also the grim illumination of hellfire. What he felt in the preceding lines, the desolation of loss of God, the resultant "pain of sense," he feels now as the damned feel it eternally, struggling in a fire of selfhood so spiritual that it is also physical, in an endless self-immolation of "their sweating selves."

The one desolate hope lies in that afterthought, "but worse"— "almost a *sotto voce* afterthought," as Boyle phrases it in his altogether fine discussion of this point.[40] In a desperately passionate prose prayer Hopkins voiced almost the same idea in his meditation notes on hell: "O Jesus, O alas Jesus Christ our Lord, we are sinners, spare us; we have done what others have been damned for, spare us; they died impenitent, they lie in hell, we are on earth, there is time yet, we are sorry for our sins, we do repent, thou spare us" (*SD* 244). The sonnet contains only a whispered remnant of that hope, and as Harris points out, the turn to Christ in prayer has been wholly omitted,[41] but it is a whisper strong enough to act as a

40. *Metaphor*, 155.
41. *Inspirations Unbidden*, 110.

somewhat paradoxical comment on the entire poem and as evidence of Hopkins' spiritual honesty and discipline.

The poem began with a dislocation of natural time and space, one that made inner time and inner darkness seem infinite by moving from "hours" to "years" to "life." But this very movement reflects, in retrospect, a hope for finite time, an echo of the consolation that "all life death does end," an assumption that temporal being must have a temporal ending. Though the sestet initially presents the self's damnation in a seemingly eternal present, that faint hope for final oblivion remains until the poem's concluding reminder that merely "seeming" infinity here must become actual infinity hereafter. The paradoxical effect of this recognition is both a desolation that is "the deeper darkened" and, even within the sonnet itself, a return to proper perspective—"But this is not really true"—and a new frail hope: "there is time yet."

Moreover, if and when we emerge from the grip of the poem's dramatic immediacy and can remember that it is an artifact, the intellectual and theological scrupulousness that dictated that final stern reminder will suggest that as man, priest, and artist Hopkins remained in some control of desolation. Even so close to the depths of the mind's mountains he catches himself up short, refuses again to feast on the "comfort" of the self's despair, and, above all, refuses to forget that while God seems absent now, his finger created his creature, man, in the past, his presence still controls him, and his time scheme, however ominous it may be, still governs the world, here and hereafter.

It is the afterthought of this sonnet, and possibly the underthought of *King Lear* also, that may have generated Hopkins' placement of "Patience hard thing!" at this point in the "unbidden" sequence, where it marks the beginning of an upward movement on the cliffs of fall. If there is "no worst" in this life, but very probably much "worse" hereafter for one who persists in self-alienation from God, there may perhaps be a "better" in this life, and one must strive for it. Specifically, there may be a "taste" other than that of bitter self, and a "word" that is not self-born, stillborn, misdirected: "Lord, blessed be thy holy word! It is sweeter to my mouth than honeycomb!"[42] Perhaps also remembered, as far closer to his own state than Thomas à Kempis, was the furious and piti-

---

42. Thomas à Kempis, *The Imitation of Christ*, translated by Richard Whitford, edited by Edward J. Klein, 209, from the chapter on desolation and consolation.

able Lear, close to his breaking point into madness, crying "You heavens, give me that patience, patience I need" (2.4.270). Doctrinally closer, however, though perhaps not emotionally so, was Ignatius. Dutifully, therefore, though with some interesting ambivalence in attitude and imagery, Hopkins attempts to follow the Ignatian injunction: "Let him who is in desolation strive to remain in patience, which is the virtue contrary to the troubles which harass him; and let him think that he will shortly be consoled, making diligent efforts against the desolation" (*SD* 204).

Reading the first quatrain, the mind's instinctive "composition of place" may imagine Hopkins looking away from the *Spiritual Exercises*, literally or psychologically, and dashing off, with some impatience and a tinge of Lear-like rebellion, his response to that advice:

> Patience, hard thing! the hard thing but to pray,
> But bid for, patience is! Patience who asks
> Wants war, wants wounds; weary his times, his tasks;
> To do without, take tosses, and obey.

The near chiasmus in the opening line emphasizes the play on two different meanings of the crucial and repeated "hard." Patience in this sonnet is not the sweet and docile virtue, the gentle fledgling "Patience exquisite, / That plumes to Peace thereafter" (51); it is cruel, even savage, requiring that total submission of all hearts that "bruise[s] them dearer" even to the point of seeming death. It is also initially viewed as a thoroughly negative virtue, one that the would-be heroic soul cannot easily bring itself to seek.

This second point, so recurrent in Hopkins' thought in the Dublin years, emerges from the new meaning of the second "hard." It is difficult for Hopkins even to bring himself to pray for patience, because such a prayer is in itself an acknowledgment of his failure as soldier of God. The next lines develop this through a deftly ironic play on the words "asks" and "wants," apparently parallel, even synonymous, but actually in contrast: the double point is that while he does indeed desire the glory and the sacrifice of combat, of "war" and heroic "wounds," a prayer for patience rises only from the lack of these.[43] As in *The Deutschland*, "The jading and jar of the cart, / Time's tasking, it is fathers that asking for ease / Of the sodden-with-its-sorrowing heart, / Not danger, electrical

43. Compare Hopkins' similar use of both "but" and "want" in "Hurrahing in Harvest": "and but the beholder wanting." See Appendix E on alternative readings of these lines.

horror." While "(Carrion Comfort)" allowed him some part in strenuous "danger," while to "take tosses" there had involved a kind of heroism, and to "obey" had meant more than resignation, the following sonnets dramatized his reduction to helpless passivity and merely sterile acceptance. That reduction he now half accepts, while at the same time, perhaps with considerable rationalization, turning the struggle for patience itself into the strenuous warfare he feels has been denied him. In earlier Retreat notes Hopkins had written: "I remembered Fr Whitty's teaching how a great part of life to the holiest of men consists in the well performance . . . of ordinary duties. And this comforted against the thought of the little I do in the way of hard penances. . . . Also since God gives me at present no great humiliations and I am not worthy of them and did not accept them well when they came [it is better] to welcome the small ones whenever such shall occur" (September 8, 1883, *SD* 253).[44] The struggle both for and against patience becomes in the sonnet a kind of "hard penance," almost a "great" humiliation.

The initially negative, anti-Ignatian rejection of patience is, paradoxically, a sign of reviving strength, but it is not the truest kind of strength, as the rest of the sonnet makes clear. The beginning of a turn in thought, as well as continued ambivalence, appears in the second quatrain:

> Rare patience roots in these, and, these away,
> Nowhere. Natural heart's-ivy Patience masks
> Our ruins of wrecked past purpose. There she basks
> Purple eyes and seas of liquid leaves all day.
>
> (Punctuation from H)

Patience remains a "hard thing" in that its only source is the bleak and rocky soil of self-denial, weary drudgery, resigned obedience, and it remains a negative thing in part, since it can only conceal, not heal, not bring to fulfillment "Our ruins of wrecked past purpose." ("There they lie . . . my old notebooks and beginnings of things . . . ruins and wrecks," April 24, 1885.) Fastening and twining itself on ruin not only as a kindly mask but also as a somewhat

---

44. An entry that continues: "I earnestly asked our Lord to watch over my compositions, not to preserve them from being lost or coming to nothing, for that I am very willing they should be, but . . . that he should have them as his own and employ or not employ them as he should see fit. And this I believe is heard" (253–54).

parasitic growth, patience is still the virtue of the failed soul, and perhaps merely a mad king's crown of wild weeds.

On the other hand, seemingly almost against his will, the speaker simultaneously recognizes both the fertility of its soil and the softly natural, effortlessly beneficent quality of the virtue itself; "roots" and especially "natural heart's-ivy" make it something neither hard in itself nor hard for the understanding heart to pray for, and in the lovely culminating image it has completely submerged all ruin, rock, and hardness in a soft and liquid shining. For the first time in the "terrible sonnets" a natural image suggests color, light, warmth, rest, hope. While still an internal image, for the first time also this one insists upon its origin in the natural fecundity of an external and daylight world. Finally, for the first time in this sonnet, "Patience" ceases to be an abstract concept, becomes personified as a kindly "she," an element of the mothering earth who acts as a mother within the fretful mind, her easy and graceful loveliness and comfort further dramatized in both syntax and sound. These last two sentences are the only ones in the poem to this point that are fluidly unbroken in movement; the last two lines are the first to replace the flintiness of staccato consonants with the lulling and liquid gentleness of the *l*- and *s*-alliteration, the wash and hush of peace. Neither the typical visual oddity of the image nor the somewhat perplexing syntax in which it is expressed can blur the new and lovely release effected by it.

These very oddities, however, stand up well to more detailed analysis of their relation to the poem's whole line of thought and movement. "Purple eyes," presumably the ivy berries (or possibly the purple flowers of one kind of English ivy), is a somewhat startling image, and even grotesque if envisioned too literally, but it does suddenly and swiftly introduce color and sight into a hitherto colorless and lightless world and may suggest both the demands and rewards of dual-natured patience, since purple is both the liturgical color of mourning and the color of royalty.[45] In the same way, Hopkins takes full advantage of the inherent duality of "basks," both in meaning and in verbal class. The typically Hopkinsian fusion of water and fire is here intrinsic to the actual denotation of the word: the root meaning (to bathe oneself) easily generates the explicit water imagery in "seas of liquid leaves" and, together with the common meaning, creates the combined sense of soothing

45. For a reading that emphasizes not the achievement of the whole ivy image but its confusion, see Harris, *Inspirations Unbidden*, 48–49.

water and genial heat always characteristic of God's gentler agents of grace. Since the word is also dual in its verbal nature, Hopkins is able to echo in syntax the point on which the entire poem hinges, the point that patience is both a passive and an active virtue. Intransitively, patience-as-a-whole, inscaped as berries (flowers) and leaves, bathes in warmth, beautifully, somnolently open to all the rays of inner and divine suns; transitively, she exposes to such warmth her shining and soothing elements, and if "leaves" also has vibrations of a second moment, as a verb parallel to "basks," her healing action becomes the more active and permanent. Finally, the movement of the entire metaphor, easily self-proliferating from roots to ruins to wrecks to seas, dramatizes the virtue's power to grow and to heal everywhere. Like God its source, its power does not end at "world's strand" but goes on to encompass "sway of the sea," to be, and to master, "ocean of a motionable mind."[46]

The conceptual and syntactical complications of these lines are therefore specifically meaningful, dramatizing patience as both somber and bright, "hard" and soothing, active and passive in origin as in effect, and, like Shelley's West Wind, "moving everywhere." Won by stern effort of the submissive will, it is yet the natural and organic result of humble passivity; growing with the seemingly effortless fertility of all organic things, it is also active and beneficently purposeful in its action.

The sestet at first intensifies, and finally in part resolves, these dualities:

> We hear our hearts grate on themselves: it kills
> To bruise them dearer. Yet the rebellious wills
> Of us wé dó bid God bend to him even so.

> And where is he who more and more distills
> Delicious kindness?—He is patient. Patience fills
> His crisp combs, and that comes those ways we know.

The objectivity, the absence of the personal "I" that has distinguished this sonnet throughout from its predecessors, is emphasized here by the use of "we" and its allied pronouns, but as the sestet opens Hopkins returns with brutal physicality of image and sound to the pain that gracious patience has not in fact healed but instead intensifies. This is "the war within" again, the inner hell where "sheath- and shelterless" thoughts grind against each other,

46. A subliminal, or perhaps even conscious, link with the sestet may have been "the sea is like his greatness, the honey like his sweetness" (*SD* 239).

where now the very source of physical and spiritual life becomes metallically fatal, softly vulnerable to that "bruising" that we again feel inwardly as with the "pain of sense."

Now, however, the God who has seemed either deliberately savage or indifferently absent from the world of the three preceding sonnets returns to salve and save, or at least Hopkins' ability to turn to him with some degree of humility and hope returns. Though "He" who is the everflowing source of consolation is still in some sense "away," since the question "And where is he ... ?" sounds still in part like muted lament for his continued absence, the manipulation of language in these concluding lines is such that consolation does not seem to remain wholly hypothetical. Most obviously, since Hopkins overtly seeks not comfort itself but the means to it, the ability to submit, that goal is at least partially achieved: earlier he could barely bring himself to "bid" for patience, to ask for it, to offer a small price for it; now he not only asks but in a sense humbly orders God to master his will—"Yet the rebellious wills / Of us we do *bid* God to bend to him even so"— and is willing to undergo the death-to-life that patience seems to involve and demand. The last two lines indicate yet more subtly the partial granting of the prayer for submission, and even for actual consolation, the first point emphasized by nuances in diction that acknowledge the nature of God and the full nature of patience, the second suggested by the very presence of the honeycomb metaphor.

"He is patient" would seem to me analogous in a muted way to the recognition "(my God!)" in "(Carrion Comfort)" and hence evidence of the poet-speaker's new will to submit. While he has been engaged first in expressing the mistaken pride that made him reluctant to pray for patience, then in an artistic attempt to define and accept the virtue's dual nature, God, source and essence of patience, and not dual at all, has been quietly waiting for human submission, and moreover has endured, tolerated, apparently forgiven, outrageous unwillingness to seek even the means to it. A second nuance in diction, the juxtaposition of "He is *patient. Patience* fills / His crisp combs," effects the final definition of the virtue and reflects Hopkins' final understanding of it.[47] In the octave, the repeated abstract noun "patience" had gradually acquired fig-

47. Following Peters, alternative readings take "He" not as God but as a general figure of the patient person, who ceases to be merely suffering, enduring, and acquires kindness, sympathy with others (*Critical Essay*, 84–85).

urative concreteness and activity and a kind of maternity in the ivy metaphor; the adjective "patient" now fully translates an abstraction into a personal, essential, active quality, into essence-in-action, so that in its final appearance the noun "Patience" is no longer that remote "hard thing" of the opening lines but is as fully concrete, as sweet, as golden as its ultimate source.

Finally, the honeycomb metaphor mutedly creates an effect that will be much more dramatically illustrated by the concluding metaphor of "My own heart." Its very presence imaginatively suggests that patience has not only been figuratively defined but has also in part been found, that the spiritual starvation on the cliffs of fall, the only reward apparently for refusal to feast on despair, has ended now, that the speaker has been granted some of the divine sustenance God possesses in such abundance, and thus has become again a partaker in sacramental union with him. Having solved in his own way Samson's riddle, "Out of the eater came forth meat, and out of the strong came forth sweetness," having answered it rightly, "What is sweeter than honey? and what is stronger than a lion?" (Judges 14:14, 18),[48] Hopkins seems to have found not only patience but actual consolation in the recognition that the lion-God, hunter and eater, is still the "Orion of light."

The sonnet does not end, however, on a completely hopeful note; metaphor is not quite strong enough here to translate imaginative potentiality into full "literal" truth, and with the final phrase the poem seems to come almost full circle, to arrive at something close to stalemate, rather than at the affirmation similar circlings have made in earlier poems. Though the circle here is not quite closed, though Hopkins has at least asserted his wish to submit, and has contemplated the sweetness of what had at first seemed only cruelly hard, he has not, by sonnet's end, actually achieved the sweet reward of patience or rediscovered a still-absent Christ. "Where is he?" receives no answer, and "those ways we know" are the austere ways the speaker has now theoretically understood but has not yet been able to follow fully. He must therefore return again to the beginning, as we do having finished the poem, must go through the process again, and perhaps, only perhaps, win beyond it. To my ear and mind, in short, there is a tone of almost weary resignation in that final phrase, and a grimness in its meaning: it recognizes that to "know" is not necessarily to do, and

48. Patricia Stubbs, "Cliffs of Fall: The Final Sonnets of Gerard Manley Hopkins," 43.

that the attempt to do may lead to an endless circularity of search and suffering.[49]

In the last of the "unbidden sonnets" the circularity of the search, of the mind's prison, is finally broken, though not until after it has been graphically redramatized. The octave of "My own heart let me more have pity on" returns again to the blind darkness of the self and expresses again, far more explicitly than "Patience, hard thing!," the point that to know, and even earnestly to will, is not immediately to do. Nevertheless, because the will is there, because Hopkins now deliberately pauses, as Adam in despair did not, "to make an act of hope" (*SD* 67), there are at the end here skies above the cliffs of fall, light upon the mind's mountains; metaphor, which has previously embodied only the actuality of desolation, or the faint possibility of hope, is here strong enough to express the actuality of possible salvation.

The opening quatrain, an exhortation, almost a prayer, addressed to himself and perhaps ultimately though obliquely to God, is in part a renewed dramatization of the ideas and motifs of earlier sonnets, but it also expresses the new "act" of spirit that will finally turn desolation to hope:

> My own heart let me more have pity on; let
> Me live to my sad self hereafter kind,
> Charitable; not live this tormented mind
> With this tormented mind tormenting yet.

The dialogue of the mind with itself continues, but with a difference. The divided "I," which could earlier find its unity only in self-loathing, and the heart, which had been merely an alter ego in suffering and an inner instrument of that torment, now become aspects of a larger self that can draw back from all its suffering elements and pity them, can choose for the response to sin felt by God, and properly felt by man toward himself, "O the pity of it!" (*SD* 134). This new identity can recognize that it has wholly failed in such compassion (hence the order of "more have pity" rather than "have more pity"), can now try to feel "This pure pity and disavowal of our past selves [which] is the state of mind of one whose sins are perfectly forgiven" (*SD* 135), and can act upon God's endorsement of the idea that "charity begins at home: true and just

---

49. In a far more optimistic reading, Cotter concludes: "And 'we know' through gnosis the ways he [Christ] comes, from all directions of the sky and earth to the honeycomb centers of men's hearts" (*Inscape*, 229). For a reading even grimmer than mine, see Harris, *Inspirations Unbidden*, 37.

selflove lies in wishing and in promoting our own best good and happiness, this is charity towards ourselves" (*SD* 51).

Second, the repeated "let," which will appear twice more with increased emphasis in the sestet, and which implies simultaneously permissive passivity and active choice, develops and transforms the activity/passivity motif of "Patience, hard thing!" and above all the concepts of resignation and renunciation that have been central to the sonnets from "No worst" on. Because Hopkins renounces now not hope but self-torment, resigns now not all choice but only the roles of Fury and of the hunter, seemingly passive resignation, abdication of action, becomes itself an "act of hope." Ultimately, the sonnet will arrive at the full expression of this active-passive act of salvation, will say without reservation "Thy will be done," abandoning not only the strenuous combat of "(Carrion Comfort)" but even the painful struggle to bend and break his will in search of the ways of patience.

Third, however, diction and syntax in the last two lines of the opening quatrain dramatize again the vicious and apparently unbreakable circle of the mind's prison. Though that prison is overtly rejected—"not live this tormented mind"—the word *mind* where we would expect *life* makes the mind-in-torment his entire existence, his only world; this is once more the torture chamber that has been the locus of all but one of the preceding sonnets. The terrible and feverish circularity of this "life" is then underscored by the repetitions of this and the following line: diction and syntax turn back upon themselves just as the mind endlessly turns upon itself, endlessly engendering "more pangs schooled at forepangs," endlessly grinding itself to a near death that never comes. "Tormenting yet" is the keynote in feeling of this quatrain, whatever its statement of change.

That the will to break out of the mind's prison is not yet sufficient to unlock its doors is further dramatized in the next quatrain. Though its statement again emphasizes the necessity of escaping the self-made torture chamber, of abandoning the futile attempt to find hope within its darkness, the imagery and the present tense return Hopkins to its circular confines—or keep him in them:

> I cast for comfort I can no more get
> By groping round my comfortless than blind
> Eyes in their dark can day or thirst can find
> Thirst's all-in-all in all a world of wet.

The characteristic coinage "my comfortless" translates a mere quality into a static condition,[50] and like "this tormented mind" it makes that condition his total world, the climate, the enclosing and only element in which he lives and gropes. Making the same point, and repeating the effect of the end of the first quatrain, is the repetitive inward-turning language of "Thirst's all-in-all in all a world of wet," again making the circle seem unbreakable. This effect is further emphasized by the complete absence of any internal punctuation in the original manuscript, to which I return in quoting this quatrain; there are no mental guideposts in this circular darkness, and no respite in the feverish hunt.

Finally, Hopkins' bewildered sense of futility, sense of exile, sense of reduction to animalism are compressed in the one word "cast." Most clearly, and almost unmetaphorically, this means simply that he turns, twists about, blindly moves around the prison walls of mind, a meaning probably linked with the more specifically mental one of "deliberate, debate with oneself, turn over in the mind"—exactly what all of these sonnets have shown him doing. He is now perhaps a fusion of the physically blinded Gloucester—who must "smell his way to Dover" (3.7.94)—and the madness-blinded Lear, groping for sanity. In conjunction with what follows, "cast" may also allude to Hopkins' own sense of satanic exile and loss; like Satan prone on the burning lake, "round he throws his baleful eyes" only to behold "No light, but rather darkness visible" (*Paradise Lost*, 1.55, 63).

Beyond, or inherent in, both denotation and allusion, however, is the probability of metaphor, since the figurative richness of "cast" seems unlikely to have escaped Hopkins' notice. The question then is which of two main metaphorical possibilities is supported by context, and by earlier stages of revision. The original version of the opening lines, "I grope for comfort I can no more get / By casting in my comfortless" (Appendix E), leaves some doubt as to dominant metaphor, if any, but tilts toward that metaphor of fishing suggested by some critics and many students and supported by the "all a world of wet" that follows. The tentative revision either shows a change in intention or more likely makes clearer the original one. It deletes the phrase that most tempts us to the fishing image ("casting in") and brings out instead the metaphor first suggested by Boyle, of hounds blindly casting "for" a lost

50. Boyle, *Metaphor*, 147. The whole of this finely reasoned discussion of the "eyes"/"thirst" metaphors should also be consulted (147–50).

scent,[51] thereby emphasizing that the poet is not mainly, if at all, the human hunter-fisherman, nor even tragic Gloucester, but the animal hunter who can only regain his humanity by choosing, as he will choose in the sestet—"call off thoughts awhile"—not to hunt. In the octave, that renunciation has not yet been fully made. He has temporarily forgotten what he had once known, that man "dogged in den" is not the divine Hound of Heaven, that the heart "hard at bay" must be the hunted, not the pursuer, and he is therefore now still blindly scenting the air for spiritual direction and light, starving for spiritual drink.

The metaphors of blindness and thirst desolately bring together two of the central metaphors of the other sonnets, in which he had blindly "thirst[ed] after daylight, draughts of daylight," in Beuno's phrase (St. Winefred's Well, 2.2.4).[52] They are also characteristically dual in implication, since their full meaning is hidden at first, as God is hidden, but will soon be seen to hold, however veiled, a source of hope.

Initially, the despair of the earlier sonnets is compressed and intensified in these metaphors. Hopkins had once either lived in night but longed for future day, physical or spiritual, or longed for the comforting darkness of sleep and death; now, though light is all around him in the present, he is irrevocably shut into the desolate darkness of his own making. He has in one earlier sonnet actually "lapped strength" and in others, thirsting for something other than the bitterness of gall and blood, for the sweetness and liquid loveliness of patience, had felt that these were either denied him by some power outside himself or were possibly to be won by stern self-discipline and effort. Now, though water lies all around him, he is a self-made Tantalus who cannot drink, though without even the humanity of that sufferer. Because his helplessness is self-engendered it is total, reducing him to hound-hunter, to blindness and thirst, not a human agent capable of acting in any way to meet its own needs.

The counterimplications of the metaphors, however, lead to the sestet's thought change. If day and water, comfort and grace, are indeed there, available, bright and abundant outside the walls of his "comfortless," realities that still exist and wait beyond the prison, this can be a source of comfort, not helpless frustration; if

51. Ibid., 147.
52. See also Caradoc's earlier "Down this darksome world cómfort whére can I find / When 'ts light I quenched" (2.1.49–50).

they are not to be reached by the blind effort of hunting within the self, perhaps abdication of that effort may serve. As he has done in other poems, Hopkins again wrings from desolation and seeming paradox hope, and a single truth:

> Soul, self; come, poor Jackself, I do advise
> You, jaded, lét be; call off thoughts awhile
> Elsewhere; leave comfort root-room; let joy size
>
> At God knows when to God knows what; whose smile
> 's not wrung, see you; unforeseentimes rather—as skies
> Betweenpie mountains—lights a lovely mile.

A new and wiser "I" than that of the preceding quatrain now addresses the imprisoned other-self, speaking with the tired but earnest tenderness of a priest advising a troubled penitent, or perhaps of a wise fool cajoling a mad king ("Prithee, nuncle, be contented"), as suggested by both Abbott and Gardner, or of an Edgar trying to strengthen his now bleakly resigned father: "Bear free and patient thoughts."[53] There is a descent in quality but an increase in pity in the movement from "Soul" to the too-hopeful appositive "self" to the sadly accurate "poor Jackself." The speaker now finds that the various parts of him—"heart," "mind," "soul"—do not compose a spiritual, kingly, tragic being, capable of purposeful human effort; even in the tragic *agon* of spiritual suffering they resolve themselves merely to the plodding workhorse self, galled by the jading and jar of the cart and able only to increase its own pain by incessant and senseless effort that rubs its soul's sores to the quick. Full humanity will only be restored to that Jackself when it ceases to be the blind plodder on the treadmill, the blind hound in darkness, when it becomes instead the master huntsman who chooses not to hunt, or at least to call off the hounds of thought from their present futile trail and to set them to some more promising scent outside the walls of self.

The result of this simultaneously active ("call off") and passive ("let be," "leave comfort root-room," "let joy size") action is that for the first time since "(Carrion Comfort)" the word *joy*, and the hope for it, enters the world of the "terrible sonnets." The very fact

53. Abbott, *LB* xxxix; Gardner, *Hopkins*, 1:177; *King Lear*, 4.6.80. Gloucester's immediately preceding lines, and his survival of symbolic suicide that generates them, bear some relation to Hopkins' whole effort and tone in this sonnet: "henceforth I'll bear / Affliction till it do cry out itself / 'Enough, enough,' and die. That thing you speak of, / I took it for a man; often 'twould say / 'The fiend, the fiend'—he led me to that place" (4.6.75–79).

that the speaker now aspires to more than resignation, more than patience, more even than "comfort," which, like patience, needs "root-room" but whose soil seems less austere, indicates the relative height to which Hopkins has managed to struggle upward on the cliffs of fall. Moreover, the nature of the imagery, which is interestingly a little at odds with its actual statement, may give us the sense that he not only hopes now for the long-sought joy but has achieved it.

Overtly, the final lines merely present a resigned hope. As Harris emphasizes, here as in the other dark sonnets there is no direct colloquy with God,[54] no renewal through direct address of the lost closeness. Instead, the lines continue the earnest and teacherly lecture to the self, only explaining why abdication of effort *may* lead to reward, without stating that it will, and simply acknowledging that neither joy nor God, its source, can be hunted down and grasped, that God is the "wringer" not the "wrung," that his action and his time scheme alone determine the moment and degree of consolation, as they have determined those of desolation—a deeply Ignatian, if not deeply consoling, acknowledgment.[55] The wryly resigned, to some ears irreverent, wit of that colloquial phrase "At God knows when to God knows what," while probably to be taken literally and seriously like most of Hopkins' apparent ironies, especially serves to underscore the hypothetical nature of the longed-for joy, and the difficult stretching out of syntax and simile makes that final light seem far distant, from both its source and its seeker.

The imaginative effect of the imagery, however, to my ear and eye, is more than, even other than, the literal statement; it transforms the merely potential into seemingly actual reality. Far from finding the figurative language a resort "to the oldest of substitutes for discursive argument" and its product "a mixed metaphor betokening God's distance,"[56] I find myself surrendering on all readings to its power. Imaginatively, the feverish aridity of the tormented mind and thirsty soul seems actually replaced by the rich growth and space implied in "root-room," and especially overwhelmed by "size"—a favorite word with Hopkins since it suggests

54. *Inspirations Unbidden*, 96.
55. "It belongs to God our Lord to give consolation to the soul without preceding cause. . . . I say without cause: without any previous . . . knowledge of any object through which such consolation would come, through one's acts of understanding and will" (Loyola, *Spiritual Exercises*, 177).
56. Harris, *Inspirations Unbidden*, 96, 51.

both organic growth and expansion.[57] The constraint of the self's dark prison does imaginatively open upon a vision of that "smile" which, if not so present or so brilliant as the "bright wings" of "God's Grandeur," nor so potently visible as the "colossal smile" of "Henry Purcell," nevertheless seems to spread its radiance over the final lines, seems actually to break upon the blind eyes with a lovely suddenness and sense of release. The "unforeseen" oddity of "whose smile / 's not wrung" and of the coinage "betweenpie" makes us see newly the new vision, and though the smile is only like the light of dappled skies appearing between, and on, dark mountains,[58] it does appear; it does show suddenly before our eyes a shaft of light, a rift in darkness, that points and beckons at least forward, perhaps upward. To the imagination, and through a final metaphor that replaces simile, it actually, not hypothetically or figuratively, "lights a lovely mile."

Neither the tone nor the quality of affirmation in this sonnet is easy to characterize, however; potential ambivalence puzzles the will of many readers and critics, though not, I suspect, of the poet-dramatist. Certainly it is a dark sonnet, intellectually and in much of its feeling. The light that imaginatively breaks upon the mind's mountains remains intellectually hypothetical and is not in any case the blazing radiance of "a crimson-cresseted east." The brief respite in time ("awhile") and the brevity in spiritual space of that one "lovely mile" may be enough for one who had expected an endless journey in pain and darkness, but neither offers assurance that the rest of the journey will be short, or easy, or lit by any constant radiance. We may feel, as Hopkins himself felt at the beginning of a Retreat in 1888, that while there is hope for happiness hereafter, "it is not happiness now. It is as if one were dazzled by a spark or star in the dark, seeing it but not seeing by it: we want a light shed on our way and happiness spread over our life" (January 2, 1888, SD 262). But neither the retreat notes, nor most of the poems of Hopkins' last years, nor "My own heart let me more have pity on" ends on this despairing note of want and darkness. The notes re-

---

57. See for example "All things rising, all things sizing" (42, "The May Magnificat," l. 25); "But when she sights the sun she grows and sizes" (103, "I am like a slip of comet," l. 6).

58. "Now where a strong shadow lay in a slack between two brows of Pendle appeared above the hill the same phenomenon I had seen twice before . . . a wedge of light faintly edged, green on the right side, red on the left, as a rainbow would be, leaning to the right and skirting the brow of the hill with a glowing edge" (May 24, 1871, JP 210).

count, and the dark sonnets dramatize, the spiritual struggle, but
both prose and poetry return in thought to trust in God and are in
tone neither aggressively triumphant nor finally hopeless, but in
the fullest sense of the word simply, and quietly, faith-full.

That it is metaphor alone that both dramatizes and controls
dualities in the last of the "unbidden" sonnets, that it is through
metaphor and not through statement that the poem acknowledges
the truth of doubt, asserts the truth of faith, and achieves its degree
of hope, is in the highest degree exemplary of Hopkins' sacramental method and of the religious vision that generated it. That vision
consistently transformed all the literal world to metaphor, then
raised it again above metaphor to the new literal truth of faith.
Therefore, in this sonnet as elsewhere, the light that "only metaphorically" breaks upon the mountains of the mind does so break,
does make actual the possibility and hope of light after darkness,
freedom after prison, sight after blindness, and perhaps even of
eternal spaces longer and lovelier than the "lovely mile." Even if
this concluding vision is equivalent to Lear's heartbreaking though
heart-restoring "Look there!," Hopkins was able to imagine and
create it, and to make it, for others at least, and one hopes for himself, a reality.

Like *The Wreck of the Deutschland*, though far more somberly,
like the whole world of Hopkins' poetry, in which the individual
poems are in a sense "moments" of that first major work, the world
of the "terrible sonnets" dramatizes tragic darkness, duality, mystery, terror, fragmentation, loss, but brings them to poetic, and
perhaps psychological, wholeness in the context of Christian tragedy, through the metaphors of Christian faith. In this microcosmic
world, God is the anvil-master still, the fearsome hunter still, but
here also his mastery is both the source of anguish and the only
source of redemption. Here too the helpless human construct feels
itself adrift and abandoned in wild waters and darkly savage nights,
"O Father, not under thy feathers," but here also the heart remembers and turns toward "*Ipse*, the only one," who remains "throned
behind / Death, with a sovereignty that heeds but hides, bodes but
abides."

Both the terror and the faith of these sonnets lie in their acknowledgment that even when God seems hidden, he is not dead;
even when distant, he is not wholly "away"; even when dark, he is
the only light in darkness. They recognize that God is a mystery indeed, but a mysterious certainty still, an Orion of light even in the
midst of his most terrible "dark descending."

Conclusion

IN OUR CENTURY, many thinkers and writers, and many critics, have come to accept as axiomatic Wittgenstein's statement, "*The limits of my language* mean the limits of my world."[1] In contrast, most of the great writers of the nineteenth century, and Hopkins in particular, acknowledged a "reserve of truth beyond what the mind reaches and still feels to be behind," and language for them could reach toward expression of that truth but could not necessarily contain or define it, certainly not determine it. They did not circumscribe the world by finite limits, nor locate the ultimate in the finite, and there remained for them as for Pascal "infinite spaces" that might both terrify the mind by their silence and summon it to new voyagings.

Hopkins' "authentic cadence" is the voice of his particular faith in those large "no-man-fathomed" mysteries of God that could not be limited or contained in language but were to him so certain that they could be sacramentally expressed by it. "Mounted in the scarlet" he saw the world and worded it in his poems, never blurring its hard actuality, but never debasing to mere actuality its ultimately mysterious "news of God." As an "incomprehensible certainty" he reverenced God, and in his best works every aspect of poetic language incarnates without limiting that inscrutable yet intensely distinct mystery that formed the center of his life and faith.

Consistency of faith thus produced one of the most consistent poetic imaginations in literature, and one most able to confront and accept the limitations of human language. While some readers see in such consistency narrowness, even poverty, of intellect, and

1. Ludwig Wittgenstein, *Tractatus Logico-Philosophicus*, trans. D. F. Pears and B. F. McGuinness (London: Routledge and Kegan Paul, 1961), 5.6, 115.

303

others almost the opposite—a facade behind which a modern mind struggled probingly, at times tragically, with modern problems —in my view it was for Hopkins, and is for any reader willing to see and share his vision, a sign of the fulfillment of his early prayer, "Let me be to Thee as the circling bird." Like Ezekiel in one of Hopkins' youthful poems, his imagination in all periods of his life "Went forth to compass mysteries" (77), though in maturity the attempt is less to compass them than to acknowledge, approach, express them as adequately as the limits of language and understanding, stretched to their furthest extremes, would allow.

The voice of his poetry is therefore the voice of splendid though sometimes dangerous extremity, since neither the human mind nor human language can easily bear the pressure of a life lived at the edge of mortal limitation. Yet it is a cadence disciplined by craftsmanship and governed by fidelity of vision, one that consistently gives utterance to the response of a "single eye" that was able to read in all times, in all inner and outer seasons, in all seeming dualities, in all bright days and harvests, even in all perplexing and terrible nights, the purposefulness and the mystery and the certainty of a God who alone makes sense of the world's mysteries.

Textual Appendixes

Appendix A
Chapter 5, "Orion of Light"

THE FOUR MAJOR manuscript sources referred to throughout were labeled by Bridges A, B, D, and H. The first is Bridges' own scrapbook collection of autographs "pasted into it as they were received" (*PB* 94), covering the years 1867–1889. B is the important collection held by the Bodleian Library (Bod.MS.Eng.poet. d.149), consisting of copies of the poems made by Bridges for Hopkins, dated, significantly revised, and added to by Hopkins himself in the years following 1883. D is a collection of letters to Canon Dixon, containing a few poems with late corrections. H, also at the Bodleian (Bod.MS.Eng.poet.d.150), is the collection of "posthumous papers" sent to Bridges by the Dublin Jesuits after Hopkins' death. "Examined, sorted, and indexed" by Bridges (*PB* 94), this scrapbook contains the major late poems, including the "terrible sonnets," as well as some unfinished poems and drafts of early poems.

References in this study to A, which I have not seen, draw on the notes of Bridges, of Gardner-MacKenzie, and of Catherine Phillips, editor of *Gerard Manley Hopkins* (Oxford Authors Series), as well as on corrections made by Hopkins in B. References to B and H are based on examination of these manuscripts, as are references to the following additional manuscript sources:

(1) the Dublin Notebook (abbreviated DN hereafter), at Campion Hall, Oxford, which includes drafts of "Spelt from Sibyl's Leaves" and of Caradoc's soliloquy from *St. Winefred's Well*, as well as diary entries;

(2) a collection of autograph drafts and copies of poems, English, Welsh, and Latin, most of them from the posthumous papers but not included by Bridges in H, including drafts of "God's Grandeur," "The Starlight Night," and "Hurrahing in Harvest" (Bod.MS.Eng.poet.c.48);

(3) letters from Hopkins to his mother and sister, covering the years from late childhood to his death in 1889, and also including

drafts of "God's Grandeur" and "The Starlight Night" (Bod.MS.Eng. lett.c.40 & 41).

I am indebted to the Bodleian Library, Oxford, for permission to reproduce photocopies of manuscripts from Eng.poet.d.149, fols. 8, 10, 15; Eng.poet.d.150, fols. 29, 31, 35, 44, 45; Eng.poet.c.48, fol 29.

The Wreck of the Deutschland

The extant drafts: A and revised B. Stressing marked in the text where it seems important is from A, the far more heavily notated manuscript, usually confirmed by B's retention of major stresses.

Stanza 1, lines 1–2. Neither A nor B gives the stressing of these lines. The best alternative to that adopted in the text is Schneider's, which places what does seem a wanted stress on "mastering" but has to omit the even more natural stress on "giver" and creates a strangely jerky effect through its stress on "God": "Thóu mástering me / Gód! giver of breath and bread" (*Dragon in the Gate*, 75).

Stanza 5, line 3. In A, "Starlight, calling him out of them"; in B, "wafting him out of it." The revision to "it" emphasizes the newly in-scaped unity of what was multiple. "Wafting" rather than "calling" seems more dual in possible antecedent, modifying both poet and star-light, thus toning down any suggestion that man can summon God at will. With the revision, nature and responsive human instressing may jointly bring God home, call him down.

Stanza 33. Alternative readings of its conclusion are basically two. (1) "The uttermost" is the subject, in apposition to "past-prayer," those furthest from salvation; these "mark" (see, "watch") Christ, who is "fetched" (seen, and/or brought to their sight, and/or "material-ized") "in the storm of his strides" (Schneider, *Dragon in the Gate*, 34; Fulweiler, *Letters*, 119). (2) As above, except that "fetched" modifies not Christ but the souls in extremity, who have been found, gathered in, reached by him (Cotter, *Inscape*, 163; Mariani, *Commentary*, 70, as the first of his two viable readings, the second being that based on "fetch" as main verb).

Stanza 35, lines 1–2. Stressing in text from A, "oúr dóor," "oúr shóals," confirmed by B's "oúr shóals." Possibly a reminder that En-glish ships and coastal towns failed to respond to the *Deutschland*'s distress signals until more than twenty-four hours after she struck, and of the plundering of the ship and the dead that followed. While God's larger purposes lay behind human failure in Hopkins' view, and while he ignored or did not know of the impossible physical conditions that delayed rescue (Mackenzie, *Reader's Guide*, 31), there is thus specific as well as doctrinal reason for the equally heavy stressing that follows: "Oh, upon Énglish sóuls!"

Chapter 6, "To Glean Our Saviour"

"God's Grandeur"
The drafts are as follows:

(1) a full draft with corrections in the posthumous papers from which Bridges compiled H, dated "Feb. 23, 1877" (Bod.MS. Eng.poet.c.48), in which the poem is entitled simply "Sonnet";

(2) a full draft that Hopkins dated "March 1, 1877" and sent to his mother on March 3, which does not incorporate all the corrections of the February version or the final revisions in B;

(3) A: two versions, in which the sonnet is entitled "God's Greatness";

(4) B: the final revised version, with revised title, dated to indicate date of inception, "St. Beuno's. Feb. 1877."

"The Starlight Night"
Abbreviations used in the text refer to the following drafts:

Feb.$_1$: the first draft in Bod.MS.Eng.poet.c.48, with tentative revisions of a few lines on the verso;

Feb.$_2$: revision of this draft;

March: the version apparently based on Feb.$_1$, not Feb.$_2$, sent to Mrs. Hopkins (Bod.MS.Eng.lett.c.41);

A: the version transcribed by Bridges in B, partially revised and then entirely crossed out by Hopkins, with the note "See later";

B: that later final version.

Line 4. The full series of revisions is as follows:

Feb.$_1$: ˣLook, the̲ elf-rings: look at the̲ out round eager eyes!

This is followed at the bottom of the page by:

^{x} { The dim woods quick with diamond wells; the elf-eyes!
The diamond wells through dim woods quick, the elf-eyes!

On the back of the page appear some further tinkerings, one of which, though rejected, first introduces the "down" idea:

in
The diamond wells quick ~~in~~ dim woods; the elf-eyes;
~~down dim woods~~
through dim woods; the elf eyes;

Feb.$_2$: he chooses the first of his tentative revisions, "The dim woods quick with diamond wells; the elf eyes!"

March: returns as usual to Feb.$_1$ but makes one slight revision, replacing "eager" with "earnest."

A's rejected version in B then begins to move toward the final form:

~~di~~ diamond wells   down in dim woods;
The ~~dim woods quick with diamond wells,~~ the elf-eyes!

The final draft in B arrives at the present version. The upshot of all this revision is (1) the major effect emphasized in the text, the fusion of the earthly and heavenly perspectives; (2) more technically, through the elimination of "wells" and the introduction of "delves," the creation of the nicely chiming internal "delves"/"elves" rhyme and the typical introduction of a noun that carries strong verbal implications; (3) the avoidance, though doubtless at some cost to Hopkins' love of vitality and dual meaning, of that slightly puzzling image of "woods" that are "quick"—with life, presumably, but also somewhat confusingly with swiftness; he will transfer "quick," with infinitely greater effect, to line 5.

where
Line 5. Feb.$_1$ has "The grey lawns cold ~~qua~~ quaking gold-dew lies!" Worse yet are the jotted alternatives on the back of this draft:

{ The grey lawns cold where ~~jaunted~~ ing gold/dew lies
there
The grey lawns cold jaunting, ~~for~~ golddew lies;
The grey lawns cold/ jaunting where golddew lies;

In Feb.$_2$, March, and A we have the original version: "The grey lawns cold where quaking gold-dew lies." But B's initial revision suddenly flashes into the inspiration of "where gold, this quickgold, lies!"—a revision only slightly altered in the final draft. This revision may have been triggered by the elimination of "quick" in the preceding line (see above, line 4) and a reluctance to give up that vital word entirely, but in any case, the result reveals Hopkins' typical method of revision at its best.

"Hurrahing in Harvest"

The drafts: "Sonnet in Harvest," Vale of Clwyd, ~~Aug~~. Sept. 1, 1877, heavily revised, and including the title revision to "Heart's Hurrahing in Harvest" (Bod.MS.Eng.poet.c.48); A; B.

Line 1. The main stresses adopted in the text seem to come closest to natural stressing and have some Hopkinsian authority, though based on A's notations, not on B's final version, which gives outrides but no stress marks. The original version of the opening phrase, together with A's clear stress on "ends," may argue for something that hovers between an anapestic lead-in—"Ĭt ĭš hárvĕšt" duplicated by "Sŭmmĕr énds now"—and the heard but diminished secondary stress on "Sŭmmer" suggested in the text. In this case, as in all but one of the possible alternative scansions, Hopkins is managing to get a good deal of stressful mileage out of the *anadiplosis* of "now/now," which carries a sense of stress in meaning, but on which he has not used up any of his five technical stresses.

Line 8. Revisions in the early draft:

> Print   or
> :~~Tongue, print,~~ pen such overwhelming replies.

The entire line and its correction are then crossed out; below, in the neater hand of later revision, appear two alternative versions:

> :Realer love's welcoming, loud greetings, rounder replies?
> :Rapturous love's greetings of realer, of rounder replies?

These revisions not only fortunately reject the flatly prosaic "overwhelming" and "loud greetings" but also show an apparent attempt to make nature's "text" speak with more human and personal eloquence, as he rejects "print" and "pen."

"Spring and Fall"

The drafts: A, dated "Lydiate, Lancashire. Sept. 7 1880," the version quoted in *LB* 120; D, sent to Dixon in January 1881, transcribed in "Additional Notes," *LD* 174; B, corrected final version, dated "Near Liverpool. 1881."

Stressing: B marks only "wíll" (l. 9, replacing A's underlining) and "What héart heárd of, ghóst guéssed" (l. 13). Additional stressing in text is derived from the other drafts as indicated.

"Thou art indeed just, Lord"

Drafts in H, A, and B. The drafts in H are as follows:

(1) Two full drafts of the poem, both entirely crossed out, to which I refer as H_1a and H_1b;

(2) Two partial drafts, heavily corrected, H_2a and H_2b: the first is a revision from the opening line through "never a work that I breed wakes," the second a revision starting with "Defeat, thwart me?" and continuing through "no, but strain";

(3) H_3: a set of nearly final corrections, from "Sir, my life on thy cause" through the final line.

B's autograph embodies all the final revisions but one. According to Bridges, A's autograph is for once the later, "being written in the peculiar faint ink of the corrections in B, and embodying them" (*PB* 121), and it is in A that "Sir, my life on thy great cause" becomes "Sir, life upon thy cause."

Line 1. Revisions:

> H_1a: Just art thou, O my God, should I contend
>   With thee; but, sir, what I shall speak is just.
>   b: Just thou art indeed, my God, should ⎱ I contend
>   would ⎰
>   With thee; but, sir, so what I speak is just.

> H_2a: Thou art indeed just, Lord, would I contend
>   so what   is
>   With thee; but, sir, ~~these words~~ I speak ~~are~~ just.
>   Lord, if I
>   B: Thou art indeed just, ~~were I to~~ contend
>   sir,   plead
>   With thee; but, ~~Lord,~~ so what I ~~speak~~ is just.

Lines 9–12. Revisions:

> H_1a: See, banks and brakes
>   Stand ~~full~~ thick with live [*sic*] now, broiderèd again
>   With fretty chervil that the spring wind shakes;
>   b: Look, banks and brakes,
>   How thick a-leaf they are, broidered all again
>   With fretty chervil which the spring wind shakes!

H_2a: Elaborate tinkerings with phrases, all crossed out and too intricate to be clearly transcribed here, the main point of interest being the introduction of the simultaneously reverent and accusing "by thee" or "from thee" ("broidered by thee again," "Leaved thick ~~by~~ from thee").

b: Straightening out the confusions of the preceding revisions, this arrives at:

> Look, banks and brakes
> Leaved thick from thee, broiderèd all again
> With fretty chervil now, and fresh wind shakes
> Them;

H₃: The nearly final revision, which eliminates what may have seemed to Hopkins the too petulant and accusing "from thee":

> Look, banks and brakes
> Leavèd how thick now! lacèd they are again
> With fretty chervil, see, and fresh wind shakes
> Them;

B:

>   See
>   ~~Look,~~ banks and brakes
> Now, leavèd   lacèd they are
> ~~Leavèd~~ how thick! ~~broiderèd all~~ again
>   look
> With fretty chervil, ~~now,~~ and fresh winds shakes
> Them;

Line 14.

H₁a: Ah life, ah life's lord, send my root some rain.

b: Then send, thou lord of life, these roots their rain.

H₃: ⎰ Mine, O thou lord of life, send my roots rain.
                                    these
    ⎱ Then send, thou lord of life, ~~my~~ roots their rain.

B: The final decision is made:
> Mine, O   send my
> ~~Then send,~~ thou lord of life, ~~these~~ roots ~~their~~ rain.

Chapter 7, "Mortal Beauty"

"Henry Purcell"

Drafts: A, with corrections in B. Metrical notations in the text from B.

For Hopkins' full paraphrase of the octave see January 4, 1883, *LB* 170–71; for that of the sestet, May 26, 1879, *LB* 83. His repeated attempts to explain "Have fair fallen" are as follows:

(1) "I *meant* 'fair fall' to mean *fair (fortune be) fall*" (January 4, 1883, *LB* 171).

(2) "This is a terrible business about my sonnet 'Have fair fallen', for I find that I still 'make myself misunderstood'. *Have* is not a plural at all, far from it. It is the singular imperative (or optative if you like) of the past, a thing possible and actual both in logic and grammar, but naturally a rare one. As in the second person we say 'Have done' or in making appointments 'Have had your dinner beforehand', so one can say in the third person not only 'Fair fall' of what is present or future but also 'Have fair fallen' of what is past" (February 3, 1883, *LB* 174). Bridges' helpful contribution, "Now fair befall your mask! fair fall the face it covers" (*Love's Labour's Lost*, 2.1.123–24), set Hopkins' mind "at rest" about allowing the line to stand, "for if it will only stand, and it will, it pleases me much" (January 28, 1883, *LB* 173).

(3) Hopkins' hardly less opaque explanation of "An age is now since passed, since parted" (l. 3) seems to say that it means both that centuries have passed since his soul passed from, parted from, his body and that it is centuries later that the poet makes this wish for him (January 4, 1883, *LB* 170–71).

"As kingfishers catch fire"

Autograph in H only, unfinished and undated. Most critics more or less confidently place it in the 1881–1882 period, as I do, because its content seems to reflect the renewal of spirit Hopkins experienced during his tertianship (October 1881–July 1882) and because the commentary on "Personality, Grace and Free Will," containing the statement crucial to the sonnet's use of "play," is of this period (*SD* 154). However, dating Hopkins' poems on the basis of mood, content, or even related prose statements is always a risky business, given his consistently dual vision in all periods. On the evidence of line spacing and format of indentation, MacKenzie argues for a date as early as 1876–1877 (*Reader's Guide*, 148).

The fact that the two partial drafts in H are in markedly different ink and handwriting—the first in a large hand and dark ink, the second in the smaller, neater hand and more faded ink (in this case over a penciled draft) characteristic of Hopkins' later corrections— suggests to me some spread of time between the two attempts on the poem. While there is no reason to suppose that a writer cannot in one day, let alone in one year, employ two different pens and change his handwriting according to mood or circumstance, it seems to me probable that the poem was begun sometime in 1877 and revised and finished much later, insofar as it was finished (there being no complete fair copy). Since it was not sent to Bridges, Dixon, or Patmore before Hopkins' death, and was not added by Hopkins himself to B, one must at least conclude that he was not satisfied with it as a finished poem in the years from 1877 to 1882, and perhaps never did finally complete it.

The stressing adopted in the text reflects Hopkins' use in the autograph of large colons to indicate stresses on the syllables immediately preceding and following.

Line 12. "Christ plays" replaced "Christ comes" only in the last of the extant revisions. This may help date that revision to 1881–1882, though it also suggests that the importance of the playing metaphor, emphasized in the text, was not in Hopkins' mind from the inception of the poem.

"The Leaden Echo and the Golden Echo"

In A, dated "Stonyhurst, Oct. 13, 1882"; in B, which contains final corrections, dated in Hopkins' own hand "Hampstead. 1881." Whatever the explanation, possibly simple forgetfulness, possibly some reference to the poem's inception date, it is clearly to be placed in the 1881–1882 period.

"Felix Randal"

Two autographs in B, one entirely canceled, dated respectively "April 28 1880, Liverpool" and "1880."

"To what serves Mortal Beauty"

Autographs in A, B, D, and the early canceled draft in H referred to in the text.

"Spelt from Sibyl's Leaves"

Uncertain in date, though within some clear time limits:

(1) The final version was sent, or at least promised, to Bridges in December 1886 (December 11, 1886, *LB* 246).

(2) The earlier drafts of the octave in the Dublin Notebook point to autumn and winter of 1884 as the months of detailed revision. MacKenzie's research has conclusively dated the first draft October 1884 (*P* xlii). The second draft seems likely to have been written in late November or December of 1884. It appears on the verso of a page containing a note that meditates on the Martyrdom of Saint Cecily, a note probably written, in accordance with Hopkins' practice in such instances, on or near the saint's feast day (November 22). On the verso of the immediately following page are entries beginning with December 20 and continuing through early January. A dating of late 1884–early 1885 therefore seems valid for at least the inception and initial development of the poem.

The note on Saint Cecily is itself worth citing, since it bears on the overall thought of the poem, especially on its concept of the heart's spiritual function:

> St. Cecily—Praise God for her martyrdom
> She told Valerian he cd. not see the angel till he was baptized. Beati mundo corde, quoniam ipsi Deum videbunt, God and the things of God. The heart is what rises towards good, shrinks from evil, recognising the good or the evil first by some eye of its own. We ought to look to God first in everything, to seek first the kingdom of God and his justice, his rightness, to be right with God and ~~him~~ God to be king or first principle . . . in us. Pray for this more, in matters of interest, of pleasure, and of will. Ask St. Cecily's help

The drafts: two of the octave only in the Dublin Notebook (DN$_1$ and DN$_2$); complete autographs in A and B; some jotted revisions of the first two lines in Bod.Eng.poet.c.48. Stressing and text of poem from B.

Line 2. While the first line remains the same in all drafts, the second underwent elaborate revisions. In DN_1 it is as follows:

          -s to be   to be
Evening strain~~ed into~~ dark, dronedark, ˄ ᴵ womb-of-all, home-of-all,
    hearse-of-all night;

After attempts on lines 3–7, Hopkins returned to this line and jotted down the revision "Evening strains to be time's-well, world's-pit." In DN_2 he is still tinkering: "Evening strains to be time's den, world's delf," and

$$
\text{Evening strains to be time's} \left\{ \begin{array}{l} \text{harbour} \\ \text{hush, world's haven} \\ \text{dock, world's den} \end{array} \right.
$$

In DN_2 he also briefly considered the more obvious internal rhyme of "doom-of-all, womb-of-all, hearse-of-all night" and, in a separate revision (Bod.), pursued the "drone" image:

$$
\left\{ \begin{array}{l} \text{Evening, dealing the dark down, time's drone, sullen hulk-of-all,} \\ \quad \text{hearse-of-all night,} \\ \text{Evening, dealing the drone-dark down, hollow hulk-of-all, home-} \\ \quad \text{of-all, hearse-of-all night,} \end{array} \right.
$$

Line 3. Evidence that "her wild hollow hoarlight" is the sickle moon rather than the blanker light argued in the text would be: (1) not only the words "hollow" and "hung" in the final version but also the earlier variants "following the height" (DN_1), and especially "willowy hoarlight" (DN_2); (2) the fact that the waxing crescent moon has been present in the sky all day, though not easily seen, a point possibly related to the whole moral argument of the poem; (3) the additional fact that the moon at this stage, like the sunset, is still very much a part of the cycle of day and evening, not of night, so that replacement of both earth-related lights with the higher stars would again be consistent with the whole theme; (4) the final substitution of "hung to the height" for "following the height" could reflect not only an attempt to make the moon a lovely pendant adornment but also a recognition that a moon that sets shortly after sunset is not rising but simply becoming brightly visible.

Behind the whole cluster of images may also lie Revelation 12, on which Hopkins had written a detailed prose commentary (November 8, 1881, *SD* 198). Especially pertinent to the poem are his discussion of the woman, interpreted not only as the Virgin but as this earth itself—"this planet, which is clothed in sunlight, ministered to more humbly by its satellite, and graced by the beauty of the zodiac and other signs of the firmament"—and his understanding of the "other sign that appeared in heaven," that of the Dragon, as "the counterpageant or counterstandard set up by Lucifer," though in the sonnet that seemingly demonic counterstandard proves to be God's, not Satan's.

Lines 7–8. In DN₂:

                              My heart rounds me right
 ⎧ Then: Evening is here ond us, over us; our night whelms,
 ⎨   whelms: when will it end us?
 ⎩ That oúr evening is over us, our night whelms, whelms: when
                       will it end us?

Chapter 8, "Sheer Plod"

"The Windhover"

Drafts: two autographs in A; corrected transcription in B, dated "St. Beuno's. May 30 1877" and adding the dedication to the title.

Dedication: "to Christ our Lord." The lateness of this addition in B makes possible opposing views of its relation or nonrelation to meaning. Critics who take the falcon as emblem or "news" of Christ, as I do, tend to find support for that interpretation in the dedication. Those who regard the bird as a natural creature only (for example, Peters, *Critical Essay*, 85–86) see the lateness of the addition as evidence that it has nothing to do with meaning but was simply added to make the sonnet an offering to Christ. To the more psychologically inclined, such as Herbert Read, it is "a patent deception," an attempt by Hopkins to overcome his scruples about "the naked sensualism of the poem" (*Collected Essays in Literary Criticism*, 336).

The most convincing explanation seems to me MacKenzie's: the dedication was a means of restoring the direct reference to Christ that had been sacrificed when Hopkins revised the somewhat ambiguous original version of the opening lines: "I caught this morning morning's minion, king / Of daylight's dauphin"; the sonnet, says MacKenzie, is essentially about the fire of that King, not the bird (*Hopkins*, 59). See also his reminder that whenever Hopkins uses dedications in the titles of poems ("The Silver Jubilee," "Spring and Fall," "To R. B."), the poems themselves contain an address to the person named (*Reader's Guide*, 79).

Line 7, "my heart in hiding." This much-discussed phrase seems to me simpler than some critics have found it. In context, it is not easy to hear it as a statement that his heart was quite properly "in hiding" with Christ or in Christ, "hidden from the devil" in Saint John's phrase

(Gardner, *Hopkins*, 1:180; Heuser, *Shaping Vision*, 53, 110; Cotter, *Inscape*, 278). (See "The Dark Night," in *The Collected Works of St. John of the Cross*, 382.) At the other extreme, and even more dubious, are the secular-psychological interpretations epitomized by Richards' statement that because of his vocation, "the poet's heart is in hiding from Life" ("Gerard Hopkins," 199), from all the temptations of the world and the senses, to which Kitchen will specifically add sexual temptations (*Hopkins*, 178). A combination of these readings was also perpetuated as if fact by David Daiches' footnotes to the poem in two widely used anthologies: "the poet's heart ('in hiding,' for the poet is a priest, with his heart hidden away from earthly things in the service of God)" (*The Norton Anthology of English Literature*, 4th ed., 2:1435*n*1; *The Norton Anthology of English Poetry*, 4th ed., 2:1790*n*2). These last interpretations distort the phrase and Hopkins' faith, since nothing in Jesuit thought or training teaches ascetic rejection of the world or cloistered withdrawal from "Life," but rather the reverse. I would think therefore that "in hiding" quietly conveys what most people feel at times and Hopkins felt often: the instinctive timidity, or at least tired inactivity, of a heart and being content to remain in secure passivity until suddenly roused by a splendid display of the opposite qualities. While the phrase almost certainly has the further metaphorical "moments" discussed in the text, its first and central meaning seems this simply human one.

Line 9. I have retained the comma after "plume," which appears in both autographs in A. If its omission in B was deliberate rather than an oversight, interpretations based on or alluding to its importance, including mine, would need qualification, though not necessarily abandonment.

Line 10. "Buckle!" Critics who defend various wholly declarative-indicative readings show a considerable range, including among others the following. Phare allows several senses of the word: (1) beauty, courage, air, act, power are "buckled within the small span of the bird's body"; (2) all its qualities "buckle to," pull together, so that the bird may fly and wheel; (3) all its qualities "give way, collapse, beneath the bird's dominant impulse" (*Poetry of Hopkins*, 131). For Thomas J. Grady ("'Windhover's' Meaning"), the meaning is simply Phare's first, "fuse." In Schneider's view, the natural world gives way, "buckles" like the plates or bulkheads of a ship in a fire at sea, and the fire of the spiritual world breaks through (*Dragon in the Gate*, 151–54). Mariani sees a description of Christ's body on the cross, "when his body buckled under its own weight" (*Commentary*, 112). For Cotter, the word describes the kestrel's contraction of wings and subsequent dive (*Inscape*, 181). Robinson stresses the new perception of reality that occurs when the abstract qualities of the bird "yield" to a new perception of its meaning (*In Extremity*, 44). MacKenzie emphasizes the coming together of the falcon's qualities as the dominant meaning but allows the closely connected "arming for battle" meanings and, most provocatively, suggests yet a further possibility: the completion of an electrical circuit, with the subsequent flash of blinding light (*Reader's Guide*, 82–83).

Critics arguing for the imperative-optative mood are fewer, but in addition to Schoder, two especially warrant mention. Milward reads "Buckle!" as addressed to the poet himself, meaning primarily "'buckle under' in humble submission to Christ the King; with the possible secondary meanings of 'buckle on,' or come together under Christ, and of 'buckle to,' or join battle with Christ against his enemies" (*Landscape and Inscape*, 52). Chevigny's different imperative meaning and persuasive reading is that "in the opening lines of the sestet . . . the heart comes out of hiding, demands that all that the bird's glory represents be caught and brought down, that it enter and be made fast to his hidden heart" ("Instress and Devotion," 147).

Line 10, "AND." Since Hopkins does not resort to such capitalization as a means of emphasis in any other mature poem, this oddity may have a pragmatic rather than a thematic explanation. In reading through Bridges' transcription in B, he could perhaps have felt a sudden irritation, at least dissatisfaction, with the flourishing ampersand Bridges everywhere used in place of *and*. While not correcting this practice elsewhere, at this point in this poem Hopkins may simply have wished to indicate loudly and clearly that this *and* was too important to be reduced to an abbreviation, without intending full capitalization to stand for all time.

Line 12. In the debate over whether "sheer plod" makes the plow shine, or the field (plow-land) shine, or both, I take the first to be overthought, though complicatedly, and the others resulting underthoughts. The dominant metaphorical logic seems to me that just as drudging farm-toil makes the plowshare shine, through friction, or simply through reflection of sunlight, so steady and faithful labor in any field makes its agent and tool, the laborer, shine ("*What I do is me*"). Also, however, just as the octave had come close to fusing splendid rider and steed and skyfields, so the metaphor here seems to fuse in shining the plowman, the plowshare, and the opened furrows these create. The point that act and agent, agent and instrument, agent and element are one is pursued and dramatized in a new way.

"St. Alphonsus Rodriguez"

The drafts: A (*LB* 293) and B, both autographs, and the two early drafts referred to in the text as Bod.$_1$ and Bod.$_2$, in the posthumous papers from which Bridges compiled H (Bod.MS.Eng.poet.c.48).

Lines 9–10.

<pre>
                          masons
Bod.₁a: But God that moulds mountain and continent
          With exquisite and   increment
          ────────────
                          quarries
      b: But God, that masons mountain, continent
          Carver, t̶h̶a̶t̶ God that
          T̶h̶a̶t̶ ̶c̶a̶r̶v̶e̶s̶,̶ ̶o̶r̶ else with exquisite increment
      c: But God that quarrieds mountains, continent
          Carveds, God that else with tiniest increment
                                  quarrier
      d: But God the mountain-mason, continent-
          Wright, world-wright, God wʰₒo with fine increment
      e: Yet God the mountain-mason, continent-
          Wright, earthsmith . . . .
          Yet he
Bod.₂: G̶o̶d̶'̶s̶ ̶h̶a̶n̶d̶ that hews oᵤt mountain, continent,
                          who,
          Earth, all, at last; y̶e̶t̶, with fine increment
A: Yet God the mountain-mason, continent-
          Quarrier, earthwright; . . . .
</pre>

Followed by, "Or, against singularity, we may try this:
          Yet God that mountain, and that continent,
          Earth, all, builds . . . .
No, this:
          Yet God that hews mountain and continent,
          Earth, all; that else, with trickling increment . . . ."
B: Yet God (that hews mountain and continent,
          Earth, all, out . . . .)

"The shepherd's brow"

The drafts, all in H, abbreviated in the text as follows:

H_1a: a complete draft, with some revisions.

b: revision of lines 1–7.

H_2a: a complete draft with revisions.

b: revision of lines 5–14.

c: revision of lines 1–9.

H_3: the final version, dated "April 3 1889."

Line 1. Versions as follows:

fronting

H_1a: The shepherd ~~fae~~ heaven's fork-lightning owns

H_1b and H_2a retain that correction.

H_2c: The shepherd's eye fronting forked lightning owns

H_3: The shepherd's brow, fronting forked lightning, owns

Line 3. In H_1a the line simply reads "The fall of awful angels fills their story"; the following versions are:

b: Of it: ~~ang~~ angels-giants falling fill their story

H_2a: Of it; angels-giants fall; they fill their story

This is then entirely crossed out and followed by:

$$\text{Of it; angels fall,} \left\{ \begin{array}{l} \text{mountains} \\ \text{towers} \\ \text{giants; and fill} \end{array} \right. \left\{ \begin{array}{l} \text{the} \\ \text{their story} \end{array} \right.$$

H_2c: Of it. Angels fall, towers, down from heaven; ~~their~~ story

H_3: Of it. Angels fall, they are towers, from heaven—a story

Line 8. The revision from "lute" to "viol" is considered immediately in H_1a and is retained in all further revisions:

$$\left\{ \begin{array}{l} \text{What bass can } \textit{his} \text{ lute bear to tragic tones?} \\ \qquad\text{has man's} \qquad \text{for} \\ \text{What bass } \underline{\text{is } \textit{his} \text{ low}} \text{ viol to tragic tones?} \end{array} \right.$$

The further change from "man's" to "our" in H_2a is also significant in a lesser way, retaining consistency in point of view with the earlier "we," saving the moment of contemptuous distancing—"He!"—for the sestet.

Lines 13–14. Context alone seems to require that "tame" be understood as adjective, not as declarative or imperative verb, but unless Hopkins changed his intent and syntax entirely in the course of revision, the variants furnish additional support for that reading. The first versions have complete sentences with full predicates that clearly use "tame" adjectivally:

or

H₁a: And I that die these deaths ~~and~~ feed this flame
　　~~Have seen my masque in spoons and found how tame~~
　　~~My tempest~~

　　　　　　　　　　　　　　　　　　　　⎧ ~~say~~
　　In spoons have seen my masque played and ⎨ how tame
　　　　　　　　　　　　　　　　　　　　⎩ say
　　My tempest and my spitfire freaks how fussy.
　　My tempest is, my spitfire freaks are fussy.
　　　　　　　　　　　　　　　　　fan
H₂a: And I that die these deaths, that ~~feed~~ this flame,
　　　　　　espy　　　poor　　　　　　～~tame~~
　　~~In spoons have seen~~ my ₌masque mirrored: ~~how~~ tame
⎧ Spy in smooth spoons　　　　　 ^
⎨　　　　　and my
⎩ My tempests ~~are and~~ spitfire frenzy fussy!
　　In smooth spoons spy my poor masque mirrored: tame
　　My tempests there, ~~and~~ my spitfire frenzy fussy.
H₂b: And I that die these deaths, that fan this flame,
　　　　　　　　　　my ⎫
　　That . . . in smooth spoons spy life's ⎬ masque mirrored:
　　　　　tame
　　My tempests there and all my ⎧ fever fussy.
　　　　　　　　　　　　　　⎩ fire

"That Nature is a Heraclitean Fire and of the comfort of the Resurrection"

A single autograph in A, giving the metrical markings used in text, dated "July 26 1888 / Co. Dublin."

Line 21. Readers may wish to set against my reading of "immortal diamond" and of the whole poem two more radical alternatives. First, Fulweiler sees in the diamond symbol some hope of reconciliation of the poem's two worlds but concludes that on the whole "the two halves of the poem do not mesh; the comfort of the Resurrection does not grow organically out of nature but is magically substituted for it" (*Letters*, 161). Second, Miller sees the ending as a major illustration of Hopkins' inability to express Christ through his permutations of language: "the ending is not some triumphant uttering of the Word as

such. It is only another metaphor, and a metaphor tautologically repeated at that . . . . a locution that in its punning doubleness confesses
to its inadequacy as a name for the Word" (*Linguistic Moment*, 260).

Appendix E
Chapter 9, "Dark Descending"

"(Carrion Comfort)"

Dating is a vexing problem because of the large discrepancy between the date of the "written in blood" letter, May 1885, and the apparent date of the first extant draft. This first canceled draft follows, on the same long page and in what appears to be identical dark ink and bold handwriting, an also-canceled draft of "To what serves Mortal Beauty?" that is clearly dated "Aug. 23 '85." The second complete draft, which continues on the verso, is in turn followed by a draft of "The Soldier," dated "Clongowes Aug. 1885," again in the same pen. From this one may draw one of three conclusions: (1) that the August version of "(Carrion Comfort)" is the first or close to first draft and that the sonnet was therefore not one of the two referred to in the May letter to Bridges; (2) that this first extant draft is a May version, but that Hopkins oddly began it a third of the way down the page, ran over to the verso, and in August or later used the space remaining at the top of the recto for "Mortal Beauty" and that remaining at the bottom of the verso for "The Soldier"; (3) that an earlier May draft, or drafts, of the sonnet has been lost. This last possibility seems by far the most probable. No other extant sonnet of May 1885, finished or fragmentary, offers itself as an adequate candidate for the one "written in blood," nor even for the second sonnet coupled with it in the May letter. Second, not only handwriting and ink but spacing suggest that "Mortal Beauty" and "(Carrion Comfort)" were fairly copied out at one stage and then revised with a different and finer pen, and that first "(Carrion Comfort)" and then "Mortal Beauty" were entirely canceled, after which Hopkins went on to a new full version of "(Carrion Comfort)"; the fact that the two variants to lines 7 and 8 of "Mortal Beauty" are squeezed in just above "(Carrion Comfort)," while neither the original transcription of the whole nor its date shows signs of such cramping, especially suggests that fair copies of both poems were made at the same time, and in the order in which they appear on the page. Finally, the first version of "(Carrion Comfort)" is a complete draft, with little initial major revision, and while it conceivably exemplifies Hopkins' practice of composing a whole poem orally in his head before "put[ting] it down with repugnance" (*FL* 379), it seems far more likely that at least one earlier, more tentative draft of May is lost. In this case, the process of "touching" this sonnet turned out to involve far more elaborate revision than Hopkins had expected when writing to Bridges in May (a speculation perhaps specifically supported by the revision from "this year" to "that year" in H_1c). If there were indeed a draft or series of drafts bringing the poem to the complete but far from final form that first appears in H, the sonnet was doubly "written in blood," artistically as well as spiritually. For arguments that not "(Carrion Comfort)" but either "I wake and feel" or "No worst" is the sonnet "written in blood," see respectively MacKenzie, *Reader's Guide*, 171, and Norman White, "Hopkins' Sonnet 'Written in Blood,'" 123–25.

Drafts and revisions are abbreviated in the text as follows, with all markings from H_3:

H_1a: the first extant draft, entirely canceled, complete, with some revisions.

b: revision of lines 12–14.

c: revision of lines 9–14.

H_2: a complete draft, but heavily revised and full of alternative revisions, which begins at the bottom of the same page as H_1 and continues on the verso, immediately above a much-revised draft of "The Soldier."

H_3: the "final" version, immediately following the only extant draft of "No worst," though carried only as far as line 10. On the preceding recto, with a canceled version of "Tom's Garland" sandwiched between them, appear lines 11 and 12.

Line 1.

Out, carrion comfort, despair! not, I'll not feast on thee;

H_1a: ~~Despair, *out*, carrion sweetness, off! *not* feast on thee;~~

H_2: Not, ~~I'll~~ I'll not, carrion comfort, despair, $\overset{o}{\underset{\wedge}{\ }}$ *nŏt* feast on thee;

　　　　　　　　　　　　　　　D

H_3: Not, I'll not, ~~ea~~ carrion comfort, despair, not feast on thee;

Line 5.

~~O yet, thou terrible,~~
H₁a: Yet why, thou terrible, wouldst thou rock *a* rude on me
H₂:　Yet, O thou terrible, why wouldst thou rude on me
H₃:　But ah, but/ O thou terrible, why wouldst thou rude on me

Lines 5–8. Two scriptural sources, the second of which Hopkins was certainly familiar with, probably influenced the imagery in this quatrain:

(1) Lamentations 3:1–20, especially "My skin and my flesh he hath made old, he hath broken my bones" (4); "He is become to me as a bear lying in wait: as a lion in secret places" (10); "He hath turned aside my paths, and hath broken me in pieces, he hath made me desolate" (11).

(2) Matthew 3:11–12, Luke 3:16–17, the baptism of Christ, on which Hopkins comments that Christ's strength is used for the sake of "hard hearts, which like sandstone, his tread may grind to power" (*SD* 268), contrasting his baptizing power with John's: "*he* baptises with breath and fire, as wheat is winnowed in the wind and sun, and uses no shell like this which only washes once but a fan that thoroughly and forever parts the wheat from the chaff. . . . The separation it makes is very visible too: the grain lies heaped on one side, the chaff blows away the other, between them the winnower stands" (*SD* 267–68).

Line 6.

　　Thy
H₁a: ~~With~~ wring-earth tread; launch lion-foot on me?
H₂:　Thy wring-earth tread rock, launch thy lion foot?

This line is then entirely crossed out and followed by:

　　　　　　　　　　　　　　lay a lionlimb against me,
Thy wring-earth right foot rock?　~~launch *a* lion hand on me?~~
　　　　　　　　　　　　　　~~launch thy lion hand?~~
H₃:　Thy wring-world ⎱ right foot rock? lay a lion limb against me?
　　　　wring-earth ⎰

Bridges' choice of the stronger, more alliterative, conceptually wider new alternative, "world," seems admirably Hopkinsian.

Line 10.

H₁a: Nay, in the toil and coil, because I kissed the rod—
~~Hand rather~~
     from
Nay ~~in~~ the storm my heart stole joy, would shout, cheer.
        the
H₁c: Nay, ~~even~~ in the toil, ~~and~~ coil, because I kissed the rod—
Hand ~~ra~~ rather—my heart from storm stole joy ho! could láugh,
   chéer—
H₂: Nay in all that ~~toil~~ toil, that coil, becaūse I kissed the rod,
Hand rather, my heart lo! lapped strength, stole joy, ~~give a~~

$$\left\{ \begin{array}{l} \text{give a laugh could} \\ \text{had a \quad laugh} \\ \text{had a laugh, a} \end{array} \right\} \quad \text{cheer.}$$

H₃: Nay in all that toil, that coil, since (seems) I kissed the rod
Hand rather, my heart lo! lapped strength, stole joy, would
   laugh,   cheer.

(The wide space between "laugh" and "cheer" results simply from the fact that he was writing around the top of the slanting cancelation line that had struck the whole early version of "Tom's Garland" below.) The relation between one stage of this sonnet and one stage of "Tom's Garland" may also be seen in that too-rollicking and "Tom-like" phrasing and stressing attempted in H₁c, "stole joy ho!" (transcribed by Harris as "Lo!" in *Inspirations Unbidden*, 149, but lower case *h* seems to me clear here).

For an alternative interpretation of the revision from "because I kissed the rod" to "since (seems)," and an argument that the poem "calls into doubt the whole of his priestly vocation," see Harris, *Inspirations Unbidden*, 100–101.

Lines 13–14.

H₁a: —I know this night, this year
Of darkness done, that I wretch wrestled, ~~I rung~~ I wrung with God.
H₁b: This night, this dark year
Now done I know that I wretch wrestled, I wrung with, God.
H₁c: That night, that dark year,
Done now, I know that I wretch wrestled, I wrung with God.
                      ≠ night,
H₂: That ~~night~~,
      that
      ~~that dark~~ year

~~in wrestle~~   ~~with~~

~~Of dárkness done, now wi*h* dóne with, I wretch wre*s*tled wrung with~~

~~our~~

Of/ now done/ darkness I wretch ~~in wrestle wrung with great God.~~

lay wrestling with (my God*!* !)

my God.

Line 14. On the issue of what is deleted in the final parentheses no definitive light is cast by similar instances in the manuscripts of other poems, though they seem to me to tip the balance toward deletion of the exclamation mark. In H's canceled version of "Tom's Garland," the exclamation in line 5 following "bed!" is neatly crossed out but not obliterated. Two other poems, however, offer almost exact duplicates of the situation in "(Carrion Comfort)." In one version of "The shepherd's brow" (H$_2$a) something that cannot have been the closing of a parenthesis is heavily crossed out in the final line: "my spitfire frenzy fussy*!*" Similarly, in a draft of "On the Portrait of Two Beautiful Young People" what has just above been clearly "time*!*" is corrected by exactly the same heavy mark as in "(Carrion Comfort)." A third possibility, perhaps, is that Hopkins was in so violent a state of private emotion that he dashed down two exclamation marks and wisely deleted one, but that sort of adolescent emphasis is wholly uncharacteristic, and I incline toward one or the other of the alternatives suggested in the text, especially the first.

"No worst, there is none"

Dating is problematical, as in the case of "(Carrion Comfort)," though here the problem may actually illuminate the dating of Hopkins' last extant copying of both sonnets. The only extant version begins directly below a canceled version of the first ten lines of "Tom's Garland," marked by Bridges "early v. of Tom"; "No worst" then continues over to the verso, where the "final" version of "(Carrion Comfort)" begins, going through "I kissed the rod"; back on the recto again, line 11 appears above "Tom's Garland," line 12 below it. Since the ink and pen of all three seem identical, and since it seems unlikely that even an "early version of Tom" (finally dated "Dromore. Sept. 1887") can have been written more than a year, and possibly more than two years, before Hopkins began asking Bridges about the use of codas (December 11, 1886, and especially November 2, 1887, *LB* 246, 263), it seems probable that he was still "touching" "(Carrion Comfort)," and perhaps had been "touching" "No worst," as late as a

year, even two years, after the May 1885 letter to Bridges on the sonnet "written in blood."

The single draft in H includes three stages:

H_a: the first two lines, with alternatives:

$$\text{No worst, there is none:} \quad \left\{ \begin{array}{l} \text{Pitched past pitch of grief} \\ \text{grief past pitch of grief,} \end{array} \right.$$

fore
More pangs at ~~pan~~ pangs schooled will wilder wring
At fore pangs more pangs schooled will wilder wring

H_b: A second revision of the opening lines:

O there   tops grief
Worst! No worst/ ~~no there~~ is none. Grief past grief
And more pangs, schooled at forepangs, wilder wring.

H_c: the last complete draft, at the end of which appear alternative versions of:

line 13: Wretch, under a comfort serves in a whirlwind: all
line 10: $\left\{ \begin{array}{l} \text{Frightful, sheer, not man's fathoming. Hold them cheap} \\ \underline{\quad\quad} \quad \underline{\quad} \quad \text{no-man-fathom\`ed.} \quad \underline{\quad\quad} \, \underline{\quad} \quad \underline{\quad} \end{array} \right.$

Except where indicated, stressing and other markings in the text are
from H_c.

Line 1. As the revisions above show, Hopkins began as he often
did with what was to be the final version of the opening line. He was
then briefly tempted by that less bleak, more dramatic, rather more
lyrically stressed "Worst! No worst O there is none," but fortunately
returned immediately to the grim finality of the original, making it
even more final by replacing the colon with a period.

Line 10. Credit must be given to both Hopkins and Bridges here.
Hopkins evidently meant to replace the rather flat original, "Frightful,
sheer down, not fathomed," with one of the two alternatives added
below the complete draft. With his sense of poetic clarity and instinct
for syntactical "decorum," Bridges selected what is probably the better
of the two, and the one closest to the original in meaning. It is possible, however, that Hopkins might have chosen the other, because of
the slight difference in thought it suggests: the second, and now
"final," phrase means simply "No man has plumbed these depths"; the
alternative "not man's fathoming" more subtly implies "No man can

plumb these depths—they are not susceptible to his probing or his understanding."

Line 13. Bridges must again be credited with a crucial choice of variants, in this case a choice that reflects both his own and Hopkins' understanding of the whole sonnet. Hopkins seems to have realized that the mind's tempest portrayed in the octave, and the image of the "cliffs of fall," demanded some culminating metaphor and, above all, that his original "under a comfort serves at worst whiles" would contradict the opening statement and the entire point of the poem. Bridges therefore chose, as Hopkins himself would almost certainly have chosen, "under a comfort serves in a whirlwind."

"To seem the stranger"
Single draft in H, with heavy revision only in the final tercet.

Lines 11–14. The revisions:

<del>But what one word</del>   Only what word
  holds <del>keeps</del> bears from heaven   baffling
Wisest my breast <del>holds still to bear</del> some ban { Wisest my heart breeds <del>dark</del>
  dumbness or death.   heaven's dark ban
Of <del>silence or of</del>   { Bars or hell's spell thwarts.
                Thoughts hoarded unheard

       hold   *or*
      <del>this to be unheard</del>
    This to hoard unheard,   { Wisest my heart breeds
<del>Heard unheeded</del>   dark heaven's baffling ban
Heard unheeded, leaves me a lonely began. { Bars etc

"I wake and feel the fell of dark"
The drafts:
 (1) An entirely canceled version of the sestet on a small sheet of writing paper, above "Strike, churl," and undatable:

     I am gall and heartburn. God's most deep decree
     Has me taste bitter, and my taste is me.
     My bones build, <del>flesh fills, bl</del> my flesh fills, blood
       feeds this curse
     Of my self stuff, by self yeast soured. I see
         with
     The lost are like this, <del>and</del> their loss to be
     Their sweating selves, as I am mine, but worse.

---

                                                    this curse—
        Self stuff, and by selfyeast so soured. I see
             by yeast^y ~~of~~ self so soured. I see

(2) The complete "final" version: two small revisions only in the octave, from "you" to "we have spent" (l. 2), from "this" or "thy" to "my lament" (l. 6); heavy revision in the sestet:

                                          deep
    I am gall, I am heartburn. God's most ~~just~~ decree
                                          was
    Bitter would have me taste: my taste ~~is~~ me;
              t   ed   med the
    Bones build in me, flesh fills, blood brims a curse.
    Selfyeast of spirit my selfstuff sours. I see   Selfyeast of spirit a
                        this   ⌠ scourge   dull dough sours. I see
    The lost are like ~~it~~, and their ⌡ loss to be
    ⌠ Their sweating selves as I am mine, but worse.
    ⌡ As I am mine, their sweating selves; but worse.

Line 14. Bridges again made the crucial choice here, but Hopkins gave some guidance. The second alternative's darkly inked revision of both word order and punctuation seems aimed at needed clarification of meaning: it is "the lost" and not himself that are modified by "but worse." See Harris, however, on a possible ambiguity remaining (*Inspirations Unbidden*, 111–12).

"Patience, hard thing!"
Single draft in H.

Line 2. Though Bridges and most succeeding editors except Phillips capitalize the first "patience" here, I have returned in the text to the manuscript's noncapitalization, which leaves the virtue abstract and unpersonified until it is newly viewed as living "Patience" in line 6. A single revision in this line, from "Ask God for" to "But bid for."

Line 3. Other critics have argued that "wants" means simply "desires" or "demands," so that the meaning of the whole quatrain is either that anyone who prays for patience is asking for suffering, is willing to pay the price of war, wounds, sacrifice (Heuser, *Shaping Vision*, 90; Boyle, *Metaphor*, 114, 137; Mariani, *Commentary*, 234; MacKenzie, *Reader's Guide*, 184, among others), or that Patience itself is the "who" that "asks" and "wants" suffering as its price (Pick,

Priest and Poet, 149). The questionable assumption of the first interpretation, that "war" and "wounds" are equivalent to "weary" times
and tasks, and the syntactical convolutions required by the second (especially the absence of an antecedent for "his," which "who" naturally
supplies), seem to me prohibitive.

Lines 5–8. Originally as follows:

Rare patience roots in these, and, these away,
Nowhere! Natural heart's-ivy it is/: it masks   [heart's-ivy Patience
                                                                              masks
Our/ ruins of wrecked past purpose. There it basks   [*or* she basks
Purple eyes and seas of liquid leaves all day.

Bridges made the choice for the alternative versions of lines 6 and
7, inserted a comma between "ivy" and "Patience," and omitted the
hyphen in "heart's-ivy." While accepting without question his choice
of "Patience masks" and "she basks," I have returned in the text to the
punctuation of the original, conjecturing that Hopkins intended not
only "heart's-ivy" but the whole "Natural heart's-ivy Patience" to be a
compound and unbroken phrase.

The handwriting of "There" (l. 7) is hard to make out. It could be
"These," in which case the transitive mood of both "basks" and
"leaves" suggested in the text would be the main meaning, though a
comma after "basks" would be essential to make this reading wholly
persuasive.

"My own heart let me more have pity on"
Single draft in H, with both above-line and marginal revisions.

Lines 5–8.

I grope for comfort I can no more get   I cast for comfort I can no more get
By casting in my comfortless than blind   By groping round
Eyes in their dark can ~~light~~ day or thirst can find
Thirst's all-in-all in all a world of wet.

Line 9.

~~Come, self,~~
~~Now, poor self, poor/d Jackself, I do advise~~   Soul, self; come, poor Jackself,
                                                                                      I do advise

Line 11.

        leave
Elsewhere; ~~give~~ comfort root-room; let joy size

Lines 13–14.

                                       whose smile
                 who
'S not wrung, see; ~~it~~ unforeseen times rather, as skies
Betweenpie mountains, lights a lovely mile.

The version of these lines chosen by Bridges, probably as he says an intended "correction," appears on a different sheet, neatly written, in the same light ink and fine hand as the "unbidden" drafts, above a revision of "Ashboughs":

'S not wrung, see you; unforeseentimes rather—as skies
Betweenpie mountains—

———————————

The original version, while more jerky and less dramatic, makes clearer the point that God, not joy, is the main antecedent of "whose smile," a point I assume to inhere also in the revision. For a different interpretation, which sees mainly a deliberate deletion of God's active immanence, see Harris, *Inspirations Unbidden*, 50–51.

Selective Bibliography

Abrams, M. H. *The Mirror and the Lamp: Romantic Theory and the Critical Tradition*. London: Oxford University Press, 1953.

Andreach, Robert J. *Studies in Structure: The Stages of the Spiritual Life in Four Modern Authors*. New York: Fordham University Press, 1964.

Bates, Ronald. "The Windhover." *Victorian Poetry* 2 (Winter 1964): 63–64.

Bender, Todd K. *Gerard Manley Hopkins: The Classical Background and Critical Reception of His Work*. Baltimore: Johns Hopkins Press, 1966.

Bergonzi, Bernard. *Gerard Manley Hopkins*. New York: Macmillan, 1977.

Bettoni, Efrem. *Duns Scotus: The Basic Principles of His Philosophy*. Translated and edited by Bernardine Bonansea. Washington: Catholic University of America Press, 1961.

Bischoff, D. Anthony, S.J. "The Manuscripts of Gerard Manley Hopkins." *Thought* 25 (Winter 1951–1952): 551–80.

Bloom, Harold. *The Visionary Company: A Reading of English Romantic Poetry*. Garden City, N.Y.: Doubleday, 1961.

Boyle, Robert, S.J. *Metaphor in Hopkins*. Chapel Hill: University of North Carolina Press, 1961.

——. "The Thought Structure of *The Wreck of the Deutschland*." In *Immortal Diamond: Studies in Gerard Manley Hopkins*, edited by Norman Weyand, S.J., 333–50. New York: Sheed & Ward, 1949.

Bridges, Robert. Introduction to the "Gerard Hopkins" selection in *The Poets and the Poetry of the Century*, edited by Alfred H. Miles, 8:161–64. 10 vols. London: Hutchinson, 1893.

Chevigny, Bell Gale. "Instress and Devotion in the Poetry of Gerard Manley Hopkins." *Victorian Studies* 9:2 (December 1965): 141–53.

Coleridge, Samuel Taylor. *Biographia Literaria.* Edited by J. Shawcross. 2 vols. London: Oxford University Press, 1907.

Cotter, James Finn. *Inscape: The Christology and Poetry of Gerard Manley Hopkins.* Pittsburgh: University of Pittsburgh Press, 1972.

Culler, Jonathan D. *The Pursuit of Signs: Semiotics, Literature, Deconstruction.* Ithaca: Cornell University Press, 1981.

Devlin, Christopher, S.J. "Hopkins and Duns Scotus." *New Verse* 14 (April 1935): 12–15.

———. "The Image and the Word—I" and "II." *The Month,* n.s. 3 (February, March 1950): 114–27, 191–202.

———. "Time's Eunuch." *The Month,* n.s. 1 (May 1949): 303–12.

Downes, David A. *Gerard Manley Hopkins: A Study of His Ignatian Spirit.* New York: Bookman Associates, 1959.

Eliot, T. S. *After Strange Gods: A Primer of Modern Heresy.* New York: Harcourt, Brace, 1934.

Ellis, Virginia Ridley. "'Authentic Cadence': The Sacramental Method of Gerard Manley Hopkins." Ph.D. diss., Brandeis University, 1969.

Empson, William. *Seven Types of Ambiguity.* London: Chatto and Windus, 1930.

Fulweiler, Howard W. *Letters from the Darkling Plain: Language and the Grounds of Knowledge in the Poetry of Arnold and Hopkins.* Columbia: University of Missouri Press, 1972.

Gardner, W. H. *Gerard Manley Hopkins (1844–1889): A Study of Poetic Idiosyncrasy in Relation to Poetic Tradition.* 2d ed., rev. 2 vols. London: Oxford University Press, 1958.

Grady, Thomas J. "'Windhover's' Meaning." *America* 70 (January 29, 1944): 465–66.

Griffith, Ll. Wyn. "The Welsh Influence." *New Verse* 14 (April 1935): 27–29.

Grigson, Geoffrey. "Blood or Bran." *New Verse* 14 (April 1935): 21–23.

———. *Gerard Manley Hopkins.* London: Longman's Green, 1955.

Gwynn, Frederick L. "Hopkins' 'The Windhover': A New Simplification." *Modern Language Notes* 66 (June 1951): 366–70.

Harris, Daniel A. *Inspirations Unbidden: The "Terrible Sonnets" of Gerard Manley Hopkins.* Berkeley and Los Angeles: University of California Press, 1982.

Hart, Sister Mary Adorita. "The Christocentric Theme in Gerard Manley Hopkins's *The Wreck of the Deutschland.*" Ph.D. diss., Catholic University, 1952.

Hartman, Geoffrey H., ed. *Hopkins: A Collection of Critical Essays.* Englewood Cliffs, N.J.: Prentice-Hall, 1966.

———. *The Unmediated Vision: An Interpretation of Wordsworth, Hopkins, Rilke, and Valéry.* New Haven: Yale University Press, 1954.

Heuser, Alan. *The Shaping Vision of Gerard Manley Hopkins.* London: Oxford University Press, 1958.

Hopkins, Gerard Manley. *The Correspondence of Gerard Manley Hopkins and Richard Watson Dixon.* Edited by Claude Colleer Abbott. 2d ed., rev. London: Oxford University Press, 1955.

———. *Further Letters of Gerard Manley Hopkins: Including His Correspondence with Coventry Patmore.* Edited by Claude Colleer Abbott. 2d ed., rev. and enl. London: Oxford University Press, 1956.

———. *The Journals and Papers of Gerard Manley Hopkins.* Edited by Humphry House, completed by Graham Storey. London: Oxford University Press, 1959.

———. *The Letters of Gerard Manley Hopkins to Robert Bridges.* Edited by Claude Colleer Abbott. 2d ed., rev. London: Oxford University Press, 1955.

———. *Poems of Gerard Manley Hopkins.* Edited by Robert Bridges. London: Humphrey Milford, printed at the Oxford University Press, 1918.

———. *The Poems of Gerard Manley Hopkins.* Edited by W. H. Gardner and N. H. MacKenzie. 4th ed., rev. London: Oxford University Press, 1967.

———. *The Sermons and Devotional Writings of Gerard Manley Hopkins.* Edited by Christopher Devlin, S.J. London: Oxford University Press, 1959.

———. Manuscript sources: "B," "H," and posthumous papers, the Bodleian Library, Oxford; the Dublin Notebook, Campion Hall, Oxford.

Humiliata, Sister Mary. "Hopkins and the Prometheus Myth." *PMLA* 70 (March 1955): 58–68.

Ignatius of Loyola, Saint. *The Spiritual Exercises.* Translated by Elder Mullan, S.J. New York: P. J. Kenedy, 1914.

Jamieson's Dictionary of the Scottish Language. Abridged by John Johnston. New ed., rev. and enl. by John Longmuir. London: William P. Nimmo, 1885.

John of the Cross, Saint [Saint Juan de la Cruz]. *The Collected Works of St. John of the Cross.* Translated by Kieran Kavanaugh and Otilio Rodriguez. Garden City, N.Y.: Doubleday, 1964.

Johnson, Wendell Stacy. *Gerard Manley Hopkins: The Poet as Victorian*. Ithaca: Cornell University Press, 1968.

Keats, John. *The Letters of John Keats*. Edited by Hyder Edward Rollins. 2 vols. Cambridge: Harvard University Press, 1958.

[Kempis, Thomas à]. *The Imitation of Christ*. Edited by Edward J. Klein, from the first edition of an English translation made circa 1530 by Richard Whitford. New York: Harper's, 1941.

Kitchen, Paddy. *Gerard Manley Hopkins*. New York: Atheneum, 1979.

Lahey, G. F., S.J. *Gerard Manley Hopkins*. 1930. 2d ed. London: Oxford University Press, 1938.

Langbaum, Robert. *The Poetry of Experience: The Dramatic Monologue in Modern Literary Tradition*. London: Chatto and Windus, 1957.

Leavis, F. R. "Metaphysical Isolation." *Gerard Manley Hopkins by the Kenyon Critics*, 115–34. Norfolk, Conn.: New Directions Books, 1945.

————. *New Bearings in English Poetry: A Study of the Contemporary Situation*. 1932. New ed. London: Chatto and Windus, 1950.

Le Gallienne, Richard. *Retrospective Reviews: A Literary Log*. 2 vols. London: John Lane, Bodley Head, 1896.

Loomis, Jeffrey B. *Dayspring in Darkness: Sacrament in Hopkins*. Lewisburg: Bucknell University Press; London and Toronto: Associated University Presses, 1988.

"The Loss of the Deutschland," *The Times*, December 9, 10, 1875.

McChesney, Donald. "The Meaning of 'Inscape.'" *The Month*, n.s. 40, nos. 1–2 (July–August 1968): 52–63.

MacKenzie, Norman H., ed. *The Early Poetic Manuscripts and Note-Books of Gerard Manley Hopkins: In Facsimile*. New York: Garland Publishing, 1989.

————. *Hopkins*. Edinburgh: Oliver and Boyd, 1968.

————. *A Reader's Guide to Gerard Manley Hopkins*. Ithaca: Cornell University Press, 1981.

McLuhan, Herbert Marshall. "The Analogical Mirrors." *Kenyon Review* 6 (Summer 1944): 322–32.

Mariani, Paul L. *A Commentary on the Complete Poems of Gerard Manley Hopkins*. Ithaca and London: Cornell University Press, 1970.

Martin, Philip M. *Mastery and Mercy: A Study of Two Religious Poems*. London: Oxford University Press, 1957.

Miller, J. Hillis. *The Disappearance of God: Five Nineteenth-Century Writers*. Cambridge: Harvard University Press, 1975.

————. *The Linguistic Moment: From Wordsworth to Stevens*. Princeton: Princeton University Press, 1985.

Milward, Peter, S.J. *A Commentary on G. M. Hopkins' The Wreck of the Deutschland*. Tokyo: Hokuseido Press, 1968.

_____. *Landscape and Inscape: Vision and Inspiration in Hopkins's Poetry*. Foreword and photography by Raymond V. Schoder, S.J. Grand Rapids, Mich.: William B. Eerdmans Publishing Co., 1975.

Murry, J. Middleton. *Aspects of Literature*. New York: Alfred A. Knopf, 1920.

Newman, John Henry, Cardinal. *Apologia Pro Vita Sua: Being a History of His Religious Opinions*. Edited by Martin J. Svaglic. Oxford: Clarendon Press, 1967.

Ong, Walter J., S.J. "Hopkins' Sprung Rhythm and the Life of English Poetry." In *Immortal Diamond: Studies in Gerard Manley Hopkins*, edited by Norman Weyand, S.J., 93–174. New York: Sheed & Ward, 1949.

_____. *Hopkins, the Self, and God*. Toronto: University of Toronto Press, 1986.

Perkins, David. *The Quest for Permanence: The Symbolism of Wordsworth, Shelley, and Keats*. Cambridge: Harvard University Press, 1959.

Peters, W. A. M., S.J. *Gerard Manley Hopkins: A Critical Essay towards the Understanding of His Poetry*. London: Oxford University Press, 1948.

Phare, Elsie Elizabeth [Duncan-Jones]. *The Poetry of Gerard Manley Hopkins: A Survey and Commentary*. Cambridge: Cambridge University Press, 1933.

Phillips, Catherine, ed. *Gerard Manley Hopkins*. Oxford Authors Series. Oxford: Oxford University Press, 1986.

Pick, John. *Gerard Manley Hopkins: Priest and Poet*. London: Oxford University Press, 1942.

Pick, John, ed. *Gerard Manley Hopkins: The Windhover*. Merrill Literary Casebook Series. Columbus, Ohio: Charles E. Merrill, 1969.

_____. *A Hopkins Reader: Selections from the Writings of Gerard Manley Hopkins*. Rev. and enl. ed. Garden City, N.Y.: Doubleday Image Books, 1966.

Read, Herbert. *Collected Essays in Literary Criticism*. London: Faber and Faber, 1938.

_____. "Poetry and Belief in Gerard Manley Hopkins." *New Verse* 1 (January 1933): 11–15.

Reeves, James. "Introduction." *Selected Poems of Gerard Manley Hopkins*. London: W. Heinemann, 1953.

Richards, I. A. "Gerard Hopkins." *Dial* 81 (September 1926): 195–203.

———. *Practical Criticism: A Study of Literary Judgment*. New York: Harcourt, Brace, 1929.

Ritz, Jean-George. *Robert Bridges and Gerard Hopkins, 1863–1889: A Literary Friendship*. London: Oxford University Press, 1960.

Roberts, Gerald, ed. *Gerard Manley Hopkins: The Critical Heritage*. London and New York: Routledge & Kegan Paul, 1987.

Robinson, John. *In Extremity: A Study of Gerard Manley Hopkins*. Cambridge: Cambridge University Press, 1978.

Ruskin, John. *The Works of John Ruskin*. Library Edition. Edited by E. T. Cook and Alexander Wedderburn. 39 vols. London: George Allen, 1903–1912.

Schneider, Elisabeth W. *The Dragon in the Gate: Studies in the Poetry of G. M. Hopkins*. Berkeley and Los Angeles: University of California Press, 1968.

Schoder, Raymond V., S.J. "Spelt from Sibyl's Leaves." *Thought* (December 1944): 633–48.

———. "What Does *The Windhover* Mean?" In *Immortal Diamond: Studies in Gerard Manley Hopkins*, edited by Norman Weyand, S.J., 275–306. New York: Sheed & Ward, 1949.

Scotus, John Duns. *Philosophical Writings*. Selected, edited, and translated by Allan Wolter. New York: Nelson, 1962.

Sprinker, Michael. *"A Counterpoint of Dissonance": The Aesthetics and Poetry of Gerard Manley Hopkins*. Baltimore and London: Johns Hopkins University Press, 1980.

Storey, Graham. *Gerard Manley Hopkins*. Writers and Their Work: A Critical and Biographical Series. Windsor, Berks.: Profile Books, 1984.

Stubbs, Patricia [Bielec]. "Cliffs of Fall: The Final Sonnets of Gerard Manley Hopkins." B.A. honors thesis, Mount Holyoke College, 1964.

Sulloway, Alison G. *Gerard Manley Hopkins and the Victorian Temper*. New York: Columbia University Press, 1972.

Taylor, Jeremy. *The Golden Grove, A Choice Manuel: Containing what is to be Believed, Practised, and Desired or Prayed for; The Prayers Being Fitted to the several days of the week. To which is added A Guide for the Penitent. Also Festival Hymns, According to the Manner of the Ancient Church. Composed for the use of the Devout, especially of younger persons*. 1655. Oxford and London: James Parker, 1868.

———. *The Rule and Exercises of Holy Dying* (1651). In *The Works of*

Jeremy Taylor, D.D., edited by the Rev. T. S. Hughes, 5:363–584. 5 vols. London: A. J. Valpy, 1831.

———. *Sermons Preached at Golden-Grove: Being for the Winter half-year, beginning on Advent-Sunday, until Whit-Sunday*. London: E. Cotes for Richard Royston, 1653.

Thomas, Alfred, S.J. *Hopkins the Jesuit: The Years of Training*. London: Oxford University Press, 1969.

Warren, Austin. "Instress of Inscape." In *Gerard Manley Hopkins by the Kenyon Critics*, 72–88. Norfolk, Conn.: New Directions Books, 1945.

Watson, Youree, S.J. "*The Loss of the Eurydice*: A Critical Analysis." In *Immortal Diamond: Studies in Gerard Manley Hopkins*, edited by Norman Weyand, S.J., 307–32. New York: Sheed & Ward, 1949.

Weyand, Norman, S.J., ed., with the assistance of Raymond V. Schoder, S.J. *Immortal Diamond: Studies in Gerard Manley Hopkins*. Introduction by John Pick. New York: Sheed & Ward, 1949.

White, Norman E. "'Hearse' in Hopkins' 'Spelt from Sibyl's Leaves.'" *English Studies* 49 (1968): 546–47.

———. "Hopkins' Sonnet 'Written in Blood.'" *English Studies* 53 (1972): 123–25.

Whitehall, Harold. "Sprung Rhythm." In *Gerard Manley Hopkins by the Kenyon Critics*, 28–54. Norfolk, Conn.: New Directions Books, 1945.

Williams, Charles. "Introduction." *Poems of Gerard Manley Hopkins*, edited by Robert Bridges. 2d ed. London: Oxford University Press, 1930.

Winters, Yvor. "The Poetry of Gerard Manley Hopkins, I" and "II." *Hudson Review* 1 (Winter 1949): 455–76; 2 (Spring 1949): 61–93.

Wolfe, Patricia A. "The Paradox of Self: A Study of Hopkins' Spiritual Conflict in the 'Terrible' Sonnets." *Victorian Poetry* 6 (Summer 1968): 85–103.

Wordsworth, William. *The Prelude*. Edited by Ernest de Selincourt. 2d ed., rev. Helen Darbishire. Oxford: Clarendon Press, 1959.

"The Wreck of the Deutschland." *The Times*, December 13, 1875.

Wright, Joseph, ed. *The English Dialect Dictionary*. 6 vols. London: Henry Frowde, 1898.

Yeats, William Butler. "Introduction." *The Oxford Book of Modern Verse, 1892–1935*, chosen by W. B. Yeats. Oxford: Clarendon Press, 1936.

Permissions

THE FOLLOWING MATERIAL has been quoted by permission:

Bodleian Library, Oxford: All manuscript illustrations.

Oxford University Press: *The Poems of Gerard Manley Hopkins*, edited by W. H. Gardner and H. H. MacKenzie, 4th ed., 1967; *The Poems of Gerard Manley Hopkins*, edited by Robert Bridges, 1918; W. H. Gardner, *Gerard Manley Hopkins (1844–1889): A Study of Poetic Idiosyncrasy in Relation to Poetic Tradition*, 1958; W. A. M. Peters, *Gerard Manley Hopkins: A Critical Essay Towards an Understanding of His Poetry*, 1948; John Pick, *Gerard Manley Hopkins: Priest and Poet*, 1942.

Oxford University Press on behalf of the Society of Jesus: *The Correspondence of Gerard Manley Hopkins and Richard Watson Dixon*, edited by Claude Colleer Abbott, 2d ed., 1955; *Further Letters of Gerard Manley Hopkins: Including His Correspondence with Coventry Patmore*, edited by Claude Colleer Abbott, 2d ed., 1956; *The Journals and Papers of Gerard Manley Hopkins*, edited by Humphry House, completed by Graham Storey, 1959; *The Letters of Gerard Manley Hopkins to Robert Bridges*, edited by Claude Colleer Abbott, 2d ed., 1955; *The Sermons and Devotional Writings of Gerard Manley Hopkins*, edited by Christopher Devlin, 1959; as well as all manuscript material quoted from Campion Hall and the Bodleian Library.

Princeton University Press: J. Hillis Miller, *The Linguistic Moment: From Wordsworth to Stevens*, copyright © 1985.

University of California Press: Daniel Harris, *Inspirations Unbidden: "The Terrible Sonnets" of Gerard Manley Hopkins*, copyright © 1982 The Regents of the University of California.

Index